FIX-IT and FORGET-IT®
Diabetic Cookbook

Fix-It and Forget-It®
Diabetic Cookbook

Slow Cooker Favorites — to include Everyone!

New York Times bestselling author
Phyllis Pellman Good
with
American Diabetes Association

Good  Books®

Intercourse, PA 17534
800/762-7171
www.goodbks.com

Although the analysts and editors have attempted full accuracy in the nutritional data and analyses included in this cookbook, many variables (including variations related to particular brands, to the refinement of products, and to the exact amounts of ingredients, as well as whether they are cooked or raw) could result in the analyses being approximate.

Because many factors influence your health, please check with your health-care expert before making substantial changes in what you eat.

Cover design and illustrations by Cheryl Benner
Design by Dawn J. Ranck

FIX-IT AND FORGET-IT DIABETIC COOKBOOK
Copyright © 2005 by Good Books, Intercourse, PA 17534

Printed in the United States of America.

ISBN 1-56148-458-X

Table of Contents

About *Fix-It and Forget-It Diabetic Coobook*

The recipes in this collection are for everyone! No more isolating persons with diabetes at mealtime. In fact, these delicious recipes offer both great taste and nutritional value—and easy preparation—the *Fix-It and Forget-It* trademark.

The American Diabetes Association joined us in this cookbook, using their know-how to adapt the recipes and analyze them so they fit into meal plans. Each recipe is followed by its Exchange List Values and its Basic Nutritional Values. Persons with diabetes need this information so they can manage their calories, and their carb, fat, and sodium counts.

Do you wish you knew more about diabetes?

Don't miss the basic information given in our introduction, "A Few Thoughts About Eating and Cooking When You Have Diabetes" (pages 5-6) and, after the recipes, "10 Most Asked Questions About Diabetes" (pages 270-271). If you want to learn more, see the "Recommended Reading List" on page 272.

Would you like a little more help to manage your own or your loved one's eating? The American Diabetes Association provides a Week of Menus on pages 255-269, using one or two recipes from this cookbook each day.

Calculating the Nutritional Analyses

If the number of servings is given as a range, we used the higher number to do the nutritional analyses calculations.

The nutritional analysis for each recipe includes all ingredients except those labeled "optional," those listed as "to taste," or those calling for a "dash." If an ingredient is listed with a second choice, the first choice was used in the analysis. If a range is given for the amount of an ingredient, the first number was used. Foods listed as "serve with" at the end of a recipe, or accompanying foods listed without an amount, were not included in the recipe's analysis. In recipes calling for cooked rice, pasta, or other grains, the analysis is based on the starch being prepared without added salt or fat, unless indicated otherwise in the recipe.

The analyses were done assuming that meats were trimmed of all visible fat, and that skin was removed from poultry, before being placed in the slow cooker.

Relax and enjoy these recipes!

Mealtimes should be refreshing. Now you can relax and enjoy these recipes because you know the content of what you're preparing and how that will affect a meal plan.

These easy-to-prepare recipes take so little time and attention, they'll help you stick to your food goals.

Diabetes need not keep us from all gathering around the table together, eating tasty, wholesome food.

After all, a diet that's healthy for persons with diabetes is healthy for everyone. And everyone can eat and enjoy it when you use recipes from *Fix-It and Forget-It Diabetic Cookbook: Slow-Cooker Favorites—to Include Everyone!*

— *Phyllis Pellman Good*

A Few Thoughts about Eating and Cooking When You Have Diabetes

No matter what the latest diet fad is, people with diabetes must always focus on carbohydrates, because carbohydrates raise blood sugar. Choosing the right foods, exercising every day (such as walking), and taking diabetes medications are the three things these people do to balance their blood sugar levels and stay healthy. (Actually, the first two are what we all should do to stay healthy!)

What Exactly Is a Carbohydrate?

Now, you may have been cooking all your life and still not be sure what a carbohydrate (carb) is. Our mothers and grandmothers showed us how to design a meal, and this is still pretty much the way we fill a plate:

meat	
starch (rice, pasta, potato, squash, corn, peas, beans)	carb
vegetable	
salad	
bread	carb
milk, water, tea	carb
dessert (fruit, cake, ice cream, etc.)	carb

You see carbohydrates (carb) in the starches (rice, pasta, potato, squash, corn, peas, or beans), in the bread and milk, the sugar in your tea, and the dessert (including fruit). These are foods we all like to eat, and none of us can—or should—go for more than about two weeks without carbohydrates in our meals. We need the nutrients that come in carbohydrate foods, which are our body's favorite fuel. The trick is in choosing which ones, because today we have so many choices that our grandmothers didn't have.

Why Vegetables Work for You

There are a few carbs in the vegetables and salad on your plate. Green leafy, red, and orange vegetables—everything but the starchy potatoes, squash, corn, peas, and beans—have carbohydrates. But they don't have much, so you can have second and third helpings before your blood sugar is affected. Don't forget that vegetables are also a powerhouse of vitamins and minerals—and that's great for your health.

Vegetables also have fiber, which slows down digestion of your food, which in turn slows down the rise in your blood sugar. (Can you see that vegetables really are the stars of the dinner plate?) Eating foods with fiber keeps your body working well.

Simply put, these are the qualities within carbs that your body prefers, whether it is a whole grain, fruit, or vegetable. These foods come to you straight from the farmer's field, so they contain lots of vitamins, minerals, and fiber. Some whole grains to look for are slow-cooking oats (sometimes called "rolled oats"), whole wheat flour, stone-ground cornmeal, and brown rice.

Watch Out for These!

Other carbs are part of the bread, starch, drink, or dessert categories, but they have traveled far from the farmer's field before getting to you. Processed grains, such as white flour and white rice, have had their germ, bran, and fiber removed. That takes out a lot of their natural vitamins and minerals, so the food manufacturer puts some artificial vitamins back in. You can read the names of these artificial vitamins on the food labels attached to the packages containing breads, cookies, and other products. Because they don't have fiber, these carbs are digested quickly, raising blood sugar more quickly, too.

Chips, cookies, and desserts are carb foods that also contain fat. Fat slows down digestion, so it helps balance the blood sugar spike caused by white flour and white sugar. But some fats are better for you than others. Most processed foods contain fats called "trans fats" that are found in the "hydrogenated vegetable oil" listed on the ingredients label. We are learning that trans fats may be the worst of the saturated fats, so food processors are starting to use other fats in their products.

Good Fats

Research shows that we all need to eat some fat every day. Our bodies just don't work right without fats. So which fats are best for your health? You probably have heard that you shouldn't eat a lot of solid fats, such as margarine, butter, marbled meat, or cheese. Vegetable oils are better, and olive oil and canola oil are the best oils because they contain balanced amounts of omega-6 and omega-3 fats. These fats are important for your heart and blood vessels (which is why you should eat more fish and freshly ground flaxseeds).

Processed foods contain a lot of omega-6 fats, but almost no omega-3 fats. You need balance. You find balance and good fats in nuts; avocados; olives; nut butters; olive and canola oils; and sesame, pumpkin, flax, and sunflower seeds. In fact, you might try a handful or two of raw almonds as a part of your daily "bread."

Remember:

- **Good carb choices:** whole grains, fruits, and vegetables.
- **Good fat choices:** olive oil, avocados, fish, nuts, and seeds.

— **American Diabetes Association.**

Beef
Main Dishes

Beef Stew

Wanda S. Curtin, Bradenton, FL
Paula King, Harrisonburg, VA
Miriam Nolt, New Holland, PA
Jean Shaner, York, PA
Mary W. Stauffer, Ephrata, PA
Alma Z. Weaver, Ephrata, PA

Makes 6 servings
(Ideal slow cooker size: 4-quart)

2 lbs. beef chuck, cubed,
    trimmed of fat
1/4-1/2 cup flour
3/4 tsp. salt
1/2 tsp. pepper
1 tsp. paprika
1 tsp. Worcestershire sauce
1 1/2 cups beef broth
half garlic clove, minced
1 bay leaf
4 medium carrots, sliced
2 medium onions, chopped
1 rib celery, sliced
3 medium potatoes, diced,
    unpeeled

1. Place meat in slow cooker.
2. Combine flour, salt, pepper, and paprika. Stir into meat until coated thoroughly.
3. Add remaining ingredients. Mix well.
4. Cover. Cook on Low 10-12 hours, or High 4-6 hours.

Exchange List Values:
Starch 1.5, Vegetable 2.0, Meat, lean 2.0

Basic Nutritional Values: Calories 278 (Calories from Fat 55), Total Fat 6 gm (Saturated Fat 1.9 gm, Polyunsat Fat 0.5 gm, Monounsat Fat 2.8 gm, Cholesterol 75 mg), Sodium 598 mg, Total Carbohydrate 28 gm, Dietary Fiber 4 gm, Sugars 7 gm, Protein 28 gm

If someone you love has diabetes, you can help by learning about the disease, talking about your feelings (because diabetes affects you, too!), offering practical help, and getting help if needed.

Bavarian Beef

Naomi E. Fast
Hesston, KS

Makes 8 servings
(Ideal slow cooker size: 4-5-quart)

3 lb. boneless beef chuck
   roast, trimmed of fat
1 Tbsp. canola oil
3 cups sliced carrots
3 cups sliced onions
2 large kosher dill pickles,
   chopped
1 cup sliced celery
1/2 cup dry red wine or
   beef broth
1/3 cup German-style
   mustard
2 tsp. coarsely ground
   black pepper
2 bay leaves
1/4 tsp. ground cloves
1 cup water
1/3 cup flour

1. Brown roast on both
sides in oil in skillet. Transfer
to slow cooker.
2. Add remaining
ingredients except flour.
3. Cover. Cook on Low 6-7
hours.
4. Remove meat and
vegetables to large platter.
Cover to keep warm.
5. Mix flour with 1 cup of
cooking broth until smooth.
Return to cooker. Turn on
High and stir, cooking until
broth is smooth and
thickened.
6. Serve over noodles or
spaetzle.

Exchange List Values:
Starch 0.5, Vegetable 2.0,
Meat, lean 3.0

Basic Nutritional Values: Calories
251 (Calories from Fat 76), Total Fat
8 gm (Saturated Fat 2.4 gm,
Polyunsat Fat 0.9 gm, Monounsat Fat
3.8 gm, Cholesterol 73 mg), Sodium
525 mg, Total Carbohydrate 17 gm,
Dietary Fiber 4 gm, Sugars 7 gm,
Protein 26 gm

Beef Stew with Shiitake Mushrooms

Kathy Hertzler
Lancaster, PA

Makes 4-6 servings
(Ideal slow cooker size: 4-5-quart)

12 new potatoes, cut into
   quarters
1/2 cup chopped onions
8-oz. pkg. baby carrots
3.4-oz. pkg. fresh shiitake
   mushrooms, sliced, or
   2 cups regular white
   mushrooms, sliced
16-oz. can whole tomatoes
14 1/2-oz. can beef broth
1/2 cup flour
1 Tbsp. Worcestershire
   sauce
1 tsp. sugar
1 tsp. dried marjoram
   leaves
1/4 tsp. pepper
1 lb. beef stewing meat,
   cubed, trimmed of fat

1. Combine all ingredients
except beef in slow cooker.
Add beef.
2. Cover. Cook on Low 8-9
hours. Stir well before serving.

Exchange List Values:
Starch 2.0, Vegetable 2.0,
Meat, lean 1.0

Basic Nutritional Values: Calories
254 (Calories from Fat 29), Total Fat
3 gm (Saturated Fat 0.9 gm,
Polyunsat Fat 0.4 gm, Monounsat Fat
1.4 gm, Cholesterol 38 mg), Sodium
534 mg, Total Carbohydrate 39 gm,
Dietary Fiber 5 gm, Sugars 8 gm,
Protein 18 gm

Dawn's Mushroom Beef Stew

Dawn Day
Westminster, CA

Makes 8-10 servings
(Ideal slow cooker size: 4-5-quart)

1 lb. sirloin, cubed,
    trimmed of fat
2 Tbsp. flour
1 Tbsp. canola oil
1 large onion, chopped
2 garlic cloves, minced
1/2 lb. button mushrooms,
    sliced
2 ribs celery, sliced
3 large carrots, sliced
3-4 large potatoes, cubed
2 tsp. seasoning salt
14 1/2-oz. can beef stock, or
    2 bouillon cubes
    dissolved in 1 2/3 cups
    water
1/2-1 cup good red wine

1. Dredge sirloin in flour and brown in oil in skillet. Reserve drippings. Place meat in slow cooker.
2. Saute onion, garlic, and mushrooms in drippings just until soft. Add to meat.
3. Add all remaining ingredients.
4. Cover. Cook on Low 6 hours. Test to see if vegetables are tender. If not, continue cooking on Low for another 1-1 1/2 hours.
5. Serve with crusty bread.

Exchange List Values:
Starch 1.5, Vegetable 2.0,
Meat, lean 1.0, Fat 0.5

Basic Nutritional Values: Calories 247 (Calories from Fat 49), Total Fat 5 gm (Saturated Fat 1.1 gm, Polyunsat Fat 1.0 gm, Monounsat Fat 2.8 gm, Cholesterol 38 mg), Sodium 572 mg, Total Carbohydrate 33 gm, Dietary Fiber 5 gm, Sugars 7 gm, Protein 17 gm

Beef Burgundy and Bacon

Joyce Kaut
Rochester, NY

Makes 6 servings
(Ideal slow cooker size: 3-4-quart)

1 slice bacon, cut in
    squares
2 lbs. sirloin tip or round
    steak, cubed, trimmed
    of fat
1 tsp. canola oil
1/4 cup flour
1/8 tsp. salt
1/2 tsp. seasoning salt
1/4 tsp. dried marjoram
1/4 tsp. dried thyme
1/4 tsp. pepper
1 garlic clove, minced
1 beef bouillon cube,
    crushed
1 cup burgundy wine
1/4 lb. fresh mushrooms,
    sliced
2 Tbsp. cornstarch
2 Tbsp. cold water

1. Cook bacon in skillet until browned. Remove bacon.
2. Coat beef with flour and brown on all sides in canola oil.
3. Combine steak, bacon drippings, bacon, seasonings, garlic, bouillon, and wine in slow cooker.
4. Cover. Cook on Low 6-8 hours.
5. Add mushrooms.
6. Dissolve cornstarch in water. Add to slow cooker.
7. Cover. Cook on High 15 minutes.
8. Serve over noodles.

Exchange List Values:
Starch 0.5, Meat, lean 3.0

Basic Nutritional Values: Calories 202 (Calories from Fat 63), Total Fat 7 gm (Saturated Fat 2.0 gm, Polyunsat Fat 0.6 gm, Monounsat Fat 3.5 gm, Cholesterol 76 mg), Sodium 389 mg, Total Carbohydrate 8 gm, Dietary Fiber 0 gm, Sugars 1 gm, Protein 25 gm

> Forget about your "ideal" weight, or how much you weighed in high school. Shoot for losing 10 pounds over 3-6 months and keeping it off!

Hungarian Barley Stew

Naomi E. Fast
Hesston, KS

Makes 8 servings
(Ideal slow cooker size: 4-quart)

2 Tbsp. canola oil
1½ lbs. beef cubes,
    trimmed of fat
2 large onions, diced
1 medium-sized green
    pepper, chopped
28-oz. can whole tomatoes
½ cup ketchup
⅔ cup dry small pearl
    barley
½ tsp. salt
½ tsp. pepper
1 Tbsp. paprika
10-oz. pkg. frozen baby
    lima beans
3 cups water
1 cup fat-free sour cream

1. Brown beef cubes in oil
in skillet. Add onions and
green peppers. Saute. Pour
into slow cooker.
    2. Add remaining
ingredients except sour
cream.
    3. Cover. Cook on High 5
hours.
    4. Stir in sour cream
before serving.
    5. Serve with your favorite
cabbage slaw.

Exchange List Values:
Starch 1.5, Vegetable 2.0,
Meat, lean 2.0

Basic Nutritional Values: Calories
286 (Calories from Fat 67), Total Fat
7 gm (Saturated Fat 1.3 gm,
Polyunsat Fat 1.5 gm, Monounsat Fat
3.6 gm, Cholesterol 44 mg), Sodium
558 mg, Total Carbohydrate 36 gm,
Dietary Fiber 6 gm, Sugars 11 gm,
Protein 20 gm

Tempting Beef Stew

Patricia Howard
Albuquerque, NM

Makes 10 servings
(Ideal slow cooker size: 4-5-quart)

2 lbs. beef stewing meat,
    trimmed of fat
3 carrots, sliced thin
1 lb. pkg. frozen green peas
    with onions
1 lb. pkg. frozen green
    beans
16-oz. can whole or stewed
    tomatoes
½ cup beef broth
½ cup white wine
¼ cup brown sugar
4 Tbsp. tapioca
½ cup bread crumbs
1½ tsp. salt
1 bay leaf
pepper to taste

1. Combine all ingredients
in slow cooker.
    2. Cover. Cook on Low 10-
12 hours.
    3. Serve over noodles, rice,
couscous, or biscuits.

Exchange List Values:
Starch 1.0, Vegetable 2.0,
Meat, lean 1.0

Basic Nutritional Values: Calories
203 (Calories from Fat 36), Total Fat
4 gm (Saturated Fat 1.1 gm,
Polyunsat Fat 0.4 gm, Monounsat Fat
1.8 gm, Cholesterol 45 mg), Sodium
588 mg, Total Carbohydrate 24 gm,
Dietary Fiber 4 gm, Sugars 12 gm,
Protein 18 gm

*Variation: In place of the
tapioca, thicken stew with
¼ cup flour dissolved in ⅓-½
cup water. Mix in and turn
cooker to High. Cover and cook
for 15-20 minutes.*

---

*Prepare this Tempting Beef
Stew before your guests arrive.
Give yourself time to relax
instead of panicking in a last-
minute rush.*

When flying, keep
your medications and
glucose meter with you
in your carry-on luggage
so there's no chance of
things being lost.

Wash-Day Stew

Naomi E. Fast
Hesston, KS

Makes 14 servings
(Ideal slow cooker size: 4-5-quart)

1¹/₂-2 lbs. lean lamb or beef,
 cubed, trimmed of fat
2 15-oz. cans garbanzo
 beans, drained
2 15-oz. cans white beans,
 drained
2 medium onions, peeled
 and quartered
1 qt. water
¹/₂ tsp. salt
1 tomato, peeled and
 quartered
1 tsp. turmeric
3 Tbsp. fresh lemon juice
8-10 pita bread pockets

1. Combine all ingredients
except pitas in slow cooker.
2. Cover. Cook on High 6-7
hours.
3. Lift stew from cooker
with a strainer spoon and
stuff in pita bread pockets.

Exchange List Values:
Starch 3.0, Meat, lean 1.0

Basic Nutritional Values: Calories
287 (Calories from Fat 38), Total Fat
4 gm (Saturated Fat 1.1 gm,
Polyunsat Fat 0.9 gm, Monounsat Fat
1.3 gm, Cholesterol 31 mg), Sodium
440 mg, Total Carbohydrate 42 gm,
Dietary Fiber 7 gm, Sugars 5 gm,
Protein 20 gm

*I learned to prepare this
nutritious meal from a student
from Iran, who was attending
graduate school at the*
*University of Nebraska.
Fatimeh explained to me that
her family prepared this dish
every wash day. Very early in
the morning, they made a fire in
a large rock-lined pit outside.
Then they placed a large
covered kettle, filled with the
above ingredients, over the coals
to cook slowly all day. At the
end of a day of doing laundry,
the food was ready with a
minimum of preparation. Of
course, they started with dry
beans and dry garbanzos,
presoaked the night before. They
served this Wash-Day Stew
spooned into pita bread and ate
it with their hands.*

1-2-3-4 Casserole

Betty K. Drescher
Quakertown, PA

Makes 8 servings
(Ideal slow cooker size: 4-quart)

1 lb. 90% lean ground beef
2 onions, sliced
3 carrots, thinly sliced
¹/₂ tsp. salt
¹/₈ tsp. pepper
1 cup cold water
¹/₂ tsp. cream of tartar
4 potatoes, thinly sliced,
 unpeeled
10³/₄-oz. can 98%-fat-free,
 reduced-sodium cream
 of mushroom soup
¹/₄ cup fat-free milk
¹/₂ tsp. salt
¹/₈ tsp. pepper

1. Layer in greased slow
cooker: ground beef, onions,
carrots, ¹/₂ tsp. salt, and
¹/₈ tsp. pepper.
2. Dissolve cream of tartar
in water in bowl. Toss sliced
potatoes with water. Drain.
3. Combine soup and milk.
Toss with potatoes. Add
remaining salt and pepper.
Arrange potatoes in slow
cooker.
4. Cover. Cook on Low 7-9
hours.

Exchange List Values:
Starch 1.5, Vegetable 1.0,
Meat, lean 1.0, Fat 0.5

Basic Nutritional Values: Calories
216 (Calories from Fat 59), Total Fat
7 gm (Saturated Fat 2.6 gm,
Polyunsat Fat 0.5 gm, Monounsat Fat
2.6 gm, Cholesterol 37 mg), Sodium
503 mg, Total Carbohydrate 24 gm,
Dietary Fiber 3 gm, Sugars 6 gm,
Protein 15 gm

Variations:
*1. Substitute sour cream for the
milk.*
*2. Top potatoes with ¹/₂ cup
shredded cheese.*

Herbed Beef Stew

Carol Findling
Princeton, IL

Makes 6-8 servings
(Ideal slow cooker size: 4-quart)

1 lb. beef round, cubed, trimmed of fat
4 Tbsp. seasoned flour*
1½ cups beef broth
1 tsp. Worcestershire sauce
1 garlic clove
1 bay leaf
4 medium carrots, sliced
3 medium potatoes, cubed, unpeeled
2 medium onions, diced
1 rounded tsp. fresh thyme, or ½ tsp. dried thyme
1 rounded tsp. chopped fresh basil, or ½ tsp. dried basil
1 Tbsp. fresh parsley, or 1 tsp. dried parsley
1 rounded tsp. fresh marjoram, or 1 tsp. dried marjoram

1. Put meat in slow cooker. Add seasoned flour. Toss with meat. Stir in remaining ingredients. Mix well.
2. Cover. Cook on High 4-6 hours, or Low 10-12 hours.

Make sure your bread really is "whole wheat"—if it doesn't have "whole wheat flour" listed as the first ingredient, it's white bread in disguise.

Exchange List Values:
Starch 1.5, Vegetable 2.0, Meat, lean 1.0

Basic Nutritional Values: Calories 220 (Calories from Fat 33), Total Fat 4 gm (Saturated Fat 1.2 gm, Polyunsat Fat 0.3 gm, Monounsat Fat 1.5 gm, Cholesterol 43 mg), Sodium 445 mg, Total Carbohydrate 28 gm, Dietary Fiber 4 gm, Sugars 7 gm, Protein 18 gm

* Seasoned Flour

1 cup flour
1 tsp. salt
1 tsp. paprika
¼ tsp. pepper

Audrey's Beef Stew

Audrey Romonosky
Austin, TX

Makes 4-6 servings
(Ideal slow cooker size: 4-quart)

3 medium carrots, sliced
3 medium potatoes, cubed, unpeeled
2 lbs. beef chuck, cubed, trimmed of fat
2 cups water
2 beef bouillon cubes
1 tsp. Worcestershire sauce
½ tsp. garlic powder
1 bay leaf
¼ tsp. salt
½ tsp. pepper
1 tsp. paprika
3 onions, chopped
1 rib celery, sliced
¼ cup flour
⅓ cup cold water

1. Combine all ingredients except flour and ⅓ cup cold water in slow cooker. Mix well.
2. Cover. Cook on Low 8 hours.
3. Dissolve flour in ⅓ cup water. Stir into meat mixture. Cook on High until thickened, about 10 minutes.

Exchange List Values:
Starch 1.5, Vegetable 2.0, Meal, lean 2.0

Basic Nutritional Values: Calories 287 (Calories from Fat 54), Total Fat 6 gm (Saturated Fat 1.8 gm, Polyunsat Fat 0.5 gm, Monounsat Fat 2.8 gm, Cholesterol 75 mg), Sodium 501 mg, Total Carbohydrate 30 gm, Dietary Fiber 5 gm, Sugars 9 gm, Protein 28 gm

Pot Roast

Carole Whaling
New Tripoli, PA

Makes 8 servings
(Ideal slow cooker size: 4-quart)

4 medium potatoes, cubed
4 medium carrots, sliced
1 medium onion, sliced
3-4 lb. rump roast, or pot roast, bone removed, trimmed of fat, and cut into serving size pieces
1 tsp. salt
½ tsp. pepper
1 bouillon cube
½ cup boiling water

1. Put vegetables and meat in slow cooker. Stir in salt and pepper.

2. Dissolve bouillon cube in water, then pour over other ingredients.

3. Cover. Cook on Low 10-12 hours.

Exchange List Values:
Starch 1.0, Vegetable 1.0, Meat, lean 3.0

Basic Nutritional Values: Calories 246 (Calories from Fat 56), Total Fat 6 gm (Saturated Fat 2.2 gm, Polyunsat Fat 0.3 gm, Monounsat Fat 2.5 gm, Cholesterol 73 mg), Sodium 485 mg, Total Carbohydrate 20 gm, Dietary Fiber 3 gm, Sugars 4 gm, Protein 27 gm

Swiss Steak
Marilyn Mowry
Irving, TX

Makes 4-6 servings
(Ideal slow cooker size: 4-quart)

3-4 Tbsp. flour
$1/2$ tsp. salt
$1/4$ tsp. pepper
$1^1/2$ tsp. dry mustard
$1^1/2$-2 lbs. round steak, trimmed of fat
1 Tbsp. canola oil
1 cup sliced onions
1 lb. carrots, sliced
$14^1/2$-oz. can whole tomatoes
1 Tbsp. brown sugar
$1^1/2$ Tbsp. Worcestershire sauce

1. Combine flour, salt, pepper, and dry mustard.

2. Cut steak in serving pieces. Dredge in flour mixture. Brown on both sides in oil in saucepan. Place in slow cooker.

3. Add onions and carrots.

4. Combine tomatoes, brown sugar, and Worcestershire sauce. Pour into slow cooker.

5. Cover. Cook on Low 8-10 hours, or High 3-5 hours.

Exchange List Values:
Vegetable 3.0, Meat, lean 3.0

Basic Nutritional Values: Calories 236 (Calories from Fat 71), Total Fat 8 gm (Saturated Fat 1.9 gm, Polyunsat Fat 1.0 gm, Monounsat Fat 3.6 gm, Cholesterol 64 mg), Sodium 426 mg, Total Carbohydrate 18 gm, Dietary Fiber 3 gm, Sugars 9 gm, Protein 23 gm

Hearty Beef Stew
Charlotte Shaffer
East Earl, PA

Makes 4-5 servings
(Ideal slow cooker size: 4-quart)

2 lbs. stewing beef, cubed, trimmed of fat
5 medium carrots, sliced
1 large onion, cut in chunks
3 ribs celery, sliced
22-oz. can stewed tomatoes
$1/2$ tsp. ground cloves
2 bay leaves
$1/4$ tsp. salt
$1/4$-$1/2$ tsp. pepper

1. Combine all ingredients in slow cooker.

2. Cover. Cook on High 5-6 hours.

Exchange List Values:
Vegetable 4.0, Meat, lean 3.0

Basic Nutritional Values: Calories 270 (Calories from Fat 66), Total Fat 7 gm (Saturated Fat 2.2 gm, Polyunsat Fat 0.5 gm, Monounsat Fat 3.4 gm, Cholesterol 90 mg), Sodium 575 mg, Total Carbohydrate 21 gm, Dietary Fiber 5 gm, Sugars 10 gm, Protein 31 gm

Variations:
1. Substitute 1 whole clove for $1/2$ tsp. ground cloves. Remove before serving.
2. Use venison instead of beef.
3. Cut back the salt and use 1 tsp. soy sauce.

Judy's Beef Stew

Judy Koczo
Plano, IL

Makes 4-6 servings
(Ideal slow cooker size: 4-quart)

2 lbs. stewing meat, cubed,
    trimmed of fat
5 medium carrots, sliced
1 medium onion, diced
3 ribs celery, diced
5 medium potatoes, cubed
28-oz. can tomatoes
$1/3$-$1/2$ cup quick-cooking
    tapioca
$1/2$ tsp. salt
$1/2$ tsp. pepper

    1. Combine all ingredients in slow cooker.
    2. Cover. Cook on Low 10-12 hours, or High 5-6 hours.

Exchange List Values:
Starch 2.0, Vegetable 3.0, Meat, lean 2.0

Basic Nutritional Values: Calories 357 (Calories from Fat 55), Total Fat 6 gm (Saturated Fat 1.8 gm, Polyunsat Fat 0.6 gm, Monounsat Fat 2.8 gm, Cholesterol 75 mg), Sodium 518 mg, Total Carbohydrate 47 gm, Dietary Fiber 7 gm, Sugars 10 gm, Protein 29 gm

Variation: Add 1 whole clove and 2 bay leaves to stew before cooking.

Slow-Cooker Stew

Trudy Kutter
Corfu, NY

Makes 6-8 servings
(Ideal slow cooker size: 4-quart)

2 lbs. boneless beef, cubed,
    trimmed of fat
4-6 celery ribs, sliced
6-8 medium carrots, sliced
6 medium potatoes, cubed,
    unpeeled
2 medium onions, sliced
28-oz. can tomatoes
$1/4$ cup minute tapioca
1 tsp. salt
$1/4$ tsp. pepper
$1/2$ tsp. dried basil, or
    oregano
1 garlic clove, pressed or
    minced

    1. Combine all ingredients in slow cooker.
    2. Cover. Cook on Low 8-10 hours.

Exchange List Values:
Starch 2.0, Vegetable 3.0, Meat, lean 1.0

Basic Nutritional Values: Calories 299 (Calories from Fat 42), Total Fat 5 gm (Saturated Fat 1.4 gm, Polyunsat Fat 0.5 gm, Monounsat Fat 2.1 gm, Cholesterol 56 mg), Sodium 549 mg, Total Carbohydrate 42 gm, Dietary Fiber 7 gm, Sugars 11 gm, Protein 23 gm

Italian Stew

Ann Gouinlock
Alexander, NY

Makes 6 servings
(Ideal slow cooker size: 4-quart)

$1^{1}/_{2}$ lbs. beef cubes
2-3 carrots, cut in 1-inch
    chunks
3-4 ribs celery, cut in
    $3/4$-1-inch pieces
1-$1^{1}/_{2}$ cups coarsely
    chopped onions
$14^{1}/_{2}$-oz. can stewed, or
    diced, tomatoes
$1/3$ cup minute tapioca
$1^{1}/_{2}$ tsp. salt
$1/4$ tsp. pepper
$1/4$ tsp. Worcestershire
    sauce
$1/2$ tsp. Italian seasoning

    1. Combine all ingredients in slow cooker.
    2. Cover. Cook on Low 8-10 hours.

Exchange List Values:
Starch 0.5, Vegetable 2.0, Meat, lean 2.0

Basic Nutritional Values: Calories 188 (Calories from Fat 41), Total Fat 5 gm (Saturated Fat 1.4 gm, Polyunsat Fat 0.3 gm, Monounsat Fat 2.1 gm, Cholesterol 56 mg), Sodium 508 mg, Total Carbohydrate 18 gm, Dietary Fiber 3 gm, Sugars 6 gm, Protein 19 gm

Venison or Beef Stew

Frances B. Musser
Newmanstown, PA

Makes 6 servings
(Ideal slow cooker size: 4-quart)

1½ lbs. venison or beef cubes
2 Tbsp. canola oil
1 medium onion, chopped
4 medium carrots, peeled and cut into 1-inch pieces
1 rib celery, cut into 1-inch pieces
4 medium potatoes, peeled and quartered
12-oz. can whole tomatoes, undrained
10½-oz. can beef broth
1 Tbsp. Worcestershire sauce
1 Tbsp. parsley flakes
1 bay leaf
¼ tsp. salt
¼ tsp. pepper
2 Tbsp. quick-cooking tapioca

1. Brown meat cubes in skillet in oil over medium heat. Transfer to slow cooker.
2. Add remaining ingredients. Mix well.
3. Cover. Cook on Low 8-9 hours.

Exchange List Values:
Starch 1.5, Vegetable 2.0, Meat, very lean 3.0, Fat 1.0

Basic Nutritional Values: Calories 313 (Calories from Fat 70), Total Fat 8 gm (Saturated Fat 1.5 gm, Polyunsat Fat 2.1 gm, Monounsat Fat 3.5 gm, Cholesterol 102 mg), Sodium 552 mg, Total Carbohydrate 29 gm, Dietary Fiber 4 gm, Sugars 7 gm, Protein 31 gm

---

Variation: For added color and flavor, add 1 cup frozen peas 5 minutes before end of cooking time.

Anything that raises your pulse and makes you breathe harder—swimming, walking, jogging, dancing, or biking—is aerobic. Find something you enjoy and do it for 30 minutes, three or four times a week.

Venison Swiss Steak

Dede Peterson
Rapid City, SD

Makes 6 servings
(Ideal slow cooker size: 4-quart)

2 lbs. round venison steak
¼ cup flour
2 tsp. salt
½ tsp. pepper
1 Tbsp. canola oil
2 medium onions, sliced
2 ribs celery, diced
1 cup carrots, diced
2 cups fresh, or stewed, tomatoes
1 Tbsp. Worcestershire sauce

1. Combine flour, salt, and pepper. Dredge steak in flour mixture. Brown in oil in skillet. Place in slow cooker.
2. Add remaining ingredients.
3. Cover. Cook on Low 7½-8½ hours.

Exchange List Values:
Starch 0.5, Vegetable 2.0, Meat, very lean 4.0, Fat 1.0

Basic Nutritional Values: Calories 277 (Calories from Fat 59), Total Fat 7 gm (Saturated Fat 1.7 gm, Polyunsat Fat 1.6 gm, Monounsat Fat 2.5 gm, Cholesterol 135 mg), Sodium 527 mg, Total Carbohydrate 14 gm, Dietary Fiber 3 gm, Sugars 6 gm, Protein 39 gm

Swiss Steak

Wanda S. Curtin, Bradenton, FL
Jeanne Hertzog, Bethlehem, PA

Makes 6 servings
(Ideal slow cooker size: 4-quart)

1½ lbs. round steak, about
  ¾" thick, trimmed of fat
2-4 tsp. flour
½-1 tsp. salt
¼ tsp. pepper
1 medium onion, sliced
1 medium carrot, chopped
1 rib celery, chopped
14½-oz. can diced
  tomatoes, or 15-oz. can
  tomato sauce

1. Cut steak into serving pieces.
2. Combine flour, salt, and pepper. Dredge meat in seasoned flour.
3. Place onions in bottom of slow cooker. Add meat. Top with carrots and celery and cover with tomatoes.
4. Cover. Cook on Low 8-10 hours, or High 3-5 hours.
5. Serve over noodles or rice.

Exchange List Values:
Vegetable 2.0, Meat, lean 2.0

Basic Nutritional Values: Calories 172 (Calories from Fat 48), Total Fat 5 gm (Saturated Fat 1.7 gm, Polyunsat Fat 0.3 gm, Monounsat Fat 2.2 gm, Cholesterol 64 mg), Sodium 381 mg, Total Carbohydrate 8 gm, Dietary Fiber 2 gm, Sugars 4 gm, Protein 22 gm

Margaret's Swiss Steak

Margaret Rich
North Newton, KS

Makes 6 servings
(Ideal slow cooker size: 4-quart)

1 cup chopped onions
½ cup chopped celery
2 lb. ½-inch thick round
  steak, trimmed of fat
¼ cup flour
3 Tbsp. oil
1 tsp. salt
¼ tsp. pepper
16-oz. can diced tomatoes
¼ cup flour
½ cup water

1. Place onions and celery in bottom of slow cooker.
2. Cut steak in serving-size pieces. Dredge in ¼ cup flour. Brown on both sides in oil in saucepan. Place in slow cooker.
3. Sprinkle with salt and pepper. Pour on tomatoes.
4. Cover. Cook on Low 9 hours. Remove meat from cooker and keep warm.
5. Turn heat to High. Blend together ¼ cup flour and water. Stir into sauce in slow cooker. Cover and cook 15 minutes. Serve with steak.

Exchange List Values:
Starch 0.5, Vegetable 1.0, Meat, lean 4.0, Fat 0.5

Basic Nutritional Values: Calories 305 (Calories from Fat 124), Total Fat 14 gm (Saturated Fat 2.8 gm, Polyunsat Fat 2.4 gm, Monounsat Fat 7.0 gm, Cholesterol 85 mg), Sodium 592 mg, Total Carbohydrate 14 gm, Dietary Fiber 2 gm, Sugars 4 gm, Protein 30 gm

Nadine & Hazel's Swiss Steak

Nadine Martinitz
Salina, KS
Hazel L. Propst
Oxford, PA

Makes 6-8 servings
(Ideal slow cooker size: 4-quart)

3 lb. round steak, trimmed
  of fat
⅓ cup flour
1 tsp. salt
½ tsp. pepper
3 Tbsp. canola oil
1 large onion, or more,
  sliced
1 large pepper, or more,
  sliced
14½-oz. can stewed
  tomatoes, or 3-4 fresh
  tomatoes, chopped
water

1. Sprinkle meat with flour, salt, and pepper. Pound both sides. Cut into 6 or 8 pieces. Brown meat in canola oil over medium heat on top of stove, about 15 minutes. Transfer to slow cooker.
2. Brown onion and pepper. Add tomatoes and bring to boil. Pour over steak.

Add water to completely cover steak.

   3. Cover. Cook on Low 6-8 hours.

Basic Nutritional Values: Calories 296 (Calories from Fat 116), Total Fat 13 gm (Saturated Fat 2.9 gm, Polyunsat Fat 1.9 gm, Monounsat Fat 6.4 gm, Cholesterol 96 mg), Sodium 547 mg, Total Carbohydrate 11 gm, Dietary Fiber 1 gm, Sugars 4 gm, Protein 33 gm

---

Variation: To add some flavor, stir in your favorite dried herbs when beginning to cook the steak, or add fresh herbs in the last hour of cooking.

Before and after working out, you should check your blood sugar levels. If you will be exercising for more than an hour, check your levels during the activity, too.

Beef, Tomatoes, & Noodles
Janice Martins
Fairbank, IA

Makes 8 servings
(Ideal slow cooker size: 4-quart)

1½ lbs. stewing beef, cubed, trimmed of fat
¼ cup flour
2 cups stewed tomatoes (if you like tomato chunks), or 2 cups crushed tomatoes (if you prefer a smoother gravy)
1 tsp. salt
¼-½ tsp. pepper
1 medium onion, chopped
water
12-oz. bag noodles

   1. Combine meat and flour until cubes are coated. Place in slow cooker.
   2. Add tomatoes, salt, pepper, and onion. Add water to cover.
   3. Cover. Simmer on Low 6-8 hours.
   4. Serve over cooked noodles.

Exchange List Values:
Starch 2.0, Vegetable 1.0, Meat, lean 2.0

Basic Nutritional Values: Calories 286 (Calories from Fat 46), Total Fat 5 gm (Saturated Fat 1.8 gm, Polyunsat Fat 0.7 gm, Monounsat Fat 2.1 gm, Cholesterol 83 mg), Sodium 490 mg, Total Carbohydrate 39 gm, Dietary Fiber 2 gm, Sugars 4 gm, Protein 20 gm

Big Beef Stew
Margaret H. Moffitt
Bartlett, TN

Makes 6-8 servings
(Ideal slow cooker size: 4-5-quart)

3 lb. beef roast, cubed, trimmed of fat
1 large onion, sliced
1 tsp. dried parsley flakes
1 medium green pepper, sliced
3 ribs celery, sliced
4 medium carrots, sliced
28-oz. can tomatoes with juice, undrained
1 garlic clove, minced
2 cups water

   1. Combine all ingredients.
   2. Cover. Cook on High 1 hour. Reduce heat to Low and cook 8 hours.
   3. Serve on rice or noodles.

Exchange List Values:
Vegetable 3.0, Meat, lean 3.0

Basic Nutritional Values: Calories 224 (Calories from Fat 61), Total Fat 7 gm (Saturated Fat 2.1 gm, Polyunsat Fat 0.4 gm, Monounsat Fat 3.1 gm, Cholesterol 85 mg), Sodium 248 mg, Total Carbohydrate 12 gm, Dietary Fiber 3 gm, Sugars 7 gm, Protein 28 gm

Note: For additional zest, add ¾ tsp. black pepper.

Spanish Round Steak

Shari Jensen
Fountain, CO

Makes 4-6 servings
(Ideal slow cooker size: 4-quart)

1 small onion, sliced
1 medium green bell
  pepper, sliced in rings
1 rib celery, chopped
2 lbs. round steak,
  trimmed of fat
2 Tbsp. chopped fresh
  parsley, or 2 tsp. dried
  parsley
1 Tbsp. Worcestershire
  sauce
1 Tbsp. dry mustard
1 Tbsp. chili powder
2 cups canned tomatoes
2 tsp. dry minced garlic
1/2 tsp. salt
1/4 tsp. pepper

1. Put half of onion, green pepper, and celery in slow cooker.
2. Cut steak into serving-size pieces. Place steak pieces in slow cooker.
3. Put remaining onion, green pepper, and celery over steak.
4. Combine remaining ingredients. Pour over meat.
5. Cover. Cook on Low 8 hours.
6. Serve over noodles or rice.

Exchange List Values:
Vegetable 2.0, Meat, lean 3.0

Basic Nutritional Values: Calories 222 (Calories from Fat 67), Total Fat 7 gm (Saturated Fat 2.3 gm, Polyunsat Fat 0.5 gm, Monounsat Fat 3.0 gm, Cholesterol 85 mg), Sodium 414 mg, Total Carbohydrate 8 gm, Dietary Fiber 2 gm, Sugars 5 gm, Protein 30 gm

Slow-Cooked Pepper Steak

Carolyn Baer, Conrath, WI
Ann Driscoll, Albuquerque, NM

Makes 6-8 servings
(Ideal slow cooker size: 4-quart)

1 1/2-2 lbs. beef round
  steak, trimmed of fat,
  cut in 3" x 1" strips
2 Tbsp. canola oil
1/4 cup soy sauce
1 garlic clove, minced
1 cup chopped onions
1 tsp. sugar
1/4 tsp. pepper
1/4 tsp. ground ginger
2 large green peppers, cut
  in strips
4 medium tomatoes cut in
  eighths, or 16-oz. can
  diced tomatoes
1/2 cup cold water
1 Tbsp. cornstarch

1. Brown beef in oil in saucepan. Transfer to slow cooker.
2. Combine soy sauce, garlic, onions, sugar, pepper, and ginger. Pour over meat.
3. Cover. Cook on Low 5-6 hours.

4. Add green peppers and tomatoes. Cook 1 hour longer.
5. Combine water and cornstarch to make paste. Stir into slow cooker. Cook on High until thickened, about 10 minutes.
6. Serve over rice or noodles.

Exchange List Values:
Vegetable 2.0, Meat, lean 2.0

Basic Nutritional Values: Calories 174 (Calories from Fat 68), Total Fat 8 gm (Saturated Fat 1.5 gm, Polyunsat Fat 1.3 gm, Monounsat Fat 3.7 gm, Cholesterol 48 mg), Sodium 546 mg, Total Carbohydrate 10 gm, Dietary Fiber 2 gm, Sugars 6 gm, Protein 17 gm

Pepper Steak Oriental

Donna Lantgen
Rapid City, SD

Makes 6 servings
(Ideal slow cooker size: 4-quart)

1 lb. round steak, trimmed
  of fat, sliced thin
3 Tbsp. light soy sauce
1/2 tsp. ground ginger
1 garlic clove, minced
1 medium green pepper,
  thinly sliced
4-oz. can mushrooms,
  drained, or 1 cup fresh
  mushrooms
1 medium onion, thinly
  sliced
1/2 tsp. crushed red pepper

1. Combine all ingredients in slow cooker.

2. Cover. Cook on Low 6-8 hours.

3. Serve as steak sandwiches topped with provolone cheese, or over rice.

Exchange List Values:
Vegetable 1.0, Meat, lean 2.0

Basic Nutritional Values: Calories 122 (Calories from Fat 32), Total Fat 4 gm (Saturated Fat 1.2 gm, Polyunsat Fat 0.2 gm, Monounsat Fat 1.5 gm, Cholesterol 43 mg), Sodium 368 mg, Total Carbohydrate 6 gm, Dietary Fiber 2 gm, Sugars 3 gm, Protein 16 gm

Powerhouse Beef Roast with Tomatoes, Onions, and Peppers

Donna Treloar, Gaston, IN

Makes 5-6 servings
(Ideal slow cooker size: 4-5-quart)

3 lb. boneless chuck roast, trimmed of fat
1 garlic clove, minced
1 Tbsp. canola oil
2-3 medium onions, sliced
2-3 sweet green and red peppers, sliced
16-oz. jar salsa
2 14½-oz. cans Mexican-style stewed tomatoes

1. Brown roast and garlic in oil in skillet. Place in slow cooker.

2. Add onions and peppers.

3. Combine salsa and tomatoes and pour over ingredients in slow cooker.

4. Cover. Cook on Low 8-10 hours.

5. Slice meat to serve.

Exchange List Values:
Vegetable 4.0, Meat, lean 4.0

Basic Nutritional Values: Calories 327 (Calories from Fat 97), Total Fat 11 gm (Saturated Fat 3.1 gm, Polyunsat Fat 1.3 gm, Monounsat Fat 4.7 gm, Cholesterol 106 mg), Sodium 565 mg, Total Carbohydrate 19 gm, Dietary Fiber 5 gm, Sugars 12 gm, Protein 38 gm

Variation: Make Beef Burritos with the leftovers. Shred the beef and heat with remaining peppers, onions, and ½ cup of the broth. Add 1 Tbsp. chili powder, 2 tsp. cumin, and salt to taste. Heat thoroughly. Fill warm flour tortillas with mixture and serve with sour cream, salsa, and guacamole.

Steak San Morco

Susan Tjon
Austin, TX

Makes 4-6 servings
(Ideal slow cooker size: 4-quart)

2 lbs. stewing meat, cubed, trimmed of fat
1 envelope sodium-free dry onion soup mix
29-oz. can peeled, or crushed, tomatoes
1 tsp. dried oregano
garlic powder to taste
2 Tbsp. canola oil
2 Tbsp. wine vinegar

1. Layer meat evenly in bottom of slow cooker.

2. Combine soup mix, tomatoes, spices, oil, and vinegar in bowl. Blend with spoon. Pour over meat.

3. Cover. Cook on High 6 hours, or Low 8-10 hours.

Exchange List Values:
Carbohydrate 0.5, Vegetable 1.0, Meat, lean 3.0

Basic Nutritional Values: Calories 237 (Calories from Fat 94), Total Fat 10 gm (Saturated Fat 2.1 gm, Polyunsat Fat 1.7 gm, Monounsat Fat 5.5 gm, Cholesterol 75 mg), Sodium 252 mg, Total Carbohydrate 10 gm, Dietary Fiber 2 gm, Sugars 5 gm, Protein 25 gm

Pat's Meat Stew

Pat Bishop, Bedminster, PA

Makes 4-5 servings
(Ideal slow cooker size: 4-quart)

1-2 lbs. beef roast, cubed,
  trimmed of fat
1 tsp. salt
1/4 tsp. pepper
2 cups water
2 small carrots, sliced
2 small onions, sliced
4-6 small potatoes,
  unpeeled, cut up in
  chunks, if desired
1/4 cup quick-cooking
  tapioca
1 bay leaf
10-oz. pkg. frozen peas, or
  mixed vegetables

1. Brown beef in nonstick
saucepan. Place in slow
cooker.
2. Sprinkle with salt and
pepper. Add remaining
ingredients except frozen
vegetables. Mix well.
3. Cover. Cook on Low
8-10 hours, or on High 4-5
hours. Add vegetables during
last 1-2 hours of cooking.

Exchange List Values:
Starch 2.0, Vegetable 1.0,
Meat, lean 1.0

Basic Nutritional Values: Calories
257 (Calories from Fat 33), Total Fat
4 gm (Saturated Fat 1.1 gm,
Polyunsat Fat 0.3 gm, Monounsat Fat
1.7 gm, Cholesterol 45 mg), Sodium
567 mg, Total Carbohydrate 36 gm,
Dietary Fiber 6 gm, Sugars 7 gm,
Protein 20 gm

Ernestine's Beef Stew

Ernestine Schrepfer
Trenton, MO

Makes 5-6 servings
(Ideal slow cooker size: 4-quart)

1 1/2 lbs. stewing meat,
  cubed, trimmed of fat
2 1/4 cups no-added-salt
  tomato juice
10 1/2-oz. can consomme
1 cup chopped celery
2 cups sliced carrots
4 Tbsp. quick-cooking
  tapioca
1 medium onion, chopped
1/4 tsp. salt
1/4 tsp. pepper

1. Combine all ingredients
in slow cooker.
2. Cover. Cook on Low 7-8
hours. (Do not peek.)

Exchange List Values:
Starch 0.5, Vegetable 2.0,
Meat, lean 2.0

Basic Nutritional Values: Calories
193 (Calories from Fat 40), Total Fat
4 gm (Saturated Fat 1.4 gm,
Polyunsat Fat 0.3 gm, Monounsat Fat
2.1 gm, Cholesterol 57 mg), Sodium
519 mg, Total Carbohydrate 17 gm,
Dietary Fiber 3 gm, Sugars 7 gm,
Protein 21 gm

Becky's Beef Stew

Becky Harder, Monument, CO

Makes 6-8 servings
(Ideal slow cooker size: 4-5-quart)

1 1/2 lbs. beef stewing meat,
  cubed, trimmed of fat
2 10-oz. pkgs. frozen
  vegetables—carrots,
  corn, peas
4 large potatoes, unpeeled,
  cubed
1 bay leaf
1 medium onion, chopped
15-oz. can stewing
  tomatoes of your
  choice—Italian,
  Mexican, or regular
8-oz. can tomato sauce
2 Tbsp. Worcestershire
  sauce
1 tsp. salt
1/4 tsp. pepper

1. Put meat on bottom of
slow cooker. Layer frozen
vegetables and potatoes over
meat.
2. Mix remaining
ingredients together in large
bowl and pour over other
ingredients.
3. Cover. Cook on Low 6-8
hours.

Exchange List Values:
Starch 2.0, Vegetable 2.0,
Meat, lean 1.0

Basic Nutritional Values: Calories
259 (Calories from Fat 31), Total Fat 3
gm (Saturated Fat 1.0 gm, Polyunsat Fat
0.4 gm, Monounsat Fat 1.6 gm,
Cholesterol 42 mg), Sodium 506
mg, Total Carbohydrate 39 gm, Dietary
Fiber 6 gm, Sugars 9 gm, Protein 19 gm

Santa Fe Stew

Jeanne Allen
Rye, CO

Makes 4-6 servings
(Ideal slow cooker size: 4-quart)

2 lbs. sirloin, or stewing
   meat, trimmed of fat,
   cubed
1 large onion, diced
2 garlic cloves, minced
2 Tbsp. canola oil
1½ cups water
1 Tbsp. dried parsley
   flakes
1 beef bouillon cube
1 tsp. ground cumin
¼ tsp. salt
3 medium carrots, sliced
1 lb. frozen green beans
1 lb. frozen corn
4-oz. can diced green
   chilies

1. Brown meat, onion, and garlic in oil in saucepan until meat is no longer pink. Place in slow cooker.
2. Stir in remaining ingredients.
3. Cover. Cook on High 30 minutes. Reduce heat to Low and cook 4-6 hours.

Exchange List Values:
Starch 1.0, Vegetable 3.0,
Meat, lean 3.0

Basic Nutritional Values: Calories 322 (Calories from Fat 99), Total Fat 11 gm (Saturated Fat 2.2 gm, Polyunsat Fat 2.0 gm, Monounsat Fat 5.6 gm, Cholesterol 75 mg), Sodium 554 mg, Total Carbohydrate 30 gm, Dietary Fiber 7 gm, Sugars 10 gm, Protein 28 gm

Eat plenty of green leafy vegetables; red, orange, and yellow fruits and vegetables; citrus fruits; nuts and seeds; and meat and fish. They are good for your heart and help prevent cancer.

Gone All-Day Casserole

Beatrice Orgish
Richardson, TX

Makes 8 servings
(Ideal slow cooker size: 4-5-quart)

1 cup uncooked wild rice,
   rinsed and drained
1 cup chopped celery
1 cup chopped carrots
2 4-oz. cans mushrooms,
   stems and pieces,
   drained
1 large onion, chopped
1 clove garlic, minced
½ cup slivered almonds
2 beef bouillon cubes
1¼ tsp. seasoned salt
2 lb. boneless round steak,
   trimmed of fat, cut into
   1-inch cubes
3 cups water

1. Place ingredients in order listed in slow cooker.
2. Cover. Cook on Low 6-8 hours or until rice is tender. Stir before serving.

Exchange List Values:
Starch 1.0, Vegetable 1.0,
Meat, lean 3.0

Basic Nutritional Values: Calories 264 (Calories from Fat 77), Total Fat 9 gm (Saturated Fat 1.7 gm, Polyunsat Fat 1.3 gm, Monounsat Fat 4.5 gm, Cholesterol 56 mg), Sodium 615 mg, Total Carbohydrate 23 gm, Dietary Fiber 4 gm, Sugars 4 gm, Protein 24 gm

Full-Flavored Beef Stew

Stacy Petersheim
Mechanicsburg, PA

Makes 6 servings
(Ideal slow cooker size: 4-quart)

2 lb. beef roast, trimmed
  of fat, cubed
2 cups sliced carrots
2 cups diced potatoes,
  unpeeled
1 medium onion, sliced
1½ cups frozen or fresh
  peas
2 tsp. quick-cooking tapioca
½ tsp. salt
½ tsp. pepper
8-oz. can tomato sauce
1 cup water
1 Tbsp. brown sugar

  1. Combine beef and
vegetables in slow cooker.
Sprinkle with tapioca, salt,
and pepper.
  2. Combine tomato sauce
and water. Pour over
ingredients in slow cooker.
Sprinkle with brown sugar.
  3. Cover. Cook on Low
8 hours.

Exchange List Values:
Starch 1.0, Vegetable 2.0,
Meat, lean 3.0

Basic Nutritional Values: Calories
271 (Calories from Fat 54), Total Fat
6 gm (Saturated Fat 1.9 gm,
Polyunsat Fat 0.4 gm, Monounsat Fat
2.8 gm, Cholesterol 75 mg), Sodium
539 mg, Total Carbohydrate 26 gm,
Dietary Fiber 5 gm, Sugars 11 gm,
Protein 28 gm

Variation: Add peas one hour
before cooking time ends to
keep their color and flavor.

Lazy Day Stew

Ruth Ann Gingrich
New Holland, PA

Makes 8 servings
(Ideal slow cooker size: 4-quart)

2 lbs. stewing beef,
  trimmed of fat, cubed
2 cups diced carrots
2 cups diced potatoes,
  unpeeled
2 medium onions, chopped
1 cup chopped celery
10-oz. pkg. lima beans
2 tsp. quick-cooking
  tapioca
1 tsp. salt
½ tsp. pepper
8-oz. can tomato sauce
1 cup water
1 Tbsp. brown sugar

  1. Place beef in bottom of
slow cooker. Add vegetables.
  2. Sprinkle tapioca, salt,
and pepper over ingredients.
  3. Mix together tomato
sauce and water. Pour over
top.
  4. Sprinkle brown sugar
over all.
  5. Cover. Cook on Low 8
hours.

Exchange List Values:
Starch 1.0, Vegetable 2.0,
Meat, lean 2.0

Basic Nutritional Values: Calories
229 (Calories from Fat 41), Total Fat
5 gm (Saturated Fat 1.4 gm,
Polyunsat Fat 0.4 gm, Monounsat Fat
2.1 gm, Cholesterol 56 mg), Sodium
558 mg, Total Carbohydrate 25 gm,
Dietary Fiber 5 gm, Sugars 8 gm,
Protein 22 gm

*Variation: Instead of lima
beans, use 1½ cups green
beans.*
    Rose M. Hoffman
    Schuylkill Haven, PA

Beef with Mushrooms

Doris Perkins
Mashpee, MA

Makes 4-6 servings
(Ideal slow cooker size: 4-quart)

1½ lbs. stewing beef,
  trimmed of fat, cubed
4-oz. can mushroom
  pieces, drained (save
  liquid)
half a garlic clove, minced
¾ cup sliced onions
3 Tbsp. canola oil
1 beef bouillon cube
1 cup hot water
8-oz. can tomato sauce
2 tsp. sugar
2 tsp. Worcestershire sauce
1 tsp. dried basil
1 tsp. dried oregano
½ tsp. salt
⅛ tsp. pepper

  1. Brown meat, mushrooms,
garlic, and onions in shortening
in skillet.

2. Dissolve bouillon cube in hot water. Add to meat mixture.

3. Stir in mushroom liquid and rest of ingredients. Mix well. Pour into slow cooker.

4. Cover. Cook on High 3 hours, or until meat is tender.

5. Serve over cooked noodles, spaghetti, or rice.

Exchange List Values:
Vegetable 2.0, Meat, lean 2.0, Fat 1.0

Basic Nutritional Values: Calories 210 (Calories from Fat 101), Total Fat 11 gm (Saturated Fat 1.8 gm, Polyunsat Fat 2.3 gm, Monounsat Fat 6.1 gm, Cholesterol 56 mg), Sodium 385 mg, Total Carbohydrate 8 gm, Dietary Fiber 2 gm, Sugars 5 gm, Protein 19 gm

Beef Pot Roast
Alexa Slonin
Harrisonburg, VA

Makes 8-10 servings
(Ideal slow cooker size: 4-5-quart)

12-oz. can whole tiny new potatoes, or 2 medium potatoes, cubed, or 2 medium sweet potatoes, cubed
8 small carrots, cut in small chunks
2 small onions, cut in wedges
2 ribs celery, cut up
2 1/2-3 lb. beef chuck, or pot roast, trimmed of fat
2 Tbsp. canola oil

3/4 cup water, dry wine, or tomato juice
1 Tbsp. Worcestershire sauce
1 tsp. instant beef bouillon granules
1 tsp. dried basil

1. Place vegetables in bottom of slow cooker.
2. Brown roast in oil in skillet. Place on top of vegetables.
3. Combine water, Worcestershire sauce, bouillon, and basil. Pour over meat and vegetables.
4. Cover. Cook on Low 10-12 hours.

Exchange List Values:
Starch 0.5, Vegetable 2.0, Meat, lean 2.0, Fat 0.5

Basic Nutritional Values: Calories 233 (Calories from Fat 78), Total Fat 9 gm (Saturated Fat 2.1 gm, Polyunsat Fat 1.3 gm, Monounsat Fat 4.1 gm, Cholesterol 61 mg), Sodium 231 mg, Total Carbohydrate 16 gm, Dietary Fiber 3 gm, Sugars 5 gm, Protein 22 gm

---

Did you know that one trip to the salad bar can add up to more than 1,000 calories? Watch out for side dishes like potato salad, pasta salad, and creamy soups; choose low-fat or fat-free dressing.

Pot Roast
Janet L. Roggie
Linville, NY

Makes 6-8 servings
(Ideal slow cooker size: 4-quart)

3 potatoes, thinly sliced
2 large carrots, thinly sliced
1 onion, thinly sliced
1 tsp. salt
1/2 tsp. pepper
3-4 lb. pot roast, trimmed of fat
1/2 cup water

1. Put vegetables in bottom of slow cooker. Stir in salt and pepper. Add roast. Pour in water.
2. Cover. Cook on Low 10-12 hours.

Exchange List Values:
Starch 1.0, Vegetable 1.0, Meat, lean 3.0

Basic Nutritional Values: Calories 219 (Calories from Fat 55), Total Fat 6 gm (Saturated Fat 2.2 gm, Polyunsat Fat 0.3 gm, Monounsat Fat 2.5 gm, Cholesterol 73 mg), Sodium 361 mg, Total Carbohydrate 14 gm, Dietary Fiber 2 gm, Sugars 3 gm, Protein 26 gm

Variations:
1. Add 1/2 tsp. dried dill, a bay leaf, and 1/2 tsp. dried rosemary for more flavor.
2. Brown roast on all sides in saucepan in 2 Tbsp. oil before placing in cooker.
Debbie Zeida
Mashpee, MA

Easy Pot Roast and Veggies

Tina Houk
Clinton, MO
Arlene Wines
Newton, KS

Makes 6 servings
(Ideal slow cooker size: 4-5-quart

3-4 lb. chuck roast,
 trimmed of fat
4 medium potatoes, cubed,
 unpeeled
4 medium carrots, sliced,
 or 1 lb. baby carrots
2 celery ribs, sliced thin,
 optional
1 envelope dry onion soup
 mix
3 cups water

1. Put roast, potatoes,
carrots, and celery in slow
cooker.
2. Add onion soup mix and
water.
3. Cover. Cook on Low 6-8
hours.

Exchange List Values:
Starch 1.5, Vegetable 1.0,
Meat, lean 3.0

Basic Nutritional Values: Calories
325 (Calories from Fat 76), Total Fat
8 gm (Saturated Fat 2.9 gm,
Polyunsat Fat 0.5 gm, Monounsat Fat
3.6 gm, Cholesterol 98 mg), Sodium
560 mg, Total Carbohydrate 26 gm,
Dietary Fiber 4 gm, Sugars 6 gm,
Protein 35 gm

Variations:
*1. To add flavor to the broth,
stir 1 tsp. kitchen bouquet,
1/2 tsp. salt, 1/2 tsp. black
pepper, and 1/2 tsp. garlic
powder into water before
pouring over meat and
vegetables.*
 Bonita Ensenberger
 Albuquerque, NM

*2. Before putting roast in
cooker, sprinkle it with the dry
soup mix, patting it on so it
adheres.*
 Betty Lahman
 Elkton, VA

Rump Roast and Vegetables

Kimberlee Greenawalt
Harrisonburg, VA

Makes 6-8 servings
(Ideal slow cooker size: 4-5-quart)

1 1/2 lbs. small potatoes
 (about 10), or medium
 potatoes (about 4),
 halved, unpeeled
2 medium carrots, cubed
1 small onion, sliced
10-oz. pkg. frozen lima
 beans
1 bay leaf
2 Tbsp. quick-cooking
 tapioca
2-2 1/2 lb. boneless beef
 round rump, round tip,
 or pot roast, trimmed of
 fat
2 Tbsp. canola oil

10 3/4-oz. can condensed
 vegetable beef soup
1/4 cup water
1/4 tsp. pepper

1. Place potatoes, carrots,
and onions in slow cooker.
Add frozen beans and bay
leaf. Sprinkle with tapioca.
2. Brown roast on all sides
in oil in skillet. Place over
vegetables in slow cooker.
3. Combine soup, water,
and pepper. Pour over roast.
4. Cover. Cook on Low 10-
12 hours, or High 5-6 hours.
5. Discard bay leaf before
serving.

Exchange List Values:
Starch 2.0, Vegetable 1.0,
Meat, lean 2.0

Basic Nutritional Values: Calories
288 (Calories from Fat 71), Total Fat
8 gm (Saturated Fat 1.9 gm,
Polyunsat Fat 1.3 gm, Monounsat Fat
3.7 gm, Cholesterol 50 mg), Sodium
349 mg, Total Carbohydrate 32 gm,
Dietary Fiber 6 gm, Sugars 5 gm,
Protein 22 gm

Hearty New England Dinner

Joette Droz
Kalona, IA

Makes 6-8 servings
(Ideal slow cooker size: 4-5-quart)

2 medium carrots, sliced
1 medium onion, sliced
1 celery rib, sliced
3 lb. boneless chuck roast, trimmed of fat
1/4 tsp. pepper
1 envelope dry onion soup mix
2 cups water
1 Tbsp. vinegar
1 bay leaf
half a small head of cabbage, cut in wedges
2 Tbsp. melted margarine, or butter
2 Tbsp. flour
1 Tbsp. dried minced onion
2 Tbsp. prepared horseradish
1/2 tsp. salt

1. Place carrots, onion, and celery in slow cooker. Place roast on top. Sprinkle with pepper. Add soup mix, water, vinegar, and bay leaf.
2. Cover. Cook on Low 7-9 hours. Remove beef and keep warm. Just before serving, cut into pieces or thin slices.
3. Discard bay leaf. Add cabbage to juice in slow cooker.
4. Cover. Cook on High 1 hour, or until cabbage is tender.

5. Melt margarine in saucepan. Stir in flour and onion. Add 1 1/2 cups liquid from slow cooker. Stir in horseradish and 1/2 tsp. salt. Bring to boil. Cook over Low heat until thick and smooth, about 2 minutes.
6. Return to cooker and blend with remaining sauce in cooker. When blended, serve over or alongside meat and vegetables.

Exchange List Values:
Vegetable 2.0, Meat, lean 3.0, Fat 0.5

Basic Nutritional Values: Calories 234 (Calories from Fat 85), Total Fat 9 gm (Saturated Fat 2.7 gm, Polyunsat Fat 1.3 gm, Monounsat Fat 4.0 gm, Cholesterol 74 mg), Sodium 607 mg, Total Carbohydrate 11 gm, Dietary Fiber 3 gm, Sugars 6 gm, Protein 26 gm

> **If you're taking a long car trip alone, take special care to avoid high or low blood sugars. Check your levels every 2-4 hours, and always keep some form of sugar with you, whether it's glucose tablets, regular soda, or a candy.**

Easy Beef Stew

Connie Johnson
Loudon, NH

Makes 6 servings
(Ideal slow cooker size: 4-5-quart)

1 lb. stewing beef
1 cup cubed turnip
2 medium potatoes, cubed, unpeeled
1 large onion, sliced
1 garlic clove, minced
2 large carrots, sliced
1/2 cup green beans, cut up
1/2 cup peas
1 bay leaf
1/2 tsp. dried thyme
1 tsp. chopped parsley
2 Tbsp. tomato paste
2 Tbsp. celery leaves
1/4 tsp. salt
1/4 tsp. pepper
1 qt., or 2 14 1/2-oz. cans, lower-sodium beef broth

1. Place meat, vegetables, and seasonings in slow cooker. Pour broth over all.
2. Cover. Cook on Low 6-8 hours.

Exchange List Values:
Starch 1.0, Vegetable 2.0, Meat, lean 1.0

Basic Nutritional Values: Calories 175 (Calories from Fat 29), Total Fat 3 gm (Saturated Fat 0.9 gm, Polyunsat Fat 0.3 gm, Monounsat Fat 1.4 gm, Cholesterol 38 mg), Sodium 466 mg, Total Carbohydrate 21 gm, Dietary Fiber 5 gm, Sugars 6 gm, Protein 16 gm

Pot Roast with Gravy and Vegetables

Irene Klaeger
Inverness, FL
Jan Pembleton
Arlington, TX

Makes 4-6 servings
(Ideal slow cooker size: 4-quart)

3-4 lb. bottom round, rump, or arm roast, trimmed of fat
1/4 tsp. salt
2-3 tsp. pepper
2 Tbsp. flour
1/4 cup cold water
1 tsp. kitchen bouquet, or gravy browning seasoning sauce
1 garlic clove, minced
2 medium onions, cut in wedges
4 medium potatoes, cubed, unpeeled
2 carrots, quartered
1 green pepper, sliced

1. Place roast in slow cooker. Sprinkle with salt and pepper.
2. Make paste of flour and cold water. Stir in kitchen bouquet and spread over roast.
3. Add garlic, onions, potatoes, carrots, and green pepper.
4. Cover. Cook on Low 8-10 hours, or High 4-5 hours.
5. Taste and adjust seasonings before serving.

Exchange List Values:
Starch 1.5, Vegetable 2.0, Meat, lean 3.0

Basic Nutritional Values: Calories 336 (Calories from Fat 75), Total Fat 8 gm (Saturated Fat 2.9 gm, Polyunsat Fat 0.5 gm, Monounsat Fat 3.4 gm, Cholesterol 98 mg), Sodium 577 mg, Total Carbohydrate 28 gm, Dietary Fiber 4 gm, Sugars 7 gm, Protein 36 gm

"Smothered" Steak
Susan Yoder Graber, Eureka, IL

Makes 6 servings
(Ideal slow cooker size: 4-quart)

1 1/2 lb. chuck, or round, steak, trimmed of fat, cut into strips
1/3 cup flour
1/4 tsp. pepper
1 large onion, sliced
1 green pepper, sliced
14 1/2-oz. can stewed tomatoes
4-oz. can mushrooms, drained
2 Tbsp. soy sauce
10-oz. pkg. frozen French-style green beans

1. Layer steak in bottom of slow cooker. Sprinkle with flour and pepper. Stir well to coat steak.
2. Add remaining ingredients. Mix together gently.
3. Cover. Cook on Low 8 hours.
4. Serve over rice.

Variations:
1. Use 8-oz. can tomato sauce instead of stewed tomatoes.
2. Substitute 1 Tbsp. Worcestershire sauce in place of soy sauce.
Mary E. Martin
Goshen, IN

Exchange List Values:
Vegetable 4.0, Meat, lean 2.0

Basic Nutritional Values: Calories 222 (Calories from Fat 50), Total Fat 6 gm (Saturated Fat 1.7 gm, Polyunsat Fat 0.4 gm, Monounsat Fat 2.3 gm, Cholesterol 64 mg), Sodium 613 mg, Total Carbohydrate 19 gm, Dietary Fiber 4 gm, Sugars 7 gm, Protein 25 gm

Veal and Peppers
Irma H. Schoen, Windsor, CT

Makes 4 servings
(Ideal slow cooker size: 4-quart)

1 1/2 lbs. boneless veal, cubed
3 green peppers, quartered
2 onions, thinly sliced
1/2 lb. fresh mushrooms, sliced
1 tsp. salt
1/2 tsp. dried basil
2 cloves garlic, minced
28-oz. can tomatoes

1. Combine all ingredients in slow cooker.
2. Cover. Cook on Low 7 hours, or on High 4 hours.
3. Serve over rice or noodles.

Basic Nutritional Values: Calories
194 (Calories from Fat 31), Total Fat
3 gm (Saturated Fat 0.9 gm,
Polyunsat Fat 0.5 gm, Monounsat Fat
1.0 gm, Cholesterol 95 mg), Sodium
555 mg, Total Carbohydrate 16 gm,
Dietary Fiber 4 gm, Sugars 9 gm,
Protein 26 gm

*Variation: Use boneless,
skinless chicken breast, cut into
chunks, instead of veal.*

Beef and Beans

Robin Schrock
Millersburg, OH

*Makes 8 servings
(Ideal slow cooker size: 4-quart)*

1 Tbsp. prepared mustard
1 Tbsp. chili powder
1/2 tsp. salt
1/4 tsp. pepper
1 1/2 lb. boneless round
 steak, trimmed of fat,
 cut into thin slices
2 14 1/2-oz. cans diced
 tomatoes, undrained
1 medium onion, chopped
1 beef bouillon cube,
 crushed
16-oz. can kidney beans,
 rinsed and drained

1. Combine mustard, chili
powder, salt, and pepper. Add
beef slices and toss to coat.
Place meat in slow cooker.
2. Add tomatoes, onion,
and bouillon.

3. Cover. Cook on Low 6-8
hours.
4. Stir in beans. Cook 30
minutes longer.
5. Serve over rice.

Basic Nutritional Values: Calories
182 (Calories from Fat 40), Total Fat
4 gm (Saturated Fat 1.3 gm,
Polyunsat Fat 0.4 gm, Monounsat Fat
1.8 gm, Cholesterol 48 mg), Sodium
582 mg, Total Carbohydrate 16 gm,
Dietary Fiber 4 gm, Sugars 6 gm,
Protein 21 gm

Three-Bean Burrito Bake

Darla Sathre
Baxter, MN

*Makes 8 servings
(Ideal slow cooker size: 4-quart)*

1 Tbsp. canola oil
1 onion, chopped
1 green bell pepper,
 chopped
2 garlic cloves, minced
16-oz. can pinto beans,
 drained
16-oz. can kidney beans,
 drained
15-oz. can black beans,
 drained
4-oz. can sliced black
 olives, drained
4-oz. can green chilies
2 15-oz. cans no-added-salt
 diced tomatoes
1 tsp. chili powder

1 tsp. ground cumin
6 6" flour tortillas
1 cup shredded Co-Jack
 cheese
sour cream

1. Saute onions, green
peppers, and garlic in large
skillet in oil.
2. Add beans, olives,
chilies, tomatoes, chili
powder, and cumin.
3. In greased slow cooker,
layer 3/4 cup vegetables, a
tortilla, 1/3 cup cheese. Repeat
layers until all those
ingredients are used, ending
with sauce.
4. Cover. Cook on Low 8-
10 hours.
5. Serve with dollops of
sour cream on individual
servings.

Basic Nutritional Values: Calories
346 (Calories from Fat 99), Total Fat
11 gm (Saturated Fat 3.3 gm,
Polyunsat Fat 1.5 gm, Monounsat Fat
4.8 gm, Cholesterol 15 mg), Sodium
573 mg, Total Carbohydrate 48 gm,
Dietary Fiber 12 gm, Sugars 8 gm,
Protein 16 gm

Beef Stew Bourguignonne

Jo Haberkamp
Fairbank, IA

Makes 6 servings
(Ideal slow cooker size: 4-quart)

2 lbs. stewing beef,
   trimmed of fat, cut in
   1-inch cubes
2 Tbsp. cooking oil
10³/4-oz. can condensed
   golden cream of
   mushroom soup
1 tsp. Worcestershire sauce
1/3 cup dry red wine
1/2 tsp. dried oregano
1/4 tsp. salt
1/2 tsp. pepper
1/2 cup chopped onions
1/2 cup chopped carrots
4-oz. can mushroom
   pieces, drained
1/2 cup cold water
1/4 cup flour

1. Brown meat in oil in saucepan. Transfer to slow cooker.
2. Mix together soup, Worcestershire sauce, wine, oregano, salt and pepper, onions, carrots, and mushrooms. Pour over meat.
3. Cover. Cook on Low 10-12 hours.
4. Combine water and flour. Stir into beef mixture. Turn cooker to High.
5. Cook and stir until thickened and bubbly.
6. Serve over noodles.

Exchange List Values:
Carbohydrate 1.0, Meat, lean 3.0, Fat 0.5

Basic Nutritional Values: Calories 266 (Calories from Fat 106), Total Fat 12 gm (Saturated Fat 2.5 gm, Polyunsat Fat 2.5 gm, Monounsat Fat 5.7 gm, Cholesterol 77 mg), Sodium 585 mg, Total Carbohydrate 12 gm, Dietary Fiber 2 gm, Sugars 2 gm, Protein 26 gm

Succulent Steak

Betty B. Dennison
Grove City, PA

Makes 4 servings
(Ideal slow cooker size: 4-quart)

1 1/2 lb. round steak,
   trimmed of fat, cut
   1/2-3/4-inch thick
1/4 cup flour
1/2 tsp. salt
1/4 tsp. pepper
1/4 tsp. paprika
2 medium onions, sliced
4-oz. can sliced
   mushrooms, drained
1/2 cup beef broth
2 tsp. Worcestershire sauce
2 Tbsp. flour
3 Tbsp. water

1. Mix together 1/4 cup flour, salt, pepper, and paprika.
2. Cut steak into 5-6 pieces. Dredge steak pieces in seasoned flour until lightly coated.
3. Layer half of onions, half of steak, and half of mushrooms into cooker. Repeat.
4. Combine beef broth and Worcestershire sauce. Pour over mixture in slow cooker.
5. Cover. Cook on Low 8-10 hours.
6. Remove steak to serving platter and keep warm. Mix together 2 Tbsp. flour and water. Stir into drippings and cook on High until thickened, about 10 minutes. Pour over steak and serve.

Exchange List Values:
Starch 0.5, Vegetable 2.0, Meat, lean 4.0

Basic Nutritional Values: Calories 295 (Calories from Fat 73), Total Fat 8 gm (Saturated Fat 2.6 gm, Polyunsat Fat 0.5 gm, Monounsat Fat 3.4 gm, Cholesterol 96 mg), Sodium 601 mg, Total Carbohydrate 18 gm, Dietary Fiber 3 gm, Sugars 6 gm, Protein 36 gm

> **Have your lipids (blood fats or cholesterol) checked once a year. HDL cholesterol is Healthy, so you want the number to be High; LDL cholesterol is Lousy, so the number should be Low.**

Steak Hi-Hat
Bonita Ensenberger
Albuquerque, NM

Makes 8-10 servings
(Ideal slow cooker size: 4-quart)

10³/4-oz. can reduced-
   sodium, 98%-fat-free
   cream of chicken soup
10³/4-oz. can reduced-
   sodium, 98%-fat-free
   cream of mushroom
   soup
1¹/2 Tbsp. Worcestershire
   sauce
¹/2 tsp. black pepper
1 tsp. paprika
2 cups onion, chopped
1 garlic clove, minced
1 cup fresh, small button
   mushrooms, quartered
2 lbs. round steak,
   trimmed of fat, cubed
1 cup fat-free sour cream
crisp bacon bits, optional

1. Combine chicken soup,
mushroom soup, Worcester-
shire sauce, pepper, paprika,
onion, garlic, and mushrooms
in slow cooker.
   2. Stir in steak.
   3. Cover. Cook on Low 8-9
hours.
   4. Stir in sour cream
during the last 20-30 minutes.
   5. Serve on hot buttered
noodles sprinkled with poppy
seeds. Garnish with bacon
bits.

Exchange List Values:
Carbohydrate 1.0, Meat,
lean 2.0

Basic Nutritional Values: Calories
178 (Calories from Fat 49), Total Fat
5 gm (Saturated Fat 1.8 gm,
Polyunsat Fat 0.6 gm, Monounsat Fat
2.0 gm, Cholesterol 56 mg), Sodium
321 mg, Total Carbohydrate 12 gm,
Dietary Fiber 1 gm, Sugars 4 gm,
Protein 19 gm

Variation: Add 1 tsp. salt with
seasonings in Step 1.

Steak Stroganoff
Marie Morucci
Glen Lyon, PA

Makes 6 servings
(Ideal slow cooker size: 4-quart)

2 Tbsp. flour
¹/2 tsp. garlic powder
¹/2 tsp. pepper
¹/4 tsp. paprika
1³/4 lb. boneless beef round
   steak, trimmed of fat
10³/4-oz. can reduced-
   sodium, 98%-fat-free
   cream of mushroom
   soup
¹/2 cup water
1 envelope sodium-free
   dried onion soup mix
9-oz. jar sliced mushrooms,
   drained
¹/2 cup fat-free sour cream
1 Tbsp. minced fresh
   parsley

1. Combine flour, garlic
powder, pepper, and paprika
in slow cooker.
   2. Cut meat into 1¹/2 x
¹/2-inch strips. Place in flour
mixture and toss until meat is
well coated.

3. Add mushroom soup,
water, and soup mix. Stir
until well blended.
   4. Cover. Cook on High
3-3¹/2 hours, or Low 6-7
hours.
   5. Stir in mushrooms, sour
cream, and parsley. Cover
and cook on High 10-15
minutes, or until heated
through.
   6. Serve with rice.

Exchange List Values:
Carbohydrate 1.0, Meat,
lean 3.0

Basic Nutritional Values: Calories
256 (Calories from Fat 66), Total Fat
7 gm (Saturated Fat 2.4 gm,
Polyunsat Fat 0.5 gm, Monounsat Fat
2.8 gm, Cholesterol 77 mg), Sodium
390 mg, Total Carbohydrate 17 gm,
Dietary Fiber 2 gm, Sugars 5 gm,
Protein 29 gm

Garlic Beef Stroganoff

Sharon Miller, Holmesville, OH

Makes 6 servings
(Ideal slow cooker size: 4-5-quart)

2 tsp. sodium-free beef
  bouillon powder
2 4½-oz. jars sliced
  mushrooms, drained
  with juice reserved
1 cup mushroom juice,
  with boiling water
  added to make a full
  cup
10¾-oz. can 98% fat-free,
  lower sodium cream of
  mushroom soup
1 large onion, chopped
3 garlic cloves, minced
1 Tbsp. Worcestershire
  sauce
1½ lb. boneless round
  steak, trimmed of fat,
  cut into thin strips
2 Tbsp. canola oil
6 ozs. fat-free cream
  cheese, cubed and
  softened

1. Dissolve bouillon in
mushroom juice and water in
slow cooker.
2. Add soup, mushrooms,
onion, garlic, and Worcestershire sauce.
3. Saute beef in oil in
skillet. Transfer to slow
cooker and stir into sauce.
4. Cover. Cook on Low 7-8
hours. Turn off heat.
5. Stir in cream cheese
until smooth.
6. Serve over noodles.

Exchange List Values:
Carbohydrate 0.5,
Vegetable 1.0, Meat, lean
2.0, Fat 0.5

Basic Nutritional Values: Calories
202 (Calories from Fat 73), Total Fat
8 gm (Saturated Fat 1.8 gm,
Polyunsat Fat 1.4 gm, Monounsat Fat
3.9 gm, Cholesterol 51 mg), Sodium
474 mg, Total Carbohydrate 10 gm,
Dietary Fiber 2 gm, Sugars 4 gm,
Protein 21 gm

Machaca Beef

Jeanne Allen
Rye, CO

Makes 12 servings
(Ideal slow cooker size: 4-quart)

1½ lb. beef roast
1 large onion, sliced
4-oz. can chopped green
  chilies
2 beef bouillon cubes
1½ tsp. dry mustard
½ tsp. garlic powder
1 tsp. seasoning salt
½ tsp. pepper
1 cup salsa

1. Combine all ingredients
except salsa in slow cooker.
Add just enough water to
cover.
2. Cover cooker and cook
on Low 10-12 hours, or until
beef is tender. Drain and
reserve liquid.
3. Shred beef using two
forks to pull it apart.
4. Combine beef, salsa,
and enough of the reserved

liquid to make of desired
consistency.
5. Use this filling for
burritos, chalupas,
quesadillas, or tacos.

Exchange List Values:
Meat, lean 1.0

Basic Nutritional Values: Calories
69 (Calories from Fat 20), Total Fat 2
gm (Saturated Fat 0.7 gm, Polyunsat
Fat 0.1 gm, Monounsat Fat 0.9 gm,
Cholesterol 24 mg), Sodium 392
mg, Total Carbohydrate 3 gm, Dietary
Fiber 1 gm, Sugars 2 gm, Protein 9
gm

Apple and Onion Beef Pot Roast

Betty K. Drescher
Quakertown, PA

Makes 8 servings
(Ideal slow cooker size: 4-quart)

3 lb. boneless beef roast,
  cut in half, trimmed of
  fat
2 Tbsp. canola oil
1 cup water
1 tsp. seasoning salt
½ tsp. soy sauce
½ tsp. Worcestershire
  sauce
¼ tsp. garlic powder
1 large tart apple,
  quartered
1 large onion, sliced
2 Tbsp. cornstarch
2 Tbsp. water

1. Brown roast on all sides in oil in skillet. Transfer to slow cooker.

2. Add water to skillet to loosen browned bits. Pour over roast.

3. Sprinkle with seasoning salt, soy sauce, Worcestershire sauce, and garlic powder.

4. Top with apple and onion.

5. Cover. Cook on Low 5-6 hours.

6. Remove roast and onion. Discard apple. Let stand 15 minutes.

7. To make gravy, pour juices from roast into saucepan and simmer until reduced to 2 cups. Combine cornstarch and water until smooth in small bowl. Stir into beef broth. Bring to boil. Cook and stir for 2 minutes until thickened.

8. Slice pot roast and serve with gravy.

Exchange List Values:
Carbohydrate 0.5, Meat, lean 3.0

Basic Nutritional Values: Calories 208 (Calories from Fat 85), Total Fat 9 gm (Saturated Fat 2.4 gm, Polyunsat Fat 1.3 gm, Monounsat Fat 4.6 gm, Cholesterol 73 mg), Sodium 265 mg, Total Carbohydrate 5 gm, Dietary Fiber 1 gm, Sugars 2 gm, Protein 24 gm

Roast
Tracey Yohn
Harrisburg, PA

Makes 6 servings
(Ideal slow cooker size: 4-quart)

2 lb. shoulder roast, trimmed of fat
1 tsp. pepper
1 tsp. garlic salt
1 small onion, sliced in rings
1 cup boiling water
1 beef bouillon cube

1. Place roast in slow cooker. Sprinkle with pepper and garlic salt. Place onion rings on top.

2. Dissolve bouillon cube in water. Pour over roast.

3. Cover. Cook on Low 10-12 hours, or on High 5-6 hours.

Exchange List Values:
Meat, lean 3.0

Basic Nutritional Values: Calories 148 (Calories from Fat 49), Total Fat 5 gm (Saturated Fat 1.9 gm, Polyunsat Fat 0.2 gm, Monounsat Fat 2.3 gm, Cholesterol 65 mg), Sodium 407 mg, Total Carbohydrate 2 gm, Dietary Fiber 0 gm, Sugars 1 gm, Protein 22 gm

Savory Sweet Roast
Martha Ann Auker
Landisburg, PA

Makes 6-8 servings
(Ideal slow cooker size: 4-quart)

3 lb. blade, or chuck, roast, trimmed of fat
2 Tbsp. canola oil
1 onion, chopped
$10^3/_4$-oz. can reduced-sodium, 99%-fat-free cream of mushroom soup
1/2 cup water
1/4 cup sugar
1/4 cup vinegar
3/4 tsp. salt
1 tsp. prepared mustard
1 tsp. Worcestershire sauce

1. Brown meat in oil on both sides in saucepan. Put in slow cooker.

2. Blend together remaining ingredients. Pour over meat.

3. Cover. Cook on Low 12-16 hours.

Exchange List Values:
Carbohydrate 1.0, Meat, lean 3.0

Basic Nutritional Values: Calories 241 (Calories from Fat 92), Total Fat 10 gm (Saturated Fat 2.7 gm, Polyunsat Fat 1.4 gm, Monounsat Fat 4.7 gm, Cholesterol 74 mg), Sodium 424 mg, Total Carbohydrate 11 gm, Dietary Fiber 0 gm, Sugars 8 gm, Protein 25 gm

Dilled Pot Roast

C.J. Slagle, Roann, IN

Makes 6 servings
(Ideal slow cooker size: 4-quart)

3 lb. beef pot roast,
  trimmed of fat
3/4 tsp. salt
1/4 tsp. pepper
2 tsp. dried dillweed,
  divided
1/4 cup water
1 Tbsp. vinegar
3 Tbsp. flour
1/2 cup water
1 cup fat-free sour cream

1. Sprinkle both sides of
meat with salt, pepper, and
1 tsp. dill. Place in slow cooker.
Add water and vinegar.
2. Cover. Cook on Low
7-9 hours, or until tender.
Remove meat from pot. Turn to
High.
3. Dissolve flour in water.
Stir into meat drippings. Stir in
additional 1 tsp. dill. Cook on
High 5 minutes. Stir in sour
cream. Cook on High another
5 minutes.
4. Slice meat and serve with
sour cream sauce over top.

Exchange List Values:
Carbohydrate 0.5, Meat,
lean 4.0

Basic Nutritional Values: Calories
260 (Calories from Fat 73), Total Fat
8 gm (Saturated Fat 2.9 gm,
Polyunsat Fat 0.3 gm, Monounsat Fat
3.4 gm, Cholesterol 101 mg), Sodium
403 mg, Total Carbohydrate 10 gm,
Dietary Fiber 0 gm, Sugars 3 gm,
Protein 34 gm

Beef Burgundy

Jacqueline Stefl
East Bethany, NY

Makes 6 servings
(Ideal slow cooker size: 4-quart)

5 medium onions, thinly
  sliced
2 lbs. stewing meat,
  trimmed of fat, cubed
1 1/2 Tbsp. flour
1/2 lb. fresh mushrooms,
  sliced
1 tsp. salt
1/4 tsp. dried marjoram
1/4 tsp. dried thyme
1/8 tsp. pepper
3/4 cup beef broth
1 1/2 cups burgundy wine

1. Place onions in slow
cooker.
2. Dredge meat in flour.
Put in slow cooker.
3. Add mushrooms, salt,
marjoram, thyme, and
pepper.
4. Pour in broth and wine.
5. Cover. Cook 8-10 hours
on Low.
6. Serve over cooked
noodles.

Exchange List Values:
Vegetable 3.0, Meat, lean
3.0

Basic Nutritional Values: Calories
219 (Calories from Fat 54), Total Fat 6
gm (Saturated Fat 1.9 gm, Polyunsat
Fat 0.4 gm, Monounsat Fat 2.8 gm,
Cholesterol 75 mg), Sodium 576
mg, Total Carbohydrate 14 gm, Dietary
Fiber 2 gm, Sugars 5 gm, Protein 26 gm

Goodtime Beef Brisket

AmyMarlene Jensen
Fountain, CO

Makes 10 servings
(Ideal slow cooker size: 4-5-quart)

3 1/2 lb. beef brisket,
  trimmed of fat
1 can beer
2 cups tomato sauce
2 tsp. prepared mustard
2 Tbsp. balsamic vinegar
2 Tbsp. Worcestershire
  sauce
1 tsp. garlic powder
1/2 tsp. ground allspice
2 Tbsp. brown sugar
1 small green, or red, bell
  pepper, chopped
1 medium onion, chopped
1/4 tsp. salt
1/2 tsp. pepper

1. Place brisket in slow
cooker.
2. Combine remaining
ingredients. Pour over meat.
3. Cover. Cook on Low 8-
10 hours.
4. Remove meat from
sauce. Slice very thin.
5. Serve on rolls or over
couscous.

Exchange List Values:
Carbohydrate 0.5, Vegetable
1.0, Meat, lean 3.0

Basic Nutritional Values: Calories
247 (Calories from Fat 85), Total Fat 9
gm (Saturated Fat 3.4 gm, Polyunsat
Fat 0.3 gm, Monounsat Fat 4.3 gm,
Cholesterol 86 mg), Sodium 472
mg, Total Carbohydrate 11 gm, Dietary
Fiber 1 gm, Sugars 9 gm, Protein 29 gm

Zippy Beef Tips

Maryann Westerberg
Rosamond, CA

Makes 6-8 servings
(Ideal slow cooker size: 4-quart)

2 lbs. stewing meat,
    trimmed of fat, cubed
2 cups sliced fresh
    mushrooms
10³/4-oz. can cream of
    mushroom soup
1 envelope fat-free dry
    onion soup mix
1 cup sugar-free 7-up, or
    other sugar-free lemon-
    lime carbonated drink

1. Place meat and
mushrooms in slow cooker.
2. Combine mushroom
soup, soup mix, and soda.
Pour over meat.
3. Cover. Cook on Low 8
hours.
4. Serve over rice.

Exchange List Values:
Carbohydrate 0.5, Meat,
lean 2.0

Basic Nutritional Values: Calories
166 (Calories from Fat 59), Total Fat
7 gm (Saturated Fat 2.1 gm,
Polyunsat Fat 1.2 gm, Monounsat Fat
2.5 gm, Cholesterol 58 mg), Sodium
349 mg, Total Carbohydrate 7 gm,
Dietary Fiber 1 gm, Sugars 2 gm,
Protein 19 gm

Horseradish Beef

Barbara Nolan
Pleasant Valley, NY

Makes 6-8 servings
(Ideal slow cooker size: 4-quart)

3 lb. pot roast, trimmed of
    fat
1 Tbsp. canola oil
¹/2 tsp. salt
¹/2 tsp. pepper
1 medium onion, chopped
6-oz. can tomato paste
¹/4 cup horseradish sauce

1. Brown roast on all sides
in oil in skillet. Place in slow
cooker. Add remaining
ingredients.
2. Cover. Cook on Low 8-
10 hours.

Exchange List Values:
Vegetable 1.0, Meat, lean
3.0, Fat 0.5

Basic Nutritional Values: Calories
220 (Calories from Fat 92), Total Fat
10 gm (Saturated Fat 3.3 gm,
Polyunsat Fat 0.9 gm, Monounsat Fat
4.0 gm, Cholesterol 77 mg), Sodium
268 mg, Total Carbohydrate 6 gm,
Dietary Fiber 1 gm, Sugars 2 gm,
Protein 25 gm

**Don't let diabetes
stop you from living life
to the fullest.**

Hungarian Goulash

Audrey Romonosky, Austin, TX

Makes 5-6 servings
(Ideal slow cooker size: 4-quart)

2 lbs. beef chuck, trimmed
    of fat, cubed
1 medium onion, sliced
¹/2 tsp. garlic powder
¹/2 cup ketchup
2 Tbsp. Worcestershire
    sauce
1 Tbsp. brown sugar
¹/4 tsp. salt
2 tsp. paprika
¹/2 tsp. dry mustard
1 cup cold water
¹/4 cup flour
¹/2 cup water

1. Place meat in slow
cooker. Add onion.
2. Combine garlic powder,
ketchup, Worcestershire
sauce, brown sugar, salt,
paprika, mustard, and 1 cup
water. Pour over meat.
3. Cover. Cook on Low 8
hours.
4. Dissolve flour in ¹/2 cup
water. Stir into meat mixture.
Cook on High until
thickened, about 10 minutes.
5. Serve over noodles.

Exchange List Values:
Carbohydrate 1.0, Meat,
lean 2.0

Basic Nutritional Values: Calories
207 (Calories from Fat 52), Total Fat
6 gm (Saturated Fat 2.0 gm,
Polyunsat Fat 0.3 gm, Monounsat Fat
2.3 gm, Cholesterol 65 mg), Sodium
444 mg, Total Carbohydrate 15 gm,
Dietary Fiber 1 gm, Sugars 7 gm,
Protein 23 gm

Chinese Pot Roast

Marsha Sabus
Fallbrook, CA

Makes 6 servings
(Ideal slow cooker size: 4-quart)

3 lb. boneless beef pot
   roast, trimmed of fat
2 Tbsp. flour
1 Tbsp. canola oil
2 large onions, chopped
1/4 cup light soy sauce
1/4 cup water
1/2 tsp. ground ginger

1. Dip roast in flour and
brown on both sides in oil in
saucepan. Place in slow
cooker.
  2. Top with onions.
  3. Combine soy sauce,
water, and ginger. Pour over
meat.
  4. Cover. Cook on High 10
minutes. Reduce heat to Low
and cook 8-10 hours.
  5. Slice and serve with rice.

Exchange List Values:
Carbohydrate 0.5, Meat,
lean 4.0

Basic Nutritional Values: Calories
272 (Calories from Fat 94), Total Fat
10 gm (Saturated Fat 3.1 gm,
Polyunsat Fat 1.1 gm, Monounsat Fat
4.7 gm, Cholesterol 98 mg), Sodium
446 mg, Total Carbohydrate 9 gm,
Dietary Fiber 1 gm, Sugars 4 gm,
Protein 34 gm

Peppery Roast

Lovina Baer
Conrath, WI

Makes 8-10 servings
(Ideal slow cooker size: 4-5-quart)

4 lb. beef, or venison,
   roast, trimmed of fat
1/2 tsp. garlic salt
1/2 tsp. onion salt
1/2 tsp. celery salt
2 tsp. Worcestershire sauce
2 tsp. pepper
1/2 cup ketchup
1 Tbsp. liquid smoke
3 Tbsp. brown sugar
1 Tbsp. dry mustard
dash of nutmeg
1 Tbsp. light soy sauce
1 Tbsp. lemon juice
3 drops hot pepper sauce

1. Place roast in slow
cooker.
  2. Combine remaining
ingredients and pour over
roast.
  3. Cover. Cook on High 6-8
hours.

Exchange List Values:
Carbohydrate 0.5, Meat,
lean 3.0

Basic Nutritional Values: Calories
202 (Calories from Fat 61), Total Fat
7 gm (Saturated Fat 2.3 gm,
Polyunsat Fat 0.3 gm, Monounsat Fat
2.7 gm, Cholesterol 78 mg), Sodium
422 mg, Total Carbohydrate 8 gm,
Dietary Fiber 0 gm, Sugars 6 gm,
Protein 26 gm

Mexican Pot Roast

Bernice A. Esau
North Newton, KS

Makes 10 servings
(Ideal slow cooker size: 4-quart)

3 lbs. boneless beef
   brisket, trimmed of fat,
   cubed
2 Tbsp. canola oil
1/2 cup slivered almonds
1 1/2 cups mild picante
   sauce, or hot, if you
   prefer
2 Tbsp. vinegar
1 tsp. garlic powder
1/4 tsp. cinnamon
1/4 tsp. dried thyme
1/4 tsp. dried oregano
1/8 tsp. ground cloves
1/8 tsp. pepper
1-1 1/4 cups water, as
   needed

1. Brown beef in oil in
skillet. Place in slow cooker.
  2. Combine remaining
ingredients. Pour over meat.
  3. Cover. Cook on Low 10-
12 hours. Add water as
needed.
  4. Serve with potatoes,
noodles, or rice.

Exchange List Values:
Vegetable 1.0, Meat, lean
3.0, Fat 1.0

Basic Nutritional Values: Calories
244 (Calories from Fat 124), Total Fat 14
gm (Saturated Fat 3.3 gm, Polyunsat Fat
1.8 gm, Monounsat Fat 7.2 gm,
Cholesterol 74 mg), Sodium 339
mg, Total Carbohydrate 4 gm, Dietary
Fiber 1 gm, Sugars 1 gm, Protein 25 gm

Chuck Wagon Beef
Charlotte Bull
Cassville, MO

Makes 10 servings
(Ideal slow cooker size: 4-quart)

4 lb. boneless chuck roast,
  trimmed of fat
1 tsp. garlic salt
1/4 tsp. black pepper
2 Tbsp. canola oil
6 garlic cloves, minced
1 large onion, sliced
1 cup water
1 bouillon cube
2 tsp. instant coffee
1 bay leaf, or 1 Tbsp.
  mixed Italian herbs
3 Tbsp. cold water
2 Tbsp. cornstarch

1. Sprinkle roast with garlic salt and pepper. Brown on all sides in oil in saucepan. Place in slow cooker. Reserve drippings.
2. Sauté garlic and onion in meat drippings in saucepan. Add 1 cup water, bouillon cube, and coffee. Cook over Low heat for several minutes, stirring until drippings loosen. Pour over meat in cooker.
3. Add bay leaf or herbs.
4. Cover. Cook on Low 8-10 hours, or until very tender. Remove bay leaf and discard. Remove meat to serving platter and keep warm.
5. Mix 3 Tbsp. water and cornstarch together until paste forms. Stir into hot liquid and onions in cooker.

Cover. Cook 10 minutes on High or until thickened.
6. Slice meat and serve with gravy over top or on the side.

Exchange List Values:
Vegetable 1.0, Meat, lean 3.0

Basic Nutritional Values: Calories 211 (Calories from Fat 83), Total Fat 9 gm (Saturated Fat 2.5 gm, Polyunsat Fat 1.1 gm, Monounsat Fat 4.3 gm, Cholesterol 78 mg), Sodium 271 mg, Total Carbohydrate 4 gm, Dietary Fiber 1 gm, Sugars 2 gm, Protein 26 gm

Exercise helps your body use insulin more efficiently, so it lowers your blood sugars more than normal—that's why insulin doses can usually be decreased before and after exercise.

French Dip Roast
Patti Boston
Newark, OH

Makes 8 servings
(Ideal slow cooker size: 4-quart)

1 large onion, sliced
3 lb. beef bottom roast,
  trimmed of fat
1/2 cup dry white wine, or
  water
1/2 of 1-oz. pkg. dry au jus
  gravy mix
2 cups lower-sodium
  100%-fat-free beef broth

1. Place onion in slow cooker. Add roast.
2. Combine wine and gravy mix. Pour over roast.
3. Add enough broth to cover roast.
4. Cover. Cook on High 5-6 hours, or Low 10-12 hours.
5. Remove meat from liquid. Let stand 5 minutes before slicing thinly across grain.

Exchange List Values:
Meat, lean 3.0

Basic Nutritional Values: Calories 177 (Calories from Fat 55), Total Fat 6 gm (Saturated Fat 2.2 gm, Polyunsat Fat 0.3 gm, Monounsat Fat 2.5 gm, Cholesterol 74 mg), Sodium 376 mg, Total Carbohydrate 3 gm, Dietary Fiber 1 gm, Sugars 2 gm, Protein 25 gm

Dripped Beef
Mitzi McGlynchey
Downingtown, PA

Makes 8 servings
(Ideal slow cooker size: 4-quart)

3 lb. chuck roast, trimmed
  of fat
1/2 tsp. salt
1 tsp. seasoned salt
1 tsp. white pepper
1 Tbsp. rosemary
1 Tbsp. dried oregano
1 Tbsp. garlic powder
1 cup water

   1. Combine all ingredients
in slow cooker.
   2. Cover. Cook on Low 6-7
hours.
   3. Shred meat using two
forks. Strain liquid and return
liquid and meat to slow
cooker. Serve meat and au jus
over mashed potatoes,
noodles, or rice.

Exchange List Values:
Meat, lean 3.0

Basic Nutritional Values: Calories
165 (Calories from Fat 56), Total Fat
6 gm (Saturated Fat 2.2 gm,
Polyunsat Fat 0.3 gm, Monounsat Fat
2.5 gm, Cholesterol 73 mg), Sodium
384 mg, Total Carbohydrate 2 gm,
Dietary Fiber 1 gm, Sugars 0 gm,
Protein 24 gm

Barbecued Roast Beef
Kim Stoltzfus, New Holland, PA

Makes 10 servings
(Ideal slow cooker size: 4-5-quart)

4 lb. chuck roast, trimmed
  of fat
1 cup no-salt-added
  ketchup
1 cup barbecue sauce
2 cups chopped celery
2 cups water
1 cup chopped onions
4 Tbsp. vinegar
2 Tbsp. brown sugar
2 Tbsp. Worcestershire
  sauce
1 tsp. chili powder
1 tsp. garlic powder
1/4 tsp. salt
5 cups cooked brown rice

   1. Combine all ingredients
except rice in large bowl.
Spoon into 5-quart cooker, or
2 3 1/2-quart cookers.
   2. Cover. Cook on Low 6-8
hours, or High 3-4 hours.
   3. Slice meat into thin
slices and serve in barbecue
sauce over rice.

Exchange List Values:
Starch 1.5, Carbohydrate
1.0, Meat, lean 3.0

Basic Nutritional Values: Calories 352
(Calories from Fat 72), Total Fat 8 gm
(Saturated Fat 2.6 gm, Polyunsat Fat 0.8
gm, Monounsat Fat 3.2 gm, Cholesterol
78 mg), Sodium 388 mg, Total
Carbohydrate 40 gm, Dietary Fiber 3
gm, Sugars 15 gm, Protein 29 gm

Sour Beef
Rosanne Hankins
Stevensville, MD

Makes 6-8 servings
(Ideal slow cooker size: 4-quart)

3 lb. pot roast, trimmed of
  fat
1/3 cup cider vinegar
1 large onion, sliced
3 bay leaves
1/2 tsp. salt
1/4 tsp. ground cloves
1/4 tsp. garlic powder

   1. Place roast in slow
cooker. Add remaining
ingredients.
   2. Cover. Cook on Low
8-10 hours.

Exchange List Values:
Meat, lean 3.0

Basic Nutritional Values: Calories
169 (Calories from Fat 55), Total Fat
6 gm (Saturated Fat 2.2 gm,
Polyunsat Fat 0.3 gm, Monounsat Fat
2.5 gm, Cholesterol 73 mg), Sodium
194 mg, Total Carbohydrate 3 gm,
Dietary Fiber 1 gm, Sugars 2 gm,
Protein 24 gm

Old World Sauerbraten

C.J. Slagle
Roann, IN
Angeline Lang
Greeley, CO

*Makes 8 servings
(Ideal slow cooker size: 4-quart)*

3¹/₂ lb. beef rump roast,
 trimmed of fat
1 cup water
1 cup vinegar
1 lemon, sliced but
 unpeeled
10 whole cloves
1 large onion, sliced
4 bay leaves
6 whole peppercorns
1 Tbsp. salt
2 Tbsp. sugar
12 gingersnaps, crumbled

1. Place meat in deep ceramic or glass bowl.
2. Combine water, vinegar, lemon, cloves, onion, bay leaves, peppercorns, salt, and sugar. Pour over meat. Cover and refrigerate 24-36 hours. Turn meat several times during marinating.
3. Place beef in slow cooker. Pour 1 cup marinade over meat.
4. Cover. Cook on Low 6-8 hours. Remove meat.
5. Strain meat juices and return to pot. Turn to High. Stir in gingersnaps. Cover and cook on High 10-14 minutes. Slice meat. Pour finished sauce over meat.

Exchange List Values:
Carbohydrate 0.5, Meat, lean 4.0

Basic Nutritional Values: Calories 235 (Calories from Fat 73), Total Fat 8 gm (Saturated Fat 2.6 gm, Polyunsat Fat 0.4 gm, Monounsat Fat 3.5 gm, Cholesterol 86 mg), Sodium 416 mg, Total Carbohydrate 10 gm, Dietary Fiber 0 gm, Sugars 4 gm, Protein 29 gm

Just for today, add up the calories from all your beverages, including alcohol. Pay special attention to serving sizes, since many sodas and juice bottles contain 2 servings, but the calories listed are for 1 serving.

Chili and Cheese on Rice

Dale and Shari Mast
Harrisonburg, VA

*Makes 6 servings
(Ideal slow cooker size: 4-quart)*

1 lb. extra-lean ground
 beef
1 medium onion, diced
1 tsp. dried basil
1 tsp. dried oregano
16-oz. can light red kidney
 beans
15¹/₂-oz. can chili beans
1¹/₂ cups stewed tomatoes,
 drained
2 cups cooked rice
6 Tbsp. fat-free grated
 cheddar cheese

1. Brown ground beef and onion in skillet. Drain. Season with basil and oregano.
2. Combine all ingredients except rice and cheese in slow cooker.
3. Cover. Cook on Low 4 hours.
4. Serve over cooked rice. Top with cheese.

Exchange List Values:
Starch 2.5, Vegetable 2.0, Meat, lean 2.0, Fat 0.5

Basic Nutritional Values: Calories 371 (Calories from Fat 78), Total Fat 9 gm (Saturated Fat 3.2 gm, Polyunsat Fat 0.6 gm, Monounsat Fat 3.6 gm, Cholesterol 49 mg), Sodium 745 mg, Total Carbohydrate 46 gm, Dietary Fiber 9 gm, Sugars 7 gm, Protein 26 gm

Loretta's Spanish Rice

Loretta Krahn
Mt. Lake, MN

Makes 8 servings
(Ideal slow cooker size: 4-5-quart)

1³/4 lbs. 90%-lean ground
  beef, browned
2 medium onions, chopped
2 medium green peppers,
  chopped
28-oz. can tomatoes
8-oz. can tomato sauce
1¹/2 cups water
2¹/2 tsp. chili powder
¹/2 tsp. salt
2 tsp. Worcestershire sauce
1¹/2 cups rice, uncooked

1. Combine all ingredients
in slow cooker.
2. Cover. Cook on Low 8-
10 hours, or High 6 hours.

Exchange List Values:
Starch 2.0, Vegetable 2.0,
Meat, lean 2.0, Fat 0.5

Basic Nutritional Values: Calories
335 (Calories from Fat 79), Total Fat
9 gm (Saturated Fat 3.3 gm,
Polyunsat Fat 0.6 gm, Monounsat Fat
3.7 gm, Cholesterol 60 mg), Sodium
550 mg, Total Carbohydrate 40 gm,
Dietary Fiber 3 gm, Sugars 8 gm,
Protein 24 gm

A Hearty Western Casserole

Karen Ashworth
Duenweg, MO

Makes 7 servings
(Ideal slow cooker size: 4-quart)

1 lb. 90%-lean ground
  beef, browned, drained
  of fat, patted dry
16-oz. can whole corn,
  drained
15-oz. can no-salt-added
  red kidney beans,
  drained
10³/4-oz. can reduced-
  sodium condensed
  tomato soup
¹/2 cup (2 ozs.) reduced-fat
  Colby cheese
¹/4 cup fat-free milk
1 tsp. minced dry onion
  flakes
¹/2 tsp. chili powder

1. Combine beef, corn,
beans, soup, cheese, milk,
onion, and chili powder in
slow cooker.
2. Cover. Cook on Low
1 hour.

Exchange List Values:
Starch 1.0, Carbohydrate
0.5, Meat, lean 2.0, Fat 0.5

Basic Nutritional Values: Calories
241 (Calories from Fat 72), Total Fat
8 gm (Saturated Fat 3.5 gm,
Polyunsat Fat 0.7 gm, Monounsat Fat
3.0 gm, Cholesterol 45 mg), Sodium
348 mg, Total Carbohydrate 23 gm,
Dietary Fiber 4 gm, Sugars 6 gm,
Protein 20 gm

Variation:
1 pkg. (of 10) refrigerator
  biscuits
2 Tbsp. margarine
¹/4 cup yellow cornmeal

Dip biscuits in margarine and
then in cornmeal. Bake 20
minutes or until brown. Top
beef mixture with biscuits
before serving.

**Eat more beans
(kidney, pinto, chick-
peas, etc.)—they're an
excellent alternative to
meat, providing protein
and fiber with no
saturated fat or
cholesterol.**

Green Chili Stew
Jeanne Allen, Rye, CO

Makes 8 servings
(Ideal slow cooker size: 4-quart)

2 Tbsp. oil
2 garlic cloves, minced
1 large onion, diced
1 lb. extra-lean ground
   sirloin
1/3 lb. ground pork
3 cups reduced-sodium
   chicken broth
2 cups water
2 4-oz. cans diced green
   chilies
4 large potatoes, diced
10-oz. pkg. frozen corn
1 tsp. black pepper
1 tsp. crushed dried
   oregano
1/2 tsp. ground cumin
1/2 tsp. salt

1. Brown garlic, onion,
sirloin, and pork in oil in
skillet. Cook until meat is no
longer pink. Drain.
2. Combine all ingredients
in slow cooker.
3. Cover. Cook on Low 4-6
hours, or until potatoes are
soft.

Exchange List Values:
Starch 2.0, Vegetable 1.0,
Meat, lean 2.0, Fat 0.5

Basic Nutritional Values: Calories
309 (Calories from Fat 99), Total Fat 11
gm (Saturated Fat 3.1 gm, Polyunsat Fat
1.6 gm, Monounsat Fat 5.3 gm,
Cholesterol 47 mg), Sodium 529
mg,Total Carbohydrate 33 gm, Dietary
Fiber 5 gm, Sugars 5 gm, Protein 20 gm

*Note: Excellent served with
warm tortillas or corn bread.*

Cowboy Casserole
Lori Berezovsky, Salina, KS

Makes 4-6 servings
(Ideal slow cooker size: 4-quart)

1 medium onion, chopped
1 1/4 lbs. 90%-lean ground
   beef, browned, drained,
   and patted dry
6 medium potatoes, sliced,
   unpeeled
1 clove garlic, minced
16-oz. can kidney beans
15-oz. can diced tomatoes
   mixed with 2 Tbsp.
   flour, or 10 3/4-oz. can
   tomato soup
1/4 tsp. salt
1/4 tsp. pepper

1. Layer onions, ground
beef, potatoes, garlic, and
beans in slow cooker.
2. Spread tomatoes or soup
over all. Sprinkle with salt
and pepper.
3. Cover. Cook on Low 5-6
hours, or until potatoes are
tender.

Exchange List Values:
Starch 2.5, Vegetable 2.0,
Meat, lean 2.0

Basic Nutritional Values: Calories
373 (Calories from Fat 73), Total Fat 8
gm (Saturated Fat 3.2 gm, Polyunsat Fat
0.6 gm, Monounsat Fat 3.4 gm,
Cholesterol 57 mg), Sodium 567
mg,Total Carbohydrate 48 gm, Dietary
Fiber 7 gm, Sugars 8 gm, Protein 27 gm

10-Layer
Slow-Cooker Dish
Norma Saltzman, Shickley, NE

Makes 8 servings
(Ideal slow cooker size: 4-quart)

6 medium potatoes, thinly
   sliced, unpeeled
1 medium onion, thinly
   sliced
15-oz. can corn, drained
15-oz. can peas, drained
1/4 cup water
1 1/2 lbs. ground beef,
   browned and drained
10 3/4-oz. can cream of
   mushroom soup

1. Layer 1: 1/4 of potatoes,
1/2 of onion
2. Layer 2: 1/2 can of corn
3. Layer 3: 1/4 of potatoes
4. Layer 4: 1/2 can peas
5. Layer 5: 1/4 of potatoes,
1/2 of onion
6. Layer 6: remaining corn
7. Layer 7: remaining
potatoes
8. Layer 8: remaining peas
and water
9. Layer 9: ground beef
10. Layer 10: soup
11. Cover. Cook on High
4 hours.

Exchange List Values:
Starch 2.5, Meat, lean 2.0,
Fat 0.5

Basic Nutritional Values: Calories
333 (Calories from Fat 101), Total Fat 11
gm (Saturated Fat 4.2 gm, Polyunsat Fat
1.6 gm, Monounsat Fat 4.2 gm,
Cholesterol 52 mg), Sodium 525
mg,Total Carbohydrate 37 gm, Dietary
Fiber 5 gm, Sugars 6 gm, Protein 22 gm

Hamburger Potatoes

Juanita Marner
Shipshewana, IN

Makes 3-4 servings
(Ideal slow cooker size: 4-quart)

3 medium potatoes, sliced, unpeeled
3 medium carrots, sliced
1 small onion, sliced
2 Tbsp. dry rice
1/4 tsp. salt
1/2 tsp. pepper
3/4 lb. 85%-lean ground beef, browned and drained
11/2-2 cups tomato juice, as needed to keep dish from getting too dry

1. Combine all ingredients in slow cooker.
2. Cover. Cook on Low 6-8 hours.

Exchange List Values:
Starch 2.0, Vegetable 1.0, Meat, lean 2.0, Fat 0.5

Basic Nutritional Values: Calories 311 (Calories from Fat 80), Total Fat 9 gm (Saturated Fat 3.4 gm, Polyunsat Fat 0.4 gm, Monounsat Fat 3.8 gm, Cholesterol 50 mg), Sodium 576 mg, Total Carbohydrate 38 gm, Dietary Fiber 5 gm, Sugars 9 gm, Protein 20 gm

Beef and Lentils

Esther Porter
Minneapolis, MN

Makes 12 servings
(Ideal slow cooker size: 4-5-quart)

1 medium onion
3 whole cloves
5 cups water
1 lb. lentils
1 tsp. salt
1 bay leaf
1 lb. (or less) ground beef, browned and drained
1/2 cup ketchup
1/4 cup molasses
2 Tbsp. brown sugar
1 tsp. dry mustard
1/4 tsp. Worcestershire sauce
1 medium onion, finely chopped

1. Stick cloves into whole onion. Set aside.
2. In large saucepan, combine water, lentils, salt, bay leaf, and whole onion with cloves. Simmer 30 minutes.
3. Meanwhile, combine all remaining ingredients in slow cooker. Stir in simmered ingredients from saucepan. Add additional water if mixture seems dry.
4. Cover. Cook on Low 6-8 hours (check to see if lentils are tender).

Exchange List Values:
Starch 1.5, Carbohydrate 0.5, Vegetable 1.0, Meat, lean 1.0

Basic Nutritional Values: Calories 230 (Calories from Fat 39), Total Fat 4 gm (Saturated Fat 1.5 gm, Polyunsat Fat 0.3 gm, Monounsat Fat 1.7 gm, Cholesterol 22 mg), Sodium 342 mg, Total Carbohydrate 32 gm, Dietary Fiber 9 gm, Sugars 11 gm, Protein 17 gm

Note: This dish freezes well.

Variation: Top with sour cream and/or salsa when serving.

Supper-in-a-Dish

Martha Hershey, Ronks, PA

Makes 8 servings
(Ideal slow cooker size: 4-quart)

1 lb. ground beef, browned and drained
11/2 cups sliced raw potatoes
1 cup sliced carrots
1 cup fresh or frozen peas
1/2 cup chopped onions
1/2 cup chopped celery
1/4 cup chopped green peppers
1/4 tsp. salt
1/4 tsp. pepper
103/4-oz. can 98%-fat-free lower-sodium cream of chicken, or mushroom, soup
1/4 cup fat-free milk
2 ozs. grated fat-free sharp cheddar cheese

1. Layer ground beef, potatoes, carrots, peas, onions, celery, green peppers, salt, and pepper in slow cooker.

2. Combine soup and milk. Pour over layered ingredients. Sprinkle with cheese.

3. Cover. Cook on High 4 hours.

Exchange List Values:
Starch 1.0, Vegetable 1.0, Meat, lean 2.0, Fat 0.5

Basic Nutritional Values: Calories 246 (Calories from Fat 79), Total Fat 9 gm (Saturated Fat 3.4 gm, Polyunsat Fat 0.7 gm, Monounsat Fat 3.5 gm, Cholesterol 50 mg), Sodium 462 mg, Total Carbohydrate 20 gm, Dietary Fiber 3 gm, Sugars 6 gm, Protein 21 gm

Meal-in-One-Casserole

Elizabeth Yoder, Millersburg, OH
Marcella Stalter, Flanagan, IL

Makes 8 servings
(Ideal slow cooker size: 4-quart)

1 lb. ground beef
1 medium onion, chopped
1 medium green pepper, chopped
15¼-oz. can whole kernel corn, drained
4-oz. can mushrooms, drained
¼ tsp. pepper
11-oz. jar salsa
5 cups uncooked medium egg noodles
28-oz. can no-added-salt diced tomatoes, undrained
1 cup shredded fat-free cheddar cheese

1. Cook beef and onion in saucepan over medium heat until meat is no longer pink. Drain. Transfer to slow cooker.

2. Top with green pepper, corn, and mushrooms. Sprinkle with pepper. Pour salsa over mushrooms. Cover and cook on Low 3 hours.

3. Cook noodles according to package in separate pan. Drain and add to slow cooker after mixture in cooker has cooked for 3 hours. Top with tomatoes. Sprinkle with cheese.

Exchange List Values:
Starch 1.5, Vegetable 2.0, Meat, lean 2.0

Basic Nutritional Values: Calories 282 (Calories from Fat 67), Total Fat 7 gm (Saturated Fat 2.7 gm, Polyunsat Fat 0.8 gm, Monounsat Fat 2.9 gm, Cholesterol 58 mg), Sodium 393 mg, Total Carbohydrate 34 gm, Dietary Fiber 4 gm, Sugars 8 gm, Protein 21 gm

Yum-e-setti

Elsie Schlabach, Millersburg, OH

Makes 9 servings
(Ideal slow cooker size: 4-5-quart)

1¼ lbs. 90%-lean ground beef, browned, drained and patted dry
10¾-oz. can 98%-fat-free, lower-sodium tomato soup
8-oz. pkg. wide noodles, cooked

10¾-oz. can 98%-fat-free, lower-sodium cream of chicken soup
1 cup chopped celery, cooked tender
1 lb. frozen mixed vegetables (including corn)
3 ozs. Velveeta Light cheese, cubed

1. Combine ground beef and tomato soup.

2. Combine noodles, chicken soup, and celery.

3. Layer beef mixture, chicken mixture, and vegetables into slow cooker. Lay cheese over top.

4. Cover. Cook on Low 2-3 hours.

Exchange List Values:
Starch 2.0, Vegetable 1.0, Meat, lean 2.0

Basic Nutritional Values: Calories 293 (Calories from Fat 76), Total Fat 8 gm (Saturated Fat 3.5 gm, Polyunsat Fat 1.0 gm, Monounsat Fat 3.0 gm, Cholesterol 68 mg), Sodium 478 mg, Total Carbohydrate 34 gm, Dietary Fiber 3 gm, Sugars 7 gm, Protein 20 gm

Variation: For more "bite," use shredded cheddar cheese instead of cubed Velveeta.

Keep healthy snacks handy! A delayed meal or change in your schedule can happen anytime, so keep snacks in your desk, briefcase, pocketbook, or glove compartment.

Meatball Stew

Nanci Keatley, Salem, OR
Ada Miller, Sugarcreek, OH

Makes 8 servings
(Ideal slow cooker size: 4-quart)

1³/₄ lbs. 98%-lean ground
   beef
¹/₂ tsp. pepper
6 medium potatoes, cubed,
   unpeeled
1 large onion, sliced
6 medium carrots, sliced
1 cup ketchup
1 cup water
1¹/₂ tsp. balsamic vinegar
1 tsp. dried basil
1 tsp. dried oregano
¹/₂ tsp. pepper

1. Combine beef, and
¹/₂ tsp. pepper. Mix well.
Shape into 1-inch balls.
Brown meatballs in saucepan
over medium heat. Drain. Pat
dry.
   2. Place potatoes, onion,
and carrots in slow cooker.
Top with meatballs.
   3. Combine ketchup,
water, vinegar, basil, oregano,
and ¹/₂ tsp. pepper. Pour over
meatballs.
   4. Cover. Cook on High
4-5 hours, or until vegetables
are tender.

Exchange List Values:
Starch 1.5, Carbohydrate
0.5, Vegetable 2.0, Meat,
lean 2.0

Basic Nutritional Values: Calories
318 (Calories from Fat 77), Total Fat
9 gm (Saturated Fat 3.3 gm,
Polyunsat Fat 0.4 gm, Monounsat Fat
3.5 gm, Cholesterol 60 mg), Sodium
610 mg, Total Carbohydrate 38 gm,
Dietary Fiber 5 gm, Sugars 9 gm,
Protein 23 gm

Mary Ellen's Barbecued Meatballs

Mary Ellen Wilcox
Scatia, NY

Makes about 60 small meatballs
(10 servings)
(Ideal slow cooker size: 4-quart)

Meatballs:
³/₄ lb. ground beef
³/₄ cup bread crumbs
1¹/₂ Tbsp. minced onion
¹/₂ tsp. horseradish
3 drops Tabasco sauce
2 eggs, beaten
¹/₄ tsp. salt
¹/₂ tsp. pepper
1 Tbsp. canola oil

Sauce:
³/₄ cup ketchup
¹/₂ cup water
¹/₄ cup cider vinegar
2 Tbsp. brown sugar
1 Tbsp. minced onion
2 tsp. horseradish
1 tsp. dry mustard
3 drops Tabasco
dash pepper

1. Combine all meatball
ingredients. Shape into
³/₄-inch balls. Brown in
nonstick skillet. Place in slow
cooker.

2. Combine all sauce
ingredients. Pour over
meatballs.
   3. Cover. Cook on Low
5 hours.

Exchange List Values:
Starch 0.5, Carbohydrate
0.5, Meat, lean 1.0, Fat 0.5

Basic Nutritional Values: Calories
148 (Calories from Fat 57), Total Fat
6 gm (Saturated Fat 1.8 gm,
Polyunsat Fat 0.8 gm, Monounsat Fat
2.8 gm, Cholesterol 63 mg), Sodium
378 mg, Total Carbohydrate 14 gm,
Dietary Fiber 1 gm, Sugars 6 gm,
Protein 9 gm

Cocktail Meatballs

Irene Klaeger
Inverness, FL

Makes 20 appetizer servings
(Ideal slow cooker size: 4-quart)

2 lbs. ground beef
1/3 cup ketchup
3 tsp. dry bread crumbs
1 egg, beaten
2 tsp. onion flakes
3/4 tsp. garlic salt
1/2 tsp. pepper
1 cup ketchup
1/2 cup packed brown sugar
6-oz. can tomato paste
1/4 cup light soy sauce
1/4 cup cider vinegar
1-1 1/2 tsp. hot pepper sauce

1. Combine ground beef, 1/3 cup ketchup, bread crumbs, egg, onion flakes, garlic salt, and pepper. Mix well. Shape into 1-inch meatballs. Place on jelly roll pan. Bake at 350° for 18 minutes, or until brown. Place in slow cooker.
2. Combine 1 cup ketchup, brown sugar, tomato paste, soy sauce, vinegar, and hot pepper sauce. Pour over meatballs.
3. Cover. Cook on Low 4 hours.

Exchange List Values:
Carbohydrate 1.0, Meat, lean 1.0

Basic Nutritional Values: Calories 128 (Calories from Fat 45), Total Fat 5 gm (Saturated Fat 1.9 gm, Polyunsat Fat 0.2 gm, Monounsat Fat 2.1 gm, Cholesterol 37 mg), Sodium 318 mg, Total Carbohydrate 12 gm, Dietary Fiber 1 gm, Sugars 8 gm, Protein 9 gm

Swedish Meatballs

Zona Mae Bontrager
Kokomo, IN

Makes 12 servings
(Ideal slow cooker size: 4-quart)

3/4 lb. ground beef
1/2 lb. ground pork
1/2 cup minced onions
3/4 cup fine dry bread crumbs
1 Tbsp. minced parsley
1 tsp. salt
1/8 tsp. pepper
1/2 tsp. garlic powder
1 Tbsp. Worcestershire sauce
1 egg
1/2 cup fat-free milk
2 Tbsp. canola oil

Gravy:
1/4 cup flour
1/4 tsp. salt
1/4 tsp. garlic powder
1/8 tsp. pepper
1 tsp. paprika
2 cups boiling water
3/4 cup fat-free sour cream

1. Combine meats, onions, bread crumbs, parsley, salt, pepper, garlic powder, Worcestershire sauce, egg, and milk.
2. Shape into balls the size of a walnut. Brown in oil in skillet. Reserve drippings, and place meatballs in slow cooker.
3. Cover. Cook on High 10-15 minutes.
4. Stir flour, salt, garlic powder, pepper, and paprika into hot drippings in skillet. Stir in water and sour cream. Pour over meatballs.
5. Cover. Reduce heat to Low. Cook 4-5 hours.
6. Serve over rice or noodles.

Exchange List Values:
Starch 1.0, Meat, lean 1.0, Fat 1.0

Basic Nutritional Values: Calories 168 (Calories from Fat 78), Total Fat 9 gm (Saturated Fat 2.5 gm, Polyunsat Fat 1.2 gm, Monounsat Fat 4.1 gm, Cholesterol 48 mg), Sodium 368 mg, Total Carbohydrate 11 gm, Dietary Fiber 0 gm, Sugars 2 gm, Protein 11 gm

Find out if your local shopping mall opens early so people can walk the mall before the stores open. If it has a walking club, join it!

Italian Meatball Subs

Bonnie Miller
Louisville, OH

Makes 9 servings
(Ideal slow cooker size: 4-5-quart)

1 egg, beaten
1/4 cup fat-free milk
1/2 cup dry bread crumbs
2 Tbsp. freshly grated
   Parmesan cheese
1/2 tsp. salt
1/4 tsp. pepper
1/8 tsp. garlic powder
3/4 lb. 85%-lean ground beef
1/2 lb. bulk pork sausage

Sauce
15-oz. can no-added-salt
   tomato sauce
6-oz. can tomato paste
1 small onion, chopped
1/2 cup chopped green bell
   pepper
1/2 cup red wine, or beef
   broth
1/3 cup water
2 garlic cloves, minced
1 tsp. dried oregano
1/2 tsp. salt
1/2 tsp. pepper
1/2 tsp. sugar

1. Make meatballs by
combining egg and milk. Add
bread crumbs, cheese, and
seasonings. Add meats. Mix
well. Shape into 1" balls.
Broil or saute until brown.
Put in slow cooker.
   2. Combine sauce
ingredients. Pour over
meatballs.

3. Cover. Cook on Low 4-6
hours.
   4. Serve on rolls with
creamy red potatoes, salad,
and dessert.

Exchange List Values:
Starch 0.5, Vegetable 1.0,
Meat, medium fat 1.0, Fat
1.0

Basic Nutritional Values: Calories
186 (Calories from Fat 81), Total Fat
9 gm (Saturated Fat 3.3 gm,
Polyunsat Fat 0.9 gm, Monounsat Fat
3.8 gm, Cholesterol 57 mg), Sodium
403 mg, Total Carbohydrate 14 gm,
Dietary Fiber 2 gm, Sugars 5 gm,
Protein 13 gm

Sweet and Sour Meatballs

Elaine Unruh
Minneapolis, MN

Makes 6-8 main-dish servings, or
20 appetizer servings
(Ideal slow cooker size: 4-quart)

Meatballs:
2 lbs. ground beef
1 1/4 cups bread crumbs
1/4 tsp. salt
1 tsp. pepper
2-3 Tbsp. Worcestershire
   sauce
1 egg
1/2 tsp. garlic salt
1/4 cup finely chopped
   onions

Sauce:
20-oz. can pineapple
   chunks, juice reserved
3 Tbsp. cornstarch
1/4 cup cold water
1 cups ketchup
2 Tbsp. Worcestershire
   sauce
1/4 tsp. salt
1/4 tsp. pepper
1/4 tsp. garlic salt
1/2 cup chopped green
   peppers

1. Combine all meatball
ingredients. Shape into 60
meatballs. Brown in nonstick
skillet, rolling so all sides are
browned. Place meatballs in
slow cooker.
   2. Pour juice from
pineapples into skillet. Stir
into drippings.
   3. Combine cornstarch and
cold water. Add to skillet and
stir until thickened.
   4. Stir in ketchup and
Worcestershire sauce. Season
with salt, pepper, and garlic
salt. Add green peppers and
pineapples. Pour over
meatballs.
   5. Cover. Cook on Low 6
hours.

Exchange List Values:
Carbohydrate 1.0, Meat,
lean 1.0, Fat 0.5

Basic Nutritional Values: Calories
150 (Calories from Fat 48), Total Fat
5 gm (Saturated Fat 1.9 gm,
Polyunsat Fat 0.3 gm, Monounsat Fat
2.2 gm, Cholesterol 37 mg), Sodium
430 mg, Total Carbohydrate 16 gm,
Dietary Fiber 1 gm, Sugars 7 gm,
Protein 10 gm

Swedish Cabbage Rolls

Fean Butzer
Batavia, NY
Pam Hochstedler
Kalona, IA

Makes 6 servings
1 serving = 2 cabbage rolls)
(Ideal slow cooker size: 4-5-quart)

12 large cabbage leaves
1 egg, beaten
1/4 cup fat-free milk
1/4 cup finely chopped
  onions
3/4 tsp. salt
1/4 tsp. pepper
1 lb. ground beef, browned
  and drained
1 cup cooked rice
8-oz. can tomato sauce
1 Tbsp. brown sugar
1 Tbsp. lemon juice
1 tsp. Worcestershire sauce

1. Immerse cabbage leaves in boiling water for about 3 minutes or until limp. Drain.
2. Combine egg, milk, onions, salt, pepper, beef, and rice. Place about 1/4 cup meat mixture in center of each leaf. Fold in sides and roll ends over meat. Place in slow cooker.
3. Combine tomato sauce, brown sugar, lemon juice, and Worcestershire sauce. Pour over cabbage rolls.
4. Cover. Cook on Low 7-9 hours.

Exchange List Values:
Starch 0.5, Vegetable 2.0,
Meat, lean 2.0, Fat 0.5

Basic Nutritional Values: Calories 219 (Calories from Fat 79), Total Fat 9 gm (Saturated Fat 3.4 gm, Polyunsat Fat 0.5 gm, Monounsat Fat 3.7 gm, Cholesterol 80 mg), Sodium 603 mg, Total Carbohydrate 18 gm, Dietary Fiber 2 gm, Sugars 7 gm, Protein 17 gm

Stuffed Cabbage

Barbara Nolan
Pleasant Valley, NY

Makes 6 servings
(Ideal slow cooker size: 4-5-quart)

4 cups water
12 large cabbage leaves
1 lb. ground beef, lamb, or
  turkey
1/2 cup cooked rice
1/2 tsp. salt
1/8 tsp. pepper
1/4 tsp. dried thyme
1/4 tsp. nutmeg
1/4 tsp. cinnamon
6-oz. can tomato paste
3/4 cup water

1. Boil 4 cups water in deep kettle. Remove kettle from heat. Soak cabbage leaves in hot water for 5 minutes, or just until softened. Remove. Drain. Cool.
2. Combine meat, rice, salt, pepper, thyme, nutmeg, and cinnamon. Place 2 Tbsp. of mixture on each leaf. Roll up firmly. Stack stuffed leaves in slow cooker.
3. Combine tomato paste and 3/4 cup water until smooth. Pour over cabbage rolls.
4. Cover. Cook on Low 6-8 hours.

Exchange List Values:
Vegetable 2.0, Meat, lean 2.0, Fat 0.5

Basic Nutritional Values: Calories 186 (Calories from Fat 73), Total Fat 8 gm (Saturated Fat 3.0 gm, Polyunsat Fat 0.4 gm, Monounsat Fat 3.4 gm, Cholesterol 45 mg), Sodium 269 mg, Total Carbohydrate 13 gm, Dietary Fiber 3 gm, Sugars 3 gm, Protein 16 gm

**Make exercise fun—
do something silly
today.**

Stuffed Green Peppers

Lois Stoltzfus
Honey Brook, PA

Makes 6 servings
(Ideal slow cooker size: 6-quart
oval, so the peppers can each sit
on the bottom of the cooker)

6 large green peppers
3/4 lb. 85%-lean ground
 beef, browned and
 drained
2 Tbsp. minced onion
1/8 tsp. salt
1/8 tsp. garlic powder
2 cups cooked rice
15-oz. can tomato sauce
1/2 cup reduced-fat
 shredded mozzarella
 cheese

1. Cut peppers in half and
remove seeds.
2. Combine all ingredients
except peppers and cheese.
3. Stuff peppers with
ground beef mixture. Place in
slow cooker.
4. Cover. Cook on Low 6-8
hours, or on High 3-4 hours.
Sprinkle with cheese during
last 30 minutes.

Exchange List Values:
Starch 1.0, Vegetable 3.0,
Meat, lean 1.0, Fat 1.0

Basic Nutritional Values: Calories
253 (Calories from Fat 69), Total Fat 8
gm (Saturated Fat 3.2 gm, Polyunsat Fat
0.5 gm, Monounsat Fat 2.8 gm,
Cholesterol 39 mg), Sodium 585
mg, Total Carbohydrate 30 gm, Dietary
Fiber 5 gm, Sugars 9 gm, Protein 17 gm

Beef Enchiladas

Jane Talso
Albuquerque, NM

Makes 12-16 servings
(Ideal slow cooker size: 5-6-quart)

4 lb. boneless chuck roast,
 trimmed of fat
2 Tbsp. canola oil
4 cups sliced onions
2 tsp. black pepper
2 tsp. cumin seeds
2 4 1/2-oz. cans peeled,
 diced green chilies
14 1/2-oz. can no-salt-added,
 peeled, diced tomatoes
8 large tortillas (10-inch
 size)
1 cup (4 ozs.) reduced-fat
 cheddar cheese,
 shredded
4 cups green, or red,
 enchilada sauce

1. Brown roast on all sides
in oil in saucepan. Place roast
in slow cooker.
2. Add remaining
ingredients except tortillas,
cheese, and sauce.
3. Cover. Cook on High 4-5
hours.
4. Shred meat with fork
and return to slow cooker.
5. Warm tortillas in oven.
Heat enchilada sauce. Fill
each tortilla with 3/4 cup beef
mixture and 1/4 cup cheese.
Roll up and serve with sauce.

Exchange List Values:
Starch 1.0, Vegetable 2.0,
Meat, lean 3.0, Fat 1.0

Basic Nutritional Values: Calories
336 (Calories from Fat 114), Total Fat
13 gm (Saturated Fat 3.5 gm,
Polyunsat Fat 1.5 gm, Monounsat Fat
5.1 gm, Cholesterol 69 mg), Sodium
542 mg, Total Carbohydrate 29 gm,
Dietary Fiber 4 gm, Sugars 5 gm,
Protein 27 gm

Variation: Use 2 lbs. ground
beef instead of chuck roast.
Brown without oil in saucepan,
along with onions.

Slow Cooker Enchiladas

Lori Berezovsky, Salina, KS
Tracy Clark, Mt. Crawford, VA
**Mary E. Herr and Michelle
Reineck**, Three Rivers, MI
Marcia S. Myer, Manheim, PA
Renee Shirk, Mt. Joy, PA
Janice Showalter, Flint, MI

Makes 8 servings
(Ideal slow cooker size: 4-quart)

1 lb. 90%-lean ground beef
1 cup chopped onions
1/2 cup chopped green
 peppers
16-oz. can no-added-salt
 red kidney beans, rinsed
 and drained
15-oz. can no-added-salt
 black beans, rinsed and
 drained
10-oz. can diced tomatoes
 with green chilies,
 undrained
1/3 cup water
1 1/2 tsp. chili powder
1/2 tsp. ground cumin
1/4 tsp. pepper

4 ozs. (1 cup) shredded fat-free sharp cheddar cheese
2 ozs. (1/2 cup) shredded reduced-fat Monterey Jack cheese
8 flour tortillas (6-7 inches in diameter)

1. Cook beef, onions, and green peppers in skillet until beef is browned and vegetables are tender. Drain. Pat dry.
2. Add next 7 ingredients and bring to a boil. Reduce heat. Cover and simmer 10 minutes.
3. Combine cheeses.
4. In slow cooker, layer about 3/4 cup beef mixture, one tortilla, and about 1/3 cup cheeses. Repeat layers.
5. Cover. Cook on Low 5-7 hours or until heated through.
6. To serve, reach to bottom with each spoonful to get all the layers, or carefully invert onto large platter and cut into wedges. Serve with sour cream and/or guacamole.

Exchange List Values:
Starch 2.0, Vegetable 1.0, Meat, lean 3.0

Basic Nutritional Values: Calories 335 (Calories from Fat 76), Total Fat 8 gm (Saturated Fat 3.5 gm, Polyunsat Fat 0.7 gm, Monounsat Fat 3.6 gm, Cholesterol 41 mg), Sodium 484 mg, Total Carbohydrate 38 gm, Dietary Fiber 6 gm, Sugars 5 gm, Protein 27 gm

Shredded Beef for Tacos
Dawn Day
Westminster, CA

Makes 6-8 servings
(Ideal slow cooker size: 4-quart)

2 lb. round roast, trimmed of fat, cut into large chunks
1 large onion, chopped
2 Tbsp. canola oil
2 serrano chilies, chopped
3 garlic cloves, minced
1 tsp. salt
1 cup water

1. Brown meat and onion in oil. Transfer to slow cooker.
2. Add chilies, garlic, salt, and water.
3. Cover. Cook on High 6-8 hours.
4. Pull meat apart with two forks until shredded.
5. Serve with fresh tortillas, lettuce, tomatoes, cheese, and guacamole.

Exchange List Values:
Meat, lean 3.0

Basic Nutritional Values: Calories 184 (Calories from Fat 79), Total Fat 9 gm (Saturated Fat 2.1 gm, Polyunsat Fat 1.2 gm, Monounsat Fat 4.2 gm, Cholesterol 64 mg), Sodium 335 mg, Total Carbohydrate 4 gm, Dietary Fiber 1 gm, Sugars 3 gm, Protein 22 gm

Tamale Pie
Jeannine Janzen
Elbing, KS

Makes 8 servings
(Ideal slow cooker size: 4-quart)

3/4 cup cornmeal
1 1/2 cups fat-free milk
1 egg, beaten
1 lb. ground beef, browned and drained
1.25-oz. envelope dry chili seasoning mix
16-oz. can diced tomatoes
16-oz. can corn, drained
1 cup grated fat-free cheddar cheese

1. Combine cornmeal, milk, and egg.
2. Stir in meat, chili seasoning mix, tomatoes, and corn until well blended. Pour into slow cooker.
3. Cover. Cook on High 1 hour, then on Low 3 hours.
4. Sprinkle with cheese. Cook another 5 minutes until cheese is melted.

Exchange List Values:
Starch 1.0, Carbohydrate 0.5, Vegetable 1.0, Meat, lean 2.0

Basic Nutritional Values: Calories 244 (Calories from Fat 65), Total Fat 7 gm (Saturated Fat 2.6 gm, Polyunsat Fat 0.6 gm, Monounsat Fat 2.9 gm, Cholesterol 63 mg), Sodium 500 mg, Total Carbohydrate 25 gm, Dietary Fiber 3 gm, Sugars 6 gm, Protein 20 gm

Mexican Corn Bread

Jeanne Heyerly
Chenoa, IL

Makes 8 servings
(Ideal slow cooker size: 4-quart)

16-oz. can no added salt
  cream-style corn
1 cup cornmeal
1/2 tsp. baking soda
1/2 tsp. salt
1/4 cup canola oil
1 cup fat-free milk
2 eggs, beaten
1/2 cup taco sauce
4 ozs. (1 cup) shredded fat-
  free cheddar cheese
1 medium onion, chopped
1 garlic clove, minced
4-oz. can diced green
  chilies
1 lb. 85%-lean ground
  beef, lightly cooked,
  drained, and patted dry

1. Combine corn, cornmeal, baking soda, salt, oil, milk, eggs, and taco sauce. Pour half of mixture into slow cooker.

2. Layer cheese, onion, garlic, green chilies, and ground beef on top of cornmeal mixture. Cover with remaining cornmeal mixture.

3. Cover. Cook on High 1 hour and on Low 3 1/2-4 hours, or only on Low 6 hours.

Exchange List Values:
Starch 2.0, Meat, lean 2.0,
Fat 1.5

Basic Nutritional Values: Calories 320 (Calories from Fat 134), Total Fat 15 gm (Saturated Fat 3.3 gm, Polyunsat Fat 2.7 gm, Monounsat Fat 7.3 gm, Cholesterol 89 mg), Sodium 575 mg, Total Carbohydrate 27 gm, Dietary Fiber 3 gm, Sugars 7 gm, Protein 20 gm

Mile-High Shredded Beef Sandwiches

Miriam Christophel
Battle Creek, MI
Mary Seielstad
Sparks, NV

Makes 8 servings
(Ideal slow cooker size: 4-quart)

3 lb. chuck roast, or round
  steak, trimmed of fat
2 Tbsp. oil
1 cup chopped onions
1/2 cup sliced celery
2 cups lower-sodium,
  98%-fat-free beef broth
1 garlic clove
3/4 cup ketchup
2 Tbsp. brown sugar
2 Tbsp. vinegar
1 tsp. dry mustard
1/2 tsp. chili powder
3 drops Tabasco sauce
1 bay leaf
1/4 tsp. paprika
1/4 tsp. garlic powder
1 tsp. Worcestershire sauce

1. In skillet brown both sides of meat in oil. Add onions and celery and sauté briefly. Transfer to slow cooker. Add broth.

2. Cover. Cook on Low 6-8 hours, or until tender. Remove meat from cooker and cool. Shred beef.

3. Remove vegetables from cooker and drain, reserving 1 1/2 cups broth. Combine vegetables and meat.

4. Return shredded meat and vegetables to cooker. Add broth and remaining ingredients and combine well.

5. Cover. Cook on High 1 hour. Remove bay leaf.

6. Pile into 8 sandwich rolls and serve.

Exchange List Values:
Carbohydrate 1.0, Meat, lean 3.0

Basic Nutritional Values: Calories 239 (Calories from Fat 88), Total Fat 10 gm (Saturated Fat 2.4 gm, Polyunsat Fat 1.3 gm, Monounsat Fat 4.6 gm, Cholesterol 73 mg), Sodium 444 mg, Total Carbohydrate 12 gm, Dietary Fiber 1 gm, Sugars 8 gm, Protein 25 gm

Jean & Tammy's Sloppy Joes

Jean Shaner, York, PA
Tammy Smoker, Cochranville, PA

Makes 14 servings
(Ideal slow cooker size: 4-quart)

2³/₄ lbs. 85%-lean ground beef, browned, drained, and patted dry
1 onion, finely chopped
1 green pepper, chopped
8-oz. can tomato sauce
8-oz. can no-salt-added tomato sauce
³/₄ cup ketchup
1 Tbsp. Worcestershire sauce
1 tsp. chili powder
¹/₄ tsp. pepper
¹/₄ tsp. garlic powder

1. Combine all ingredients in slow cooker.
2. Cover. Cook on Low 8-10 hours, or on High 3-4 hours.
3. Serve in sandwich rolls.

Exchange List Values:
Carbohydrate 0.5, Meat, lean 3.0, Fat 0.5

Basic Nutritional Values: Calories 227 (Calories from Fat 104), Total Fat 12 gm (Saturated Fat 4.5 gm, Polyunsat Fat 0.4 gm, Monounsat Fat 5.0 gm, Cholesterol 67 mg), Sodium 383 mg, Total Carbohydrate 9 gm, Dietary Fiber 1 gm, Sugars 5 gm, Protein 21 gm

Corned Beef

Elaine Vigoda
Rochester, NY

Makes 12 servings
(Ideal slow cooker size: 4-5-quart)

3 large carrots, cut into chunks
1 cup chopped celery
¹/₂ tsp. pepper
1 cup water
2 lb. piece of corned beef, trimmed of fat
1 large onion, cut into pieces
half a small head of cabbage, cut in wedges
4 medium potatoes, peeled and chunked

1. Place carrots, celery, pepper, and water in slow cooker.
2. Add beef. Cover with onions.
3. Cover. Cook on Low 8-10 hours, or on High 5-6 hours.
4. Lift corned beef out of cooker and add cabbage and potatoes, pushing them to bottom of slow cooker. Return beef to cooker.
5. Cover. Cook on High 2 hours.
6. Remove corned beef. Cool and slice on the diagonal. Serve surrounded by vegetables.

Exchange List Values:
Starch 0.5, Vegetable 1.0, Meat, medium fat 1.0, Fat 1.0

Basic Nutritional Values: Calories 194 (Calories from Fat 93), Total Fat 10 gm (Saturated Fat 3.4 gm, Polyunsat Fat 0.5 gm, Monounsat Fat 4.9 gm, Cholesterol 52 mg), Sodium 639 mg, Total Carbohydrate 14 gm, Dietary Fiber 3 gm, Sugars 4 gm, Protein 11 gm

In addition to your regular doctor, have someone—a certified diabetes educator, nurse practitioner, or nurse case manager—whom you can contact on short notice to discuss problems or questions that come up, such as unexplained high blood sugars or sudden illness.

Corned Beef and Cabbage

Rhoda Burgoon
Collingswood, NJ
Jo Ellen Moore
Pendleton, IN

Makes 12 servings
(Ideal slow cooker size: 4-5-quart)

3 carrots, cut in 3" pieces
2-lb. corned beef brisket, trimmed of all fat
2-3 medium onions, quartered
3/4-1 1/4 cups water
half a small head of cabbage, cut in wedges

1. Layer all ingredients except cabbage in slow cooker.
2. Cover. Cook on Low 8-10 hours, or on High 5-6 hours.
3. Add cabbage wedges to liquid, pushing down to moisten. Turn to High and cook an additional 2-3 hours.

Exchange List Values:
Vegetable 1.0, Meat, medium fat 2.0

Basic Nutritional Values: Calories 159 (Calories from Fat 93), Total Fat 10 gm (Saturated Fat 3.4 gm, Polyunsat Fat 0.4 gm, Monounsat Fat 4.9 gm, Cholesterol 52 mg), Sodium 624 mg, Total Carbohydrate 6 gm, Dietary Fiber 2 gm, Sugars 3 gm, Protein 11 gm

Note: To cook more cabbage than slow cooker will hold, cook separately in skillet. Remove 1 cup broth from slow cooker during last hour of cooking. Pour over cabbage wedges in skillet. Cover and cook slowly for 20-30 minutes.

Variations:
1. Add 4 medium potatoes, halved, with the onions.
2. Top individual servings with mixture of sour cream and horseradish.
Kathi Rogge
Alexandria, IN

Corned Beef

Margaret Jarrett
Anderson, In

Makes 12 servings
(Ideal slow cooker size: 4-quart)

2 lb. cut of marinated corned beef
2-3 garlic cloves, minced
10-12 peppercorns

1. Place meat in bottom of cooker. Top with garlic and peppercorns. Cover with water.
2. Cover. Cook on High 4-5 hours, or until tender.
3. Cool meat, slice thin, and use to make Reuben sandwiches.

Exchange List Values:
Meat, medium fat 2.0

Basic Nutritional Values: Calories 135 (Calories from Fat 91), Total Fat 10 gm (Saturated Fat 3.4 gm, Polyunsat Fat 0.4 gm, Monounsat Fat 4.9 gm, Cholesterol 52 mg), Sodium 605 mg, Total Carbohydrate 0 gm, Dietary Fiber 0 gm, Sugars 0 gm, Protein 10 gm

We suggest your sandwiches include a slice of Swiss cheese, sauerkraut, and Thousand Island dressing on toasted pumpernickel bread.

Pork
Main Dishes

Cranberry Pork Roast

Barbara Aston
Ashdown, AR

Makes 9 servings
(Ideal slow cooker size: 4-quart)

2¾ lb. boneless pork roast, trimmed of fat
pepper to taste
1 cup ground, or finely chopped, cranberries
3 Tbsp. honey
1 tsp. grated orange peel
⅛ tsp. ground cloves
⅛ tsp. ground nutmeg

1. Sprinkle roast with pepper. Place in slow cooker.
2. Combine remaining ingredients. Pour over roast.
3. Cover. Cook on Low 8-10 hours.

Exchange List Values:
Carbohydrate 0.5, Meat, lean 3.0

Basic Nutritional Values: Calories 214 (Calories from Fat 81), Total Fat 9 gm (Saturated Fat 3.5 gm, Polyunsat Fat 0.6 gm, Monounsat Fat 4.3 gm, Cholesterol 63 mg), Sodium 37 mg, Total Carbohydrate 7 gm, Dietary Fiber 1 gm, Sugars 7 gm, Protein 25 gm

You may want to add a little salt to this recipe if you generally use it in your diet.

Drinking less alcohol, quitting smoking, and getting more exercise are not only better for your health, they will also save you money on health care, since you may be able to use less insulin.

Barbara Jean's Whole Pork Tenderloin

Barbara Jean Fabel, Wausau, WI

Makes 6-8 servings
(Ideal slow cooker size: 4-5-quart)

1/2 cup sliced celery
1/4 lb. fresh mushrooms, quartered
1 medium onion, sliced
2 Tbsp. margarine
2 1 1/4 lb. pork tenderloins, trimmed of fat
1 Tbsp. canola oil
1/2 cup beef broth
3/4 tsp. salt
1/4 tsp. pepper
1/2 tsp. sodium-free beef-flavored instant bouillon
1 Tbsp. flour

1. Placed celery, mushrooms, onion, and margarine in slow cooker.
2. Brown tenderloins in skillet in 1 Tbsp. canola oil. Layer over vegetables in slow cooker.
3. Pour beef broth over tenderloins. Sprinkle with salt and pepper.
4. Combine bouillon and flour. Pour over tenderloins.
5. Cover. Cook on High 3 hours or on Low 4-5 hours.

Exchange List Values:
Meat, lean 4.0

Basic Nutritional Values: Calories 228 (Calories from Fat 87), Total Fat 10 gm (Saturated Fat 2.4 gm, Polyunsat Fat 1.9 gm, Monounsat Fat 4.3 gm,

Cholesterol 82 mg), Sodium 385 mg, Total Carbohydrate 3 gm, Dietary Fiber 1 gm, Sugars 2 gm, Protein 30 gm

Autumn Harvest Pork Loin

Stacy Schmucker Stoltzfus
Enola, PA

Makes 4-6 servings
(Ideal slow cooker size: 4-quart)

1 cup cider or apple juice
1 1/2 lb. boneless pork loin, trimmed of fat
1/2 tsp. salt
1/4 tsp. pepper
2 large Granny Smith apples, peeled and sliced
1 1/2 whole medium butternut squashes, peeled and cubed
2 Tbsp. brown sugar
1/4 tsp. cinnamon
1/4 tsp. dried thyme
1/4 tsp. dried sage

1. Heat cider in hot skillet. Sear pork loin on all sides in cider.
2. Sprinkle meat with salt and pepper on all sides. Place in slow cooker, along with juices.
3. Combine apples and squash. Sprinkle with sugar and herbs. Stir. Place around pork loin.
4. Cover. Cook on Low 5-6 hours.
5. Remove pork from cooker. Let stand 10-15

minutes. Slice into 1/2"-thick slices.
6. Serve topped with apples and squash.

Exchange List Values:
Starch 1.0, Fruit 1.0, Meat, lean 2.0, Fat 0.5

Basic Nutritional Values: Calories 280 (Calories from Fat 68), Total Fat 8 gm (Saturated Fat 2.7 gm, Polyunsat Fat 0.7 gm, Monounsat Fat 3.3 gm, Cholesterol 63 mg), Sodium 241 mg, Total Carbohydrate 31 gm, Dietary Fiber 3 gm, Sugars 19 gm, Protein 24 gm

Teriyaki Pork Roast

Janice Yoskovich, Carmichaels, PA

Makes 10 servings
(Ideal slow cooker size: 4-quart)

3/4 cup unsweetened apple juice
2 Tbsp. sugar
2 Tbsp. soy sauce
1 Tbsp. vinegar
1 tsp. ground ginger
1/4 tsp. garlic powder
1/8 tsp. pepper
3 lb. boneless pork loin roast, halved, trimmed of fat
2 1/2 Tbsp. cornstarch
3 Tbsp. cold water

1. Combine apple juice sugar, soy sauce, vinegar, ginger, garlic powder, and pepper in greased slow cooker

2. Add roast. Turn to coat.

3. Cover. Cook on Low 7-8 hours. Remove roast and keep warm.

4. In saucepan, combine cornstarch and cold water until smooth. Stir in juices from roast. Bring to boil. Cook and stir for 2 minutes or until thickened. Serve with roast.

Exchange List Values:
Carbohydrate 0.5, Meat, lean 3.0

Basic Nutritional Values: Calories 211 (Calories from Fat 79), Total Fat 9 gm (Saturated Fat 3.4 gm, Polyunsat Fat 0.6 gm, Monounsat Fat 4.2 gm, Cholesterol 62 mg), Sodium 241 mg, Total Carbohydrate 7 gm, Dietary Fiber 0 gm, Sugars 5 gm, Protein 24 gm

Pork Roast with Potatoes and Onions

Trudy Kutter, Corfu, NY

Makes 6-8 servings
(Ideal slow cooker size: 4-quart)

2^1/2-3 lb. boneless pork loin roast, trimmed of fat
1 large garlic clove, slivered
5 potatoes, cubed, unpeeled
1 large onion, sliced
^{3}/4 cup broth, tomato juice, or water
1^1/2 Tbsp. soy sauce
1 Tbsp. cornstarch
1 Tbsp. cold water

1. Make slits in roast and insert slivers of garlic. Put under broiler to brown.

2. Put potatoes in slow cooker. Add half of onions. Place roast on onions and potatoes. Cover with remaining onions.

3. Combine broth and soy sauce. Pour over roast.

4. Cover. Cook on Low 8 hours. Remove roast and vegetables from liquid.

5. Combine cornstarch and water. Add to liquid in slow cooker. Turn to High until thickened. Serve over sliced meat and vegetables.

Exchange List Values:
Starch 1.5, Meat, lean 3.0

Basic Nutritional Values: Calories 289 (Calories from Fat 83), Total Fat 9 gm (Saturated Fat 3.6 gm, Polyunsat Fat 0.7 gm, Monounsat Fat 4.4 gm, Cholesterol 64 mg), Sodium 339 mg, Total Carbohydrate 22 gm, Dietary Fiber 3 gm, Sugars 4 gm, Protein 28 gm

---

Variation: Use sweet potatoes instead of white potatoes.

Savory Pork Roast

Betty A. Holt, St. Charles, MO

Makes 8-10 servings
(Ideal slow cooker size: 4-quart)

3 lb. boneless pork loin roast, trimmed of fat
large onion, sliced
1 bay leaf
2 Tbsp. soy sauce
1 Tbsp. garlic powder

1. Place roast and onion in slow cooker. Add bay leaf, soy sauce, and garlic powder.

2. Cover. Cook on High 1 hour and then on Low 6 hours.

3. Slice and serve.

Exchange List Values:
Meat, lean 3.0

Basic Nutritional Values: Calories 187 (Calories from Fat 79), Total Fat 9 gm (Saturated Fat 3.4 gm, Polyunsat Fat 0.6 gm, Monounsat Fat 4.2 gm, Cholesterol 62 mg), Sodium 241 mg, Total Carbohydrate 1 gm, Dietary Fiber 0 gm, Sugars 0 gm, Protein 24 gm

Are you taking a drug that could be interfering with another drug you take? Make an appointment with your pharmacist for a pill check; most will do it for free or for a small fee.

Flautas with Pork Filling

Donna Lantgen
Rapid City, SD

Makes 6-8 servings
(Ideal slow cooker size: 4-quart)

1 lb. pork roast or chops, cubed
1/4 cup chopped onions
4-oz. can diced green chilies
7-oz. can green chile salsa or chile salsa
1 tsp. cocoa powder
16-oz. can chili with beans

1. Brown cubed pork in nonstick skillet. Drain. Place in slow cooker.
2. Add remaining ingredients except chili.
3. Cover. Cook on Low 2-3 hours.
4. Add chili. Cook 2-3 hours longer on Low.
5. Serve on flour tortillas with guacamole dip.

Exchange List Values:
Starch 0.5, Meat, lean 2.0

Basic Nutritional Values: Calories 153 (Calories from Fat 62), Total Fat 7 gm (Saturated Fat 2.8 gm, Polyunsat Fat 0.5 gm, Monounsat Fat 3.1 gm, Cholesterol 35 mg), Sodium 566 mg, Total Carbohydrate 9 gm, Dietary Fiber 3 gm, Sugars 2 gm, Protein 14 gm

Note: This is especially good on spinach-herb tortillas.

Shepherd's Pie

Melanie Thrower, McPherson, KS

Makes 6 servings
(Ideal slow cooker size: 3-4-quart)

3/4 lb. ground pork
1 Tbsp. vinegar
3/4 tsp. salt
1/4 tsp. hot pepper
1 tsp. paprika
1/4 tsp. dried oregano
1/4 tsp. black pepper
1 tsp. chili powder
1 small onion, chopped
15-oz. can corn, drained
3 large potatoes, unpeeled
1/4 cup fat-free milk
1 tsp. margarine
1/4 tsp. salt
dash of pepper
shredded cheese

1. Combine pork, vinegar, and spices. Cook in skillet until brown. Add onion and cook until onions begin to glaze. Spread in bottom of slow cooker.
2. Spread corn over meat.
3. Boil potatoes until soft. Mash with milk, butter, 1/4 tsp. salt, and dash of pepper. Spread over meat and corn.
4. Cover. Cook on Low 3 hours. Sprinkle top with cheese a few minutes before serving.

Exchange List Values:
Starch 2.0, Meat, lean 1.0, Fat 1.0

Basic Nutritional Values: Calories 269 (Calories from Fat 85), Total Fat 9 gm (Saturated Fat 3.2 gm, Polyunsat Fat 1.3 gm, Monounsat Fat 4.0 gm, Cholesterol 38 mg), Sodium 538 mg, Total Carbohydrate 33 gm, Dietary Fiber 4 gm, Sugars 5 gm, Protein 15 gm

Variation: You can substitute ground beef for the pork. This is my 9-year-old son's favorite dish.

Verenike Casserole

Jennifer Yoder Sommers
Harrisonburg, VA

Makes 8-10 servings
(Ideal slow cooker size: 4-5-quart)

24 ozs. 1% (low-fat) cottage cheese
3 eggs
1 tsp. salt
1/2 tsp. pepper
1 cup fat-free sour cream
2 cups fat-free evaporated milk
2 cups cubed, cooked, extra-lean, lower-sodium ham
7 dry lasagna noodles

1. Combine all ingredients except noodles.
2. Place half of creamy ham mixture in bottom of cooker. Add uncooked noodles. Cover with remaining half of creamy ham sauce. Be sure noodles are fully submerged in sauce.
3. Cover. Cook on Low 5-6 hours.
4. Serve with green salad, peas, and zwiebach or bread.

Basic Nutritional Values: Calories 222 (Calories from Fat 28), Total Fat 3 gm (Saturated Fat 0.8 gm, Polyunsat Fat 0.4 gm, Monounsat Fat 1.0 gm, Cholesterol 81 mg), Sodium 604 mg, Total Carbohydrate 26 gm, Dietary Fiber 1 gm, Sugars 11 gm, Protein 22 gm

Chalupa

Jeannine Janzen, Elbing, KS

Makes 12-16 servings
(Ideal slow cooker size: 5-quart)

3 lb. pork roast, trimmed of fat
1 lb. dry pinto beans
2 garlic cloves, minced
1 Tbsp. ground cumin
1 Tbsp. dried oregano
2 Tbsp. chili powder
1 Tbsp. salt
4-oz. can chopped green chilies
water

1. Cover beans with water and soak overnight in slow cooker.
2. In the morning, remove beans (reserve soaking water) and put roast in bottom of cooker. Add remaining ingredients (including the beans and their soaking water) and more water if needed to cover all the ingredients.
3. Cook on High 1 hour, and then on Low 6 hours. Remove meat and shred with two forks. Return meat to slow cooker.
4. Cook on High 1 more hour.
5. Serve over a bed of lettuce. Top with grated cheese and chopped onions and tomatoes.

Basic Nutritional Values: Calories 200 (Calories from Fat 55), Total Fat 6 gm (Saturated Fat 2.2 gm, Polyunsat Fat 0.6 gm, Monounsat Fat 2.8 gm, Cholesterol 38 mg), Sodium 501 mg, Total Carbohydrate 16 gm, Dietary Fiber 6 gm, Sugars 2 gm, Protein 20 gm

Tangy Pork Chops

Tracy Clark, Mt. Crawford, VA
Lois M. Martin, Lititz, PA
Becky Oswald, Broadway, PA

Makes 4 servings
(Ideal slow cooker size: 4-quart)

4 $1/2$-inch-thick pork chops, bone in, trimmed of fat
$1/8$ tsp. pepper
2 medium onions, chopped
2 celery ribs, chopped
1 large green pepper, sliced
$14 1/2$-oz. can stewed tomatoes, no salt added
$1/3$ cup ketchup
2 Tbsp. cider vinegar
2 Tbsp. brown sugar
2 Tbsp. Worcestershire sauce
1 Tbsp. lemon juice
1 reduced-sodium beef bouillon cube
2 Tbsp. cornstarch
2 Tbsp. water

1. Place chops in slow cooker. Sprinkle with pepper.
2. Add onions, celery, pepper, and tomatoes.
3. Combine ketchup, vinegar, brown sugar, Worcestershire sauce, lemon juice, and bouillon. Pour over vegetables.
4. Cover. Cook on Low 5-6 hours.
5. Combine cornstarch and water until smooth. Stir into slow cooker.
6. Cover. Cook on High 30 minutes, or until thickened.
7. Serve over rice.

Basic Nutritional Values: Calories 254 (Calories from Fat 47), Total Fat 5 gm (Saturated Fat 1.7 gm, Polyunsat Fat 0.5 gm, Monounsat Fat 2.1 gm, Cholesterol 47 mg), Sodium 546 mg, Total Carbohydrate 35 gm, Dietary Fiber 4 gm, Sugars 20 gm, Protein 19 gm

Variation: Use chunks of beef or chicken legs and thighs instead of pork.

Exercise is like a miracle drug—it boosts your metabolism, increases muscle mass so you burn more calories, improves your body's response to insulin, and naturally lowers glucose.

Chops and Beans

Mary L. Casey, Scranton, PA

Makes 4-6 servings
(Ideal slow cooker size: 4-quart)

2 1-lb. cans pork and
 beans
1/4 cup no-salt-added
 ketchup
2 slices bacon, browned
 and crumbled
1/2 cup chopped onions,
 sauteed
1 Tbsp. Worcestershire
 sauce
1 Tbsp. brown sugar
brown sugar substitute to
 equal 1 Tbsp
6 (1 1/2 lbs.) pork chops,
 bone in, trimmed of fat
2 tsp. prepared mustard
1 Tbsp. brown sugar
2 Tbsp. no-salt-added
 ketchup
one lemon

1. Combine beans, 1/4 cup
ketchup, bacon, onions,
Worcestershire sauce, 1 Tbsp.
brown sugar, and 1 Tbsp.
brown sugar substitute in
slow cooker.
2. Brown chops in
nonstick skillet. In separate
bowl, mix together 2 tsp.
mustard, 1 Tbsp. brown
sugar, and 2 Tbsp. ketchup.
Brush each chop with sauce,
then carefully stack into
cooker, placing a slice of
lemon on each chop.
Submerge in bean/bacon
mixture.
3. Cover. Cook on Low 4-6
hours.

Exchange List Values:
Starch 2.0, Carbohydrate
0.5, Meat, lean 2.0, Fat 0.5

Basic Nutritional Values: Calories
323 (Calories from Fat 73), Total Fat
8 gm (Saturated Fat 2.0 gm,
Polyunsat Fat 1.0 gm, Monounsat Fat
3.5 gm, Cholesterol 55 mg), Sodium
790 mg, Total Carbohydrate 40 gm,
Dietary Fiber 8 gm, Sugars 20 gm,
Protein 23 gm

Perfect Pork Chops

Brenda Pope
Dundee, OH

Makes 2 servings
(Ideal slow cooker size: 4-quart)

2 small onions
1/2 lb. boneless, center loin
 pork chops, frozen,
 trimmed of fat
fresh ground pepper to
 taste
3/4 tsp. reduced-sodium
 bouillon granules
1/4 cup hot water
2 Tbsp. prepared mustard
 with white wine
fresh parsley sprigs, or
 lemon slices, optional

1. Cut off ends of onions
and peel. Cut onions in half
crosswise to make 4 thick
wheels. Place in bottom of
slow cooker.
2. Sear both sides of frozen
chops in heavy skillet. Place
in cooker on top of onions.
Sprinkle with pepper.
3. Dissolve bouillon

granules in hot water. Stir in
mustard. Pour into slow
cooker.
4. Cover. Cook on High 3-4
hours.
5. Serve topped with fresh
parsley sprigs or lemon slices,
if desired.

Exchange List Values:
Carbohydrate 0.5, Meat,
lean 3.0

Basic Nutritional Values: Calories
204 (Calories from Fat 72), Total Fat
8 gm (Saturated Fat 2.9 gm,
Polyunsat Fat 0.7 gm, Monounsat Fat
3.9 gm, Cholesterol 51 mg), Sodium
392 mg, Total Carbohydrate 11 gm,
Dietary Fiber 2 gm, Sugars 7 gm,
Protein 22 gm

Pork Chops with Mushroom Sauce

Jennifer J. Gehman
Harrisburg, PA

Makes 6 servings
(Ideal slow cooker size: 4-quart)

6 1/2"-thick (1/4 lb. each)
 boneless pork chops
10 3/4-oz. can reduced-
 sodium, 98%-fat-free
 cream of mushroom soup
3/4 cup white wine
4-oz. can sliced
 mushrooms
2 Tbsp. quick cooking
 tapioca
2 tsp. Worcestershire sauce
1 tsp. beef bouillon
 granules, or 1 beef
 bouillon cube

¼ tsp. minced garlic
¾ tsp. dried thyme,
  optional

1. Place pork chops in slow cooker.
2. Combine remaining ingredients and pour over pork chops.
3. Cook on Low 8-10 hours, or on High 4½-5 hours.

Exchange List Values:
Carbohydrate 0.5, Meat, lean 3.0

Basic Nutritional Values: Calories 207 (Calories from Fat 76), Total Fat 8 gm (Saturated Fat 3.3 gm, Polyunsat Fat 0.8 gm, Monounsat Fat 3.7 gm, Cholesterol 52 mg), Sodium 452 mg, Total Carbohydrate 9 gm, Dietary Fiber 1 gm, Sugars 2 gm, Protein 22 gm

Pork Chops on Rice
Hannah D. Burkholder
Bridgewater, VA

Makes 4 servings
(Ideal slow cooker size: 4-quart)

½ cup brown rice, uncooked
⅔ cup converted white rice, uncooked
1 Tbsp. olive oil
½ cup chopped onions
4-oz. can sliced mushrooms, drained
½ tsp. dried thyme
½ tsp. sage
¼ tsp. black pepper
4 small (about 4 ozs. each)

boneless pork chops
¾ cup beef consommé
½ cup water
2 Tbsp. Worcestershire sauce
½ tsp. dried thyme
½ tsp. paprika
¼ tsp. ground nutmeg

1. Saute white and brown rice in olive oil in skillet until rice is golden brown.
2. Remove from heat and stir in onions, mushrooms, ½ tsp. thyme, sage, and pepper. Pour into greased slow cooker.
3. Arrange chops over rice.
4. Combine consommé, water, and Worcestershire sauce. Pour over chops.
5. Combine ½ tsp. thyme, paprika, and nutmeg. Sprinkle over chops.
6. Cover. Cook on Low 7-9 hours or on High 4-5 hours.

Exchange List Values:
Starch 3.0, Vegetable 1.0, Meat, lean 2.0, Fat 1.0

Basic Nutritional Values: Calories 425 (Calories from Fat 107), Total Fat 12 gm (Saturated Fat 3.5 gm, Polyunsat Fat 1.2 gm, Monounsat Fat 6.3 gm, Cholesterol 52 mg), Sodium 528 mg, Total Carbohydrate 50 gm, Dietary Fiber 3 gm, Sugars 4 gm, Protein 28 gm

---

Make a back-up plan of things you will do when you are tempted to overeat or smoke — take a walk, play some music and dance, suck on a mint, or knit.

Pork and Cabbage Dinner
Mrs. Paul Gray, Beatrice, NE

Makes 8 servings
(Ideal slow cooker size: 4-5-quart)

2 lbs. pork steaks, or chops, or shoulder, bone-in, trimmed of fat
¾ cup chopped onions
¼ cup chopped fresh parsley, or 2 Tbsp. dried parsley
4 cups shredded cabbage
1 tsp. salt
⅛ tsp. pepper
½ tsp. caraway seeds
⅛ tsp. allspice
½ cup beef broth
2 medium cooking apples, cored and sliced ¼-inch thick

1. Place pork in slow cooker. Layer onions, parsley, and cabbage over pork.
2. Combine salt, pepper, caraway seeds, and allspice. Sprinkle over cabbage. Pour broth over cabbage.
3. Cover. Cook on Low 5-6 hours.
4. Add apple slices 30 minutes before serving.

Exchange List Values:
Fruit 0.5, Vegetable 1.0, Meat, lean 2.0

Basic Nutritional Values: Calories 149 (Calories from Fat 44), Total Fat 5 gm (Saturated Fat 1.7 gm, Polyunsat Fat 0.4 gm, Monounsat Fat 2.1 gm, Cholesterol 47 mg), Sodium 382 mg, Total Carbohydrate 9 gm, Dietary Fiber 2 gm, Sugars 6 gm, Protein 18 gm

Creamy Ham Topping (for baked potatoes)

Judy Buller, Bluffton, OH

Makes 12 servings
(Ideal slow cooker size: 4-quart)

2 Tbsp. margarine
1/4 cup flour
2 cups fat-free milk
1/4 cup fat-free half-and-half
1 Tbsp. chopped parsley
1 Tbsp. sodium-free chicken bouillon granules
1/2 tsp. Italian seasoning
2 cups diced cooked ham
1/4 cup Romano cheese, grated
1 cup sliced mushrooms

1. Melt butter in saucepan. Stir in flour. Add milk and half-and-half.
2. Stir in remaining ingredients. Pour into slow cooker.
3. Cover. Cook on Low 1-2 hours.
4. Serve over baked potatoes. Top with shredded cheese and sour cream if you wish.

Exchange List Values:
Carbohydrate 0.5, Meat, lean 1.0

Basic Nutritional Values: Calories 93 (Calories from Fat 36), Total Fat 4 gm (Saturated Fat 1.3 gm, Polyunsat Fat 0.8 gm, Monounsat Fat 1.6 gm, Cholesterol 17 mg), Sodium 386 mg, Total Carbohydrate 5 gm, Dietary Fiber 0 gm, Sugars 3

Black Beans with Ham

Colleen Heatwole, Burton, MI

Makes 8-10 servings
(Ideal slow cooker size: 5-quart)

4 cups dry black beans
1 cups diced ham
1 tsp. cumin
1/2-1 cup minced onion
2 garlic cloves, minced
3 bay leaves
1 qt. fresh diced tomatoes
1 Tbsp. brown sugar

1. Cover black beans with water and soak for 8 hours, or overnight. Drain and pour beans into slow cooker.
2. Add all remaining ingredients and stir well. Cover with water.
3. Cover cooker. Cook on Low 10-12 hours.
4. Serve over rice.

Exchange List Values:
Starch 3.0, Vegetable 1.0, Meat, very lean 1.0

Basic Nutritional Values: Calories 302 (Calories from Fat 19), Total Fat 2 gm (Saturated Fat 0.5 gm, Polyunsat Fat 0.6 gm, Monounsat Fat 0.5 gm, Cholesterol 8 mg), Sodium 196 mg, Total Carbohydrate 51 gm, Dietary Fiber 18 gm, Sugars 8 gm, Protein 21 gm

This is our favorite black bean recipe. We make it frequently in the winter.

Ham and Lima Beans

Charlotte Shaffer
East Earl, PA

Makes 6 servings
(Ideal slow cooker size: 4-quart)

1 lb. dry lima beans
1 medium onion, chopped
1 medium bell pepper, chopped
1 tsp. dry mustard
1 tsp. pepper
6 ozs. ham, finely cubed
1 cup water
10 3/4-oz. can 98%-fat-free, reduced-sodium tomato soup

1. Cover beans with water. Soak 8 hours. Drain.
2. Combine ingredients in slow cooker.
3. Cover. Cook on Low 7 hours or High 4 hours.
4. If mixture begins to dry out, add 1/2 cup water or more and stir well.
5. This is delicious served with hot corn bread.

Exchange List Values:
Starch 2.5, Carbohydrate 0.5, Vegetable 1.0, Meat, lean 1.0

Basic Nutritional Values: Calories 313 (Calories from Fat 27), Total Fat 3 gm (Saturated Fat 0.9 gm, Polyunsat Fat 0.8 gm, Monounsat Fat 0.8 gm, Cholesterol 16 mg), Sodium 561 mg, Total Carbohydrate 50 gm, Dietary Fiber 15 gm, Sugars 12 gm, Protein 23 gm

Ham and Corn Slow Cooker Casserole

Vicki Dinkel, Sharon Springs, KS

Makes 8 servings
(Ideal slow cooker size: 4-5-quart)

¼ cup canola oil
1 small green pepper, chopped
1 medium onion, chopped
½ cup flour
½ tsp. paprika
½ tsp. pepper
¼ tsp. dried thyme
1 tsp. dry mustard
4 cups fat-free milk
8-oz. can cream-style corn
2 cups diced, slightly cooked potatoes
3 cups diced, cooked, extra-lean, reduced-sodium ham
3 ozs. shredded reduced-fat cheddar cheese

1. Saute green pepper and onion in canola oil in skillet.
2. Stir in flour and seasonings.
3. Gradually stir in milk and cook until thickened. Pour into slow cooker.
4. Stir in remaining ingredients.
5. Cover. Cook on Low 8 hours or High 4 hours.

Exchange List Values:
Starch 1.0, Milk, fat-free 0.5, Meat, lean 2.0, Fat 0.5

Basic Nutritional Values: Calories 255 (Calories from Fat 95), Total Fat 11 gm (Saturated Fat 2.3 gm, Polyunsat Fat 2.4 gm, Monounsat Fat 5.3 gm, Cholesterol 34 mg), Sodium 596 mg, Total Carbohydrate 24 gm, Dietary Fiber 2 gm, Sugars 11 gm, Protein 18 gm Jamie Schwankl

Ham and Scalloped Potatoes

Penny Blosser, Beavercreek, OH
Jo Haberkamp, Fairbank, IA
Ruth Hofstetter, Versailles, MO
Rachel Kauffman, Alto, MI
Mary E. Martin, Goshen, IN
Brenda Pope, Dundee, OH
Joyce Slaymaker, Strasburg, PA

Makes 6-8 servings
(Ideal slow cooker size: 4-5-quart)

6-8 (1 lb. total) slices ham
8 medium potatoes, thinly sliced
2 medium onions, thinly sliced
1 cup reduced-fat grated cheddar, or American, cheese
10¾-oz. can 98%-fat-free, reduced-sodium cream of celery, or mushroom, soup
paprika

1. Put half of ham, potatoes, and onions in slow cooker. Sprinkle with cheese. Repeat layers.
2. Spoon soup over top. Sprinkle with paprika.
3. Cover. Cook on Low 8-10 hours, or High 4 hours.

Exchange List Values:
Starch 2.0, Meat, lean 2.0

Basic Nutritional Values: Calories 229 (Calories from Fat 45), Total Fat 5 gm (Saturated Fat 2.5 gm, Polyunsat Fat 0.6 gm, Monounsat Fat 1.4 gm, Cholesterol 36 mg), Sodium 733 mg, Total Carbohydrate 32 gm, Dietary Fiber 3 gm, Sugars 7 gm, Protein 17 gm

You may want to add salt and pepper to taste if you generally use them in your diet.

Variation: If you like a lot of creamy sauce with your ham and potatoes, stir ¾ soup-can of milk into the soup before pouring it over the layers.
Alma Z. Weaver, Ephrata, PA

Two tablespoons (one ladle) of salad dressing alone can add 150-200 calories to your salad. Instead, choose low-calorie salad dressing or add a little oil and vinegar.

Ham in Cider
Dorothy M. Van Deest
Memphis, TN

Makes 6-8 servings
(Ideal slow cooker size: 4-5-quart)

3-lb. boneless, precooked,
  extra-lean, lower-sodium
  ham, trimmed of fat
4 cups sweet cider, or
  apple juice
1/4 cup brown sugar
brown sugar substitute to
  equal 1/4 cup
2 tsp. dry mustard
1 tsp. ground cloves
1 cup white seedless
  raisins

1. Place ham and cider in slow cooker.
2. Cover. Cook on Low 8-10 hours.
3. Remove ham from cider and place in baking pan.
4. Make a paste of sugar, sugar substitute, mustard, cloves, and a little hot cider. Brush over ham. Pour 1/2 cup of juice from slow cooker into baking pan. Stir in raisins.
5. Bake at 375° for 30 minutes, until the paste has turned into a glaze.

Exchange List Values:
Carbohydrate 2.0, Meat, very lean 3.0

Basic Nutritional Values: Calories 255 (Calories from Fat 26), Total Fat 3 gm (Saturated Fat 1.0 gm, Polyunsat Fat 0.6 gm, Monounsat Fat 1.0 gm, Cholesterol 67 mg), Sodium 1194 mg, Total Carbohydrate 31 gm, Dietary Fiber 1 gm, Sugars 28 gm, Protein 27 gm

Sweet-Sour Pork
Mary W. Stauffer
Ephrata, PA

Makes 4-6 servings
(Ideal slow cooker size: 4-quart)

2 lbs. boneless pork
  shoulder, cut in strips,
  trimmed of fat
1 green pepper, cut in
  strips
half a medium onion,
  thinly sliced
3/4 cup shredded carrots
2 Tbsp. coarsely chopped
  sweet pickles
2 Tbsp. brown sugar
brown sugar substitute to
  equal 1 Tbsp.
2 Tbsp. cornstarch
1/4 cup water
1 cup pineapple juice
  (reserved from
  pineapple chunks)
1/4 cup cider vinegar
1 Tbsp. soy sauce
2 cups (20-oz. can)
  pineapple chunks,
  canned in juice

1. Place pork strips in slow cooker.
2. Add green pepper, onion, carrots, and pickles.
3. In bowl, mix together brown sugar, sugar substitute, and cornstarch. Add water, pineapple juice, vinegar, and soy sauce. Stir until smooth.
4. Pour over ingredients in slow cooker.
5. Cover. Cook on Low 5-7 hours. One hour before serving, add pineapple chunks. Stir.

6. Serve over buttered noodles with an additional dash of vinegar or garlic to taste.

Exchange List Values:
Fruit 1.0, Carbohydrate 0.5, Vegetable 1.0, Meat, lean 3.0

Basic Nutritional Values: Calories 270 (Calories from Fat 74), Total Fat 8 gm (Saturated Fat 2.8 gm, Polyunsat Fat 0.8 gm, Monounsat Fat 3.8 gm, Cholesterol 75 mg), Sodium 285 mg, Total Carbohydrate 27 gm, Dietary Fiber 2 gm, Sugars 21 gm, Protein 22 gm

Schnitz und Knepp
Jean Robinson, Cinnaminson, NJ

Makes 12 servings
(Ideal slow cooker size: 5-quart)

Snitz:
1 qt. dried sweet apples
3 lbs. extra-lean, lower-
  sodium, boneless ham
  slices, cut into 2" cubes
2 Tbsp. brown sugar
1 cinnamon stick

Knepp (Dumplings):
2 cups flour
4 tsp. baking powder
1 egg, well beaten
3 Tbsp. melted margarine
scant 1/2 cup fat-free milk
1/4 tsp. pepper

1. Cover apples with water in large bowl and let soak for a few hours.
2. Place ham in slow cooker. Cover with water.

3. Cover cooker. Cook on High 2 hours.

4. Add apples and water in which they have been soaking.

5. Add brown sugar and cinnamon stick. Mix until dissolved.

6. Cover. Cook on Low 3 hours.

7. Combine dumpling ingredients in bowl. Drop into hot liquid in cooker by tablespoonfuls. Turn to High. Cover. Do not lift lid for 15 minutes.

8. Serve piping hot on a large platter. A celery-carrot jello salad rounds out the meal well.

Exchange List Values:
Starch 1.5, Fruit 1.0, Meat, lean 2.0

Basic Nutritional Values: Calories 293 (Calories from Fat 48), Total Fat 5 gm (Saturated Fat 1.4 gm, Polyunsat Fat 1.4 gm, Monounsat Fat 2.1 gm, Cholesterol 63 mg), Sodium 980 mg, Total Carbohydrate 41 gm, Dietary Fiber 3 gm, Sugars 19 gm, Protein 20 gm

---

This was my grandmother's recipe and she had no slow cooker. Schnitz und Knepp cooked on the back of the woodstove till the quilting was done. I was allowed to drop in the dumplings.

Keep a bottle of uncoated aspirin handy. If someone shows signs of having a heart attack, give the person an aspirin with water while you call 911.

Barbecued Pork

Grace Ketcham, Marietta, GA
Mary Seielstad, Sparks, NV

Makes 10 servings
(Ideal slow cooker size: 4-quart)

3 lbs. pork, trimmed of fat, cubed
2 cups chopped onions
3 medium green peppers, chopped
1/4 cup brown sugar
brown sugar substitute to equal 2 Tbsp.
1/4 cup vinegar
6-oz. can tomato paste
1 1/2 Tbsp. chili powder
1 tsp. dry mustard
2 tsp. Worcestershire sauce
1 1/4 tsp. salt

1. Combine all ingredients in slow cooker.

2. Cover. Cook on High 8 hours.

3. Shred meat with fork. Mix into sauce and heat through.

4. Serve on hamburger buns with grated cheese and cole slaw on top.

Exchange List Values:
Carbohydrate 0.5, Vegetable 2.0, Meat, lean 3.0

Basic Nutritional Values: Calories 246 (Calories from Fat 84), Total Fat 9 gm (Saturated Fat 3.5 gm, Polyunsat Fat 0.8 gm, Monounsat Fat 4.3 gm, Cholesterol 62 mg), Sodium 367 mg, Total Carbohydrate 15 gm, Dietary Fiber 3 gm, Sugars 9 gm, Protein 26 gm

Variation: Substitute cubed chuck roast or stewing beef for the pork, or use half beef, half pork.

Rice and Beans— and Sausage

Marcia S. Myer, Manheim, PA

Makes 8 servings
(Ideal slow cooker size: 4-quart)

3 celery ribs, chopped
1 onion, chopped
2 garlic cloves, minced
1 3/4 cups tomato juice
2 16-oz. cans kidney beans, drained
3/4 tsp. dried oregano
3/4 tsp. dried thyme
1/4 tsp. red pepper flakes
1/4 tsp. pepper
1/2 lb. (or more) fully cooked smoked turkey sausage, or kielbasa, cut into 1/4" slices
3 cups cooked rice
shredded cheese, optional

1. Combine all ingredients except rice and shredded cheese in slow cooker.

2. Cover. Cook on Low 4-6 hours.

3. Serve over rice. Garnish with shredded cheese, if you wish.

Exchange List Values:
Starch 2.5, Vegetable 1.0, Meat, lean 1.0

Basic Nutritional Values: Calories 241 (Calories from Fat 33), Total Fat 4 gm (Saturated Fat 1.0 gm, Polyunsat Fat 0.8 gm, Monounsat Fat 0.8 gm, Cholesterol 18 mg), Sodium 611 mg, Total Carbohydrate 42 gm, Dietary Fiber 6 gm, Sugars 6 gm, Protein 13 gm

Sausage-Potato Slow Cooker Dinner

Deborah Swartz
Grottoes, VA

Makes 6-8 servings
(Ideal slow cooker size: 4-5-quart)

1 cup water
1/2 tsp. cream of tartar
6 medium potatoes,
    unpeeled, thinly sliced
3/4 lb. sausage, casings
    removed and browned
1 onion, chopped
1/4 cup flour
salt to taste
pepper to taste
1 1/2 cups grated fat-free
    cheddar cheese, divided
1 Tbsp. margarine
10 3/4-oz. can 98%-fat-free,
    reduced-sodium cream
    of mushroom soup

1. Combine water and cream of tartar. Toss sliced potatoes in water. Drain.
2. Layer half of the potatoes, sausage, onion, and flour, a sprinkling of salt and pepper, and one-third of cheddar cheese in slow cooker. Repeat layers until ingredients are used, reserving one-third of cheese for top.
3. Dot butter over top. Pour soup over all.
4. Cover. Cook on Low 7-9 hours or on High 3-4 hours.
5. Sprinkle reserved cheese over top just before serving.

Exchange List Values:
Starch 2.0, Meat, medium fat 1.0, Fat 0.5

Basic Nutritional Values: Calories 262 (Calories from Fat 77), Total Fat 9 gm (Saturated Fat 2.8 gm, Polyunsat Fat 1.5 gm, Monounsat Fat 3.6 gm, Cholesterol 19 mg), Sodium 579 mg, Total Carbohydrate 32 gm, Dietary Fiber 3 gm, Sugars 5 gm, Protein 15 gm

Election Lunch

Alix Nancy Botsford
Seminole, OK

Makes 12 servings
(Ideal slow cooker size: 6-quart)

2 Tbsp. olive oil
1 large onion, chopped
1 lb. sausage, cut into thin
    slices, or casings
    removed and crumbled
1 rib celery, sliced
1 Tbsp. Worcestershire
    sauce
1 1/2 tsp. dry mustard
2 Tbsp. honey
1 Tbsp. sugar substitute
10-oz. can tomatoes with
    green chili peppers
1 lb. can lima or butter
    beans, drained, with
    liquid reserved
1 lb. can red kidney beans,
    drained, with liquid
    reserved
1 lb. can garbanzo beans,
    drained, rinsed

1. Brown onion and sausage in oil.

2. Combine ingredients in 6-qt. slow cooker, or divide between 2 4-qt. cookers and stir to combine. Add reserved juice from lima and kidney beans if there's enough room in the cooker(s).
3. Cover. Cook on Low 2-4 hours.

Exchange List Values:
Starch 1.5, Meat, medium fat 1.0, Fat 0.5

Basic Nutritional Values: Calories 204 (Calories from Fat 79), Total Fat 9 gm (Saturated Fat 2.4 gm, Polyunsat Fat 1.3 gm, Monounsat Fat 4.3 gm, Cholesterol 14 mg), Sodium 613 mg, Total Carbohydrate 23 gm, Dietary Fiber 5 gm, Sugars 8 gm, Protein 9 gm

I mixed up this hearty stew the night before Election Day and took it to the voting site the next morning. I plugged it in, and all day long we could smell the stew cooking. I work at a very sparsely populated, country poling place and ended up giving out the recipe and little water-cup samples to many voters!

I have four different sizes of slow cookers. One is very tiny, with only an on and off switch, for keeping cheese sauce hot. One I use for heating gravy. Another I often use to keep mashed potatoes warm.

Golden Autumn Stew

Naomi E. Fast, Hesston, KS

Makes 8-10 servings
(Ideal slow cooker size: 4-5-quart)

2 cups cubed Yukon gold
   potatoes
2 cups cubed, peeled sweet
   potatoes
2 cups cubed, peeled
   butternut squash
1 cup cubed, peeled
   rutabaga
1 cup diced carrots
1 cup sliced celery
1 lb. Low-fat smoked
   sausage
2 cups apple juice or cider
1 tart apple, thinly sliced
salt to taste
pepper to taste
1 Tbsp. sugar or honey

1. Combine vegetables in slow cooker.
2. Place ring of sausage on top.
3. Add apple juice and apple slices.
4. Cover. Cook on High 2 hours and on Low 4 hours, or until vegetables are tender. Do not stir.
5. To serve, remove sausage ring. Season with salt, pepper, and sugar as desired. Place vegetables in bowl. Slice meat into rings and place on top.
6. Serve with hot baking-powder biscuits and honey, and a green salad or cole slaw.

Exchange List Values:
Starch 1.0, Fruit 0.5,
Vegetable 1.0, Meat, lean
1.0

Basic Nutritional Values: Calories 172 (Calories from Fat 21), Total Fat 2 gm (Saturated Fat 0.8 gm, Polyunsat Fat 0.9 gm, Monounsat Fat 0.5 gm, Cholesterol 19 mg), Sodium 413 mg,Total Carbohydrate 31 gm, Dietary Fiber 3 gm, Sugars 15 gm, Protein 7 gm

Don't omit the rutabaga! Get acquainted with its rich uniqueness. It will surprise and please your taste buds.

Melt-in-your-Mouth Sausages

Ruth Ann Gingrich,
New Holland, PA
Ruth Hershey, Paradise, PA
Carol Sherwood, Batavia, NY
Nancy Zimmerman,
Loysville, PA

Makes 8 servings
(Ideal slow cooker size: 4-quart)

1¾ lbs. sweet turkey
   Italian sausage, cut into
   5-inch lengths
48-oz. jar fat-free, low-
   sodium pasta sauce
6-oz. can no-added-salt
   tomato paste
1 large green pepper,
   thinly sliced
1 large onion, thinly sliced
1 Tbsp. grated Parmesan
   cheese
1 tsp. dried parsley,
   or 1 Tbsp. chopped
   fresh parsley
1 cup water

1. Place sausage in skillet. Cover with water. Simmer 10 minutes. Drain.
2. Combine remaining ingredients in slow cooker. Add sausage.
3. Cover. Cook on Low 6 hours.
4. Serve in buns, or cut sausage into bite-sized pieces and serve over cooked spaghetti. Sprinkle with more Parmesan cheese if you wish.

Exchange List Values:
Carbohydrate 1.5, Meat,
lean 3.0, Fat 0.5

Basic Nutritional Values: Calories 288 (Calories from Fat 111), Total Fat 12 gm (Saturated Fat 3.5 gm, Polyunsat Fat 1.5 gm, Monounsat Fat 2.2 gm, Cholesterol 79 mg), Sodium 692 mg,Total Carbohydrate 21 gm, Dietary Fiber 3 gm, Sugars 12 gm, Protein 25 gm

Many people resist going on insulin injections, even though their doctor wants them to, but it may be just what they need to feel their best, ensure tight control, and avoid future complications.

Polish Kraut 'n Apples

Lori Berezovsky, Salina, KS
Marie Morucci, Glen Lyon, PA

Makes 6 servings
(Ideal slow cooker size: 4-quart)

1 lb. fresh, or canned, sauerkraut
1 lb. low-fat, smoked Polish sausage
3 tart cooking apples, unpeeled, thinly sliced
2 Tbsp. brown sugar
brown sugar substitute to equal 3 Tbsp.
1/8 tsp. pepper
1/2 tsp. caraway seeds, optional
3/4 cup apple juice, or cider

1. Rinse sauerkraut and squeeze dry. Place half in slow cooker.
2. Cut sausage into 2-inch lengths and add to cooker.
3. Continue to layer remaining ingredients in slow cooker in order given. Top with remaining sauerkraut. Do not stir.
4. Cover. Cook on High 3-3½ hours, or Low 6-7 hours.

Exchange List Values:
Fruit 1.0, Carbohydrate 1.0, Meat, lean 1.0

Basic Nutritional Values: Calories 195 (Calories from Fat 33), Total Fat 4 gm (Saturated Fat 1.4 gm, Polyunsat Fat 0.3 gm, Monounsat Fat 1.9 gm, Cholesterol 35 mg), Sodium 945 mg, Total Carbohydrate 31 gm, Dietary Fiber 4 gm, Sugars 20 gm, Protein 10 gm

Dawn's Sausage and Peppers

Dawn Day, Westminster, CA

Makes 8-10 servings
(Ideal slow cooker size: 4-5-quart)

3 medium onions, sliced
1 medium sweet red pepper, sliced
1 medium sweet green pepper, sliced
1 medium sweet yellow pepper, sliced
4 garlic cloves, minced
1 Tbsp. canola oil
28-oz. can no-added-salt chopped tomatoes
1/2 tsp. red crushed pepper
2 lbs. fresh turkey sweet Italian sausage, cut into 3" pieces

1. Saute onions, peppers, and garlic in oil in skillet. When just softened, place in slow cooker.
2. Add tomatoes and crushed red pepper. Mix well.
3. Add sausage links.
4. Cover. Cook on Low 6 hours.
5. Serve on rolls, or over pasta or baked potatoes.

Exchange List Values:
Vegetable 2.0, Meat, medium fat 2.0, Fat 0.5

Basic Nutritional Values: Calories 237 (Calories from Fat 112), Total Fat 12 gm (Saturated Fat 3.1 gm, Polyunsat Fat 1.8 gm, Monounsat Fat 2.7 gm, Cholesterol 72 mg), Sodium 619 mg, Total Carbohydrate 12 gm, Dietary Fiber 3 gm, Sugars 7 gm, Protein 21 gm

Variation: For a thicker sauce, stir in 3 Tbsp. ClearJell during the last 15 minutes of the cooking time.

Sausage Sauerkraut Supper

Ruth Ann Hoover
New Holland, PA
Robin Schrock
Millersburg, OH

Makes 10-12 servings
(Ideal slow cooker size: 4-5-quart)

4 cups cubed carrots
4 cups cubed red potatoes
2 14-oz. cans sauerkraut, rinsed and drained
1 lb. fresh Polish sausage, cut into 3-inch pieces
1 medium onion, thinly sliced
3 garlic cloves, minced
1½ cups dry white wine, or chicken broth
1/2 tsp. pepper
1 tsp. caraway seeds

1. Layer carrots, potatoes, and sauerkraut in slow cooker.
2. Brown sausage in skillet. Transfer to slow cooker. Reserve 1 Tbsp. drippings in skillet.
3. Saute onion and garlic in drippings until tender. Stir in wine. Bring to boil. Stir to loosen brown bits. Stir in pepper and caraway seeds. Pour over sausage.
4. Cover. Cook on Low 8-9 hours.

Basic Nutritional Values: Calories
195 (Calories from Fat 86), Total Fat
10 gm (Saturated Fat 3.4 gm,
Polyunsat Fat 1.0 gm, Monounsat Fat
5.2 gm, Cholesterol 24 mg), Sodium
689 mg, Total Carbohydrate 18 gm,
Dietary Fiber 5 gm, Sugars 5 gm,
Protein 8 gm

Kielbasa and Cabbage

Barbara McGinnis

Jupiter, FL

Makes 6 servings
(Ideal slow cooker size: 4-5-quart)

1½ lb.-head green cabbage,
  shredded
2 medium onions, chopped
3 medium red potatoes,
  peeled and cubed
1 red bell pepper, chopped
2 garlic cloves, minced
2/3 cup dry white wine
1 lb. Low-fat Polish
  kielbasa, cut into 3-inch
  long links
28-oz. can cut-up no-
  added-salt tomatoes
  with juice
1 Tbsp. Dijon mustard
3/4 tsp. caraway seeds
1/2 tsp. pepper

1. Combine all ingredients
in slow cooker.
2. Cover. Cook on Low 7-8
hours, or until cabbage is tender.

Basic Nutritional Values: Calories
226 (Calories from Fat 39), Total Fat
4 gm (Saturated Fat 1.4 gm,
Polyunsat Fat 0.6 gm, Monounsat Fat
2.0 gm, Cholesterol 35 mg), Sodium
781 mg, Total Carbohydrate 34 gm,
Dietary Fiber 7 gm, Sugars 15 gm,
Protein 14 gm

Aunt Lavina's Sauerkraut

Pat Unternahrer

Wayland, IA

Makes 8-12 servings
(Ideal slow cooker size: 4-quart)

2 lbs. smoked Low-fat
  sausage, cut into 1-inch
  pieces
2 Tbsp. water, or oil
2 bell peppers, chopped
2 onions, sliced
1/2 lb. fresh mushrooms,
  sliced
1 qt. sauerkraut, drained
2 14½-oz. cans no-added-
  salt diced tomatoes with
  green peppers
1/2 tsp. pepper
2 Tbsp. brown sugar

1. Place sausage in slow
cooker. Heat on Low while
you prepare other ingredients.
2. Saute peppers, onions,
and mushrooms in small
amount of water or oil in
saucepan.
3. Combine all ingredients
in slow cooker.
4. Cover. Cook on Low 5-6
hours, or High 3-4 hours.
5. Serve with mashed potatoes.

Basic Nutritional Values: Calories
163 (Calories from Fat 34), Total Fat
4 gm (Saturated Fat 1.4 gm,
Polyunsat Fat 1.5 gm, Monounsat Fat
0.8 gm, Cholesterol 32 mg), Sodium
984 mg, Total Carbohydrate 21 gm,
Dietary Fiber 4 gm, Sugars 11 gm,
Protein 12 gm

Check your blood
sugar as soon as you get
up, before you do
anything else, and then
treat as needed. Starting
the day with a normal
blood sugar level will
make it easier to keep
your level under control
throughout the day.

Pork Spareribs with Sauerkraut

Char Hagner
Montague, MI

Makes 4-6 servings
(Ideal slow cooker size: 4-quart)

2 small cooking apples,
  sliced in rings
1¹/₂-2 lbs. country-style
  spareribs, trimmed of
  fat, cut into serving-size
  pieces and browned
2 cups canned sauerkraut,
  drained and rinsed
¹/₂ cup apple cider, or juice
¹/₂ tsp. caraway seeds,
  optional

1. Layer apples, ribs, and
sauerkraut into slow cooker.
Pour on juice. Sprinkle with
caraway seeds.
2. Cover. Cook on Low 8
hours, or High 4 hours.

Exchange List Values:
Fruit 0.5, Vegetable 1.0,
Meat, medium fat 2.0

Basic Nutritional Values: Calories
198 (Calories from Fat 82), Total Fat
9 gm (Saturated Fat 3.3 gm,
Polyunsat Fat 0.8 gm, Monounsat Fat
3.9 gm, Cholesterol 57 mg), Sodium
356 mg,Total Carbohydrate 11 gm,
Dietary Fiber 3 gm, Sugars 7 gm,
Protein 18 gm

Sauerkraut and Ribs

Margaret H. Moffitt
Bartlett, TN

Makes 6 servings
(Ideal slow cooker size: 4-quart)

27-oz. can sauerkraut,
  drained and rinsed
1 small onion, chopped
2 lbs. country-style pork
  ribs, trimmed of fat, cut
  into serving-size pieces
¹/₄ tsp. pepper
half a sauerkraut can of
  water

1. Pour sauerkraut and
juice into slow cooker. Add
onion.
2. Season ribs with pepper.
Place on top of kraut. Add
water.
3. Cover. Cook on High
until mixture boils. Reduce
heat to Low and cook 4
hours.
4. Serve with mashed potatoes.

Exchange List Values:
Vegetable 1.0, Meat,
medium fat 2.0

Basic Nutritional Values: Calories
185 (Calories from Fat 82), Total Fat
9 gm (Saturated Fat 3.3 gm,
Polyunsat Fat 0.8 gm, Monounsat Fat
3.9 gm, Cholesterol 57 mg), Sodium
548 mg,Total Carbohydrate 7 gm,
Dietary Fiber 4 gm, Sugars 3 gm,
Protein 19 gm

Chops and Kraut

Willard E. Roth
Elkhart, IN

Makes 6 servings
(Ideal slow cooker size: 4-quart)

1 lb. bag fresh sauerkraut,
  drained and rinsed
2 large Vidalia onions,
  sliced
6 (¹/₄ lb. each) pork chops,
  bone-in, trimmed of fat
¹/₃ cup water

1. Make 3 layers in well-
greased cooker: kraut, onions,
and chops. Pour water over
top.
2. Cover. Cook on Low 6
hours.
3. Serve with mashed potatoes and applesauce or cranberry sauce.

Exchange List Values:
Vegetable 2.0, Meat, lean
2.0

Basic Nutritional Values: Calories
156 (Calories from Fat 43), Total Fat
5 gm (Saturated Fat 1.7 gm,
Polyunsat Fat 0.4 gm, Monounsat Fat
2.1 gm, Cholesterol 47 mg), Sodium
336 mg,Total Carbohydrate 10 gm,
Dietary Fiber 3 gm, Sugars 6 gm,
Protein 18 gm

Smothered Lentils

Tracey B. Stenger
Gretna, LA

Makes 6 servings
(Ideal slow cooker size: 4-quart)

2 cups dry lentils, rinsed
   and sorted
1 medium onion, chopped
1/2 cup chopped celery
2 garlic cloves, minced
1 cup ham, cooked and
   chopped
1/2 cup chopped carrots
1 cup diced fresh tomatoes
1 tsp. dried marjoram
1 tsp. ground coriander
3 cups water

1. Combine all ingredients
in slow cooker.
2. Cover. Cook on Low 8
hours. (Check lentils after 5
hours of cooking. If they've
absorbed all the water, stir in
1 more cup water.)

Exchange List Values:
Starch 2.0, Vegetable 1.0,
Meat, very lean 2.0

Basic Nutritional Values: Calories
239 (Calories from Fat 19), Total Fat
2 gm (Saturated Fat 0.5 gm,
Polyunsat Fat 0.5 gm, Monounsat Fat
0.7 gm, Cholesterol 13 mg), Sodium
333 mg,Total Carbohydrate 36 gm,
Dietary Fiber 14 gm, Sugars 6 gm,
Protein 21 gm

*You may want to add salt and
pepper if you regularly use them
in your diet.*

Green Beans and Sausage

Alma Weaver
Ephrata, PA

Makes 4-6 servings
(Ideal slow cooker size: 4-quart)

1 qt. green beans, cut into
   2-inch pieces
1 carrot, chopped
1 small green pepper,
   chopped
8-oz. can no-added-salt
   tomato sauce
1/4 tsp. dried thyme
1/4 tsp. salt
1/2 lb. bulk pork sausage,
   browned and drained

1. Combine all ingredients
except sausage in slow
cooker.
2. Cover. Cook on High 3-4
hours. Add sausage and cook
another 2 hours on Low.

Exchange List Values:
Vegetable 2.0, Meat,
medium fat 1.0

Basic Nutritional Values: Calories
114 (Calories from Fat 53), Total Fat
6 gm (Saturated Fat 2.0 gm,
Polyunsat Fat 0.8 gm, Monounsat Fat
2.5 gm, Cholesterol 14 mg), Sodium
350 mg,Total Carbohydrate 11 gm,
Dietary Fiber 4 gm, Sugars 5 gm,
Protein 6 gm

Brats and Spuds

Kathi Rogge, Alexandria, IN

Makes 6 servings
(Ideal slow cooker size: 4-quart)

5-6 bratwurst links, cut
   into 1" pieces
5 medium-sized potatoes,
   peeled and cubed
27-oz. can sauerkraut,
   rinsed and drained
1 medium tart apple,
   unpeeled, chopped
1 small onion, chopped
2 Tbsp. brown sugar
brown sugar substitute to
   equal 1 Tbsp.

1. Brown bratwurst on all
sides in skillet.
2. Combine remaining
ingredients in slow cooker.
Stir in bratwurst.
3. Cover. Cook on High 4-6
hours, or until potatoes and
apples are tender.

Exchange List Values:
Starch 1.5, Carbohydrate
0.5, Vegetable 1.0, Meat,
high fat 1.0

Basic Nutritional Values: Calories
273 (Calories from Fat 88), Total Fat
10 gm (Saturated Fat 3.5 gm,
Polyunsat Fat 1.1 gm, Monounsat Fat
5.4 gm, Cholesterol 25 mg), Sodium
920 mg,Total Carbohydrate 36 gm,
Dietary Fiber 6 gm, Sugars 13 gm,
Protein 10 gm

*Variation: Add a small
amount of caraway seeds or
crisp bacon pieces, just before
serving.*

Ham Balls

Jo Haberkamp
Fairbank, IA

Makes 24 servings
(Ideal slow cooker size: 6-quart)

Ham Balls:
3 eggs
3 cups crushed graham crackers
2 cups milk
2 tsp. dried minced onion
1/4 tsp. pepper
2 lbs. extra-lean, reduced-sodium ground ham
1 1/2 lbs. 90%-lean ground beef
1 1/2 lbs. ground pork, trimmed of fat

Topping:
1/2 cup no-salt-added ketchup
1/4 cup water
1/2 cup brown sugar
1/4 cup plus 2 Tbsp. vinegar
1/2 tsp. dry mustard

1. Beat eggs slightly in large bowl. Add graham crackers, milk, minced onion, pepper, and ground meats. Mix well.
2. Form into 24 balls, using a 1/2-cup measuring cup for each ball.
3. Combine topping ingredients.
4. Layer meatballs and topping in greased slow cooker.
5. Cover. Cook on High 1 hour. Reduce heat to Low and cook 3-4 hours more.

Exchange List Values:
Carbohydrate 1.0, Meat, medium fat 2.0

Basic Nutritional Values: Calories 220 (Calories from Fat 63), Total Fat 7 gm (Saturated Fat 2.5 gm, Polyunsat Fat 0.9 gm, Monounsat Fat 2.9 gm, Cholesterol 82 mg), Sodium 429 mg, Total Carbohydrate 17 gm, Dietary Fiber 0 gm, Sugars 10 gm, Protein 21 gm

Hot Dogs and Noodles

Dolores Kratz, Souderton, PA

Makes 6 servings
(Ideal slow cooker size: 4-quart)

8-oz. pkg. medium egg noodles, cooked and drained
1 cup freshly grated Parmesan cheese
1 cup fat-free milk
1 Tbsp. flour
1 lb. pkg. fat-free hot dogs, sliced
2 Tbsp. brown sugar brown sugar substitute to equal 1 Tbsp.
1/4 cup fat-free mayonnaise
2 Tbsp. prepared mustard

1. Place noodles, cheese, milk, and flour in slow cooker. Mix well.
2. Combine hot dogs with remaining ingredients. Spoon evenly over noodles.
3. Cover. Cook on Low 5-6 hours.

Exchange List Values:
Starch 2.0, Carbohydrate 1.0, Meat, lean 2.0

Basic Nutritional Values: Calories 326 (Calories from Fat 59), Total Fat 7 gm (Saturated Fat 3.4 gm, Polyunsat Fat 0.8 gm, Monounsat Fat 2.2 gm, Cholesterol 65 mg), Sodium 1036 mg, Total Carbohydrate 44 gm, Dietary Fiber 1 gm, Sugars 12 gm, Protein 22 gm

> **Foods with trans fats are bad for your heart. If the label says partially hydrogenated vegetable oil, shortening, or margarine, beware!**

Chicken & Turkey Main Dishes

Chicken and Sausage Cacciatore

Joyce Kaut
Rochester, NY

Makes 4-6 servings
(Ideal slow cooker size: 4-quart)

1 large green pepper, sliced
   in 1″ strips
1 cup sliced mushrooms
1 medium onion, sliced in
   rings
1 lb. skinless, boneless
   chicken breasts,
   browned
1 lb. lean fresh, sweet
   Italian turkey sausage
   links, browned
1/2 tsp. dried oregano
1/2 tsp. dried basil
2 Tbsp. Italian Seasoning
   Mix (see page 254 for
   recipe.
1 1/2 cups no-added-salt
   tomato sauce

1. Layer vegetables in slow cooker.
2. Top with meat.
3. Sprinkle with oregano, basil, and Italian seasoning mix.
4. Top with tomato sauce.
5. Cover. Cook on Low 8 hours.
6. Remove cover during last 30 minutes of cooking time to allow sauce to cook-off and thicken.
7. Serve over cooked spiral pasta.

Exchange List Values:
Vegetable 2.0, Meat, lean 4.0

Basic Nutritional Values: Calories 278 (Calories from Fat 100), Total Fat 11 gm (Saturated Fat 3.1 gm, Polyunsat Fat 1.5 gm, Monounsat Fat 2.3 gm, Cholesterol 105 mg), Sodium 547 mg,Total Carbohydrate 10 gm, Dietary Fiber 2 gm, Sugars 6 gm, Protein 34 gm

Wild Rice Hot Dish

Barbara Tenney
Delta, PA

Makes 8-10 side dish servings
(Ideal slow cooker size: 4-quart)

2 cups wild rice, uncooked
1/2 cup slivered almonds
1/2 cup chopped onions
1/2 cup chopped celery
8-12-oz. can mushrooms,
  drained
2 cups cut-up, cooked
  chicken
6 cups reduced-sodium,
  98%-fat-free chicken
  broth
1/4 tsp. pepper
1/4 tsp. garlic powder
1 Tbsp. parsley

1. Wash and drain rice.
2. Combine all ingredients in slow cooker. Mix well.
3. Cover. Cook on Low 4-6 hours, or until rice is finished. Do not remove lid before rice has cooked 4 hours.

Exchange List Values:
Starch 2.0, Meat, lean 1.0,
Fat 0.5

Basic Nutritional Values: Calories 227 (Calories from Fat 51), Total Fat 6 gm (Saturated Fat 0.8 gm, Polyunsat Fat 1.4 gm, Monounsat Fat 2.7 gm, Cholesterol 25 mg), Sodium 403 mg, Total Carbohydrate 28 gm, Dietary Fiber 4 gm, Sugars 2 gm, Protein 17 gm

Frances' Roast Chicken

Frances Schrag
Newton, KS

Makes 6 servings
(Ideal slow cooker size: 4-5-quart)

3 lb. whole frying chicken
salt to taste
pepper to taste
1/2 tsp. poultry seasoning
half an onion, chopped
1 rib celery, chopped
1/4 tsp. dried basil

1. Sprinkle chicken cavity with salt, pepper, and poultry seasoning. Put onion and celery inside cavity. Put chicken in slow cooker. Sprinkle with basil.
2. Cover. Cook on Low 8-10 hours, or High 4-6 hours.
3. Remove skin from chicken and discard liquid.

Exchange List Values:
Meat, lean 3.0

Basic Nutritional Values: Calories 140 (Calories from Fat 48), Total Fat 5 gm (Saturated Fat 1.4 gm, Polyunsat Fat 1.2 gm, Monounsat Fat 1.9 gm, Cholesterol 65 mg), Sodium 56 mg, Total Carbohydrate 0 gm, Dietary Fiber 0 gm, Sugars 0 gm, Protein 21 gm

Donna's Cooked Chicken

Donna Treloar
Gaston, IN

(Ideal slow cooker size: 5-quart)

1 medium onion, sliced
2 1/2 lb. boneless, skinless
  chicken breasts
1/2 tsp. seasoned salt
1/4 tsp. pepper
1/2 tsp. garlic powder

1. Layer onion in bottom of slow cooker. Add chicken and sprinkle with seasoned salt, pepper, and garlic powder.
2. Cook on Low 4 hours or until done but not dry.
3. Use in stir-frys, chicken salads, or casseroles, slice for sandwiches, shred for enchiladas, or cut up and freeze for later use.

Exchange List Values:
Meat, very lean 4.0

Basic Nutritional Values: Calories 138 (Calories from Fat 24), Total Fat 3 gm (Saturated Fat 0.7 gm, Polyunsat Fat 0.6 gm, Monounsat Fat 0.9 gm, Cholesterol 67 mg), Sodium 131 mg, Total Carbohydrate 1 gm, Dietary Fiber 0 gm, Sugars 1 gm, Protein 25 gm

Variation: Splash chicken with 2 Tbsp. light soy sauce before cooking.

Chicken in a Pot

Carolyn Baer, Conrath, WI
Evie Hershey, Atglen, PA
Judy Koczo, Plano, IL
Mary Puskar, Forest Hill, MD
Mary Wheatley, Mashpee, MA

Makes 6 servings
(Ideal slow cooker size: 5-quart)

2 medium carrots, sliced
2 medium onions, sliced
2 celery ribs, cut in 1-inch
   pieces
3 lb. chicken, whole or cut
   up, skin removed
3/4 tsp. salt
1/2 tsp. dried coarse black
   pepper
1 tsp. dried basil
1/2 cup water, chicken
   broth, or white cooking
   wine

1. Place vegetables in bottom of slow cooker. Place chicken on top of vegetables. Add seasonings and water.

2. Cover. Cook on Low 8-10 hours, or High 3½ hours (use 1 cup liquid if cooking on High).

3. This is a great foundation for soups—chicken vegetable, chicken noodle, chicken rice, chicken corn, and other favorites.

Exchange List Values:
Vegetable 1.0, Meat, lean 3.0

Basic Nutritional Values: Calories 172 (Calories from Fat 49), Total Fat 5 gm (Saturated Fat 1.5 gm, Polyunsat Fat 1.3 gm, Monounsat Fat 1.9 gm, Cholesterol 65 mg), Sodium 381 mg, Total Carbohydrate 8 gm, Dietary Fiber 2 gm, Sugars 4 gm, Protein 22 gm

Note: To make this a full meal, add 2 medium-sized potatoes, quartered, to vegetables before cooking.

Another Chicken in a Pot

Jennifer J. Gehman
Harrisburg, PA

Makes 4-6 servings
(Ideal slow cooker size: 4-5-quart)

1 lb. bag baby carrots
1 small onion, diced
10-oz. pkg. frozen green
   beans, thawed
3 lb. whole chicken, cut
   into serving-size pieces,
   skin and fat removed
1/2 tsp. salt
1/2 tsp. black pepper
1/2 cup chicken broth
1/4 cup white wine
1/2-1 tsp. dried basil

1. Put carrots, onion, and beans on bottom of slow cooker. Add chicken. Top with salt, pepper, broth, and wine. Sprinkle with basil.

2. Cover. Cook on Low 8-10 hours, or High 3½-5 hours.

Exchange List Values:
Vegetable 2.0, Meat, lean 3.0

Basic Nutritional Values: Calories 194 (Calories from Fat 51), Total Fat 6 gm (Saturated Fat 1.5 gm, Polyunsat Fat 1.4 gm, Monounsat Fat 2.0 gm, Cholesterol 66 mg), Sodium 434 mg, Total Carbohydrate 12 gm, Dietary Fiber 4 gm, Sugars 6 gm, Protein 23 gm

If you lose just 10 pounds and keep it off, your blood pressure, blood sugars, and cholesterol levels are likely to improve.

Savory Slow-Cooker Chicken

Sara Harter Fredette
Williamsburg, MA

Makes 4 servings
(Ideal slow cooker size: 4-5-quart)

2½ lbs. chicken pieces, skinned
1 lb. fresh tomatoes, chopped, or 15-oz. can stewed tomatoes
2 Tbsp. white wine
1 bay leaf
¼ tsp. pepper
2 garlic cloves, minced
1 onion, chopped
½ cup chicken broth
1 tsp. dried thyme
¼ tsp. salt
2 cups broccoli, cut into bite-sized pieces

1. Combine all ingredients except broccoli in slow cooker.
2. Cover. Cook on Low 8-10 hours.
3. Add broccoli 30 minutes before serving.

Exchange List Values:
Vegetable 2.0, Meat, lean 3.0

Basic Nutritional Values: Calories 230 (Calories from Fat 67), Total Fat 7 gm (Saturated Fat 1.9 gm, Polyunsat Fat 1.8 gm, Monounsat Fat 2.5 gm, Cholesterol 82 mg), Sodium 427 mg, Total Carbohydrate 11 gm, Dietary Fiber 3 gm, Sugars 7 gm, Protein 30 gm

Chicken and Vegetables

Rosanne Hankins
Stevensville, MD

Makes 6 servings
(Ideal slow cooker size: 4-5-quart)

3 lbs. chicken, cut up, skin and visible fat removed
salt to taste
pepper to taste
1 bay leaf
2 tsp. lemon juice
¼ cup diced onions
¼ cup diced celery
1 lb. frozen mixed vegetables including corn

1. Sprinkle salt and pepper over chicken and place chicken in slow cooker. Add bay leaf and lemon juice.
2. Cover. Cook on Low 6-8 hours, or High 3-5 hours. Remove chicken from bones. Reserve liquid, skimming fat if desired.
3. Cook ½ cup liquid, onions, and celery in microwave on High for 2 minutes. Add frozen vegetables and microwave until cooked through.
4. Return all ingredients to slow cooker and cook on High 30 minutes.
5. Serve over cooked rice.

Exchange List Values:
Vegetable 2.0, Meat, lean 3.0

Basic Nutritional Values: Calories 187 (Calories from Fat 49), Total Fat 5 gm (Saturated Fat 1.4 gm, Polyunsat Fat 1.3 gm, Monounsat Fat 1.9 gm, Cholesterol 65 mg), Sodium 105 mg, Total Carbohydrate 11 gm, Dietary Fiber 2 gm, Sugars 3 gm, Protein 24 gm

When you eat out, ask for a to-go box. Before you take a single bite of your meal, put half of it in the box. Out of sight, out of mind!

Baked Chicken Breasts

Janice Crist
Quinter, KS
Tracy Supcoe
Barclay, MD

Makes 4-6 servings
(Ideal slow cooker size: 4-quart)

3 whole chicken breasts, halved
10¾-oz. can 98%-fat-free, reduced-sodium cream of chicken soup
½ cup dry sherry
1 tsp. dried tarragon, or rosemary, or both
1 tsp. Worcestershire sauce
¼ tsp. garlic powder
4-oz. can sliced mushrooms, drained

1. Place chicken breasts in slow cooker.
2. In saucepan, combine remaining ingredients. Heat until smooth and hot. Pour over chicken.
3. Cover. Cook on Low 8-10 hours.

Exchange List Values:
Carbohydrate 0.5, Meat, very lean 4.0, Fat 0.5

Basic Nutritional Values: Calories 214 (Calories from Fat 40), Total Fat 4 gm (Saturated Fat 1.3 gm, Polyunsat Fat 1.2 gm, Monounsat Fat 1.3 gm, Cholesterol 88 mg), Sodium 339 mg, Total Carbohydrate 7 gm, Dietary Fiber 1 gm, Sugars 2 gm, Protein 34 gm

Chicken Delicious

Janice Crist
Quinter, KS

Makes 8-12 servings
(Ideal slow cooker size: 4-5-quart)

6 whole boneless, skinless chicken breasts, halved, visible fat removed
10¾-oz. can 98%-fat-free, lower-sodium cream of mushroom soup
10¾-oz. can cream of celery soup
⅓ cup dry sherry, or white wine

1. Place chicken in slow cooker.
2. Combine soups with sherry. Pour over chicken.
3. Cover. Cook on Low 8-10 hours.
4. Serve with rice.

Exchange List Values:
Carbohydrate 0.5, Meat, very lean 4.0, Fat 0.5

Basic Nutritional Values: Calories 203 (Calories from Fat 48), Total Fat 5 gm (Saturated Fat 1.6 gm, Polyunsat Fat 1.4 gm, Monounsat Fat 1.5 gm, Cholesterol 85 mg), Sodium 352 mg, Total Carbohydrate 4 gm, Dietary Fiber 0 gm, Sugars 1 gm, Protein 32 gm

This recipe is best if seasoned with lemon juice, salt, pepper, celery salt, and paprika before cooking. You can also sprinkle with grated Parmesan cheese.

Chicken in Wine

Mary Seielstad
Sparks, NV

Makes 4-6 servings
(Ideal slow cooker size: 4-quart)

2 lbs. chicken breasts, or pieces, trimmed of skin and fat
10¾-oz. can 98%-fat-free, reduced-sodium cream of mushroom soup
10¾-oz. can French onion soup
1 cup dry white wine, or chicken broth

1. Put chicken in slow cooker.
2. Combine soups and wine. Pour over chicken.
3. Cover. Cook on Low 6-8 hours.
4. Serve over rice, pasta, or potatoes.

Exchange List Values:
Carbohydrate 0.5, Meat, very lean 5.0

Basic Nutritional Values: Calories 225 (Calories from Fat 47), Total Fat 5 gm (Saturated Fat 1.4 gm, Polyunsat Fat 1.2 gm, Monounsat Fat 1.6 gm, Cholesterol 91 mg), Sodium 645 mg, Total Carbohydrate 7 gm, Dietary Fiber 1 gm, Sugars 3 gm, Protein 35 gm

Creamy Chicken and Noodles

Rhonda Burgoon
Collingswood, NJ

Makes 4-6 servings
(Ideal slow cooker size: 4-quart)

2 cups sliced carrots
1½ cups chopped onions
1 cup sliced celery
2 Tbsp. snipped fresh parsley
bay leaf
3 medium-sized chicken
    legs and thighs (about
    2 lbs.), skin removed
2 10¾-oz. cans 98%-fat-
    free, reduced-sodium
    cream of chicken soup
½ cup water
1 tsp. dried thyme
¼ tsp. salt
¼ tsp. pepper
1 cup peas
8 ozs. dry wide noodles,
    cooked

1. Place carrots, onions, celery, parsley, and bay leaf in bottom of slow cooker.
2. Place chicken on top of vegetables.
3. Combine soup, water, thyme, salt, and pepper. Pour over chicken and vegetables.
4. Cover. Cook on Low 8-9 hours or on High 4-4½ hours.
5. Remove chicken from slow cooker. Cool slightly. Remove from bones, cut into bite-sized pieces, and return to slow cooker.
6. Remove and discard bay leaf.

7. Stir peas into mixture in slow cooker. Allow to cook for 5-10 more minutes.
8. Pour over cooked noodles. Toss gently to combine.
9. Serve with crusty bread and a salad.

Exchange List Values:
Starch 2.0, Carbohydrate 0.5, Vegetable 2.0, Meat, lean 2.0

Basic Nutritional Values: Calories 357 (Calories from Fat 71), Total Fat 8 gm (Saturated Fat 2.4 gm, Polyunsat Fat 2.3 gm, Monounsat Fat 2.3 gm, Cholesterol 87 mg), Sodium 614 mg, Total Carbohydrate 48 gm, Dietary Fiber 5 gm, Sugars 9 gm, Protein 22 gm

Chicken in Mushroom Gravy

Rosemarie Fitzgerald
Gibsonia, PA
Audrey L. Kneer
Wllliamsfield, IL

Makes 6 servings
(Ideal slow cooker size: 4-quart)

6 (5 ozs. each) boneless,
    skinless chicken breast
    halves
salt to taste
pepper to taste
¼ cup dry white wine, or
    chicken broth
10¾-oz. can 98%-fat-free,
    reduced-sodium cream
    of mushroom soup
4-oz. can sliced
    mushrooms, drained

1. Place chicken in slow cooker. Season with salt and pepper.
2. Combine wine and soup. Pour over chicken. Top with mushrooms.
3. Cover. Cook on Low 7-9 hours.

Exchange List Values:
Carbohydrate 0.5, Meat, very lean 4.0, Fat 0.5

Basic Nutritional Values: Calories 204 (Calories from Fat 40), Total Fat 4 gm (Saturated Fat 1.4 gm, Polyunsat Fat 1.0 gm, Monounsat Fat 1.3 gm, Cholesterol 85 mg), Sodium 320 mg, Total Carbohydrate 6 gm, Dietary Fiber 1 gm, Sugars 1 gm, Protein 34 gm

Mushroom Chicken in Sour Cream Sauce

Lavina Hochstedler
Grand Blanc, MI
Joyce Shackelford
Green Bay, WI

Makes 6 servings
(Ideal slow cooker size: 4-quart)

1/4 tsp. salt
1/4 tsp. pepper
1/2 tsp. paprika
1/4 tsp. lemon pepper
1 tsp. garlic powder
6 skinless, bone-in chicken breast halves
10 3/4-oz. can 98%-fat-free, reduced-sodium cream of mushroom soup
8-oz. container fat-free sour cream
1/2 cup dry white wine, or chicken broth
1/2 lb. fresh mushrooms, sliced

1. Combine salt, pepper, paprika, lemon pepper, and garlic powder. Rub over chicken. Place in slow cooker.
2. Combine soup, sour cream, and wine or broth. Stir in mushrooms. Pour over chicken.
3. Cover. Cook on Low 6-8 hours or High 5 hours.
4. Serve over potatoes, rice, or couscous. Delicious accompanied with broccoli-cauliflower salad and applesauce.

Exchange List Values:
Carbohydrate 1.0, Meat, very lean 4.0

Basic Nutritional Values: Calories 217 (Calories from Fat 37), Total Fat 4 gm (Saturated Fat 1.2 gm, Polyunsat Fat 0.9 gm, Monounsat Fat 1.2 gm, Cholesterol 76 mg), Sodium 407 mg, Total Carbohydrate 12 gm, Dietary Fiber 1 gm, Sugars 4 gm, Protein 30 gm

Chicken Azteca

Katrine Rose
Woodbridge, VA

Makes 10-12 servings
(Ideal slow cooker size: 5-6-quart)

2 15-oz. cans black beans, drained
4 cups frozen corn kernels
2 garlic cloves, minced
3/4 tsp. ground cumin
2 cups chunky salsa, divided
10 skinless, boneless chicken breast halves
12 ozs. fat-free cream cheese, cubed

1. Combine beans, corn, garlic, cumin, and half of salsa in slow cooker.
2. Arrange chicken breasts over top. Pour remaining salsa over top.
3. Cover. Cook on High 2-3 hours or on Low 4-6 hours.
4. Remove chicken and cut into bite-sized pieces. Return to cooker.
5. Stir in cream cheese. Cook on High until cream cheese melts.
6. Spoon chicken and sauce over cooked rice. Top with shredded cheddar cheese if you wish.

Exchange List Values:
Starch 1.5, Meat, very lean 4.0

Basic Nutritional Values: Calories 252 (Calories from Fat 27), Total Fat 3 gm (Saturated Fat 0.8 gm, Polyunsat Fat 0.8 gm, Monounsat Fat 0.9 gm, Cholesterol 64 mg), Sodium 366 mg, Total Carbohydrate 24 gm, Dietary Fiber 5 gm, Sugars 4 gm, Protein 33 gm

Did you know that people who eat a lot of whole grains have fewer heart attacks?

Tamale Chicken

Jeanne Allen
Rye, CO

Makes 8 servings
(Ideal slow cooker size: 4-5-quart)

1 medium onion, chopped
4-oz. can chopped green
  chilies
1 Tbsp. canola oil
10¾-oz. can 98%-fat-free,
  reduced-sodium cream
  of chicken soup
1 cup fat-free sour cream
1 cup sliced ripe olives
1 cup chopped no-added-
  salt stewed tomatoes
1¼ cups shredded fat-free
  cheddar cheese, divided
8 chicken breast halves,
  cooked and chopped
16-oz. can beef tamales,
  chopped
1 tsp. chili powder
1 tsp. garlic powder
1 tsp. pepper

1. Saute onion and chilies
in oil in skillet.
2. Combine all ingredients
except ¼ cup shredded
cheese. Pour into slow cooker.
3. Top with remaining
cheese.
4. Cover. Cook on High 3-4
hours.
5. Pass chopped fresh
tomatoes, shredded lettuce,
sour cream, salsa, and/or
guacamole so guests can top
their Tamale Chicken with
these condiments.

Exchange List Values:
Starch 0.5, Carbohydrate
0.5, Vegetable 1.0, Meat,
lean 4.0, Fat 0.5

Basic Nutritional Values: Calories
341 (Calories from Fat 98), Total Fat
11 gm (Saturated Fat 2.7 gm,
Polyunsat Fat 2.1 gm, Monounsat Fat
4.9 gm, Cholesterol 87 mg), Sodium
848 mg, Total Carbohydrate 21 gm,
Dietary Fiber 3 gm, Sugars 5 gm,
Protein 37 gm

Tex-Mex Chicken and Rice

Kelly Evenson
Pittsboro, NC

Makes 8 servings
(Ideal slow cooker size: 4-5-quart)

1 cup converted white rice,
  uncooked
28-oz. can diced peeled
  tomatoes
6-oz. can tomato paste
3 cups hot water
1 pkg. dry taco seasoning
  mix
4 whole boneless, skinless
  chicken breasts,
  uncooked and cut into
  ½" cubes
2 medium onions, chopped
1 green pepper, chopped
4-oz. can diced green chilies
1 tsp. garlic powder
½ tsp. pepper

1. Combine all ingredients
except chilies, garlic powder,
and pepper in large slow
cooker.

2. Cover. Cook on Low
4-4½ hours, or until rice is
tender and chicken is cooked.
3. Stir in green chilies and
reserved seasonings and
serve.
4. Serve with mixed green
leafy salad and refried beans.

Exchange List Values:
Starch 1.5, Vegetable 3.0,
Meat, very lean 3.0

Basic Nutritional Values: Calories
300 (Calories from Fat 32), Total Fat
4 gm (Saturated Fat 0.8 gm,
Polyunsat Fat 0.9 gm, Monounsat Fat
1.1 gm, Cholesterol 73 mg), Sodium
656 mg, Total Carbohydrate 34 gm,
Dietary Fiber 4 gm, Sugars 7 gm,
Protein 32 gm

Wanda's Chicken and Rice Casserole

Wanda Roth, Napoleon, OH

Makes 6-8 servings
(Ideal slow cooker size: 4-5-quart)

1 cup long-grain rice,
  uncooked
3 cups water
2 tsp. chicken bouillon
  granules
10¾-oz can 98%-fat-free,
  reduced-sodium cream
  of chicken soup
16-oz. bag frozen broccoli
2 cups chopped, cooked
  chicken
½ tsp. garlic powder
¼ tsp. onion salt
1 cup grated fat-free
  cheddar cheese

1. Combine all ingredients in slow cooker.

2. Cook on High 3-4 hours.

Exchange List Values:
Starch 1.5, Vegetable 1.0, Meat, lean 1.0

Basic Nutritional Values: Calories 214 (Calories from Fat 33), Total Fat 4 gm (Saturated Fat 1.0 gm, Polyunsat Fat 1.0 gm, Monounsat Fat 1.1 gm, Cholesterol 36 mg), Sodium 559 mg, Total Carbohydrate 26 gm, Dietary Fiber 2 gm, Sugars 3 gm, Protein 19 gm

Note: If casserole is too runny, remove lid from slow cooker for 15 minutes while continuing to cook on High.

Sharon's Chicken and Rice Casserole

Sharon Anders
Alburtis, PA

Makes 4 servings
(Ideal slow cooker size: 3-4-quart)

10³/4-oz. can cream of
  celery soup
2-oz. can sliced
  mushrooms, drained
¹/2 cup raw long-grain rice
4 chicken breast halves,
  skinned and boned
1 Tbsp. sodium-free dried
  onion soup mix (see
  recipe on page 254)

1. Combine soup, mush-rooms, and rice in greased slow cooker. Mix well.

2. Layer chicken breasts on top of mixture. Sprinkle with onion soup mix.

3. Cover. Cook on Low 4-6 hours.

Exchange List Values:
Starch 2.0, Meat, very lean 4.0, Fat 1.0

Basic Nutritional Values: Calories 330 (Calories from Fat 71), Total Fat 8 gm (Saturated Fat 2.4 gm, Polyunsat Fat 2.5 gm, Monounsat Fat 2.0 gm, Cholesterol 86 mg), Sodium 677 mg, Total Carbohydrate 26 gm, Dietary Fiber 2 gm, Sugars 2 gm, Protein 35 gm

Scalloped Potatoes and Chicken

Carol Sommers
Millersburg, OH

Makes 6-8 servings
(Ideal slow cooker size: 4-quart)

¹/4 cup chopped green
  peppers
¹/2 cup chopped onions
1¹/2 cups diced Velveeta
  Light cheese
7 medium potatoes,
  unpeeled, sliced
3 (about 10 ozs. each)
  whole boneless, skinless
  chicken breasts
salt to taste
10³/4-oz. can cream of
  celery soup
1 soup-can fat-free milk

1. Place layers of green peppers, onions, cheese, and potatoes in slow cooker.

2. Sprinkle salt over chicken breasts and lay on top of potatoes.

3. Combine soup and milk and pour into slow cooker, pushing meat down into liquid.

4. Cover. Cook on High 1¹/2 hours. Reduce temperature to Low and cook 3-4 hours. Test that potatoes are soft. If not, continue cooking on Low another hour and test again, continuing to cook until potatoes are finished.

Exchange List Values:
Starch 1.5, Carbohydrate 0.5, Meat, very lean 4.0, Fat 1.0

Basic Nutritional Values: Calories 336 (Calories from Fat 63), Total Fat 7 gm (Saturated Fat 3.0 gm, Polyunsat Fat 1.6 gm, Monounsat Fat 2.0 gm, Cholesterol 73 mg), Sodium 677 mg, Total Carbohydrate 34 gm, Dietary Fiber 3 gm, Sugars 8 gm, Protein 34 gm

Buy a pedometer and seek out ways to take more steps today—shoot for 10,000 a day.

Scalloped Chicken

Carolyn W. Carmichael
Berkeley Heights, NJ

Makes 4 servings
(Ideal slow cooker size: 4-quart)

5-oz. pkg. scalloped
  potatoes
scalloped potatoes dry
  seasoning pack
2 chicken breast halves
2 chicken legs
10-oz. pkg. frozen peas
2 cups water

1. Put potatoes, seasoning pack, chicken, and peas in slow cooker. Pour water over all.
2. Cover. Cook on Low 8-10 hours, or on High 4 hours.

Exchange List Values:
Starch 2.0, Meat, lean 3.0

Basic Nutritional Values: Calories 336 (Calories from Fat 64), Total Fat 7 gm (Saturated Fat 2.0 gm, Polyunsat Fat 2.1 gm, Monounsat Fat 2.1 gm, Cholesterol 87 mg), Sodium 861 mg, Total Carbohydrate 34 gm, Dietary Fiber 5 gm, Sugars 5 gm, Protein 35 gm

> Even if you have limited mobility, you should still try to work some activity into your daily schedule. Many senior centers often offer armchair aerobics or yoga, for instance.

Chicken and Vegetables

Jeanne Heyerly, Chenoa, IL

Makes 2 servings
(Ideal slow cooker size: 4-quart)

2 medium potatoes,
  quartered
2-3 carrots, sliced
5 ozs. frozen chicken
  breasts
1 frozen drumstick and
  thigh, split
salt to taste
pepper to taste
1 medium onion, chopped
2 garlic cloves, minced
1 cup shredded cabbage
2 tsp. salt-free bouillon
  powder
2 cups water

1. Place potatoes and carrots in slow cooker. Layer chicken on top. Sprinkle with salt, pepper, onion, and garlic. Top with cabbage. Carefully pour chicken bouillon combined with water around edges.
2. Cover. Cook on Low 8-9 hours.

Exchange List Values:
Starch 2.0, Vegetable 3.0, Meat, lean 2.0

Basic Nutritional Values: Calories 335 (Calories from Fat 30), Total Fat 3 gm (Saturated Fat 0.8 gm, Polyunsat Fat 1.0 gm, Monounsat Fat 1.0 gm, Cholesterol 62 mg), Sodium 129 mg, Total Carbohydrate 48 gm, Dietary Fiber 8 gm, Sugars 14 gm, Protein 28 gm

California Chicken

Shirley Sears
Tiskilwa, IL

Makes 4-6 servings
(Ideal slow cooker size: 4-quart)

3 lb. chicken, quartered,
  skin removed, trimmed
  of visible fat
1 cup orange juice
1/3 cup chili sauce
2 Tbsp. light soy sauce
1 Tbsp. molasses
1 tsp. dry mustard
1/4 tsp. garlic powder
1/4 tsp. onion powder
2 Tbsp. chopped green
  peppers
3 medium oranges, peeled
  and separated into
  slices, or 13 1/2-oz. can
  mandarin oranges

1. Arrange chicken in slow cooker.
2. In separate bowl, combine juice, chili sauce, soy sauce, molasses, dry mustard, garlic, and onion powder. Pour over chicken.
3. Cover. Cook on Low 8-9 hours.
4. Stir in green peppers and oranges. Heat 30 minutes longer.

Exchange List Values:
Fruit 1.0, Vegetable 1.0,
Meat, lean 3.0

Basic Nutritional Values: Calories
224 (Calories from Fat 50), Total Fat
6 gm (Saturated Fat 1.5 gm,
Polyunsat Fat 1.3 gm, Monounsat Fat
1.9 gm, Cholesterol 65 mg), Sodium
426 mg, Total Carbohydrate 20 gm,
Dietary Fiber 2 gm, Sugars 15 gm,
Protein 24 gm

*Variation: Stir 1 tsp. curry
powder in with sauces and
seasonings. Stir 1 small can
pineapple chunks and juice in
with green peppers and
oranges.*

Dad's Spicy
Chicken Curry

Tom & Sue Ruth
Lancaster, PA

*Makes 8 servings
(Ideal slow cooker size: 4-5-quart)*

**4 lbs. chicken pieces, with
bones, trimmed of skin
and fat**
water
2 medium onions, diced
**10-oz. pkg. frozen chopped
spinach, thawed and
squeezed dry**
1 cup plain low-fat yogurt
2-3 diced red potatoes
1 tsp. salt
1 tsp. garlic powder
1 tsp. ground ginger
1 tsp. ground cumin
1 tsp. ground coriander
1 tsp. pepper
1 tsp. ground cloves
1 tsp. ground cardamom
1 tsp. ground cinnamon
1/2 tsp. chili powder
1 tsp. red pepper flakes
3 tsp. turmeric

1. Place chicken in large
slow cooker. Cover with water.
2. Cover. Cook on High 2
hours, or until tender.
3. Drain chicken. Remove
from slow cooker. Cool briefly
and cut/shred into small
pieces. Return to slow cooker.
4. Add remaining ingred-
ients.
5. Cover. Cook on Low 4-6
hours, or until potatoes are
tender.
6. Serve on rice. Accom-
pany with fresh mango slices
or mango chutney.

Exchange List Values:
Carbohydrate 1.0, Meat,
lean 3.0

Basic Nutritional Values: Calories
221 (Calories from Fat 56), Total Fat
6 gm (Saturated Fat 1.8 gm,
Polyunsat Fat 1.4 gm, Monounsat Fat
2.1 gm, Cholesterol 67 mg), Sodium
402 mg, Total Carbohydrate 16 gm,
Dietary Fiber 3 gm, Sugars 4 gm,
Protein 25 gm

*Variation: Substitute 5 tsp.
curry powder for the garlic,
ginger, cumin, coriander, and
pepper.*

Orange Chicken Leg Quarters

Kimberly Jensen
Bailey, CO

Makes 5 servings
(Ideal slow cooker size: 4-quart)

4 chicken drumsticks, all visible fat removed
4 chicken thighs, all visible fat removed
1 cup strips of green and red bell peppers
1/2 cup canned chicken broth
1/2 cup prepared orange juice
1/2 cup no-salt-added ketchup
2 Tbsp. light soy sauce
1 Tbsp. light molasses
1 Tbsp. prepared mustard
1/4 tsp. garlic powder
11-oz. can mandarin oranges
2 tsp. cornstarch
1 cup frozen peas
2 green onions, sliced

1. Place chicken in slow cooker. Top with pepper strips.
2. Combine broth, juice, ketchup, soy sauce, molasses, mustard, and garlic powder. Pour over chicken.
3. Cover. Cook on Low 6-7 hours.
4. Remove chicken and vegetables from slow cooker. Keep warm.
5. Measure out 1 cup of cooking sauce. Put in saucepan and bring to boil.

Discard remaining cooking sauce.
6. Drain oranges, reserving 1 Tbsp. juice. Stir cornstarch into reserved juice. Add to boiling sauce in pan.
7. Add peas to sauce and cook, stirring for 2-3 minutes until sauce thickens and peas are warm. Stir in oranges.
8. Arrange chicken pieces on platter of cooked white rice, fried cellophane noodles, or lo mein noodles. Pour orange sauce over chicken and rice or noodles. Top with sliced green onions.

Exchange List Values:
Carbohydrate 1.5, Meat, lean 3.0

Basic Nutritional Values: Calories 285 (Calories from Fat 77), Total Fat 9 gm (Saturated Fat 2.3 gm, Polyunsat Fat 2.0 gm, Monounsat Fat 3.1 gm, Cholesterol 90 mg), Sodium 382 mg, Total Carbohydrate 21 gm, Dietary Fiber 3 gm, Sugars 14 gm, Protein 30 gm

Creamy Nutmeg Chicken

Amber Swarey,
Donalds, SC

Makes 6 servings
(Ideal slow cooker size: 4-quart)

6 boneless chicken breast halves, skin and visible fat removed
1 Tbsp. canola oil
1/4 cup chopped onions
1/4 cup minced parsley
2 10³/4-oz. cans 98%-fat-free, reduced-sodium cream of mushroom soup
1/2 cup fat-free sour cream
1/2 cup fat-free milk
1 Tbsp. ground nutmeg
1/4 tsp. sage
1/4 tsp. dried thyme
1/4 tsp. crushed rosemary

1. Brown chicken in skillet in oil. Reserve drippings and place chicken in slow cooker.
2. Saute onions and parsley in drippings until onions are tender.
3. Stir in remaining ingredients. Mix well. Pour over chicken.
4. Cover. Cook on Low 3 hours, or until juices run clear.
5. Serve over mashed or fried potatoes or rice.

Exchange List Values:
Carbohydrate 1.0, Meat, very lean 4.0, Fat 1.0

Basic Nutritional Values: Calories 264 (Calories from Fat 69), Total Fat 8 gm (Saturated Fat 1.9 gm, Polyunsat Fat 2.1 gm, Monounsat Fat 2.8 gm, Cholesterol 83 mg), Sodium 495 mg, Total Carbohydrate 15 gm, Dietary Fiber 1 gm, Sugars 5 gm, Protein 31 gm

Orange Chicken and Sweet Potatoes

Kimberlee Greenawalt
Harrisonburg, VA

Makes 6 servings
(Ideal slow cooker size: 4-quart)

2 (5¹/₂ ozs. each) sweet potatoes, peeled and sliced
3 whole boneless, skinless chicken breasts, halved, all visible fat removed
²/₃ cup flour
1 tsp. nutmeg
¹/₂ tsp. cinnamon
10³/₄-oz. can condensed, 98%-fat-free, reduced-sodium cream of chicken, soup
~~4-oz. can sliced mushrooms, drained.~~
¹/₂ cup orange juice
¹/₂ tsp. grated orange rind
2 tsp. brown sugar
3 Tbsp. flour

1. Place sweet potatoes in bottom of slow cooker.
2. Rinse chicken breasts and pat dry. Combine flour, nutmeg, and cinnamon. Thoroughly coat chicken in seasoned flour mixture. Place on top of sweet potatoes.
3. Combine soup with remaining ingredients. Stir well. Pour over chicken breasts.
4. Cover. Cook on Low 8-10 hours, or High 3-4 hours.
5. Serve over rice.

Exchange List Values:
Starch 2.0, Carbohydrate 0.5, Meat, very lean 4.0

Basic Nutritional Values: Calories 337 (Calories from Fat 44), Total Fat 5 gm (Saturated Fat 1.4 gm, Polyunsat Fat 1.3 gm, Monounsat Fat 1.4 gm, Cholesterol 88 mg), Sodium 335 mg, Total Carbohydrate 34 gm, Dietary Fiber 3 gm, Sugars 8 gm, Protein 36 gm

---

Quitting smoking is not easy—it often takes several tries. This time may just be the one that works!

Chicken with Applesauce

Kelly Evenson, Pittsboro, NC

Makes 4 servings
(Ideal slow cooker size: 4-quart)

4 boneless, skinless chicken breast halves
salt to taste
pepper to taste
2 Tbsp. oil
2 cups applesauce, unsweetened
¹/₄ cup barbecue sauce
¹/₂ tsp. poultry seasoning
2 tsp. honey
¹/₂ tsp. lemon juice

1. Season chicken with salt and pepper. Brown in oil for 5 minutes per side.
2. Cut up chicken into 1″ chunks and transfer to slow cooker.
3. Combine remaining ingredients. Pour over chicken and mix together well.
4. Cover. Cook on High 2-3 hours, or until chicken is tender.
5. Serve over rice or noodles.

Exchange List Values:
Fruit 1.0, Meat, very lean 4.0, Fat 2.0

Basic Nutritional Values: Calories 301 (Calories from Fat 94), Total Fat 10 gm (Saturated Fat 1.5 gm, Polyunsat Fat 2.9 gm, Monounsat Fat 5.3 gm, Cholesterol 84 mg), Sodium 199 mg, Total Carbohydrate 19 gm, Dietary Fiber 2 gm, Sugars 16 gm, Protein 32 gm

Maui Chicken

John D. Allen
Rye, CO

Makes 6 servings
(Ideal slow cooker size: 4-quart)

6 boneless chicken breast
  halves, trimmed of skin
  and fat
2 Tbsp. oil
14¹⁄₂-oz. can chicken broth
20-oz. can pineapple
  chunks
¹⁄₄ cup vinegar
2 Tbsp. brown sugar
2 tsp. soy sauce
1 garlic clove, minced
1 medium green bell
  pepper, chopped
3 Tbsp. cornstarch
¹⁄₄ cup water

1. Brown chicken in oil.
Transfer chicken to slow
cooker.
2. Combine remaining
ingredients. Pour over
chicken.
3. Cover. Cook on High 4-6
hours.
4. Serve over rice.

Exchange List Values:
Fruit 1.0, Carbohydrate
0.5, Meat, very lean 4.0,
Fat 1.5

Basic Nutritional Values: Calories
305 (Calories from Fat 75), Total Fat
8 gm (Saturated Fat 1.4 gm,
Polyunsat Fat 2.2 gm, Monounsat Fat
4.0 gm, Cholesterol 82 mg), Sodium
601 mg, Total Carbohydrate 25 gm,
Dietary Fiber 1 gm, Sugars 19 gm,
Protein 32 gm

Sweet and Sour Chicken

Bernice A. Esau
North Newton, KS

Makes 6 servings
(Ideal slow cooker size: 4-quart)

1¹⁄₂ cups sliced carrots
1 large green pepper,
  chopped
1 medium onion, chopped
2 Tbsp. quick-cooking
  tapioca
2¹⁄₂ lbs. chicken, cut into
  serving-size pieces, skin
  removed, trimmed of fat
8-oz. can pineapple chunks
  in juice
3 Tbsp. brown sugar
brown sugar substitute to
  equal 1¹⁄₂ Tbsp.
¹⁄₃ cup vinegar
1 Tbsp. soy sauce
¹⁄₂ tsp. instant chicken
  bouillon
¹⁄₄ tsp. garlic powder
¹⁄₄ tsp. ground ginger,
  or ¹⁄₂ tsp. freshly grated
  ginger
¹⁄₈ tsp. salt

1. Place vegetables in bottom of slow cooker. Sprinkle
with tapioca. Add chicken.
2. In separate bowl, com-
bine pineapple, brown sugar,
brown sugar substitute,
vinegar, soy sauce, bouillon,
garlic powder, ginger, and
salt. Pour over chicken.
3. Cover. Cook on Low 8-
10 hours.
4. Serve over cooked rice.

Exchange List Values:
Fruit 0.5, Carbohydrate
0.5, Vegetable 1.0, Meat,
lean 2.0

Basic Nutritional Values: Calories 208
(Calories from Fat 41), Total Fat 5 gm
(Saturated Fat 1.2 gm, Polyunsat Fat 1.1
gm, Monounsat Fat 1.6 gm, Cholesterol
54 mg), Sodium 365 mg, Total
Carbohydrate 23 gm, Dietary Fiber 2
gm, Sugars 16 gm, Protein 19 gm

Ann's Chicken Cacciatore

Ann Driscoll, Albuquerque, NM

Makes 6-8 servings
(Ideal slow cooker size: 4-quart)

1 large onion, thinly sliced
3 lbs. chicken, cut up, skin
  removed, trimmed of fat
2 6-oz. cans tomato paste
4-oz. can sliced
  mushrooms, drained
1 tsp. salt
1/4 cup dry white wine
1/4 tsp. pepper
1-2 garlic cloves, minced
1-2 tsp. dried oregano
1/2 tsp. dried basil
1/2 tsp. celery seed,
  optional
1 bay leaf

1. Place onion in slow cooker. Add chicken.
2. Combine remaining ingredients. Pour over chicken.
3. Cover. Cook on Low 7-9 hours, or High 3-4 hours.
4. Serve over spaghetti.

Exchange List Values:
Vegetable 3.0, Meat, lean 2.0

Basic Nutritional Values: Calories 161 (Calories from Fat 40), Total Fat 4 gm (Saturated Fat 1.1 gm, Polyunsat Fat 1.1 gm, Monounsat Fat 1.5 gm, Cholesterol 49 mg), Sodium 405 mg, Total Carbohydrate 12 gm, Dietary Fiber 3 gm, Sugars 3 gm, Protein 19 gm

Coq au Vin

Kimberlee Greenawalt
Harrisonburg, VA

Makes 6 servings
(Ideal slow cooker size: 4-quart)

2 cups frozen pearl onions,
  thawed
4 thick slices bacon, fried,
  drained, patted dry, and
  crumbled
1 cup sliced button
  mushrooms
1 garlic clove, minced
1 tsp. dried thyme leaves
1/8 tsp. black pepper
6 (5 ozs. each) boneless,
  skinless chicken breast
  halves, trimmed of fat
1/2 cup dry red wine
3/4 cup chicken broth
1/4 cup tomato paste
3 Tbsp. flour

1. Layer ingredients in slow cooker in the following order: onions, bacon, mushrooms, garlic, thyme, pepper, chicken, wine, broth.
2. Cover. Cook on Low 6-8 hours.
3. Remove chicken and vegetables. Cover and keep warm.
4. Ladle 1/2 cup cooking liquid into small bowl. Cool slightly. Turn slow cooker to High. Cover. Mix reserved liquid, tomato paste, and flour until smooth. Return mixture to slow cooker, cover, and cook 15 minutes, or until thickened.
5. Serve chicken, vegetables, and sauce over noodles.

Exchange List Values:
Vegetable 2.0, Meat, very lean 4.0, Fat 1.5

Basic Nutritional Values: Calories 258 (Calories from Fat 66), Total Fat 7 gm (Saturated Fat 2.2 gm, Polyunsat Fat 1.2 gm, Monounsat Fat 2.9 gm, Cholesterol 91 mg), Sodium 388 mg, Total Carbohydrate 10 gm, Dietary Fiber 2 gm, Sugars 4 gm, Protein 36 gm

---

If you think you are having a heart attack (or someone you care about is), don't wait until you're "sure." Call 911 right away.

Lemon Garlic Chicken

Cindy Krestynick
Glen Lyon, PA

Makes 6 servings
(Ideal slow cooker size: 4-quart)

1 tsp. dried oregano
1/2 tsp. seasoned salt
1/4 tsp. pepper
6 (5 ozs. each) chicken
   breast halves, skinned
   and rinsed
2 Tbsp. canola oil
1/4 cup water
3 Tbsp. lemon juice
2 garlic cloves, minced
1 tsp. chicken bouillon
   granules
1 tsp. minced fresh parsley

1. Combine oregano, salt, and pepper. Rub all of mixture into chicken. Brown chicken in canola oil in skillet. Transfer to slow cooker.
2. Place water, lemon juice, garlic, and bouillon cubes in skillet. Bring to boil, loosening browned bits from skillet. Pour over chicken.
3. Cover. Cook on High 2-2 1/2 hours, or Low 4-5 hours.
4. Add parsley and baste chicken. Cover. Cook on High 15-30 minutes, until chicken is tender.

Exchange List Values:
Meat, very lean 4.0, Fat 1.5

Basic Nutritional Values: Calories 210 (Calories from Fat 71), Total Fat 8 gm (Saturated Fat 1.2 gm, Polyunsat Fat 2.1 gm, Monounsat Fat 3.8 gm, Cholesterol 84 mg), Sodium 283 mg, Total Carbohydrate 1 gm, Dietary Fiber 0 gm, Sugars 1 gm, Protein 32 gm

Melanie's Chicken Cordon Bleu

Melanie Thrower
McPherson, KS

Makes 6 servings
(Ideal slow cooker size: 4-quart)

3 (1 1/2 lbs.) whole boneless,
   skinless chicken breasts
6 (1/2-oz. per slice) pieces
   thinly sliced ham
6 (1/2-oz. per slice) thin
   slices reduced-fat Swiss
   cheese
salt to taste
pepper to taste
6 slices bacon, gently
   browned but not crispy,
   drained, and patted dry
1/4 cup water
1 tsp. salt-free chicken
   bouillon powder
1/2 cup white cooking wine
1 tsp. cornstarch
1/4 cup cold water

1. Flatten chicken to 1/8-1/4-inch thickness. Place a slice of ham and a slice of cheese on top of each flattened breast. Sprinkle with salt and pepper. Roll up and wrap with strip of bacon. Secure with toothpick. Place in slow cooker.
2. Combine 1/4 cup water, granules, and wine. Pour into slow cooker.
3. Cover. Cook on High 4 hours.
4. Combine cornstarch and 1/4 cup cold water. Add to slow cooker. Cook until sauce thickens.

Exchange List Values:
Meat, very lean 5.0, Fat 1.0

Basic Nutritional Values: Calories 231 (Calories from Fat 77), Total Fat 9 gm (Saturated Fat 3.1 gm, Polyunsat Fat 1.1 gm, Monounsat Fat 3.3 gm, Cholesterol 86 mg), Sodium 424 mg, Total Carbohydrate 1 gm, Dietary Fiber 0 gm, Sugars 0 gm, Protein 35 gm

Marcy's Barbecued Chicken

Marcy Engle, Harrisonburg, VA

Makes 6 servings
(Ideal slow cooker size: 4-quart)

2 lbs. chicken pieces, skin
   and all visible fat
   removed
1/4 cup flour
1 cup ketchup
2 cups water
1/3 cup Worcestershire
   sauce
1 tsp. chili powder
1/2 tsp. salt
1/2 tsp. pepper
2 drops Tabasco sauce
1/4 tsp. garlic salt
1/4 tsp. onion salt

1. Dust chicken with flour. Transfer to slow cooker.

2. Combine remaining ingredients. Pour over chicken.

3. Cover. Cook on Low 5 hours.

Exchange List Values:
Carbohydrate 1.5, Meat, lean 2.0

Basic Nutritional Values: Calories 219 (Calories from Fat 37), Total Fat 4 gm (Saturated Fat 1.1 gm, Polyunsat Fat 0.9 gm, Monounsat Fat 1.4 gm, Cholesterol 66 mg), Sodium 348 mg, Total Carbohydrate 20 gm, Dietary Fiber 1 gm, Sugars 14 gm, Protein 24 gm

Tracy's Barbecued Chicken Wings

Tracy Supcoe, Barclay, MD

Makes 8 full-sized servings
(Ideal slow cooker size: 4-quart)

4 lbs. chicken wings, skin removed
2 large onions, chopped
2 6-oz. cans tomato paste
2 large garlic cloves, minced
1/4 cup Worcestershire sauce
1/4 cup cider vinegar
1/4 cup brown sugar
brown sugar substitute to equal 2 Tbsp.
1/2 cup sweet pickle relish
1/2 cup red, or white, wine
1/4 tsp. salt
2 tsp. dry mustard

1. Cut off wing tips. Cut wings at joint. Place in slow cooker.

2. Combine remaining ingredients. Add to slow cooker. Stir.

3. Cover. Cook on Low 5-6 hours.

Exchange List Values:
Carbohydrate 0.5, Vegetable 3.0, Meat, lean 2.0

Basic Nutritional Values: Calories 226 (Calories from Fat 45), Total Fat 5 gm (Saturated Fat 1.2 gm, Polyunsat Fat 1.1 gm, Monounsat Fat 1.5 gm, Cholesterol 44 mg), Sodium 369 mg, Total Carbohydrate 27 gm, Dietary Fiber 3 gm, Sugars 19 gm, Protein 19 gm

Levi's Sesame Chicken Wings

Shirley Unternahrer Hinh
Wayland, IA

Makes 16 appetizer servings
(Ideal slow cooker size: 4-quart)

3 lbs. chicken wings
salt to taste
pepper to taste
1 cup honey
sugar substitute to equal 6 Tbsp.
3/4 cup light soy sauce
1/2 cup no-salt-added ketchup
2 Tbsp. canola oil
2 Tbsp. sesame oil
2 garlic cloves, minced
toasted sesame seeds

1. Rinse wings. Cut at joint. Sprinkle with salt and pepper. Place on broiler pan.

2. Broil 5 inches from broiler, 10 minutes on each side. Place chicken in slow cooker.

3. Combine remaining ingredients except sesame seeds. Pour over chicken.

4. Cover. Cook on Low 5 hours or High 2½ hours.

5. Sprinkle sesame seeds over top just before serving.

6. Serve as appetizer, or with white or brown rice and shredded lettuce to turn this appetizer into a meal.

Exchange List Values:
Carbohydrate 1.5, Meat, high fat 1.0

Basic Nutritional Values: Calories 192 (Calories from Fat 77), Total Fat 9 gm (Saturated Fat 1.8 gm, Polyunsat Fat 2.3 gm, Monounsat Fat 3.7 gm, Cholesterol 22 mg), Sodium 453 mg, Total Carbohydrate 21 gm, Dietary Fiber 0 gm, Sugars 21 gm, Protein 9 gm

My husband and his co-workers have a "pot-luck-lunch" at work. I think this is a nice way to break the monotony of the week or month. And it gives them a chance to share. What better way to keep it ready than in a slow cooker!

> **Eat 3 vegetables and 2 fruits today—fresh or frozen is best.**

Chicken and Seafood Gumbo

Dianna Milhizer
Brighton, MI

Makes 12 servings
(Ideal slow cooker size: 5-6-quart)

1 cup chopped celery
1 cup chopped onions
½ cup chopped green
  peppers
¼ cup olive oil
¼ cup, plus 1 Tbsp., flour
6 cups 100%-fat-free,
  30-50% lower-sodium
  chicken broth
2 lbs. chicken, cut up, skin
  and visible fat removed
3 bay leaves
1½ cups sliced okra
12-oz. can diced tomatoes
1 tsp. Tabasco sauce
salt to taste
pepper to taste
1 lb. ready-to-eat shrimp
½ cup snipped fresh
  parsley

1. Saute celery, onions, and
peppers in oil. Blend in flour
and chicken broth until
smooth. Cook 5 minutes.
Pour into slow cooker.
2. Add remaining
ingredients except seafood
and parsley.
3. Cover. Cook on Low
10-12 hours.
4. One hour before serving
add shrimp and parsley.
5. Remove bay leaves
before serving.
6. Serve with white rice.

Exchange List Values:
Vegetable 2.0, Meat, lean
2.0

Basic Nutritional Values: Calories
162 (Calories from Fat 61), Total Fat
7 gm (Saturated Fat 1.2 gm,
Polyunsat Fat 1.0 gm, Monounsat Fat
4.0 gm, Cholesterol 95 mg), Sodium
424 mg, Total Carbohydrate 7 gm,
Dietary Fiber 1 gm, Sugars 3 gm,
Protein 17 gm

Szechwan-Style Chicken and Broccoli

Jane Meiser, Harrisonburg, VA

Makes 4 servings
(Ideal slow cooker size: 4-quart)

2 whole boneless, skinless
  chicken or turkey breasts
1 Tbsp. canola oil
½ cup picante sauce
2 Tbsp. light soy sauce
½ tsp. sugar
½ Tbsp. quick-cooking
  tapioca
1 medium onion, chopped
2 garlic cloves, minced
½ tsp. ground ginger
2 cups broccoli florets
1 medium red pepper, cut
  into pieces

1. Cut meat into 1" cubes
and brown lightly in oil in
skillet. Place in slow cooker.
2. Stir in remaining
ingredients.
3. Cover. Cook on High
1-1½ hours or on Low 2-3
hours.

Exchange List Values:
Vegetable 2.0, Meat, very
lean 4.0, Fat 1.0

Basic Nutritional Values: Calories
254 (Calories from Fat 64), Total Fat
7 gm (Saturated Fat 1.2 gm,
Polyunsat Fat 1.9 gm, Monounsat Fat
3.2 gm, Cholesterol 84 mg), Sodium
619 mg, Total Carbohydrate 12 gm,
Dietary Fiber 3 gm, Sugars 7 gm,
Protein 35 gm

Chicken Casablanca

Joyce Kaut
Rochester, NY

Makes 6-8 servings
(Ideal slow cooker size: 4-5-quart)

2 Tbsp. canola oil
2 large onions, sliced
1 tsp. ground ginger
3 garlic cloves, minced
3 large carrots, diced
2 large potatoes, unpeeled, diced
3 lbs. skinless chicken pieces
1/2 tsp. ground cumin
1/2 tsp. salt
1/2 tsp. pepper
1/4 tsp. cinnamon
2 Tbsp. raisins
14 1/2-oz. can chopped tomatoes
3 small zucchini, sliced
15-oz. can garbanzo beans, drained
2 Tbsp. chopped parsley

You can cut back on the number of calories you get each day and still eat your favorite foods—just reduce how much of them you eat. Control your portion sizes to control your weight!

1. Saute onions, ginger, and garlic in oil in skillet. (Reserve oil.) Transfer to slow cooker. Add carrots and potatoes. Transfer to slow cooker, reserving oil.
2. Brown chicken over medium heat in reserved oil. Transfer to slow cooker. Mix gently with vegetables.
3. Combine seasonings in separate bowl. Sprinkle over chicken and vegetables. Add raisins and tomatoes.
4. Cover. Cook on High 4-6 hours.
5. Add sliced zucchini, beans, and parsley 30 minutes before serving.
6. Serve over cooked rice or couscous.

Exchange List Values:
Starch 2.0, Vegetable 2.0, Meat, lean 3.0, Fat 0.5

Basic Nutritional Values: Calories 395 (Calories from Fat 93), Total Fat 10 gm (Saturated Fat 1.9 gm, Polyunsat Fat 2.9 gm, Monounsat Fat 4.3 gm, Cholesterol 87 mg), Sodium 390 mg, Total Carbohydrate 40 gm, Dietary Fiber 8 gm, Sugars 12 gm, Protein 36 gm

Variation: Add 1/2 tsp. turmeric and 1/4 tsp. cayenne pepper to Step 3.
Michelle Mann
Mt. Joy, PA

Greek Chicken

Judy Govotsus
Monrovia, MD

Makes 4-6 servings
(Ideal slow cooker size: 4-quart)

4 potatoes, unpeeled, quartered
2 lbs. chicken pieces, trimmed of skin and fat
2 large onions, quartered
1 whole bulb garlic, minced
3 tsp. dried oregano
3/4 tsp. salt
1/2 tsp. pepper
1 Tbsp. olive oil

1. Place potatoes in bottom of slow cooker. Add chicken, onions, and garlic. Sprinkle with seasonings. Top with oil.
2. Cover. Cook on High 5-6 hours, or on Low 9-10 hours.

Exchange List Values:
Starch 1.5, Vegetable 2.0, Meat, lean 2.0

Basic Nutritional Values: Calories 278 (Calories from Fat 56), Total Fat 6 gm (Saturated Fat 1.3 gm, Polyunsat Fat 1.1 gm, Monounsat Fat 3.0 gm, Cholesterol 65 mg), Sodium 358 mg, Total Carbohydrate 29 gm, Dietary Fiber 4 gm, Sugars 9 gm, Protein 27 gm

Cathy's Chicken Creole

Cathy Boshart
Lebanon, PA

Makes 6 servings
(Ideal slow cooker size: 4-quart)

2 Tbsp. canola oil
half a medium green
  pepper, chopped
2 medium onions, chopped
1/2 cup chopped celery
1 lb. 4-oz.-can tomatoes
1/2 tsp. pepper, or your
  choice of dried herbs
1/8 tsp. red pepper
3/4 tsp. salt, or your choice of
  dried herbs
1 cup water
2 Tbsp. cornstarch
1 tsp. sugar
1 1/2 Tbsp. cold water
2 cups cooked and cubed
  chicken
6 green, or black, olives,
  sliced
1/2 cup sliced mushrooms

1. Place oil in slow cooker.
Add green pepper, onions,
and celery. Heat.
2. Add tomatoes, peppers,
salt, and 1 cup water.
3. Cover. Cook on High
while preparing remaining
ingredients.
4. Combine cornstarch and
sugar. Add 1 1/2 Tbsp. cold
water and make a smooth
paste. Stir into mixture in
slow cooker. Add chicken,
olives, and mushrooms.
5. Cover. Cook on Low
2-3 hours.

Mulligan Stew

Carol Ambrose, Ripon, CA

Makes 8 servings
(Ideal slow cooker size: 4-5-quart)

3 lbs. stewing chicken, cut
  up, trimmed of skin and
  fat
1/2 tsp. salt
1 oz. salt pork, or bacon,
  cut in 1-inch squares
4 cups tomatoes, peeled
  and sliced
2 cups fresh corn, or 1 lb.
  pkg. frozen corn
1 cup coarsely chopped
  potatoes
10-oz. pkg. lima beans,
  frozen
1/2 cup chopped onions
1 tsp. salt
1/4 tsp. pepper
dash of cayenne pepper

1. Place chicken in very
large slow cooker. Add water
to cover. Add 1/2 tsp. salt.
2. Cover. Cook on Low
2 hours. Add more water if
needed.

3. Add remaining ingredi-
ents. (If you don't have a
large cooker, divide the stew
between 2 average-sized
ones.) Simmer on Low 5
hours longer.

Notes:
*1. Flavor improves if stew is
refrigerated and reheated the
next day. May also be made in
advance and frozen.*
*2. You can debone the chicken
after the first cooking for 2
hours. Stir chicken pieces back
into cooker with other
ingredients and continue with
directions above.*

Marsha's Chicken Enchilada Casserole

Marsha Sabus, Falibrook, CA

Makes 4-6 servings
(Ideal slow cooker size: 4-5-quart)

1 onion, chopped
1 garlic clove, minced
1 Tbsp. oil
10-oz. can enchilada sauce
8-oz. can no-salt-added tomato sauce
salt to taste
pepper to taste
8 corn tortillas
3 boneless chicken breast halves, cooked and cubed
15-oz. can ranch-style beans, drained
11-oz. can Mexicorn, drained
4 ozs. reduced-fat cheddar cheese, grated
2¼-oz. can sliced black olives, drained

1. Saute onion and garlic in oil in saucepan. Stir in enchilada sauce and tomato sauce. Season with salt and pepper.
2. Place two tortillas in bottom of slow cooker. Layer one-third of chicken on top. Top with one-third sauce mixture, one-third beans, one-third corn, one-third cheese, and one-third black olives. Repeat layers 2 more times. Top with 2 tortillas.
3. Cover. Cook on Low 6-8 hours.

Exchange List Values:
Starch 2.5, Vegetable 1.0, Meat, lean 2.0, Fat 1.0

Basic Nutritional Values: Calories 370 (Calories from Fat 110), Total Fat 12 gm (Saturated Fat 3.3 gm, Polyunsat Fat 2.2 gm, Monounsat Fat 4.6 gm, Cholesterol 55 mg), Sodium 619 mg, Total Carbohydrate 43 gm, Dietary Fiber 8 gm, Sugars 7 gm, Protein 28 gm

Variation: Substitute 1 lb. cooked and drained hamburger for the chicken.

Gran's Big Potluck

Carol Ambrose
Ripon, CA

Makes 10 servings
(Ideal slow cooker size: 5-6-quart)

2½ lb. stewing hen, cut into pieces, trimmed of skin and fat
½ lb. stewing beef, cubed, trimmed of skin and fat
½ lb. veal shoulder, or roast, trimmed of skin and fat, cubed
1½ qts. water
½ lb. small red potatoes, cubed
½ lb. small onions, cut in half
1 cup sliced carrots
1 cup chopped celery
1 medium green pepper, chopped
1 lb. pkg. frozen lima beans
1 cup okra, whole or diced, fresh or frozen
1 cup frozen whole-kernel corn
8-oz. can whole tomatoes with juice
15-oz. can tomato puree
1 tsp. salt
¼-½ tsp. pepper
1 tsp. dry mustard
½ tsp. chili powder
¼ cup chopped fresh parsley

1. Combine all ingredients except last 5 seasonings in one very large slow cooker, or divide between two medium-sized ones.
2. Cover. Cook on Low 10-12 hours. Add seasonings during last hour of cooking.

Exchange List Values:
Starch 1.0, Vegetable 2.0, Meat, lean 2.0

Basic Nutritional Values: Calories 242 (Calories from Fat 42), Total Fat 5 gm (Saturated Fat 1.2 gm, Polyunsat Fat 0.9 gm, Monounsat Fat 1.6 gm, Cholesterol 63 mg), Sodium 535 mg, Total Carbohydrate 26 gm, Dietary Fiber 6 gm, Sugars 7 gm, Protein 25 gm

Note: You may want to debone the chicken and mix it back into the cooker before serving the meal.

> Cut the fat in at least one meal today.

89

Joyce's Chicken Tetrazzini

Joyce Slaymaker, Strasburg, PA

Makes 4 servings
(Ideal slow cooker size: 3-4-quart)

2 cups diced cooked
 chicken
2 tsp. salt-free chicken
 bouillon powder
2 cups water
1 small onion, chopped
1/4 cup sauterne, white
 wine, or milk
1/2 cup slivered almonds
2 4-oz. cans sliced
 mushrooms, drained
103/4-oz. can 98%-fat-free,
 reduced-sodium cream
 of mushroom soup
6 ozs. raw spaghetti,
 cooked

1. Combine all ingredients
except spaghetti in slow
cooker.
2. Cover. Cook on Low 6-8
hours.
3. Serve over spaghetti.
Sprinkle with Parmesan
cheese if you wish.

Exchange List Values:
Starch 2.0, Carbohydrate
1.0, Vegetable 1.0, Meat,
lean 3.0, Fat 1.0

Basic Nutritional Values: Calories
469 (Calories from Fat 139), Total Fat
15 gm (Saturated Fat 2.8 gm,
Polyunsat Fat 3.7 gm, Monounsat Fat
7.1 gm, Cholesterol 63 mg), Sodium
528 mg, Total Carbohydrate 48 gm,
Dietary Fiber 6 gm, Sugars 6 gm,
Protein 33 gm

Variations:
1. Place spaghetti in large
baking dish. Pour sauce in
center. Sprinkle with Parmesan
cheese. Broil until lightly
browned.
2. Add 10-oz. pkg. frozen peas
to Step 1.

Darlene Raber
Wellman, IA

Chicken and Stuffing

Janice Yoskovich
Carmichaels, PA
Jo Ellen Moore
Pendleton, IN

Makes 14-16 side dish servings
(Ideal slow cooker size: 6-quart)

21/2 tsp. salt-free chicken
 bouillon powder
21/2 cups water
1/4 cup canola oil
1/2 cup chopped onions
1/2 cup chopped celery
4-oz. can mushrooms,
 stems and pieces,
 drained
1/4 cup dried parsley flakes
11/2 tsp. rubbed sage
1 tsp. poultry seasoning
1/2 tsp. salt
1/2 tsp. pepper
12 cups day-old bread
 cubes (1/2-inch pieces)
2 eggs
103/4-oz. can 98%-fat-free,
 reduced-sodium cream
 of chicken soup
5 cups cubed cooked
 chicken

1. Combine all ingredients
except bread, eggs, soup, and
chicken in large saucepan.
Simmer for 10 minutes.
2. Place bread cubes in
large bowl.
3. Combine eggs and soup.
Stir into broth mixture until
smooth. Pour over bread and
toss well.
4. Layer half of stuffing
and then half of chicken into
very large slow cooker (or
two medium-sized cookers).
Repeat layers.
5. Cover. Cook on Low
41/2-5 hours.

Exchange List Values:
Starch 1.0, Meat, lean 2.0,
Fat 0.5

Basic Nutritional Values: Calories
215 (Calories from Fat 78), Total Fat
9 gm (Saturated Fat 1.6 gm,
Polyunsat Fat 2.5 gm, Monounsat Fat
3.7 gm, Cholesterol 67 mg), Sodium
362 mg, Total Carbohydrate 16 gm,
Dietary Fiber 1 gm, Sugars 2 gm,
Protein 16 gm

Chicken and Dumplings

Elva Ever, North English, IA

Makes 8-10 servings
(Ideal slow cooker size: 4-quart)

4 whole chicken breasts,
 or 1 small chicken
3/4 cup sliced carrots
1/4 cup chopped onions
1/4 cup chopped celery
11/2 cups peas

4-6 Tbsp. flour
1 cup water
salt to taste
pepper to taste
1 cup buttermilk baking
    mix to make dumplings
paprika to taste

1. Cook chicken in water in soup pot. Cool, skin, and debone chicken. Return broth to boiling in soup pot.
2. Cook vegetables in microwave on High for 5 minutes.
3. Meanwhile, combine flour and water until smooth. Add to boiling chicken broth. Add enough extra water to make 4 cups broth, making sure gravy is fairly thick. Season with salt and pepper.
4. Combine chicken, vegetables, and gravy in slow cooker.
5. Mix dumplings as directed on baking mix box. Place dumplings on top of chicken in slow cooker. Sprinkle with paprika.
6. Cover. Cook on High 3 hours.

Exchange List Values:
Starch 1.0, Meat, very lean 4.0

Basic Nutritional Values: Calories 222 (Calories from Fat 43), Total Fat 5 gm (Saturated Fat 0.8 gm, Polyunsat Fat 1.4 gm, Monounsat Fat 1.6 gm, Cholesterol 67 mg), Sodium 248 mg, Total Carbohydrate 15 gm, Dietary Fiber 2 gm, Sugars 3 gm, Protein 28 gm

Barbecue Chicken for Buns
Linda Sluiter, Schererville, IN

Makes 16-20 servings
(Ideal slow cooker size: 4-quart)

6 cups diced cooked
    chicken
2 cups chopped celery
1 cup chopped onions
1 cup chopped green
    peppers
2 Tbsp. canola oil
2 cups ketchup
2 cups water
2 Tbsp. brown sugar
4 Tbsp. vinegar
2 tsp. dry mustard
1 tsp. pepper
1/2 tsp. salt

1. Combine all ingredients in slow cooker.
2. Cover. Cook on Low 8 hours.
3. Stir chicken until it shreds.
4. Pile into steak rolls and serve.

Exchange List Values:
Carbohydrate 0.5, Meat, lean 2.0

Basic Nutritional Values: Calories 131 (Calories from Fat 43), Total Fat 5 gm (Saturated Fat 1.0 gm, Polyunsat Fat 1.1 gm, Monounsat Fat 1.9 gm, Cholesterol 37 mg), Sodium 391 mg, Total Carbohydrate 10 gm, Dietary Fiber 1 gm, Sugars 5 gm, Protein 13 gm

Chicken Reuben Bake
Gail Bush, Landenberg, PA

Makes 6 servings
(Ideal slow cooker size: 4-quart)

4 boneless, skinless
    chicken breast halves
1 lb. bag sauerkraut,
    drained and rinsed
4-5 (1-oz. each) slices Swiss
    cheese
3/4 cup fat-free Thousand
    Island salad dressing
2 Tbsp. chopped fresh
    parsley

1. Place chicken in slow cooker. Layer sauerkraut over chicken. Add cheese. Top with salad dressing. Sprinkle with parsley.
2. Cover. Cook on Low 6-8 hours.

Exchange List Values:
Carbohydrate 1.0, Meat, very lean 4.0

Basic Nutritional Values: Calories 217 (Calories from Fat 41), Total Fat 5 gm (Saturated Fat 2.0 gm, Polyunsat Fat 0.6 gm, Monounsat Fat 1.4 gm, Cholesterol 63 mg), Sodium 693 mg, Total Carbohydrate 13 gm, Dietary Fiber 2 gm, Sugars 6 gm, Protein 28 gm

Order a vegetarian meal the next time you fly—they're tasty and usually low in cholesterol and saturated fat.

Turkey in a Pot
Dorothy M. Pittman
Pickens, SC

Makes 10-12 servings
(Ideal slow cooker size: 6-quart)

4-5 lb. turkey breast, skin
removed (if frozen, it
doesn't have to be
thawed)
1 medium onion, chopped
1 rib celery, chopped
¼ cup melted margarine
1½ cups chicken broth

1. Wash turkey breast. Pat
dry. Place in greased slow
cooker. Put onion and celery
in cavity.
2. Pour margarine over
turkey. Pour broth around
turkey.
3. Cover. Cook on High 6
hours. Let stand 10 minutes
before carving.

Exchange List Values:
Meat, very lean 4.0, Fat 0.5

Basic Nutritional Values: Calories
160 (Calories from Fat 45), Total Fat
5 gm (Saturated Fat 0.8 gm,
Polyunsat Fat 1.3 gm, Monounsat Fat
1.8 gm, Cholesterol 70 mg), Sodium
287 mg, Total Carbohydrate 1 gm,
Dietary Fiber 0 gm, Sugars 1 gm,
Protein 26 gm

*Optional: You may wish to
season the turkey with salt and
lemon-pepper seasoning to
taste.*

Turkey Breast
Barbara Katrine Rose
Woodbridge, VA

Makes 6-8 servings
(Ideal slow cooker size: 6-quart)

1 large (4½ lbs.) boneless
turkey breast, skin
removed
¼ cup apple cider, or juice
1 tsp. salt
¼ tsp. pepper

1. Put turkey breast in
slow cooker. Drizzle apple
cider over turkey. Sprinkle on
both sides with salt and pepper.
2. Cover. Cook on High 3-4
hours.
3. Remove turkey breast.
Let stand for 15 minutes
before slicing.

Exchange List Values:
Meat, very lean 4.0

Basic Nutritional Values: Calories
150 (Calories from Fat 10), Total Fat
1 gm (Saturated Fat 0.0 gm,
Polyunsat Fat 0.0 gm, Monounsat Fat
0.0 gm, Cholesterol 89 mg), Sodium
252 mg, Total Carbohydrate 1 gm,
Dietary Fiber 0 gm, Sugars 1 gm,
Protein 33 gm

**What's your best
weapon in the fight
against diabetes?
Exercise!**

Easy and Delicious Turkey Breast
Gail Bush
Landenberg, PA

Makes 12 servings
(Ideal slow cooker size: 6-quart)

5 lb. turkey breast, bone
in, skin removed
15-oz. can whole berry
cranberry sauce
1 envelope dry onion soup
mix
½ cup orange juice
½ tsp. salt
¼ tsp. pepper

1. Place turkey in slow
cooker.
2. Combine remaining
ingredients. Pour over turkey.
3. Cover. Cook on Low 6-8
hours.

Exchange List Values:
Carbohydrate 1.0, Meat,
very lean 4.0

Basic Nutritional Values: Calories
210 (Calories from Fat 12), Total Fat
1 gm (Saturated Fat 0.0 gm,
Polyunsat Fat 0.1 gm, Monounsat Fat
0.1 gm, Cholesterol 87 mg), Sodium
391 mg, Total Carbohydrate 16 gm,
Dietary Fiber 1 gm, Sugars 15 gm,
Protein 33 gm

Slow Cooker Turkey Breast

Liz Ann Yoder
Hartville, OH

Makes 12 servings
(Ideal slow cooker size: 6-7-quart)

**6 lb. turkey breast, skin
    and visible fat removed
2 tsp. oil
salt to taste
pepper to taste
1 medium onion,
    quartered
4 garlic cloves, peeled
1/2 cup water**

1. Rinse turkey and pat dry with paper towels.
2. Rub oil over turkey. Sprinkle with salt and pepper. Place, meaty side up, in large slow cooker.
3. Place onion and garlic around sides of cooker.
4. Cover. Cook on Low 9-10 hours, or until meat thermometer stuck in meaty part of breast registers 170°.
5. Remove from slow cooker and let stand 10 minutes before slicing.
6. Serve with mashed potatoes, cranberry salad, and corn or green beans.

Exchange List Values:
Meat, very lean 5.0

Basic Nutritional Values: Calories 187 (Calories from Fat 16), Total Fat 2 gm (Saturated Fat 0.4 gm, Polyunsat Fat 0.5 gm, Monounsat Fat 0.6 gm, Cholesterol 107 mg), Sodium 68 mg, Total Carbohydrate 1 gm, Dietary Fiber 0 gm, Sugars 1 gm, Protein 39 gm

Variations:
1. Add carrot chunks and chopped celery to Step 3 to add more flavor to the turkey broth.
2. Reserve broth for soups, or thicken with flour-water paste and serve as gravy over sliced turkey.
3. Freeze broth in pint-sized containers for future use.
4. Debone turkey and freeze in pint-sized containers for future use. Or freeze any leftover turkey after serving the meal described above.

Turkey Breast with Orange Sauce

Jean Butzer, Batavia, NY

Makes 4-6 servings
(Ideal slow cooker size: 4-5-quart)

**1 large onion, chopped
3 garlic cloves, minced
1 tsp. dried rosemary
1/2 tsp. pepper
2 lb. boneless, skinless
    turkey breast
1 1/2 cups orange juice**

1. Place onions in slow cooker.
2. Combine garlic, rosemary, and pepper.
3. Make gashes in turkey, about 3/4 of the way through at 2" intervals. Stuff with herb mixture. Place turkey in slow cooker.
4. Pour juice over turkey.
5. Cover. Cook on Low 7-8 hours, or until turkey is no longer pink in center.

Exchange List Values:
Fruit 0.5, Meat, very lean 4.0

Basic Nutritional Values: Calories 178 (Calories from Fat 8), Total Fat 1 gm (Saturated Fat 0.3 gm, Polyunsat Fat 0.3 gm, Monounsat Fat 0.2 gm, Cholesterol 81 mg), Sodium 53 mg, Total Carbohydrate 10 gm, Dietary Fiber 1 gm, Sugars 9 gm, Protein 30 gm

This very easy, impressive-looking and -tasting recipe is perfect for company.

Stuffed Turkey Breast

Jean Butzer
Batavia, NY

Makes 12 servings
(Ideal slow cooker size: 5-6-quart)

1/4 cup margarine, melted
1 small onion, finely
    chopped
1/2 cup finely chopped
    celery
2 1/2-oz. pkg. croutons with
    real bacon bits
1 cup chicken broth
2 Tbsp. fresh minced
    parsley
1/2 tsp. poultry seasoning
1 whole uncooked turkey
    breast, or 2 halves
    (about 5 lbs.), skin and
    visible fat removed
salt to taste
pepper to taste
24" x 26" piece of
    cheesecloth for each
    breast half
dry white wine

1. Combine margarine,
onion, celery, croutons, broth,
parsley, and poultry
seasoning.
2. Cut turkey breast in
thick slices from breastbone
to rib cage, leaving slices
attached to bone (crosswise
across breast).
3. Sprinkle turkey with salt
and pepper.
4. Soak cheesecloth in
wine. Place turkey on
cheesecloth. Stuff bread
mixture into slits between
turkey slices. Fold one end of
cheesecloth over the other to
cover meat. Place on metal
rack or trivet in 5- or 6-qt.
slow cooker.
5. Cover. Cook on Low 7-9
hours or until tender. Pour
additional wine over turkey
during cooking.
6. Remove from pot and
remove cheesecloth
immediately. If you prefer the
breast to be browner, remove
from pot and brown in 400°
oven for 15-20 minutes. Let
stand 10 minutes before
slicing through and serving.

Exchange List Values:
Starch 0.5, Meat, very lean
5.0, Fat 0.5

Basic Nutritional Values: Calories
216 (Calories from Fat 57), Total Fat
6 gm (Saturated Fat 1.0 gm,
Polyunsat Fat 1.4 gm, Monounsat Fat
2.4 gm, Cholesterol 89 mg), Sodium
341 mg, Total Carbohydrate 5 gm,
Dietary Fiber 1 gm, Sugars 1 gm,
Protein 34 gm

Variation: Thicken the
drippings, if you wish, for gravy.
Mix together 3 Tbsp.
cornstarch and 1/4 cup cold
water. When smooth, stir into
broth (with turkey removed
from cooker). Turn cooker to
High and stir until cornstarch
paste is dissolved. Allow to
cook for about 10 minutes, until
broth is thickened and smooth.

Slow Cooker Turkey and Dressing

Carol Sherwood
Batavia, NY

Makes 8 servings
(Ideal slow cooker size: 5-6-quart)

8-oz. pkg. herb-flavored
    stuffing mix
1/2 cup hot water
2 Tbsp. butter, softened
1 onion, chopped
1/2 cup chopped celery
1/4 cup sweetened, dried
    cranberries
3 lb. boneless turkey
    breast
1/4 tsp. dried basil
1/2 tsp. pepper

1. Spread dry stuffing mix
in greased slow cooker.
2. Add water, butter,
onion, celery, and cranberries. Mix well.
3. Sprinkle turkey breast
with basil, and pepper. Place
over stuffing mixture.
4. Cover. Cook on Low 5-6
hours, or until turkey is done
but not dry.
5. Remove turkey. Slice
and set aside.
6. Gently stir stuffing and
allow to sit for 5 minutes
before serving.
7. Place stuffing on platter,
topped with sliced turkey.

Exchange List Values:
Starch 2.0, Meat, very lean 4.0

Basic Nutritional Values: Calories 307 (Calories from Fat 34), Total Fat 4 gm (Saturated Fat 2.1 gm, Polyunsat Fat 0.3 gm, Monounsat Fat 1.0 gm, Cholesterol 99 mg), Sodium 488 mg, Total Carbohydrate 26 gm, Dietary Fiber 3 gm, Sugars 5 gm, Protein 37 gm

Keep track of the total grams of fiber you eat today—you should get around 25-35 grams a day.

Zucchini and Turkey Dish
Dolores Kratz
Souderton, PA

Makes 6 servings
(Ideal slow cooker size: 3-4-quart)

3 cups zucchini, sliced
1 small onion, chopped
1/4 tsp. salt
1 cup cubed cooked turkey
2 fresh tomatoes, sliced, or 14 1/2-oz. can diced tomatoes
1/2 tsp. dried oregano
1 tsp. dried basil
1/4 cup freshly grated Parmesan cheese
6 Tbsp. shredded provolone cheese
3/4 cup Pepperidge Farms stuffing

1. Combine zucchini, onion, salt, turkey, tomatoes, oregano, and basil in slow cooker. Mix well.
2. Top with cheeses and stuffing.
3. Cover. Cook on Low 8-9 hours.

Exchange List Values:
Starch 0.5, Vegetable 1.0, Meat, lean 1.0

Basic Nutritional Values: Calories 128 (Calories from Fat 39), Total Fat 4 gm (Saturated Fat 2.3 gm, Polyunsat Fat 0.5 gm, Monounsat Fat 1.2 gm, Cholesterol 23 mg), Sodium 312 mg, Total Carbohydrate 12 gm, Dietary Fiber 2 gm, Sugars 4 gm, Protein 11 gm

Slow-Cooked Turkey Dinner
Miriam Nolt
New Holland, PA

Makes 6 servings
(Ideal slow cooker size: 4-5-quart)

1 onion, diced
6 (1 lb. total) small red potatoes, quartered
2 cups sliced carrots
1 1/2 lbs. boneless, skinless turkey thighs
1/4 cup flour
2 Tbsp. salt-free dry onion soup mix (see recipe on page 254)
10 3/4-oz. can 98%-fat-free, reduced-sodium cream of mushroom soup
2/3 cup fat-free, reduced-sodium chicken broth

1. Place vegetables in bottom of slow cooker.
2. Place turkey thighs over vegetables.
3. Combine remaining ingredients. Pour over turkey.
4. Cover. Cook on High 30 minutes. Reduce heat to Low and cook 7 hours.

Exchange List Values:
Starch 1.5, Vegetable 1.0, Meat, lean 2.0

Basic Nutritional Values: Calories 274 (Calories from Fat 58), Total Fat 6 gm (Saturated Fat 2.2 gm, Polyunsat Fat 1.9 gm, Monounsat Fat 1.4 gm, Cholesterol 61 mg), Sodium 571 mg, Total Carbohydrate 29 gm, Dietary Fiber 4 gm, Sugars 6 gm, Protein 25 gm

Barbecued Turkey Legs
Barbara Walker
Sturgis, SC

Makes 4-6 servings
(Ideal slow cooker size: 4-5-quart)

4 small skinless turkey
 drumsticks
1/4-1/2 tsp. pepper
1/4 cup molasses
1/4 cup vinegar
1/2 cup ketchup
3 Tbsp. Worcestershire
 sauce
3/4 tsp. hickory smoke
2 Tbsp. instant minced
 onion

1. Sprinkle turkey with
pepper. Place in slow cooker.
2. Combine remaining
ingredients. Pour over turkey.
3. Cover. Cook on Low 5-7
hours.

Exchange List Values:
Carbohydrate 1.0, Meat,
lean 4.0

Basic Nutritional Values: Calories
319 (Calories from Fat 87), Total Fat
10 gm (Saturated Fat 3.2 gm,
Polyunsat Fat 2.9 gm, Monounsat Fat
2.2 gm, Cholesterol 112 mg), Sodium
445 mg, Total Carbohydrate 18 gm,
Dietary Fiber 0 gm, Sugars 13 gm,
Protein 38 gm

Barbecued Turkey Cutlets
Maricarol Magill
Freehold, NJ

Makes 6-8 servings
(Ideal slow cooker size: 4-quart)

6-8 (2 lbs.) turkey cutlets
1/4 cup molasses
1/4 cup cider vinegar
1/4 cup ketchup
3 Tbsp. Worcestershire
 sauce
1 tsp. garlic salt
3 Tbsp. chopped onion
2 Tbsp. brown sugar
1/4 tsp. pepper

1. Place turkey cutlets in
slow cooker.
2. Combine remaining
ingredients. Pour over turkey.
3. Cover. Cook on Low 4
hours.
4. Serve over white or
brown rice.

Exchange List Values:
Carbohydrate 1.0, Meat,
very lean 3.0

Basic Nutritional Values: Calories
155 (Calories from Fat 5), Total Fat 1
gm (Saturated Fat 0.2 gm, Polyunsat
Fat 0.2 gm, Monounsat Fat 0.1 gm,
Cholesterol 61 mg), Sodium 365
mg, Total Carbohydrate 14 gm,
Dietary Fiber 0 gm, Sugars 12 gm,
Protein 22 gm

Turkey and Sweet Potato Casserole
Michele Ruvola
Selden, NY

Makes 4 servings
(Ideal slow cooker size: 4-quart)

3 medium (6 1/4-6 1/2 ozs.
 each) sweet potatoes,
 peeled and cut into 2"
 pieces
10-oz. pkg. frozen cut
 green beans
1 1/2 lbs. turkey cutlets
12-oz. jar home-style
 turkey gravy
2 Tbsp. flour
1 tsp. parsley flakes
1/4-1/2 tsp. dried rosemary
 leaves, crumbled
1/8 tsp. pepper

1. Layer sweet potatoes,
green beans, and turkey in
slow cooker.
2. Combine remaining
ingredients until smooth.
Pour over mixture in slow
cooker.
3. Cover. Cook on Low 8-
10 hours.
4. Remove turkey and
vegetables and keep warm.
Stir sauce. Serve with sauce
over meat and vegetables, or
with sauce in a gravy boat.
5. Serve with biscuits and
cranberry sauce.

Exchange List Values:
Starch 2.0, Vegetable 1.0,
Meat, very lean 4.0

Basic Nutritional Values: Calories 318 (Calories from Fat 24), Total Fat 3 gm (Saturated Fat 0.3 gm, Polyunsat Fat 0.7 gm, Monounsat Fat 0.9 gm, Cholesterol 93 mg), Sodium 473 mg, Total Carbohydrate 35 gm, Dietary Fiber 4 gm, Sugars 7 gm, Protein 37 gm

Savory Turkey Meatballs in Italian Sauce

Marla Folkerts
Holland, OH

Makes 8 servings
(Ideal slow cooker size: 4-quart)

28-oz. can crushed
   tomatoes
1 Tbsp. red wine vinegar
1 medium onion, finely
   chopped
2 garlic cloves, minced
1/4 tsp. Italian herb
   seasoning
1 tsp. dried basil
1 lb. ground turkey
1/8 tsp. garlic powder
1/8 tsp. black pepper
1/3 cup dried parsley
2 egg whites
1/4 tsp. dried minced onion
1/3 cup quick oats
1/4 cup grated Parmesan
   cheese
1/4 cup flour
2 Tbsp. canola oil

1. Combine tomatoes, vinegar, onions, garlic, Italian seasonings, and basil in slow cooker. Turn to Low.

2. Combine remaining ingredients, except flour and oil. Form into 1″ balls. Dredge each ball in flour. Brown in oil in skillet over medium heat. Drain. Transfer to slow cooker. Stir into sauce.

3. Cover. Cook on Low 6-8 hours.

4. Serve over pasta or rice.

Exchange List Values:
Starch 0.5, Vegetable 2.0, Meat, lean 2.0, Fat 0.5

Basic Nutritional Values: Calories 226 (Calories from Fat 94), Total Fat 10 gm (Saturated Fat 2.4 gm, Polyunsat Fat 2.5 gm, Monounsat Fat 4.5 gm, Cholesterol 46 mg), Sodium 402 mg, Total Carbohydrate 16 gm, Dietary Fiber 3 gm, Sugars 7 gm, Protein 17 gm

Note: The meatballs and sauce freeze well.

People with diabetes should see their doctor at least twice a year.

Turkey Sloppy Joes

Marla Folkerts
Holland, OH

Makes 6 servings

1 red onion, chopped
1 sweet pepper, chopped
1 1/2 lbs. boneless cooked
   turkey, finely chopped
1 cup no-salt-added
   ketchup
1/2 tsp. salt
1 garlic clove, minced
1 tsp. Dijon-style mustard
1/8 tsp. pepper
6 (1 1/2 ozs. each) multigrain
   sandwich rolls

1. Place onion, sweet pepper, and turkey in slow cooker.

2. Combine ketchup, salt, garlic, mustard, and pepper. Pour over turkey mixture. Mix well.

3. Cover. Cook on Low 4 1/2-6 hours.

4. Serve on sandwich rolls.

Exchange List Values:
Starch 1.5, Vegetable 3.0, Meat, lean 1.0, Fat 0.5

Basic Nutritional Values: Calories 271 (Calories from Fat 49), Total Fat 5 gm (Saturated Fat 1.6 gm, Polyunsat Fat 1.3 gm, Monounsat Fat 1.8 gm, Cholesterol 40 mg), Sodium 457 mg, Total Carbohydrate 36 gm, Dietary Fiber 3 gm, Sugars 16 gm, Protein 21 gm

Tricia's Cranberry Turkey Meatballs

Shirley Unternahrer Hinh
Wayland, IA

Makes 12 servings
(Ideal slow cooker size: 4-quart)

16-oz. can jelled cranberry
  sauce
1/2 cup ketchup or
  barbecue sauce
1 egg
1 lb. ground turkey
half a small onion,
  chopped
1 tsp. salt
1/4 tsp. black pepper
1-2 tsp. grated orange peel,
  optional

1. Combine cranberry
sauce and ketchup in slow
cooker.
2. Cover. Cook on High
until sauce is mixed.
3. Combine remaining
ingredients. Shape into 24
balls.
4. Cook over medium heat
in skillet for 8-10 minutes, or
just until browned. Add to
sauce in slow cooker.
5. Cover. Cook on Low 3
hours.
6. Serve with rice and a
steamed vegetable.

Exchange List Values:
Carbohydrate 1.0, Meat,
lean 1.0

Basic Nutritional Values: Calories
134 (Calories from Fat 34), Total Fat
4 gm (Saturated Fat 0.9 gm,
Polyunsat Fat 0.9 gm, Monounsat Fat
1.4 gm, Cholesterol 28 mg), Sodium
353 mg, Total Carbohydrate 18 gm,
Dietary Fiber 1 gm, Sugars 15 gm,
Protein 8 gm

Turkey Meatballs and Gravy

Betty Sue Good, Broadway, VA

Makes 10 servings
(Ideal slow cooker size: 4-quart)

2 eggs, beaten
3/4 cup bread crumbs
1/2 cup finely chopped
  onions
1/2 cup finely chopped
  celery
2 Tbsp. chopped fresh
  parsley
1/4 tsp. pepper
1/8 tsp. garlic powder
1 1/2 lbs. ground raw turkey
1 1/2 Tbsp. canola oil
10 3/4-oz. can 99%-fat-free,
  reduced-sodium cream
  of mushroom soup
1 cup water
7/8-oz. pkg. turkey gravy
  mix
1/2 tsp. dried thyme
2 bay leaves

1. Combine eggs, bread
crumbs, onions, celery,
parsley, pepper, garlic
powder, and meat. Shape into
3/4" balls.
2. Brown meatballs in oil
in skillet. Drain meatballs

and pat dry. Transfer to slow
cooker.
3. Combine soup, water,
dry gravy mix, thyme, and
bay leaves. Pour over
meatballs.
4. Cover. Cook on Low 6-8
hours or High 3-4 hours.
Discard bay leaves before
serving.
5. Serve over mashed
potatoes or buttered noodles.

Exchange List Values:
Starch 0.5, Carbohydrate
0.5, Meat, lean 2.0, Fat 0.5

Basic Nutritional Values: Calories
212 (Calories from Fat 97), Total Fat
11 gm (Saturated Fat 2.5 gm,
Polyunsat Fat 2.7 gm, Monounsat Fat
4.4 gm, Cholesterol 94 mg), Sodium
365 mg, Total Carbohydrate 11 gm,
Dietary Fiber 1 gm, Sugars 2 gm,
Protein 17 gm

**Oils are good for your
heart. The solid fats—
butter, margarine,
shortening, and lard—
are bad for your heart.**

Bean and Other Main Dishes

New England Baked Beans

Mary Wheatley
Mashpee, MA
Jean Butzer
Batavia, NY

Makes 8 servings
(Ideal slow cooker size: 4-quart)

1 lb. dried beans—Great Northern, pea beans, or navy beans
2 ozs. salt pork, sliced or diced
1 qt. water
1 tsp. salt
1 Tbsp. brown sugar
1/2 cup molasses
1/2 tsp. dry mustard
1/2 tsp. baking soda
1 onion, coarsely chopped
5 cups water

1. Wash beans and remove any stones or shriveled beans.
2. Meanwhile, simmer salt pork in 1 quart water in saucepan for 10 minutes. Drain. Do not reserve liquid.
3. Combine all ingredients in slow cooker.
4. Cook on High until contents come to boil. Turn to Low. Cook 14-16 hours, or until beans are tender.

Exchange List Values:
Starch 2.0, Carbohydrate 1.0

Basic Nutritional Values: Calories 269 (Calories from Fat 41), Total Fat 5 gm (Saturated Fat 1.6 gm, Polyunsat Fat 0.7 gm, Monounsat Fat 1.9 gm, Cholesterol 4 mg), Sodium 444 mg, Total Carbohydrate 47 gm, Dietary Fiber 10 gm, Sugars 18 gm, Protein 12 gm

Variations:
1. Add 1/2 tsp. pepper to Step 3.
Rachel Kauffman
Alton, MI

2. Add 1/4 cup ketchup to Step 3.
Cheri Jantzen
Houston, TX

To keep yourself motivated once you start a weight-loss program, reward yourself by buying a new CD, getting a new exercise outfit, or going to the movies.

"Famous" Baked Beans

Katrine Rose
Woodbridge, VA

Makes 15 servings
(Ideal slow cooker size: 4-5-quart)

1 lb. ground beef
1/4 cup minced onions
1 cup no-salt-added
　ketchup
4 15-oz. cans pork and
　beans
1/3 cup brown sugar
brown sugar substitute to
　equal 1/4 cup
2 Tbsp. liquid smoke
1 Tbsp. Worcestershire
　sauce

1. Brown beef and onions in skillet. Drain. Spoon meat and onions into slow cooker.
2. Add remaining ingredients and stir well.
3. Cover. Cook on High 3 hours or on Low 5-6 hours.

Exchange List Values:
Starch 1.0, Carbohydrate 1.0, Meat, lean 1.0

Basic Nutritional Values: Calories 207 (Calories from Fat 44), Total Fat 5 gm (Saturated Fat 1.2 gm, Polyunsat Fat 0.5 gm, Monounsat Fat 2.0 gm, Cholesterol 22 mg), Sodium 539 mg, Total Carbohydrate 32 gm, Dietary Fiber 5 gm, Sugars 17 gm, Protein 10 gm

There are many worthy baked bean recipes, but these are both easy and absolutely delicious. The secret to this recipe is the liquid smoke. I get many requests for this recipe, and some friends have added the word "famous" to its name.

Deb's Baked Beans

Deborah Swartz
Grottoes, VA

Makes 8 servings
(Ideal slow cooker size: 4-quart)

4 slices bacon, fried and
　drained
1 Tbsp. reserved drippings
1/2 cup chopped onions
2 15-oz. cans pork and
　beans
1/2 tsp. salt, optional
2 Tbsp. brown sugar
1 Tbsp. Worcestershire
　sauce
1 tsp. prepared mustard

1. Fry bacon in skillet until crisp. Reserve 2 Tbsp. drippings. Crumble bacon.
3. Cook onions in bacon drippings.
4. Combine all ingredients in slow cooker.
5. Cover. Cook on High 1 1/2-2 hours.

Exchange List Values:
Starch 1.5, Fat 1.0

Basic Nutritional Values: Calories 158 (Calories from Fat 43), Total Fat 5 gm (Saturated Fat 1.3 gm, Polyunsat Fat 0.7 gm, Monounsat Fat 2.1 gm, Cholesterol 8 mg), Sodium 549 mg, Total Carbohydrate 24 gm, Dietary Fiber 5 gm, Sugars 11 gm, Protein 5 gm

Barbecued Lima Beans

Hazel L. Propst
Oxford, PA

Makes 20 servings
(Ideal slow cooker size: 4-5-quart)

1 1/2 lbs. dried lima beans
6 cups water
2 1/4 cups chopped onions
1/2 cup brown sugar
brown sugar substitute to
　equal 6 Tbsp.
1 1/2 cups ketchup
13 drops Tabasco sauce
1/2 cup dark corn syrup
1 tsp. salt
1/4 lb. bacon, diced

1. Soak washed beans in water overnight. Do not drain.
2. Add onion. Bring to boil. Simmer 30-60 minutes, or until beans are tender. Drain beans, reserving liquid.
3. Combine all ingredients except bean liquid in slow cooker. Mix well. Pour in enough liquid so that beans are barely covered.
4. Cover. Cook on Low 10 hours, or High 4-6 hours. Stir occasionally.

Basic Nutritional Values: Calories
195 (Calories from Fat 27), Total Fat
3 gm (Saturated Fat 0.9 gm,
Polyunsat Fat 0.4 gm, Monounsat Fat
1.2 gm, Cholesterol 4 mg), Sodium
393 mg, Total Carbohydrate 36 gm,
Dietary Fiber 7 gm, Sugars 15 gm,
Protein 8 gm

Refried Beans with Bacon

Arlene Wengerd
Millersburg, OH

Makes 8 servings
(Ideal slow cooker size: 4-quart)

2 cups dried red, or pinto,
    beans
6 cups water
2 garlic cloves, minced
1 large tomato, peeled,
    seeded, and chopped
1 tsp. salt
2 ozs. bacon

1. Combine beans, water,
garlic, tomato, and salt in
slow cooker.
2. Cover. Cook on High 5
hours, stirring occasionally.
When the beans become soft,
drain off some liquid.
3. While the beans cook,
brown bacon in skillet. Drain,
reserving drippings. Crumble
bacon. Add half of bacon and
1½ Tbsp. drippings to beans.
Stir.
4. Mash or puree beans

with a food processor. Fry the
mashed bean mixture in the
remaining bacon drippings.
Add more salt to taste.
    5. To serve, sprinkle the
remaining bacon on top of
beans.

Basic Nutritional Values: Calories
171 (Calories from Fat 34), Total Fat
4 gm (Saturated Fat 1.2 gm,
Polyunsat Fat 0.6 gm, Monounsat Fat
1.5 gm, Cholesterol 5 mg), Sodium
354 mg, Total Carbohydrate 26 gm,
Dietary Fiber 9 gm, Sugars 3 gm,
Protein 9 gm

Variations:
1. Instead of draining off liquid,
add ⅓ cup dry minute rice and
continue cooking about 20
minutes. Add a dash of hot
sauce and a dollop of sour
cream to individual servings.
2. Instead of frying the mashed
bean mixture, place several
spoonfuls on flour tortillas, roll
up, and serve.
        Susan McClure
        Dayton, VA

If you sometimes
forget to take your pills,
an inexpensive pill
organizer may help you
keep track.

Red Beans and Pasta

Naomi E. Fast, Hesston, KS

Makes 6-8 servings
(Ideal slow cooker size: 4-5-quart)

3 14½ oz. cans 100%-fat-
    free, reduced-sodium
    chicken broth
½ tsp. ground cumin
1 Tbsp. chili powder
1 garlic clove, minced
8 ozs. uncooked spiral pasta
half a large green pepper,
    diced
half a large red pepper,
    diced
1 medium onion, diced
15-oz. can red beans, rinsed
    and drained
chopped fresh parsley
chopped fresh cilantro

1. Combine broth, cumin,
chili powder, and garlic in
slow cooker.
2. Cover. Cook on High
until mixture comes to boil.
3. Add pasta, vegetables,
and beans. Stir together well.
4. Cover. Cook on Low 3-4
hours.
5. Add parsley and cilantro
before serving.

Basic Nutritional Values: Calories
180 (Calories from Fat 9), Total Fat 1
gm (Saturated Fat 0.0 gm, Polyunsat
Fat 0.4 gm, Monounsat Fat 0.2 gm,
Cholesterol 0 mg), Sodium 448
mg, Total Carbohydrate 34 gm,
Dietary Fiber 4 gm, Sugars 4 gm,
Protein 9 gm

Red Beans and Rice

Margaret A. Moffitt
Bartlett, TN

Makes 10 servings
(Ideal slow cooker size: 4-5-quart)

1 lb. pkg. dried red beans
water
4 ozs. smoked sausage
1/2 tsp. salt
1 tsp. pepper
3-4 cups water
6-oz. can tomato paste
8-oz. can tomato sauce
4 garlic cloves, minced

1. Soak beans for 8 hours. Drain. Discard soaking water.
2. Mix together all ingredients in slow cooker.
3. Cover. Cook on Low 10-12 hours, or until beans are soft. Serve over rice.

Exchange List Values:
Starch 1.5, Vegetable 1.0, Meat, lean 1.0

Basic Nutritional Values: Calories 198 (Calories from Fat 36), Total Fat 4 gm (Saturated Fat 1.2 gm, Polyunsat Fat 0.8 gm, Monounsat Fat 1.5 gm, Cholesterol 7 mg), Sodium 370 mg, Total Carbohydrate 30 gm, Dietary Fiber 8 gm, Sugars 4 gm, Protein 12 gm

Variation: Use canned red kidney beans. Cook 1 hour on High and then 3 hours on Low.

Note: These beans freeze well.

Party-Time Beans

Beatrice Martin
Goshen, IN

Makes 14 servings
(Ideal slow cooker size: 6-quart)

1 1/2 cups ketchup
1 onion, chopped
1 green pepper, chopped
1 sweet red pepper, chopped
1/2 cup water
1/4 cup packed brown sugar
brown sugar substitute to equal 2 Tbsp.
2 bay leaves
2-3 tsp. cider vinegar
1 tsp. ground mustard
1/8 tsp. pepper
16-oz. can kidney beans, rinsed and drained
15 1/2-oz. can Great Northern beans, rinsed and drained
15-oz. can lima beans, rinsed and drained
15-oz. can black beans, rinsed and drained
15 1/2-oz. can black-eyed peas, rinsed and drained

1. Combine first 11 ingredients in slow cooker. Mix well.
2. Add remaining ingredients. Mix well.
3. Cover. Cook on Low 5-7 hours, or until onion and peppers are tender.
4. Remove bay leaves before serving.
5. Serve with grilled hamburgers, tossed salad or veggie tray, chips, fruit, and cookies.

Exchange List Values:
Starch 1.5, Carbohydrate 0.5

Basic Nutritional Values: Calories 172 (Calories from Fat 7), Total Fat 1 gm (Saturated Fat 0.1 gm, Polyunsat Fat 0.2 gm, Monounsat Fat 0.0 gm, Cholesterol 0 mg), Sodium 493 mg, Total Carbohydrate 35 gm, Dietary Fiber 8 gm, Sugars 11 gm, Protein 9 gm

New Mexico Pinto Beans

John D. Allen, Rye, CO

Makes 10 servings
(Ideal slow cooker size: 4-quart)

2 1/2 cups dried pinto beans
3 qts. water
1/2 cup ham, or salt pork, diced, or a small ham shank
2 garlic cloves, crushed
1 tsp. crushed red chili peppers, optional

1. Sort beans. Discard pebbles, shriveled beans, and floaters. Wash beans under running water. Place in saucepan, cover with 3 quarts water, and soak overnight.
2. Drain beans and discard soaking water. Pour beans into slow cooker. Cover with fresh water.
3. Add meat, garlic, and chili peppers. Cook on Low 6-10 hours, or until beans are soft.

Basic Nutritional Values: Calories 145 (Calories from Fat 8), Total Fat 1 gm (Saturated Fat 0.2 gm, Polyunsat Fat 0.2 gm, Monounsat Fat 0.3 gm, Cholesterol 4 mg), Sodium 95 mg, Total Carbohydrate 25 gm, Dietary Fiber 8 gm, Sugars 2 gm, Protein 10 gm

Scandinavian Beans
Virginia Bender, Dover, DE

Makes 8 servings
(Ideal slow cooker size: 4-5-quart)

1 lb. dried pinto beans
6 cups water
1/4 lb. bacon, or 1 ham hock
1 onion, chopped
2-3 garlic cloves, minced
1/4 tsp. pepper
1/4 tsp. salt
2 Tbsp. molasses
1 cup ketchup
Tabasco to taste
1 tsp. Worcestershire sauce
1/4 cup brown sugar
brown sugar substitute to equal 1/4 cup
1/3 cup cider vinegar
1/4 tsp. dry mustard

1. Soak beans in water in soup pot for 8 hours. Bring beans to boil and cook 1 1/2-2 hours, or until soft. Drain, reserving liquid.
2. Combine all ingredients in slow cooker, using just enough bean liquid to cover everything. Cook on Low 5-6 hours.

Exchange List Values:
Starch 2.0, Carbohydrate 1.0, Vegetable 1.0, Fat 0.5

Basic Nutritional Values: Calories 305 (Calories from Fat 65), Total Fat 7 gm (Saturated Fat 2.2 gm, Polyunsat Fat 0.9 gm, Monounsat Fat 3.0 gm, Cholesterol 10 mg), Sodium 564 mg, Total Carbohydrate 51 gm, Dietary Fiber 11 gm, Sugars 18 gm, Protein 12 gm

Calico Beans
Alice Miller, Stuarts Draft, VA

Makes 12 servings
(Ideal slow cooker size: 6-quart)

1/2 lb. ground beef
1/4 lb. bacon, chopped
1/2 cup chopped onions
1/2 cup no-added-salt ketchup
1/3 cup brown sugar
brown sugar substitute to equal 3 Tbsp.
2 Tbsp. sugar
1 Tbsp. vinegar
1 tsp. dry mustard
16-oz. can pork and beans, undrained
16-oz. can red kidney beans, undrained
16-oz. can yellow limas, undrained
16-oz. can navy beans, undrained

1. Brown ground beef, bacon, and onions together in skillet. Drain. Spoon meat and onions into slow cooker.
2. Stir ketchup, brown sugar, sugar substitute, sugar, vinegar and mustard. Mix together well. Add to slow cooker.
3. Pour beans into slow cooker and combine all ingredients thoroughly.
4. Cover. Cook on High 3-4 hours.
5. Serve over rice, or take to a picnic as is.

Exchange List Values:
Starch 2.5, Meat, lean 1.0

Basic Nutritional Values: Calories 233 (Calories from Fat 39), Total Fat 4 gm (Saturated Fat 1.3 gm, Polyunsat Fat 0.5 gm, Monounsat Fat 1.7 gm, Cholesterol 15 mg), Sodium 620 mg, Total Carbohydrate 37 gm, Dietary Fiber 7 gm, Sugars 16 gm, Protein 12 gm

Instead of rice or potatoes, try couscous or quinoa [KEEN-wa], whole grains that cook fast, are easy to make, and taste great!

New Orleans Red Beans

Cheri Jantzen
Houston, TX

Makes 6 servings
(Ideal slow cooker size: 4-quart)

2 cups dried kidney beans
5 cups water
8 ozs. low-fat smoked
  sausage, cut in small
  pieces
2 medium onions, chopped
2 cloves garlic, minced
1/4 tsp. salt

1. Wash and sort beans. In saucepan, combine beans and water. Boil 2 minutes. Remove from heat. Soak 1 hour.
2. Brown sausage slowly in a skillet. (If needed, use nonfat cooking spray.) Add onions, garlic, and salt and saute until tender.
3. Combine all ingredients, including the bean water, in slow cooker.
4. Cover. Cook on Low 8-10 hours. During last 20 minutes of cooking, stir frequently and mash lightly with spoon.
5. Serve over hot cooked white rice.

Exchange List Values:
Starch 2.5, Vegetable 1.0, Meat, very lean 1.0

Basic Nutritional Values: Calories 260 (Calories from Fat 23), Total Fat 3 gm (Saturated Fat 0.8 gm,

Polyunsat Fat 1.1 gm, Monounsat Fat 0.5 gm, Cholesterol 16 mg), Sodium 422 mg, Total Carbohydrate 42 gm, Dietary Fiber 10 gm, Sugars 8 gm, Protein 18 gm

Pioneer Beans

Kay Magruder
Seminole, OK

Makes 8 servings
(Ideal slow cooker size: 4-quart)

1 lb. dry lima beans
1 bunch green onions,
  chopped
3 tsp. salt-free beef
  bouillon powder
6 cups water
1 lb. Low-fat smoked
  sausage
1/2 tsp. garlic powder
3/4 tsp. Tabasco sauce

1. Combine all ingredients in slow cooker. Mix well.
2. Cover. Cook on High 8-9 hours, or until beans are soft but not mushy.
3. Serve with home-baked bread.

Exchange List Values:
Starch 2.5, Meat, very lean 2.0

Basic Nutritional Values: Calories 252 (Calories from Fat 28), Total Fat 3 gm (Saturated Fat 1.1 gm, Polyunsat Fat 1.3 gm, Monounsat Fat 0.7 gm, Cholesterol 24 mg), Sodium 487 mg, Total Carbohydrate 38 gm, Dietary Fiber 10 gm, Sugars 7 gm, Protein 18 gm

Cowboy Beans

Sharon Timpe, Mequon, WI

Makes 12 servings
(Ideal slow cooker size: 5-6-quart)

6 slices bacon, cut in
  pieces
1/2 cup onions, chopped
1 garlic clove, minced
16-oz. can baked beans
16-oz. can kidney beans,
  drained
15-oz. can butter beans or
  pinto beans, drained
2 Tbsp. dill pickle relish or
  chopped dill pickles
1/3 cup chili sauce or
  ketchup
2 tsp. Worcestershire sauce
1/4 cup brown sugar
brown sugar substitute to
  equal 2 Tbsp.
1/8 tsp. hot pepper sauce,
  optional

1. Lightly brown bacon, onions, and garlic in skillet. Drain.
2. Combine all ingredients in slow cooker. Mix well.
3. Cover. Cook on Low 5-7 hours or High 3-4 hours.

Exchange List Values:
Starch 1.0, Carbohydrate 0.5, Fat 0.5

Basic Nutritional Values: Calories 138 (Calories from Fat 17), Total Fat 2 gm (Saturated Fat 0.6 gm, Polyunsat Fat 0.3 gm, Monounsat Fat 0.7 gm, Cholesterol 3 mg), Sodium 441 mg, Total Carbohydrate 25 gm, Dietary Fiber 5 gm, Sugars 9 gm, Protein 7 gm

Four Beans and Sausage

Mary Seielstad
Sparks, NV

Makes 8 servings
(Ideal slow cooker size: 5-quart)

15-oz. can Great Northern beans, drained
15½-oz. can black beans, rinsed and drained
16-oz. can red kidney beans, drained
15-oz. can butter beans, drained
1½ cups no-salt-added ketchup
½ cup chopped onions
1 medium green pepper, chopped
1 lb. low-fat smoked sausage, cooked and cut into ½-inch slices
2 Tbsp. brown sugar
brown sugar substitute to equal 1 Tbsp.
2 garlic cloves, minced
1 tsp. Worcestershire sauce
½ tsp. dry mustard
½ tsp. Tabasco sauce

1. Combine all ingredients in slow cooker.
2. Cover. Cook on Low 9-10 hours, or High 4-5 hours.

Exchange List Values:
Starch 2.0, Carbohydrate 1.5, Meat, lean 1.0

Basic Nutritional Values: Calories 328 (Calories from Fat 31), Total Fat 3 gm (Saturated Fat 1.2 gm, Polyunsat Fat 1.4 gm, Monounsat Fat 0.7 gm, Cholesterol 24 mg), Sodium 764 mg, Total Carbohydrate 56 gm, Dietary Fiber 11 gm, Sugars 22 gm, Protein 19 gm

Creole Black Beans

Joyce Kaut
Rochester, NY

Makes 8 servings
(Ideal slow cooker size: 4-quart)

14 ozs. low-fat smoked sausage, sliced in ½″ pieces, browned
3 15-oz. cans black beans, drained
1½ cups chopped onions
1½ cups chopped green peppers
1½ cups chopped celery
4 garlic cloves, minced
2 tsp. dried thyme
1½ tsp. dried oregano
1½ tsp. pepper
1 tsp. salt-free chicken bouillon powder
3 bay leaves
8-oz. can no-added-salt tomato sauce
1 cup water

1. Combine all ingredients in slow cooker.
2. Cover. Cook on Low 8 hours or on High 4 hours.
3. Remove bay leaves.
4. Serve over rice, with a salad and fresh fruit for dessert.

Exchange List Values:
Starch 1.5, Vegetable 2.0, Meat, lean 1.0

Basic Nutritional Values: Calories 223 (Calories from Fat 27), Total Fat 3 gm (Saturated Fat 1.0 gm, Polyunsat Fat 1.2 gm, Monounsat Fat 0.6 gm, Cholesterol 21 mg), Sodium 566 mg, Total Carbohydrate 34 gm, Dietary Fiber 10 gm, Sugars 9 gm, Protein 15 gm

Variation: You may substitute a 14½-oz. can of stewed tomatoes for the tomato sauce.

For many people, diabetes still means you cannot eat sugar. Be patient; it takes years for new information to reach the general public, and years to change old ways of thinking.

Pizza Beans

Kelly Evenson
Pittsboro, NC

Makes 6 servings
(Ideal slow cooker size: 4-quart)

16-oz. can pinto beans,
  drained
16-oz. can kidney beans,
  drained
2¼-oz. can ripe olives
  sliced, drained
28-oz. can no-added-salt
  stewed or whole
  tomatoes
¾ lb. bulk lean turkey
  Italian sausage
1 Tbsp. oil
1 green pepper, chopped
1 medium onion, chopped
1 garlic clove, minced
1 tsp. dried oregano
1 tsp. dried basil

1. Combine beans, olives,
and tomatoes in slow cooker.
2. Brown sausage in
½ Tbsp. oil in skillet. Drain.
Transfer sausage to slow
cooker.
3. Saute green pepper in
½ Tablespoon oil for 1
minute, stirring constantly.
Add onions and continue
stirring until onions start to
become translucent. Add
garlic and cook 1 more
minute. Transfer to slow
cooker.
4. Stir in seasonings.
5. Cover. Cook on Low 7-9
hours.
6. To serve, sprinkle with
Parmesan cheese if you wish.

Exchange List Values:
Starch 1.5, Vegetable 3.0,
Meat, lean 2.0, Fat 1.0

Basic Nutritional Values: Calories
335 (Calories from Fat 104), Total Fat
12 gm (Saturated Fat 2.2 gm,
Polyunsat Fat 2.0 gm, Monounsat Fat
3.7 gm, Cholesterol 45 mg), Sodium
632 mg,Total Carbohydrate 39 gm,
Dietary Fiber 10 gm, Sugars 8 gm,
Protein 23 gm

*Variation: For a thicker soup,
20 minutes before serving
remove ¼ cup liquid from
cooker and add 1 Tbsp.
cornstarch to it. Stir until
dissolved. Return to soup. Cook
on High for 15 minutes, or until
thickened.*

Cajun Sausage and Beans

Melanie Thrower
McPherson, KS

Makes 6 servings
(Ideal slow cooker size: 4-quart)

1 lb. Low-fat smoked
  sausage, sliced into
  ¼-inch pieces
16-oz. can no-salt-added red
  kidney beans
16-oz. can crushed tomatoes
  with green chilies
1 cup chopped celery
half an onion, chopped
2 Tbsp. Italian seasoning
Tabasco sauce to taste

1. Combine all ingredients
in slow cooker.

2. Cover. Cook on Low 8
hours.
3. Serve over rice or as a
thick zesty soup.

Exchange List Values:
Starch 1.0, Vegetable 1.0,
Meat, lean 1.0

Basic Nutritional Values: Calories
158 (Calories from Fat 22), Total Fat
2 gm (Saturated Fat 0.8 gm,
Polyunsat Fat 1.0 gm, Monounsat Fat
0.5 gm, Cholesterol 18 mg), Sodium
588 mg,Total Carbohydrate 23 gm,
Dietary Fiber 7 gm, Sugars 7 gm,
Protein 11 gm

Beans with Rice

Miriam Christophel
Battle Creek, MI

Makes 8 servings
(Ideal slow cooker size: 5-6-quart)

3 cups dried small red
  beans
8 cups water
3 garlic cloves, minced
1 large onion, chopped
8 cups fresh water
1 ham hock
½ cup ketchup
½ tsp. salt
pinch of pepper
1½-2 tsp. ground cumin
1 Tbsp. parsley
1-2 bay leaves

1. Soak beans overnight in
8 cups water. Drain. Place
soaked beans in slow cooker
with garlic, onion, 8 cups
fresh water, and ham hock.

2. Cover. Cook on High 12-14 hours.

3. Take ham hock out of cooker and allow to cool. Remove meat from bones. Remove and discard visible fat and skin. Cut up ham and return to slow cooker. Add remaining ingredients.

4. Cover. Cook on High 2-3 hours.

5. Serve over rice with dollop of sour cream, if you wish.

Exchange List Values:
Starch 1.5, Fat 0.5

Basic Nutritional Values: Calories 148 (Calories from Fat 25), Total Fat 3 gm (Saturated Fat 0.8 gm, Polyunsat Fat 0.5 gm, Monounsat Fat 1.0 gm, Cholesterol 4 mg), Sodium 382 mg, Total Carbohydrate 24 gm, Dietary Fiber 6 gm, Sugars 5 gm, Protein 8 gm

Time and again, studies have shown that getting your blood sugars down to near-normal levels lowers your risk of developing diabetes complications.

Six-Bean Barbecued Beans
Gladys Longacre
Susquehanna, PA

Makes 24 (1/2 cup) servings
(Ideal slow cooker size: 6-quart)

1-lb. can kidney beans, drained
1-lb. can pinto beans, drained
1-lb. can Great Northern beans, drained
1-lb. can butter beans, drained
1-lb. can navy beans, drained
1-lb. can pork and beans
1/4 cup barbecue sauce
1/3 cup prepared mustard
1/3 cup ketchup
2 Tbsp. Worcestershire sauce
1 small onion, chopped
1 small pepper, chopped
2 Tbsp. molasses, or sorghum molasses
1/2 cup brown sugar
brown sugar substitute to equal 1/4 cup

1. Mix together all ingredients in slow cooker.

2. Cook on Low 4-6 hours.

Exchange List Values:
Starch 1.5

Basic Nutritional Values: Calories 122 (Calories from Fat 6), Total Fat 1 gm (Saturated Fat 0.1 gm, Polyunsat Fat 0.2 gm, Monounsat Fat 0.2 gm, Cholesterol 1 mg), Sodium 322 mg, Total Carbohydrate 24 gm, Dietary Fiber 6 gm, Sugars 7 gm, Protein 6 gm

Sweet and Sour Beans
Julette Leaman, Harrisonburg, VA

Makes 8 servings
(Ideal slow cooker size: 4-5-quart)

5 slices bacon
4 medium onions, cut in rings
1/4 cup brown sugar
brown sugar substitute to equal 2 Tbsp.
1 tsp. dry mustard
1/2 tsp. salt
1/4 cup cider vinegar
1-lb. can green beans, drained
2 1-lb. cans butter beans, drained
2 14 1/2-oz. cans baked beans, no added salt

1. Brown bacon in skillet and crumble. Drain all but 3 tsp. bacon drippings. Stir in onions, brown sugar, sugar substitute, mustard, salt, and vinegar. Simmer 20 minutes.

2. Combine all ingredients in slow cooker.

3. Cover. Cook on Low 3 hours.

Exchange List Values:
Starch 2.0, Carbohydrate 1.0, Vegetable 1.0, Meat, lean 1.0

Basic Nutritional Values: Calories 289 (Calories from Fat 40), Total Fat 4 gm (Saturated Fat 1.5 gm, Polyunsat Fat 0.7 gm, Monounsat Fat 1.7 gm, Cholesterol 5 mg), Sodium 519 mg, Total Carbohydrate 51 gm, Dietary Fiber 13 gm, Sugars 22 gm, Protein 13 gm

Four-Bean Medley

Sharon Brubaker
Myerstown, PA

Makes 8 servings
(Ideal slow cooker size: 4-5-quart)

8 bacon slices, diced and
  browned until crisp
2 medium onions, chopped
6 Tbsp. brown sugar
brown sugar substitute to
  equal 3 Tbsp.
1/2 cup vinegar
1 tsp. dry mustard
1/2 tsp. garlic powder
16-oz. can baked beans,
  undrained
16-oz. can kidney beans,
  drained
15 1/2-oz. can butter beans,
  drained
14 1/2-oz. can green beans,
  drained
2 Tbsp. ketchup

1. Mix together all ingredients. Pour into slow cooker.
2. Cover. Cook on Low 6-8 hours.

Exchange List Values:
Starch 2.0, Carbohydrate
0.5, Vegetable 1.0, Fat 0.5

Basic Nutritional Values: Calories
242 (Calories from Fat 34), Total Fat 4
gm (Saturated Fat 1.1 gm, Polyunsat Fat
0.6 gm, Monounsat Fat 1.5 gm, Cholesterol 5 mg), Sodium 619 mg, Total
Carbohydrate 44 gm, Dietary Fiber 9
gm, Sugars 19 gm, Protein 11 gm

Variation: Make this a main
dish by adding 1 lb. hamburger to
the bacon, browning it along with
the bacon and chopped onions in
a skillet, then adding that
mixture to the rest of the
ingredients before pouring into
the slow cooker.

Main Dish Baked Beans

Sue Pennington
Bridgewater, VA

Makes 8 servings
(Ideal slow cooker size: 4-quart)

1 lb. ground beef
28-oz. can baked beans
8-oz. can pineapple tidbits
  packed in juice, drained
4 1/2-oz. can sliced
  mushrooms, drained
1 large onion, chopped
1 large green pepper,
  chopped
1/2 cup Phyllis's Low-
  Sodium Barbecue Sauce
  (see recipe on page 254)
2 Tbsp. light soy sauce
1 clove garlic, minced
1/4 tsp. pepper

1. Brown ground beef in
skillet. Drain. Place in slow
cooker.
2. Stir in remaining ingredients. Mix well.
3. Cover. Cook on Low 4-8
hours, or until bubbly. Serve
in soup bowls.

Exchange List Values:
Starch 1.0, Carbohydrate
0.5, Vegetable 1.0, Meat,
lean 1.0, Fat 1.0

Basic Nutritional Values: Calories
238 (Calories from Fat 58), Total Fat
6 gm (Saturated Fat 2.4 gm,
Polyunsat Fat 0.5 gm, Monounsat Fat
2.6 gm, Cholesterol 34 mg), Sodium
663 mg, Total Carbohydrate 31 gm,
Dietary Fiber 7 gm, Sugars 13 gm,
Protein 17 gm

Slow Cooker Kidney Beans

Jeanette Oberholtzer
Manheim, PA

Makes 12 servings
(Ideal slow cooker size: 4-quart)

2 30-oz. cans kidney beans,
  rinsed and drained
28-oz. can no-salt-added
  diced tomatoes, drained
2 medium-sized red bell
  peppers, chopped
1 cup ketchup
1/4 cup brown sugar
brown sugar substitute to
  equal 2 Tbsp.
2 Tbsp. honey
2 Tbsp. molasses
1 Tbsp. Worcestershire
  sauce
1 tsp. dry mustard
2 medium red apples,
  cored, cut into pieces

1. Combine all ingredients,
except apples, in slow cooker.
2. Cover. Cook on Low 4-5
hours.

3. Stir in apples.

4. Cover. Cook 2 more hours on Low.

Starch 1.5, Carbohydrate 1.0, Vegetable 1.0

Basic Nutritional Values: Calories 216 (Calories from Fat 8), Total Fat 1 gm (Saturated Fat 0.0 gm, Polyunsat Fat 0.4 gm, Monounsat Fat 0.1 gm, Cholesterol 0 mg), Sodium 445 mg, Total Carbohydrate 46 gm, Dietary Fiber 9 gm, Sugars 20 gm, Protein 10 gm

One-Pot Dinner
Vicki Dinkel, Sharon Springs, KS

Makes 8 servings
(Ideal slow cooker size: 4-quart)

1/2 lb. ground beef
1/4 lb. bacon, cut in pieces
1 cup chopped onions
2 16-oz. cans pork and beans
16-oz. can kidney beans, drained
1 cup no-salt-added ketchup
16-oz. can butter beans, drained
2 Tbsp. brown sugar
brown sugar substitute to equal 1 Tbsp.
1 Tbsp. liquid smoke
2 Tbsp. white vinegar
dash of pepper

1. Brown ground beef in skillet. Drain off drippings. Place beef in slow cooker.

2. Brown bacon and onions in skillet. Drain off drippings. Pat dry with absorbent towling. Add bacon and onions to slow cooker.

3. Stir remaining ingredients into cooker.

4. Cover. Cook on Low 5-9 hours or High 3 hours.

Exchange List Values:
Starch 2.5, Carbohydrate 1.0, Meat, lean 1.0

Basic Nutritional Values: Calories 338 (Calories from Fat 68), Total Fat 8 gm (Saturated Fat 2.1 gm, Polyunsat Fat 0.9 gm, Monounsat Fat 3.2 gm, Cholesterol 25 mg), Sodium 763 mg, Total Carbohydrate 52 gm, Dietary Fiber 11 gm, Sugars 22 gm, Protein 17 gm

Fruity Baked Bean Casserole
Elaine Unruh, Minneapolis, MN

Makes 8 servings
(Ideal slow cooker size: 4-5-quart)

1/2 lb. bacon
3 medium onions, chopped
16-oz. can lima beans, drained
16-oz. can kidney beans, drained
16-oz. can baked beans
14 1/2-oz. can baked beans, no added salt
15 1/2-oz. can pineapple chunks, canned in juice
2 Tbsp. brown sugar
brown sugar substitute to equal 2 Tbsp.

1/4 cup cider vinegar
2 Tbsp. molasses
1/2 cup ketchup
2 Tbsp. prepared mustard
1/2 tsp. garlic powder
1 medium green pepper, chopped

1. Cook bacon in skillet. Crumble. Place bacon in slow cooker. Rinse skillet.

2. Saute onions in skillet with fat-free non-stick cooking spray until soft. Drain. Add to bacon in slow cooker.

3. Add beans and pineapple to cooker. Mix well.

4. Combine brown sugar, sugar substitute, vinegar, molasses, ketchup, mustard, garlic powder and green pepper. Mix well. Stir into mixture in slow cooker.

5. Cover. Cook on High 2-3 hours.

Exchange List Values:
Starch 2.5, Fruit 0.5, Carbohydrate 1.0, Vegetable 1.0

Basic Nutritional Values: Calories 350 (Calories from Fat 46), Total Fat 5 gm (Saturated Fat 1.5 gm, Polyunsat Fat 0.9 gm, Monounsat Fat 2.0 gm, Cholesterol 7 mg), Sodium 577 mg, Total Carbohydrate 65 gm, Dietary Fiber 13 gm, Sugars 32 gm, Protein 15 gm

Swimming or water aerobics are just two activities that don't stress the joints. You'll be surprised at how much more energy you have!

Apple Bean Bake

Barbara A. Yoder, Goshen, IN

Makes 12 side dish servings
(Ideal slow cooker size: 4-5-quart)

4 Tbsp. margarine
2 large Granny Smith
  apples, unpeeled, cubed
1/4 cup brown sugar
brown sugar substitute to
  equal 2 Tbsp.
2 Tbsp. sugar
white sugar substitute to
  equal 1 Tbsp.
1/2 cup no-added-salt
  ketchup
1 tsp. cinnamon
1 Tbsp. molasses
24-oz. can Great Northern
  beans, undrained
24-oz. can pinto beans,
  undrained

1. Melt margarine in
skillet. Add apples and cook
until tender.
2. Stir in brown sugar,
sugar, and sugar substitutes.
Cook until they melt. Stir in
ketchup, cinnamon, and
molasses.
3. Add beans. Mix well.
Pour into slow cooker.
4. Cover. Cook on High 2-4
hours.

Exchange List Values:
Starch 1.0, Fruit 0.5,
Carbohydrate 0.5, Fat 1.0

Basic Nutritional Values: Calories
195 (Calories from Fat 44), Total Fat
5 gm (Saturated Fat 0.8 gm,
Polyunsat Fat 1.5 gm, Monounsat Fat
1.8 gm, Cholesterol 0 mg), Sodium

399 mg,Total Carbohydrate 32 gm,
Dietary Fiber 6 gm, Sugars 17 gm,
Protein 6 gm

Ann's Boston Baked Beans

Ann Driscoll
Albuquerque, MN

Makes 20 side dish servings
(Ideal slow cooker size: 4-5-quart)

1 cup raisins
2 small onions, diced
2 tart apples, unpeeled,
  diced
1 cup chili sauce
1 cup chopped extra-lean,
  reduced-sodium ham
1 lb. 15-oz. can baked
  beans
2 14 1/2-oz. cans baked
  beans, no-added-salt
3 tsp. dry mustard
1/2 cup sweet pickle relish

1. Mix together all ingredients.
2. Cover. Cook on Low 6-8
hours.

Exchange List Values:
Starch 1.0, Fruit 0.5,
Carbohydrate 0.5

Basic Nutritional Values: Calories
148 (Calories from Fat 6), Total Fat 1
gm (Saturated Fat 0.1 gm, Polyunsat
Fat 0.2 gm, Monounsat Fat 0.1 gm,
Cholesterol 3 mg), Sodium 443
mg,Total Carbohydrate 32 gm,
Dietary Fiber 6 gm, Sugars 16 gm,
Protein 6 gm

Pheasant a la Elizabeth

Elizabeth L. Richards
Rapid City, SD

Makes 8 servings
(Ideal slow cooker size: 4-quart)

6 half (6 1/2 ozs. each)
  boneless, skinless
  pheasant breasts, cubed
3/4 cup teriyaki sauce
1/3 cup flour
1 1/2 tsp. garlic salt
pepper to taste
2 Tbsp. olive oil
1 large onion, sliced
12-oz. can beer
3/4 cup fresh mushrooms,
  sliced

1. Marinate pheasant in
teriyaki sauce for 2-4 hours.
Remove breasts from teriyaki
sauce (teriyaki sauce should
be disposed of).
2. Combine flour, garlic
salt, and pepper. Dredge
pheasant in flour. Brown in
olive oil in skillet. Add onion
and saute for 3 minutes, stirring frequently. Transfer to
slow cooker.
3. Add beer and mush-
rooms.
4. Cover. Cook on Low 6-8
hours.

Exchange List Values:
Carbohydrate 0.5, Meat,
lean 4.0

Basic Nutritional Values: Calories
260(Calories from Fat 75), Total Fat 8
gm (Saturated Fat 0.5 gm, Polyunsat Fat

1.3 gm, Monounsat Fat 3.9 gm, Cholesterol 92 mg), Sodium 357 mg, Total Carbohydrate 10 gm, Dietary Fiber 1 gm, Sugars 5 gm, Protein 34 gm

Variation: Instead of pheasant, use chicken.

Pot-Roasted Rabbit
Donna Treloar, Gaston, IN

Makes 6 servings
(Ideal slow cooker size: 4-quart)

2 onions, sliced
4-lb. roasting rabbit, skinned
1 garlic clove, sliced
2 bay leaves
1 whole clove
1 cup hot water
2 Tbsp. soy sauce
2 Tbsp. flour
½ cup cold water

1. Place onion in bottom of slow cooker.
2. Insert garlic in rabbit cavity. Place rabbit in slow cooker.
3. Add bay leaves, clove, hot water, and soy sauce to slow cooker.
4. Cover. Cook on Low 10-12 hours.
5. Remove rabbit and thicken gravy by stirring 2 Tbsp. flour blended into ½ cup water into simmering juices in cooker. Continue stirring until gravy thickens. Cut rabbit into serving-size pieces and serve with gravy.

Exchange List Values:
Carbohydrate 0.5, Meat, lean 5.0

Basic Nutritional Values: Calories 294 (Calories from Fat 97), Total Fat 11 gm (Saturated Fat 3.2 gm, Polyunsat Fat 2.1 gm, Monounsat Fat 2.9 gm, Cholesterol 110 mg), Sodium 390 mg, Total Carbohydrate 7 gm, Dietary Fiber 1 gm, Sugars 4 gm, Protein 40 gm

Venison in Sauce
Anona M. Teel, Bangor, PA

Makes 12 sandwiches
(Ideal slow cooker size: 5-quart)

3-4 lb. venison roast
¼ cup vinegar
2 garlic cloves, minced
¼ tsp. salt
cold water
2 Tbsp. oil
1 large onion, sliced
half a green pepper, sliced
2 ribs celery, sliced
1-2 garlic cloves, minced
1½-2 tsp. salt
¼ tsp. pepper
½ tsp. dried oregano
¼ cup ketchup
1 cup tomato juice

1. Combine vinegar, garlic cloves, and ¼ tsp. salt. Pour over venison. Add water until meat is covered. Marinate 6-8 hours.
3. Cut meat into pieces. Brown in oil in skillet. Place in slow cooker.
4. Mix remaining ingredients together; then pour into cooker. Stir in meat.
5. Cover. Cook on Low 8-10 hours.
6. Using two forks, pull the meat apart and then stir it through the sauce.
7. Serve on sandwich rolls, or over rice or pasta.

Exchange List Values:
Vegetable 1.0, Meat, very lean 3.0, Fat 1.0

Basic Nutritional Values: Calories 176 (Calories from Fat 46), Total Fat 5 gm (Saturated Fat 1.4 gm, Polyunsat Fat 1.3 gm, Monounsat Fat 2.0 gm, Cholesterol 96 mg), Sodium 429 mg, Total Carbohydrate 5 gm, Dietary Fiber 1 gm, Sugars 3 gm, Protein 26 gm

Eat some avocado, olives, almonds, or sesame seeds today. Small amounts give your body the good fat that it needs.

Venison Roast
Colleen Heatwole, Burton, MI

Makes 10 servings
(Ideal slow cooker size: 4-5-quart)

3-lb. venison roast
1/4 cup vinegar
2 garlic cloves, minced
1 tsp. salt
1/2 cup chopped onions
15-oz. can no-added-salt
 tomato sauce
1 Tbsp. ground mustard
1 pkg. brown gravy mix
1/2 tsp. salt
1/4 cup water

1. Place venison in deep bowl. Combine vinegar, garlic, and salt. Pour over venison. Add enough cold water to cover venison. Marinate for at least 8 hours in refrigerator.
2. Rinse and drain venison. Place in slow cooker.
3. Combine remaining ingredients and pour over venison.
4. Cover. Cook on Low 10-12 hours.
5. If you wish, serve with a green salad, potatoes, and rolls to make a complete meal.

Exchange List Values:
Vegetable 1.0, Meat, very lean 4.0

Basic Nutritional Values: Calories 186 (Calories from Fat 31), Total Fat 3 gm (Saturated Fat 1.4 gm, Polyunsat Fat 0.7 gm, Monounsat Fat 0.7 gm, Cholesterol 115 mg), Sodium 530 mg, Total

Carbohydrate 5 gm, Dietary Fiber 1 gm, Sugars 4 gm, Protein 31 gm

Note: The sauce on this roast works well for any meat.

This is an easy meal to have for a Saturday dinner with guests or extended family. There is usually a lot of sauce, so make plenty of potatoes, noodles, or rice.

Beef-Venison Barbecue
Gladys Longacre, Susquehanna, PA

Makes 8 servings
(Ideal slow cooker size: 4-quart)

1 1/2 lbs. ground beef
1/2 lb. ground venison
1 medium onion, chopped
1/2 cup chopped green
 peppers
1 garlic clove, minced
1/4 tsp. pepper
1/2 tsp. dried thyme
1 tsp. dried oregano
1 tsp. dried basil
1/4 cup brown sugar
1/4 cup vinegar
1 Tbsp. dry mustard
1 cup ketchup
1/2-1 Tbsp. hickory-smoked
 barbecue sauce
8 hamburger rolls

1. Brown meat in skillet. Place in slow cooker.
2. Add remaining ingredients except rolls. Mix well.
3. Cover. Cook on High 1 hour or Low 2-3 hours.

4. Serve barbecue in hamburger rolls.

Exchange List Values:
Starch 2.0, Carbohydrate 0.5, Meat, lean 3.0

Basic Nutritional Values: Calories 366 (Calories from Fat 111), Total Fat 12 gm (Saturated Fat 4.3 gm, Polyunsat Fat 0.9 gm, Monounsat Fat 5.2 gm, Cholesterol 76 mg), Sodium 634 mg, Total Carbohydrate 37 gm, Dietary Fiber 3 gm, Sugars 15 gm, Protein 27 gm

Note: This recipe can be made in larger quantities to freeze and then reheat when needed.

This barbecue recipe was made in large quantities and served at the concession stand for our farm machinery sale in 1987. They used ice cream dippers to scoop the meat into the sandwich rolls.

Put on some classical music and conduct a pretend orchestra from your chair at home—it can be quite a workout!

Baked Lamb Shanks

Irma H. Schoen, Windsor, CT

Makes 6 servings
(Ideal slow cooker size: 4-quart)

1 medium onion, thinly sliced
2 small carrots, cut in thin strips
1 rib celery, chopped
3 (1 lb. each) lamb shanks, cracked, trimmed of fat
1-2 cloves garlic, split
1/8 tsp. salt
1/4 tsp. pepper
1 tsp. dried oregano
1 tsp. dried thyme
2 bay leaves, crumbled
1/2 cup dry white wine
8-oz. can tomato sauce

1. Place onions, carrots, and celery in slow cooker.
2. Rub lamb with garlic and season with salt and pepper. Add to slow cooker.
3. Mix remaining ingredients together in separate bowl and add to meat and vegetables.
4. Cover. Cook on Low 8-10 hours, or High 4-6 hours.

Exchange List Values:
Vegetable 1.0, Meat, very lean 4.0, Fat 0.5

Basic Nutritional Values: Calories 182 (Calories from Fat 44), Total Fat 5 gm (Saturated Fat 1.7 gm, Polyunsat Fat 0.3 gm, Monounsat Fat 2.1 gm, Cholesterol 83 mg), Sodium 386 mg, Total Carbohydrate 7 gm, Dietary Fiber 2 gm, Sugars 4 gm, Protein 26 gm

Lamb Stew

Dottie Schmidt, Kansas City, MO

Makes 6 servings
(Ideal slow cooker size: 4-quart)

2 lbs. lamb, cubed
1/2 tsp. sugar
2 Tbsp. oil
2 tsp. salt
1/4 tsp. pepper
1/4 cup flour
2 cups water
3/4 cup red cooking wine
1/4 tsp. powdered garlic
2 tsp. Worcestershire sauce
6 medium carrots, sliced
4 small onions, quartered
4 ribs celery, sliced
3 medium potatoes, unpeeled, diced

1. Sprinkle lamb with sugar. Brown in oil in skillet.
2. Remove lamb and place in cooker, reserving drippings. Stir salt, pepper, and flour into drippings until smooth. Stir in water and wine until smooth, stirring until broth simmers and thickens.
3. Pour into cooker. Add remaining ingredients and stir until well mixed.
4. Cover. Cook on Low 8-10 hours.
5. Serve with crusty bread.

Exchange List Values:
Starch 1.5, Vegetable 2.0, Meat, lean 4.0

Basic Nutritional Values: Calories 388 (Calories from Fat 116), Total Fat 13 gm (Saturated Fat 3.2 gm, Polyunsat Fat 2.3 gm, Monounsat Fat 5.9 gm, Cholesterol 98 mg), Sodium 943 mg, Total Carbohydrate 32 gm, Dietary Fiber 5 gm, Sugars 9 gm, Protein 35 gm

Lamb Chops

Shirley Sears, Tiskilwa, IL

Makes 6-8 servings
(Ideal slow cooker size: 4-quart)

1 medium onion, sliced
1 tsp. dried oregano
1/2 tsp. dried thyme
1/2 tsp. garlic powder
1/4 tsp. salt
1/8 tsp. pepper
8 loin lamb chops (13/4-2 lbs.), bone-in, trimmed of visible fat
2 garlic cloves, minced
1/4 cup water

1. Place onion in slow cooker.
2. Combine oregano, thyme, garlic powder, salt, and pepper. Rub over lamb chops. Place in slow cooker. Top with garlic. Pour water down along side of cooker, so as not to disturb the rub on the chops.
3. Cover. Cook on Low 4-6 hours.

Exchange List Values:
Meat, lean 2.0

Basic Nutritional Values: Calories 117 (Calories from Fat 44), Total Fat 5 gm (Saturated Fat 1.7 gm, Polyunsat Fat 0.3 gm, Monounsat Fat 2.1 gm, Cholesterol 48 mg), Sodium 116 mg, Total Carbohydrate 2 gm, Dietary Fiber 0 gm, Sugars 1 gm, Protein 15 gm

Herb Potato-Fish Bake

Barbara Sparks
Glen Burnie, MD

Makes 4 servings
(Ideal slow cooker size: 4-quart)

10³/₄-oz. can cream of celery soup
¹/₂ cup water
1-lb. perch fillet, fresh or thawed
2 cups cooked, diced potatoes, drained
¹/₄ cup freshly grated Parmesan cheese
1 Tbsp. chopped parsley
¹/₂ tsp. dried basil
¹/₄ tsp. dried oregano

1. Combine soup and water. Pour half in slow cooker. Spread fillet on top. Place potatoes on fillet. Pour remaining soup mix over top.

2. Combine cheese and herbs. Sprinkle over ingredients in slow cooker.

3. Cover. Cook on High 1-2 hours, being careful not to overcook fish.

Exchange List Values:
Starch 1.0, Carbohydrate 0.5, Meat, lean 3.0

Basic Nutritional Values: Calories 269 (Calories from Fat 73), Total Fat 8 gm (Saturated Fat 2.8 gm, Polyunsat Fat 2.3 gm, Monounsat Fat 2.2 gm, Cholesterol 56 mg), Sodium 696 mg, Total Carbohydrate 22 gm, Dietary Fiber 2 gm, Sugars 2 gm, Protein 26 gm

Shrimp Jambalaya

Karen Ashworth
Duenweg, MO

Makes 8 servings
(Ideal slow cooker size: 4-quart)

2 Tbsp. margarine
2 medium onions, chopped
2 green bell peppers, chopped
3 ribs celery, chopped
1 cup chopped extra-lean, lower-sodium cooked ham
2 garlic cloves, chopped
1¹/₂ cups minute rice
1¹/₂ cups 99%-fat-free, lower-sodium beef broth
28-oz. can chopped tomatoes
2 Tbsp. chopped parsley
1 tsp. dried basil
¹/₂ tsp. dried thyme
¹/₄ tsp. pepper
¹/₈ tsp. cayenne pepper
1 lb. shelled, deveined, medium-size shrimp
1 Tbsp. chopped parsley for garnish

1. Melt margarine in slow cooker set on High. Add onions, peppers, celery, ham, and garlic. Cook 30 minutes.

2. Add rice. Cover and cook 15 minutes.

3. Add broth, tomatoes, 2 Tbsp. parsley, and remaining seasonings. Cover and cook on High 1 hour.

4. Add shrimp. Cook on High 30 minutes, or until liquid is absorbed.

5. Garnish with 1 Tbsp. parsley.

Exchange List Values:
Starch 1.0, Vegetable 2.0, Meat, lean 1.0, Fat 0.5

Basic Nutritional Values: Calories 205 (Calories from Fat 36), Total Fat 4 gm (Saturated Fat 0.8 gm, Polyunsat Fat 1.3 gm, Monounsat Fat 1.5 gm, Cholesterol 95 mg), Sodium 529 mg, Total Carbohydrate 26 gm, Dietary Fiber 3 gm, Sugars 7 gm, Protein 16 gm

Jambalaya

Doris M. Coyle-Zipp
South Ozone Park, NY

Makes 5-6 servings
(Ideal slow cooker size: 4-quart)

3¹/₂-4-lb. roasting chicken, trimmed of skin and fat, cut up
3 onions, diced
1 carrot, sliced
3-4 garlic cloves, minced
1 tsp. dried oregano
1 tsp. dried basil
¹/₂ tsp. salt
¹/₈ tsp. white pepper
14-oz. can crushed tomatoes
1 lb. shelled raw shrimp
2 cups cooked rice

1. Combine all ingredients except shrimp and rice in slow cooker.

2. Cover. Cook on Low 2-3¹/₂ hours, or until chicken is tender.

3. Add shrimp and rice.

4. Cover. Cook on High 15-20 minutes, or until shrimp are done.

Exchange List Values:
Starch 1.0, Vegetable 3.0, Meat, lean 4.0

Basic Nutritional Values: Calories 354 (Calories from Fat 65), Total Fat 7 gm (Saturated Fat 1.9 gm, Polyunsat Fat 1.8 gm, Monounsat Fat 2.4 gm, Cholesterol 192 mg), Sodium 589 mg, Total Carbohydrate 29 gm, Dietary Fiber 4 gm, Sugars 9 gm, Protein 41 gm

Shrimp Creole
Carol Findling
Princeton, IL

Makes 8-10 servings
(Ideal slow cooker size: 4-5-quart)

1/4 cup canola oil
1/3 cup flour
1 3/4 cups sliced onions
1 cup diced green peppers
1 cup diced celery
1 1/2 large carrots, shredded
2 3/4-lb. can tomatoes
3/4 cup water
1/2 tsp. dried thyme
1 garlic clove, minced
pinch of rosemary
1 Tbsp. sugar
3 bay leaves
1 Tbsp. Worcestershire sauce
3/4 tsp. salt
1/8 tsp. dried oregano
2 lbs. shelled shrimp, deveined

1. Combine canola oil and flour in a skillet. Brown, stirring constantly. Add onions, green peppers, celery, and carrots. Cook 5-10 minutes. Transfer to slow cooker.

2. Add remaining ingredients, except shrimp, and stir well.

3. Cover. Cook on Low 6-8 hours.

4. Add shrimp during last hour.

5. Serve over rice.

Exchange List Values:
Vegetable 3.0, Meat, very lean 2.0, Fat 1.0

Basic Nutritional Values: Calories 187 (Calories from Fat 59), Total Fat 7 gm (Saturated Fat 0.6 gm, Polyunsat Fat 2.1 gm, Monounsat Fat 3.4 gm, Cholesterol 140 mg), Sodium 563 mg, Total Carbohydrate 15 gm, Dietary Fiber 3 gm, Sugars 8 gm, Protein 17 gm

Talk positively to yourself; don't talk down. If your sugar level was high, think, "I was high, and I treated it," rather than "I was high; I failed."

Oriental Shrimp Casserole
Sharon Wantland
Menomonee Falls, WI

Makes 10 servings
(Ideal slow cooker size: 4-quart)

4 cups cooked rice
2 cups cooked or canned shrimp
1 cup cooked or canned chicken
1-lb. can (2 cups) Chinese vegetables
10 3/4-oz. can cream of celery soup
1/2 cup milk
1/2 cup chopped green peppers
1 Tbsp. soy sauce
3-oz. can dried Chinese noodles

1. Combine all ingredients except noodles in slow cooker.

2. Cover. Cook on Low 45 minutes.

3. Top with noodles just before serving.

Exchange List Values:
Starch 2.0, Meat, lean 1.0

Basic Nutritional Values: Calories 216 (Calories from Fat 54), Total Fat 6 gm (Saturated Fat 1.5 gm, Polyunsat Fat 2.5 gm, Monounsat Fat 1.5 gm, Cholesterol 58 mg), Sodium 452 mg, Total Carbohydrate 27 gm, Dietary Fiber 1 gm, Sugars 1 gm, Protein 12 gm

Seafood Gumbo

Barbara Katrine Rose
Woodbridge, VA

Makes 6 servings
(Ideal slow cooker size: 4-5-quart)

1 Tbsp. canola oil
1 lb. okra, sliced
2 Tbsp. canola oil
1/4 cup flour
1 bunch green onions, sliced
1/2 cup chopped celery
2 garlic cloves, minced
16-oz. can tomatoes and
  juice
1 bay leaf
1 Tbsp. chopped fresh
  parsley
1 fresh thyme sprig
1/2 tsp. salt
1/2-1 tsp. red pepper
3-5 cups water, depending
  upon the consistency you
  like
1 lb. peeled and deveined
  fresh shrimp
1/2 lb. fresh crabmeat

1. Saute okra in 1 Tbsp. canola oil until okra is lightly browned. Transfer to slow cooker.
2. Combine 2 Tbsp. canola oil and flour in skillet. Cook over medium heat, stirring constantly until roux is the color of chocolate, 20-25 minutes. Stir in green onions, celery, and garlic. Cook until vegetables are tender. Add to slow cooker. Gently stir in remaining ingredients.
3. Cover. Cook on High 3-4 hours.
4. Serve over rice.

Exchange List Values:
egetable 3.0, Meat, very
lean 2.0, Fat 1.5

Basic Nutritional Values: Calories 221 (Calories from Fat 75), Total Fat 8 gm (Saturated Fat 0.7 gm, Polyunsat Fat 2.6 gm, Monounsat Fat 4.3 gm, Cholesterol 148 mg), Sodium 548 mg, Total Carbohydrate 15 gm, Dietary Fiber 3 gm, Sugars 5 gm, Protein 22 gm

Curried Shrimp

Charlotte Shaffer, East Earl, PA

Makes 5 servings
(Ideal slow cooker size: 3-4-quart)

1 small onion, chopped
2 cups cooked shrimp
1 tsp. curry powder
10 3/4-oz. can 98%-fat-free,
  lower-sodium cream of
  mushroom soup
1 cup fat-free sour cream

1. Combine all ingredients except sour cream in slow cooker.
2. Cover. Cook on Low 4-6 hours.
3. Ten minutes before serving, stir in sour cream.
4. Serve over rice or puff pastry.

Exchange List Values:
Starch 2.0, Meat, lean 1.0

Basic Nutritional Values: Calories 130 (Calories from Fat 16), Total Fat 2 gm (Saturated Fat 0.6 gm, Polyunsat Fat 0.5 gm, Monounsat Fat 0.4 gm, Cholesterol 92 mg), Sodium 390

mg, Total Carbohydrate 15 gm, Dietary Fiber 1 gm, Sugars 5 gm, Protein 12 gm

Variation: Add another 1/2 tsp. curry for some added flavor.

Company Seafood Pasta

Jennifer Yoder Sommers
Harrisonburg, VA

Makes 8 servings
(Ideal slow cooker size: 4-quart)

2 cups fat-free sour cream
5 ozs. (1 1/4 cups) shredded
  reduced-fat Monterey
  Jack cheese
1 Tbsp. light, soft tub
  margarine, melted
1/2 lb. fresh crabmeat
1/8 tsp. pepper
1/2 lb. bay scallops, lightly
  cooked
1 lb. medium shrimp,
  cooked and peeled
4 cups cooked linguine

1. Combine sour cream, cheese, and margarine in slow cooker.
2. Stir in remaining ingredients, except linguine.
3. Cover. Cook on Low 1-2 hours.
4. Serve immediately over linguine. Garnish with fresh parsley.

Exchange List Values:
Starch 2.0, Meat, lean 3.0

Basic Nutritional Values: Calories 308 (Calories from Fat 59), Total Fat 7 gm (Saturated Fat 3.1 gm, Polyunsat Fat

1.1 gm, Monounsat Fat 2.1 gm, Cholesterol 127 mg), Sodium 449 mg,Total Carbohydrate 31 gm, Dietary Fiber 1 gm, Sugars 5 gm, Protein 29 gm

Seafood Medley

Susan Alexander,
Baltimore, MD

Makes 12 servings
(Ideal slow cooker size: 4-quart)

1 lb. peeled and deveined shrimp
1 lb. crabmeat
1 lb. bay scallops
2 10³/4-oz. cans cream of celery soup
2 soup cans fat-free milk
3 tsp. margarine
1 tsp. Old Bay seasoning
1/4 tsp. pepper

1. Layer shrimp, crab, and scallops in slow cooker.
2. Combine soup and milk. Pour over seafood.
3. Mix together margarine and spices and pour over top.
4. Cover. Cook on Low 3-4 hours.
5. Serve over rice or noodles.

Exchange List Values:
Carbohydrate 0.5, Meat, very lean 3.0, Fat 0.5

Basic Nutritional Values: Calories 168 (Calories from Fat 51), Total Fat 6 gm (Saturated Fat 1.6 gm, Polyunsat Fat 2.1 gm, Monounsat Fat 1.5 gm, Cholesterol 106 mg), Sodium 679 mg,Total Carbohydrate 7 gm, Dietary Fiber 0 gm, Sugars 3 gm, Protein 20 gm

Salmon Cheese Casserole

Wanda S. Curtin
Bradenton, FL

Makes 6 servings
(Ideal slow cooker size: 4-quart)

14³/4-oz. can salmon, canned without salt, but with liquid
4-oz. can mushrooms, drained
1 1/2 cups bread crumbs
2 eggs, beaten
1/2 cup grated reduced-fat cheddar cheese
1 Tbsp. lemon juice
1 Tbsp. minced onion

1. Flake fish in bowl, removing bones. Stir in remaining ingredients. Pour into lightly greased slow cooker.
2. Cover. Cook on Low 3-4 hours.

Exchange List Values:
Starch 1.5, Meat, medium fat 2.0

Basic Nutritional Values: Calories 257 (Calories from Fat 85), Total Fat 9 gm (Saturated Fat 2.9 gm, Polyunsat Fat 2.2 gm, Monounsat Fat 3.0 gm, Cholesterol 116 mg), Sodium 442 mg,Total Carbohydrate 21 gm, Dietary Fiber 1 gm, Sugars 2 gm, Protein 23 gm

Tuna Barbecue

Esther Martin
Ephrata, PA

Makes 4 servings
(Ideal slow cooker size: 3-4-quart)

12-oz. can tuna, packed in water, drained
2 cups no-salt-added tomato juice
1 medium green pepper, finely chopped
2 Tbsp. onion flakes
2 Tbsp. Worcestershire sauce
3 Tbsp. vinegar
2 Tbsp. sugar
1 Tbsp. prepared mustard
1 rib celery, chopped
dash chili powder
1/2 tsp. cinnamon
dash hot sauce, optional

1. Combine all ingredients in slow cooker.
2. Cover. Cook on Low 8-10 hours, or High 4-5 hours. If mixture becomes too dry while cooking, add 1/2 cup tomato juice.
3. Serve on buns.

Exchange List Values:
Carbohydrate 0.5, Vegetable 2.0, Meat, very lean 2.0

Basic Nutritional Values: Calories 162 (Calories from Fat 8), Total Fat 1 gm (Saturated Fat 0.2 gm, Polyunsat Fat 0.3 gm, Monounsat Fat 0.3 gm, Cholesterol 23 mg), Sodium 423 mg,Total Carbohydrate 18 gm, Dietary Fiber 2 gm, Sugars 14 gm, Protein 21 gm

Tuna Noodle Casserole

Leona Miller
Millersburg, OH

Makes 6 servings
(Ideal slow cooker size: 4-quart)

2 6^1/$_2$-oz. cans water-packed tuna, drained
2 10^1/$_2$-oz. cans 98%-fat-free, lower-sodium cream of mushroom soup
1 cup milk
2 Tbsp. dried parsley
10-oz. pkg. frozen mixed vegetables, thawed
8-oz. pkg. noodles, cooked and drained
^{1}/$_2$ cup toasted sliced almonds

1. Combine tuna, soup, milk, parsley, and vegetables. Fold in noodles. Pour into greased slow cooker. Top with almonds.
2. Cover. Cook on Low 7-9 hours, or High 3-4 hours.

Exchange List Values:
Starch 2.0, Carbohydrate 1.0, Meat, lean 3.0

Basic Nutritional Values: Calories 395 (Calories from Fat 101), Total Fat 11 gm (Saturated Fat 1.9 gm, Polyunsat Fat 2.5 gm, Monounsat Fat 5.7 gm, Cholesterol 21 mg), Sodium 637 mg, Total Carbohydrate 46 gm, Dietary Fiber 5 gm, Sugars 8 gm, Protein 27 gm

Easy Stuffed Shells

Rebecca Plank Leichty
Harrisonburg, VA

Makes 7 servings
(Ideal slow cooker size: 4-quart)

20-oz. bag frozen stuffed shells
15-oz. can marinara or spaghetti sauce
15-oz. can green beans, drained

1. Place shells around edge of greased slow cooker.
2. Cover with marinara sauce.
3. Pour green beans in center.
4. Cover. Cook on Low 8 hours or on High 3 hours.
5. Serve with garlic toast and salad.

Exchange List Values:
Starch 1.0, Vegetable 2.0, Fat 1.5

Basic Nutritional Values: Calories 221 (Calories from Fat 66), Total Fat 7 gm (Saturated Fat 3.2 gm, Polyunsat Fat 0.9 gm, Monounsat Fat 2.2 gm, Cholesterol 66 mg), Sodium 728 mg, Total Carbohydrate 27 gm, Dietary Fiber 3 gm, Sugars 7 gm, Protein 10 gm

Variation: Reverse Steps 2 and 3. Double the amount of marinara sauce and pour over both the shells and the beans.

Tempeh-Stuffed Peppers

Sara Harter Fredette
Williamsburg, MA

Makes 4 servings
(Ideal slow cooker size: 6-quart oval, so the peppers can each sit on the bottom of slow cooker)

4 ozs. tempeh, cubed
1 garlic clove, minced
2 14^1/$_2$-oz. cans diced tomatoes, no-salt-added
2 tsp. soy sauce
^{1}/$_4$ cup chopped onions
1^1/$_2$ cups cooked rice
1 cup shredded fat-free cheddar cheese
Tabasco sauce, optional
4 green, red, or yellow, bell peppers, tops removed and seeded
^{1}/$_4$ cup shredded fat-free cheddar cheese

1. Steam tempeh 10 minutes in saucepan. Mash in bowl with garlic, half the tomatoes, and soy sauce.
2. Stir in onions, rice, 1 cup cheese, and Tabasco sauce. Stuff into peppers.
3. Place peppers in slow cooker. Pour remaining half of tomatoes over peppers.
4. Cover. Cook on Low 6-8 hours, or High 3-4 hours. Top with ^{1}/$_4$ cup cheese in last 30 minutes.

Exchange List Values:
Starch 2.0, Vegetable 3.0, Meat, lean 1.0

Basic Nutritional Values: Calories 266 (Calories from Fat 26), Total Fat 3 gm (Saturated Fat 0.1 gm, Polyunsat Fat 1.5 gm, Monounsat Fat 0.6 gm, Cholesterol 4 mg), Sodium 510 mg, Total Carbohydrate 42 gm, Dietary Fiber 6 gm, Sugars 17 gm, Protein 21 gm

Minestra Di Ceci

Jeanette Oberholtzer
Manheim, PA

Makes 8 servings
(Ideal slow cooker size: 4-quart)

1 lb. dry chickpeas
water
1 sprig fresh rosemary
10 leaves fresh sage
1 Tbsp. salt
water
1-2 large garlic cloves, minced
1 tsp. canola oil
1 cup small dry pasta, your choice of shape

1. Wash chickpeas. Place in slow cooker. Soak for 8 hours in full pot of water, along with rosemary, sage, and salt.
2. Drain water. Remove herbs.
3. Refill slow cooker with water to 1" above peas.
4. Cover. Cook on Low 5 hours.
5. Saute garlic in olive oil in skillet until clear.
6. Puree half of peas, along with several cups of broth from cooker, in blender. Return puree to slow cooker.

Add garlic and oil.
7. Boil pasta in saucepan until al dente, about 5 minutes. Drain. Add to peas.
8. Cover. Cook on High 30-60 minutes, or until pasta is tender and heated through, but not mushy.

Exchange List Values:
Starch 2.5, Meat, very lean 1.0

Basic Nutritional Values: Calories 236 (Calories from Fat 34), Total Fat 4 gm (Saturated Fat 0.4 gm, Polyunsat Fat 1.5 gm, Monounsat Fat 1.1 gm, Cholesterol 0 mg), Sodium 445 mg, Total Carbohydrate 40 gm, Dietary Fiber 9 gm, Sugars 7 gm, Protein 12 gm

Variation: Add 1/2 tsp. black pepper to Step 1, if you like.

Wear a medical alert bracelet or necklace that says "diabetes"—not to call attention to your condition, but to tell medical personnel to check your sugar level if an emergency happened.

Barbecued Lentils

Sue Hamilton
Minooka, IL

Makes 8 servings
(Ideal slow cooker size: 4-quart)

2 cups Phyllis' Low-Sodium Barbecue Sauce (recipe on page 254)
3 1/2 cups water
1 lb. dry lentils
9.7-oz. pkg. vegetarian hot dogs, sliced

1. Combine all ingredients in slow cooker.
2. Cover. Cook on Low 6-8 hours.

Exchange List Values:
Starch 2.0, Vegetable 2.0, Meat, very lean 2.0

Basic Nutritional Values: Calories 270 (Calories from Fat 9), Total Fat 1 gm (Saturated Fat 0.1 gm, Polyunsat Fat 0.5 gm, Monounsat Fat 0.2 gm, Cholesterol 0 mg), Sodium 464 mg, Total Carbohydrate 43 gm, Dietary Fiber 15 gm, Sugars 12 gm, Protein 23 gm

Arroz Con Queso

Nadine L. Martinitz, Salina, KS

Makes 6-8 servings
(Ideal slow cooker size: 4-quart)

14½-oz. can whole
  tomatoes, mashed
15-oz. can Mexican style
  beans, undrained
1½ cups uncooked long
  grain rice
3 ozs. grated reduced-fat
  Monterey Jack cheese
1 large onion, finely
  chopped
1 cup Low-fat cottage
  cheese
4¼-oz. can chopped green
  chili peppers, drained
1 Tbsp. canola oil
3 garlic cloves, minced
3 ozs. grated reduced-fat
  Monterey Jack cheese

1. Combine all ingredients
except final 3 ozs. of cheese.
Pour into well greased slow
cooker.
   2. Cover. Cook on Low 6-9
hours.
   3. Sprinkle with remaining
cheese before serving.
   4. Serve with salsa.

Exchange List Values:
Starch 2.5, Vegetable 1.0,
Meat, medium fat 1.0

Basic Nutritional Values: Calories
294 (Calories from Fat 59), Total Fat
7 gm (Saturated Fat 3.3 gm,
Polyunsat Fat 0.9 gm, Monounsat Fat
2.3 gm, Cholesterol 16 mg), Sodium
589 mg, Total Carbohydrate 42 gm,
Dietary Fiber 4 gm, Sugars 6 gm,
Protein 16 gm

Cheese Souffle Casserole

Vicki Dinkel
Sharon Spring, KS

Makes 8 servings
(Ideal slow cooker size: 4-quart)

14 slices fresh bread,
  crusts removed, divided
5 ozs. (1¼ cups) grated
  reduced-fat sharp
  cheddar cheese, divided
1 Tbsp. light, soft tub
  margarine, melted,
  divided
3 eggs
4 egg whites
2 cups fat-free milk,
  scalded
1 cup fat-free half-and-half
2 tsp. Worcestershire sauce
paprika

1. Tear bread into small
pieces. Place half in well-
greased slow cooker. Add half
the grated cheese and half the
butter. Repeat layers.
   2. Beat together eggs and
egg whites, milk, half-and-
half, and Worcestershire
sauce. Pour over bread and
cheese. Sprinkle top with
paprika.
   3. Cover. Cook on Low 4-6
hours.

Exchange List Values:
Starch 1.0, Milk, fat-free
0.5, Meat, medium fat 1.0

Basic Nutritional Values: Calories
205 (Calories from Fat 70), Total Fat
8 gm (Saturated Fat 3.4 gm,

Polyunsat Fat 1.1 gm, Monounsat Fat
2.3 gm, Cholesterol 96 mg), Sodium
468 mg, Total Carbohydrate 23 gm,
Dietary Fiber 1 gm, Sugars 7 gm,
Protein 14 gm

Macaroni and Cheese

Sherry L. Lapp
Lancaster, PA

Makes 10 servings
(Ideal slow cooker size: 4-5-quart)

8-oz. pkg. elbow macaroni,
  cooked al dente
12-oz. can fat-free
  evaporated milk
1 cup fat-free half-and-half
2 Tbsp. light, soft tub
  margarine, melted
2 large eggs, slightly beaten
6 ozs. (1½ cups) grated
  sharp reduced-fat
  cheddar cheese, divided
⅛ tsp. white pepper
¼ cup grated Parmesan
  cheese

1. In slow cooker, combine
lightly cooked macaroni,
evaporated milk, half-and-
half, melted margarine, eggs,
1 cup cheddar cheese, and
pepper.
   2. Top with remaining
cheddar and Parmesan
cheeses.
   3. Cover. Cook on Low
3 hours.

Exchange List Values:
Starch 1.0, Milk, fat-free
0.5, Meat, lean 1.0, Fat 0.5

Basic Nutritional Values: Calories
200 (Calories from Fat 64), Total Fat
7 gm (Saturated Fat 3.3 gm,
Polyunsat Fat 0.6 gm, Monounsat Fat
2.3 gm, Cholesterol 59 mg), Sodium
310 mg, Total Carbohydrate 24 gm,
Dietary Fiber 1 gm, Sugars 6 gm,
Protein 13 gm

Crockpot Macaroni

Lisa F. Good
Harrisonburg, VA

Makes 6 servings
(Ideal slow cooker size: 4-quart)

1½ cups dry macaroni
1½ Tbsp. light, soft tub
   margarine
6 ozs. light Velveeta cheese,
   sliced
2 cups fat-free milk
1 cup fat-free half-and-half

1. Combine macaroni, and
butter.
2. Layer cheese over top.
3. Pour in milk and half-
and-half.
4. Cover. Cook on High 3-4
hours, or until macaroni are
soft.

Exchange List Values:
Starch 1.0, Milk, fat-free
1.0, Fat 1.0

Basic Nutritional Values: Calories
208 (Calories from Fat 45), Total Fat
5 gm (Saturated Fat 2.5 gm,
Polyunsat Fat 0.5 gm, Monounsat Fat

1.6 gm, Cholesterol 15 mg), Sodium
555 mg, Total Carbohydrate 27 gm,
Dietary Fiber 0 gm, Sugars 12 gm,
Protein 14 gm

Spaghetti Sauce

Doris Perkins
Mashpee, MA

Makes 20 servings
(Ideal slow cooker size: 4-5-quart)

2 slices bacon, diced
1¼ lbs. ground beef
½ lb. ground pork
1 cup chopped onions
½ cup chopped green
   peppers
3 garlic cloves, minced
2 2 lb. 3-oz. cans Italian
   tomatoes
2 6-oz. cans tomato paste
1 cup dry red wine, or
   water
2½ tsp. dried oregano
2½ tsp. dried basil
1 bay leaf, crumbled
¾ cup water
¼ cup chopped fresh
   parsley
1 tsp. dried thyme
1 tsp. salt
¼ tsp. pepper
¼ cup dry red wine, or
   water

1. Brown bacon in skillet
until crisp. Drain. Remove.
Add ground beef and pork.
Crumble and cook until
brown. Stir in onions, green
peppers, and garlic. Cook 10
minutes. Drain fat and pat
dry with absorbent toweling.

2. Pour tomatoes into slow
cooker and crush with back
of spoon.
3. Add all other ingredi-
ents, except ¼ cup wine, in
slow cooker.
4. Cover. Bring to boil on
High. Reduce heat to Low for
3-4 hours.
5. During last 30 minutes,
stir in wine or water.

Exchange List Values:
Vegetable 2.0, Meat,
medium fat 1.0

Basic Nutritional Values: Calories
115 (Calories from Fat 46), Total Fat
5 gm (Saturated Fat 1.8 gm,
Polyunsat Fat 0.4 gm, Monounsat Fat
2.2 gm, Cholesterol 25 mg), Sodium
309 mg, Total Carbohydrate 9 gm,
Dietary Fiber 2 gm, Sugars 4 gm,
Protein 9 gm

**Did you know that
fat-free foods can
sometimes be higher in
calories and carbohy-
drates than the original
version? Read the two
labels and compare.**

Chunky Spaghetti Sauce

Patti Boston
Newark, OH

Makes 12 cups
(Ideal slow cooker size: 4-quart)

1 lb. ground beef, browned
  and drained
1/2 lb. bulk sausage,
  browned and drained
14 1/2-oz. can no-added-salt
  Italian tomatoes with
  basil
15-oz. can Italian tomato
  sauce
1 medium onion, chopped
1 green pepper, chopped
8-oz. can sliced
  mushrooms
1/2 cup dry red wine
2 tsp. sugar
1 tsp. minced garlic
1 1/2 tsp. dried basil

1. Combine all ingredients
in slow cooker.
2. Cover. Cook on High
3 1/2-4 hours, or Low 7-8
hours.

Basic Nutritional Values: Calories
134 (Calories from Fat 61), Total Fat
7 gm (Saturated Fat 2.5 gm,
Polyunsat Fat 0.5 gm, Monounsat Fat
2.9 gm, Cholesterol 30 mg), Sodium
397 mg, Total Carbohydrate 8 gm,
Dietary Fiber 2 gm, Sugars 4 gm,
Protein 11 gm

Variations:
1. For added texture and zest,
add 3 fresh, medium-sized
tomatoes, chopped, and 4 large
fresh basil leaves, torn. Stir in
1 tsp. salt and 1/2 tsp. pepper.
2. To any leftover sauce, add
chickpeas or kidney beans and
serve chili!

Sausage-Beef Spaghetti Sauce

Jeannine Janzen
Elbing, KS

Makes 16-20 servings
(Ideal slow cooker size: 4-quart)

1 lb. ground beef
1 lb. Italian sausage, sliced
2 28-oz. cans crushed
  tomatoes
3/4 can (28-oz. tomato can)
  water
2 tsp. garlic powder
1 tsp. pepper
2 Tbsp. or more parsley
2 Tbsp. dried oregano
2 12-oz. cans tomato paste
2 12-oz. cans tomato puree

1. Brown ground beef and
sausage in skillet. Drain.
Transfer to large slow cooker.
2. Add crushed tomatoes,
water, garlic powder, pepper,
parsley, and oregano.
3. Cover. Cook on High 30
minutes. Add tomato paste
and tomato puree. Cook on
Low 6 hours.

Basic Nutritional Values: Calories
176 (Calories from Fat 71), Total Fat
8 gm (Saturated Fat 2.7 gm,
Polyunsat Fat 0.8 gm, Monounsat Fat
3.1 gm, Cholesterol 27 mg), Sodium
408 mg, Total Carbohydrate 17 gm,
Dietary Fiber 4 gm, Sugars 6 gm,
Protein 10 gm

Note: Leftovers freeze well.

Easy-Does-It Spaghetti

Rachel Kauffman, Alto, MI
Lois Stoltzfus, Honey Brook, PA
Deb Unternahrer, Wayland, IA

Makes 12 servings
(Ideal slow cooker size: 4-quart)

2 lbs. 85%-lean ground
  chuck, browned and
  drained
1 cup chopped onions
2 cloves garlic, minced
2 15-oz. cans no-salt-added
  tomato sauce
3 tsp. Italian seasoning
1/4 tsp. pepper
2 4-oz. cans sliced
  mushrooms, drained
6 cups tomato juice
16 ozs. dry spaghetti,
  broken into 4-5-inch
  pieces

1. Combine all ingredients
except spaghetti in slow
cooker.

2. Cover. Cook on Low 6-8 hours, or High 3-5 hours. Turn to High during last 30 minutes and stir in dry spaghetti. (If spaghetti is not fully cooked, continue cooking another 10 minutes, checking to make sure it is not becoming over-cooked.)

3. Sprinkle individual servings with Parmesan cheese if diets permit.

Exchange List Values:
Starch 2.0, Vegetable 2.0, Meat, lean 2.0

Basic Nutritional Values: Calories 328 (Calories from Fat 78), Total Fat 9 gm (Saturated Fat 3.0 gm, Polyunsat Fat 0.6 gm, Monounsat Fat 3.5 gm, Cholesterol 45 mg), Sodium 547 mg, Total Carbohydrate 42 gm, Dietary Fiber 3 gm, Sugars 10 gm, Protein 22 gm

Variation: Add 1 tsp. dry mustard and 1/2 tsp. allspice in Step 1.

Kathy Hertzler
Lancaster, PA

Mom's Meatballs

Mary C. Casey, Scranton, PA

Makes 8-10 servings
(Ideal slow cooker size: 4-5-quart)

Sauce:
2 Tbsp. canola oil
1/4-1/2 cup chopped onions
3 garlic cloves, minced
29-oz. can tomato puree
29-oz. can water

12-oz. can tomato paste
12-oz. can water
1 Tbsp. sugar
2 tsp. dried oregano
1/4 tsp. Italian seasoning
1/2 tsp. dried basil
1/8 tsp. pepper
1/4 cup diced green peppers

Meatballs:
1 lb. 85%-lean ground beef
1 egg
2 Tbsp. water
3/4 cup Italian bread crumbs
1/8 tsp. black pepper
1/8 tsp. salt
1 Tbsp. canola oil

1. Saute onions and garlic in oil in saucepan.

2. Combine all sauce ingredients in slow cooker.

3. Cover. Cook on Low while making meatballs.

4. Mix together all meatball ingredients except oil. Form into small meatballs, then brown on all sides in oil in saucepan. Drain on paper towels. Add to sauce.

5. Cover. Cook on Low 4-5 hours.

Exchange List Values:
Starch 0.5, Vegetable 3.0, Meat, medium fat 1.0, Fat 1.0

Basic Nutritional Values: Calories 221 (Calories from Fat 91), Total Fat 10 gm (Saturated Fat 2.4 gm, Polyunsat Fat 1.7 gm, Monounsat Fat 4.9 gm, Cholesterol 48 mg), Sodium 540 mg, Total Carbohydrate 22 gm, Dietary Fiber 4 gm, Sugars 7 gm, Protein 13 gm

Nancy's Spaghetti Sauce

Nancy Graves
Manhattan, KS

Makes 4-6 servings
(Ideal slow cooker size: 4-quart)

1/4 cup minced onion
garlic powder to taste
3 cups chopped fresh tomatoes
6-oz. can tomato paste
1/2 tsp. salt
dash of pepper
1 basil leaf
1 chopped green pepper
1 lb. ground beef, browned and drained
4-oz. can sliced mushrooms, undrained

1. Combine all ingredients in slow cooker.

2. Cover. Cook on Low 3 hours.

Exchange List Values:
Vegetable 2.0, Meat, lean 2.0, Fat 0.5

Basic Nutritional Values: Calories 186 (Calories from Fat 75), Total Fat 8 gm (Saturated Fat 3.0 gm, Polyunsat Fat 0.5 gm, Monounsat Fat 3.4 gm, Cholesterol 45 mg), Sodium 372 mg, Total Carbohydrate 12 gm, Dietary Fiber 3 gm, Sugars 4 gm, Protein 17 gm

Take a walk after dinner instead of watching TV.

Spaghetti with Meat Sauce

Esther Lehman, Croghan, NY

Makes 8-10 servings
(Ideal slow cooker size: 4-5-quart)

1 lb. ground beef, browned
2 28-oz. cans tomatoes
2 medium onions,
    quartered
2 medium carrots, cut into
    chunks
2 garlic cloves, minced
6-oz. can tomato paste
2 Tbsp. chopped fresh
    parsley
1 bay leaf
1 Tbsp. sugar
1 tsp. dried basil
1/2 tsp. salt
1/2 tsp. dried oregano
dash pepper
2 Tbsp. cold water
2 Tbsp. cornstarch

1. Place meat in slow cooker.
2. In blender, combine 1 can tomatoes, onions, carrots, and garlic. Cover and blend until finely chopped. Stir into meat.
3. Cut up the remaining can of tomatoes. Stir into meat mixture. Add tomato paste, parsley, bay leaf, sugar, basil, salt, oregano, and pepper. Mix well.
4. Cover. Cook on Low 8-10 hours.
5. To serve, turn to High. Remove bay leaf. Cover and heat until bubbly, about 10 minutes.

6. Combine water and cornstarch. Stir into tomato mixture. Cook 10 minutes longer.
7. Serve with spaghetti and Parmesan cheese.

Exchange List Values:
Vegetable 3.0, Meat, lean 1.0, Fat 0.5

Basic Nutritional Values: Calories 151 (Calories from Fat 46), Total Fat 5 gm (Saturated Fat 1.8 gm, Polyunsat Fat 0.4 gm, Monounsat Fat 2.1 gm, Cholesterol 27 mg), Sodium 403 mg, Total Carbohydrate 17 gm, Dietary Fiber 3 gm, Sugars 8 gm, Protein 11 gm

Pasta Sauce with Meat and Veggies

Maria Foikerts
Holland, OH

Makes 6 servings
(Ideal slow cooker size: 4-quart)

1/2 lb. ground turkey,
    browned and drained
1/2 lb. ground beef,
    browned and drained
1 rib celery, chopped
2 medium carrots,
    chopped
1 garlic clove, minced
1 medium onion, chopped
28-oz. can diced tomatoes
    with juice
1/4 tsp. salt
1/4 tsp. dried thyme
6-oz. can tomato paste
1/8 tsp. pepper

1. Combine turkey, beef, celery, carrots, garlic, and onion in slow cooker.
2. Add remaining ingredients. Mix well.
3. Cover. Cook on Low 7-8 hours.
4. Serve over pasta or rice.

Exchange List Values:
Vegetable 3.0, Meat, lean 2.0, Fat 0.5

Basic Nutritional Values: Calories 200 (Calories from Fat 72), Total Fat 8 gm (Saturated Fat 2.4 gm, Polyunsat Fat 1.3 gm, Monounsat Fat 3.1 gm, Cholesterol 50 mg), Sodium 391 mg, Total Carbohydrate 16 gm, Dietary Fiber 4 gm, Sugars 7 gm, Protein 17 gm

Katelyn's Spaghetti Sauce

Katelyn Bailey
Mechanicsburg, PA

Makes 10-12 servings
(Ideal slow cooker size: 4-5-quart)

1 lb. ground beef, browned
    and drained
3/4 cup chopped onions
1 garlic clove, minced
3 Tbsp. oil
2 6-oz. cans tomato paste
1 Tbsp. sugar
1 1/2 tsp. salt
1-1 1/2 tsp. dried oregano
1/2 tsp. pepper
1 bay leaf
2 qts. fresh tomatoes, or
    tomato sauce

1. Combine all ingredients in slow cooker.

2. Cover. Cook on Low 8-10 hours. Remove bay leaf before serving.

Basic Nutritional Values: Calories 151 (Calories from Fat 71), Total Fat 8 gm (Saturated Fat 1.7 gm, Polyunsat Fat 1.4 gm, Monounsat Fat 3.8 gm, Cholesterol 22 mg), Sodium 342 mg, Total Carbohydrate 13 gm, Dietary Fiber 3 gm, Sugars 6 gm, Protein 9 gm

Note: This sauce freezes well.

Creamy Spaghetti
Dale Peterson, Rapid City, SD

Makes 8 servings
(Ideal slow cooker size: 5-quart)

1 cup chopped onions
1 cup chopped green peppers
1 Tbsp. olive oil
28-oz. can tomatoes with juice
4-oz. can mushrooms, chopped and drained
2¼-oz. can sliced ripe olives, drained
2 tsp. dried oregano
1 lb. ground beef, browned and drained
12 ozs. spaghetti, cooked and drained
10¾-oz. can reduced-sodium, 98%-fat-free cream of mushroom soup

½ cup water
1½ cups (6 ozs.) shredded fat-free cheddar cheese
¼ cup freshly grated Parmesan cheese

1. Saute onions and green peppers in olive oil in skillet until tender. Add tomatoes, mushrooms, olives, oregano, and beef. Simmer for 10 minutes. Transfer to slow cooker.

2. Add spaghetti. Mix well.

3. Combine soup and water. Pour over casserole. Sprinkle with cheeses.

4. Cover. Cook on Low 4-6 hours.

Basic Nutritional Values: Calories 390 (Calories from Fat 103), Total Fat 11 gm (Saturated Fat 3.5 gm, Polyunsat Fat 1.1 gm, Monounsat Fat 5.2 gm, Cholesterol 39 mg), Sodium 607 mg, Total Carbohydrate 45 gm, Dietary Fiber 4 gm, Sugars 7 gm, Protein 26 gm

Italian Vegetable Pasta Sauce
Sherril Bieberly, Sauna, KS

Makes 20, ½ cup servings
(Ideal slow cooker size: 4-5-quart)

3 Tbsp. olive oil
1 cup packed chopped fresh parsley
3 ribs celery, chopped
1 medium onion, chopped

2 garlic cloves, minced
2-inch sprig fresh rosemary, or ½ tsp. dried rosemary
2 small fresh sage leaves, or ½ tsp. dried sage
32-oz. can tomato sauce
32-oz. can chopped tomatoes
1 small dried hot chili pepper
¼ lb. fresh mushrooms, sliced, or 8-oz. can sliced mushrooms, drained
½ tsp. salt

1. Heat oil in skillet. Add parsley, celery, onion, garlic, rosemary, and sage. Saute until vegetables are tender. Place in slow cooker.

2. Add tomatoes, chili pepper, mushrooms, and salt.

3. Cover. Cook on Low 12-18 hours, or on High 5-6 hours.

Basic Nutritional Values: Calories 49 (Calories from Fat 20), Total Fat 2 gm (Saturated Fat 0.3 gm, Polyunsat Fat 0.3 gm, Monounsat Fat 1.5 gm, Cholesterol 0 mg), Sodium 402 mg, Total Carbohydrate 7 gm, Dietary Fiber 2 gm, Sugars 4 gm, Protein 1 gm

Variation: Add 2 lbs. browned ground beef to olive oil and sauted vegetables. Continue with recipe.

> **Eat salmon—it has a type of fat that's great for your heart.**

Louise's Vegetable Spaghetti Sauce

Louise Stackhouse
Benton, PA

Makes 4-6 servings
(Ideal slow cooker size: 4-quart)

6 fresh medium tomatoes, peeled and crushed
1 medium onion, chopped
2 medium green peppers, chopped
2 cloves garlic, minced
1/2 tsp. dried basil
1/2 tsp. dried oregano
1/4 tsp. salt
2 Tbsp. sugar
sweetener substitute to equal 1 Tbsp. sugar

1. Combine all ingredients in slow cooker.
2. Cover. Cook on Low 8-10 hours. If the sauce is too watery for your liking, stir in a 6-oz. can of tomato paste during the last hour of cooking.
3. Serve over cooked spaghetti or other pasta.

Exchange List Values:
Vegetable 3.0

Basic Nutritional Values: Calories 69 (Calories from Fat 6), Total Fat 1 gm (Saturated Fat 0.0 gm, Polyunsat Fat 0.2 gm, Monounsat Fat 0.1 gm, Cholesterol 0 mg), Sodium 113 mg, Total Carbohydrate 16 gm, Dietary Fiber 3 gm, Sugars 11 gm, Protein 2 gm

Pizza in a Pot

Marianne J. Troyer
Millersburg, OH

Makes 6-8 servings
(Ideal slow cooker size: 4-quart)

1 lb. bulk lean sweet Italian turkey sausage, browned and drained
28-oz. can crushed tomatoes
15 1/2-oz. can chili beans
2 1/4-oz. can sliced black olives, drained
1 medium onion, chopped
1 small green pepper, chopped
2 garlic cloves, minced
1/4 cup grated Parmesan cheese
1 Tbsp. quick-cooking tapioca
1 Tbsp. dried basil
1 bay leaf

1. Combine all ingredients in slow cooker.
2. Cover. Cook on Low 8-9 hours.
3. Discard bay leaf. Stir well.
4. Serve over pasta. Top with mozzarella cheese.

Exchange List Values:
Starch 1.0, Vegetable 2.0, Meat, lean 2.0, Fat 0.5

Basic Nutritional Values: Calories 251 (Calories from Fat 87), Total Fat 10 gm (Saturated Fat 2.8 gm, Polyunsat Fat 1.1 gm, Monounsat Fat 2.3 gm, Cholesterol 49 mg), Sodium 937 mg, Total Carbohydrate 23 gm, Dietary Fiber 7 gm, Sugars 8 gm, Protein 18 gm

Pizza Rice

Sue Hamilton
Minooka, IL

Makes 14 servings
(Idea slow cooker size: 3-4-quart)

2 cups white or brown rice, uncooked
2 cups chunky pizza sauce
3 1/2 cups water
7-oz. can mushrooms, drained and rinsed
3 ozs. turkey pepperoni, sliced
1 cup grated reduced-fat cheddar cheese

1. Combine rice, sauce, water, mushrooms, and pepperoni in slow cooker. Stir.
2. Cover. Cook on Low 4-6 hours, or on High 3-5 hours.
3. Sprinkle with cheese before serving.

Exchange List Values:
Starch 1.5, Fat 0.5

Basic Nutritional Values: Calories 151 (Calories from Fat 30), Total Fat 3 gm (Saturated Fat 1.4 gm, Polyunsat Fat 0.5 gm, Monounsat Fat 0.9 gm, Cholesterol 14 mg), Sodium 365 mg, Total Carbohydrate 24 gm, Dietary Fiber 1 gm, Sugars 2 gm, Protein 7 gm

Soups

Frances' Hearty Vegetable Soup

Frances Schrag
Newton, KS

Makes 10 servings
(Ideal slow cooker size: 6-quart)

1 lb. round steak, cut into
  $1/2$-inch pieces
$14^1/2$-oz. can diced
  tomatoes
3 cups water
2 potatoes, peeled and
  cubed
2 onions, sliced
3 celery ribs, sliced
2 carrots, sliced
3 beef bouillon cubes
$1/2$ tsp. dried basil
$1/2$ tsp. dried oregano
$1/4$ tsp. pepper
$1^1/2$ cups frozen mixed
  vegetables, or your
  choice of frozen
  vegetables

1. Combine first 3 ingredients in slow cooker.

2. Cover. Cook on High 6 hours.

3. Add remaining ingredients. Cover and cook on High 2 hours more, or until meat and vegetables are tender.

Exchange List Values:
Starch 0.5, Vegetable 1.0,
Meat, lean 1.0

Basic Nutritional Values: Calories 117 (Calories from Fat 20), Total Fat 2 gm (Saturated Fat 0.7 gm, Polyunsat Fat 0.2 gm, Monounsat Fat 0.9 gm, Cholesterol 26 mg), Sodium 405 mg, Total Carbohydrate 14 gm, Dietary Fiber 3 gm, Sugars 5 gm, Protein 11 gm

Variation: Increase dried basil to 1 tsp. and dried oregano to 1 tsp.

Tracy Clark
Mt. Crawford, VA

If you tend to develop nighttime lows, set your alarm and check your blood sugar level at 3:00 a.m. each night.

Nancy's Vegetable Beef Soup

Nancy Graves, Manhattan, KS

Makes 6-8 servings
(Ideal slow cooker size: 5-6-quart)

2 lb. roast cut into bite-sized pieces, or 2 lbs. stewing meat
15-oz. can corn
15-oz. can green beans
1 lb. bag frozen peas
40-oz. can no-added-salt stewed tomatoes
5 tsp. salt-free beef bouillon powder
Tabasco to taste
1/2 tsp. salt

1. Combine all ingredients in slow cooker. Do not drain vegetables.
2. Add water to fill slow cooker to within 3 inches of top.
3. Cover. Cook on Low 8 hours, or until meat is tender and vegetables are soft.

Exchange List Values:
Starch 1.0, Vegetable 2.0, Meat, lean 2.0

Basic Nutritional Values: Calories 229 (Calories from Fat 46), Total Fat 5 gm (Saturated Fat 1.4 gm, Polyunsat Fat 0.5 gm, Monounsat Fat 2.2 gm, Cholesterol 56 mg), Sodium 545 mg, Total Carbohydrate 24 gm, Dietary Fiber 6 gm, Sugars 10 gm, Protein 23 gm

Variation: Add 1 large onion, sliced, 2 cups sliced carrots, and 3/4 cup pearl barley to mixture before cooking.

Anona's Beef Vegetable Soup

Anona M. Teel
Bangor, PA

Makes 6 servings
(Ideal slow cooker size: 4-quart)

1-1½ lb. soup bone
1 lb. stewing beef cubes
1½ qts. cold water
1/2 tsp. salt
3/4 cup diced celery
3/4 cup diced carrots
3/4 cup diced potatoes
3/4 cup diced onion
1 cup frozen mixed vegetables of your choice
1 lb. can tomatoes
1/8 tsp. pepper
1 Tbsp. chopped dried parsley

1. Put all ingredients in slow cooker.
2. Cover. Cook on Low 8-10 hours. Remove bone before serving.

Exchange List Values:
Starch 0.5, Vegetable 1.0, Meat, lean 1.0

Basic Nutritional Values: Calories 134 (Calories from Fat 28), Total Fat 3 gm (Saturated Fat 0.9 gm, Polyunsat Fat 0.3 gm, Monounsat Fat 1.4 gm, Cholesterol 38 mg), Sodium 407 mg, Total Carbohydrate 13 gm, Dietary Fiber 3 gm, Sugars 6 gm, Protein 14 gm

"Absent Cook" Stew

Kathy Hertzler
Lancaster, PA

Makes 5-6 servings
(Ideal slow cooker size: 4-quart)

2 lbs. stewing beef, cubed
2-3 carrots, sliced
1 onion, chopped
3 large potatoes, cubed
3 ribs celery, sliced
10¾-oz. can tomato soup
1 soup can water
1/8 tsp. salt
dash of pepper
2 Tbsp. vinegar

1. Combine all ingredients in slow cooker.
2. Cover. Cook on Low 10-12 hours.

Exchange List Values:
Starch 2.0, Vegetable 1.0, Meat, lean 2.0

Basic Nutritional Values: Calories 314 (Calories from Fat 59), Total Fat 7 gm (Saturated Fat 2.0 gm, Polyunsat Fat 0.8 gm, Monounsat Fat 2.9 gm, Cholesterol 75 mg), Sodium 427 mg, Total Carbohydrate 35 gm, Dietary Fiber 5 gm, Sugars 9 gm, Protein 28 gm

Lilli's Vegetable Beef Soup

Lilli Peters
Dodge City, KS

Makes 10-12 servings
(Ideal slow cooker size: 4-5-quart)

3 lbs. stewing meat, cut in
  1-inch pieces
2 Tbsp. canola oil
4 potatoes, cubed
4 carrots, sliced
3 ribs celery, sliced
14-oz. can diced tomatoes
14-oz. can Italian
  tomatoes, crushed
2 medium onions, chopped
2 wedges cabbage, sliced
  thin
2 tsp. salt-free beef
  bouillon powder
2 Tbsp. fresh parsley
1 tsp. seasoned salt
1 tsp. garlic salt
1/2 tsp. pepper
water

1. Brown meat in oil in
skillet. Drain.
2. Combine all ingredients
except water in large slow
cooker. Cover with water.
3. Cover. Cook on Low
8-10 hours.

Exchange List Values:
Starch 0.5, Vegetable 2.0,
Meat, lean 2.0, Fat 0.5

Basic Nutritional Values: Calories
223 (Calories from Fat 61), Total Fat
7 gm (Saturated Fat 1.5 gm,
Polyunsat Fat 1.0 gm, Monounsat Fat
3.4 gm, Cholesterol 56 mg), Sodium
465 mg, Total Carbohydrate 20 gm,
Dietary Fiber 4 gm, Sugars 7 gm,
Protein 21 gm

Jeanne's Vegetable Beef Borscht

Jeanne Heyerly
Chenoa, IL

Makes 8 servings
(Ideal slow cooker size: 5-quart)

1 lb. beef roast, cooked
  and cubed
half a head of cabbage,
  sliced thin
3 medium potatoes, diced
4 carrots, sliced
1 large onion, diced
1 cup tomatoes, diced
1 cup corn
1 cup green beans
2 cups 98%-fat-free, lower-
  sodium beef broth
2 cups tomato juice
1/4 tsp. garlic powder
1/4 tsp. dill seed
1/2 tsp. pepper
water
sour cream

1. Mix together all ingredients except water and sour
cream. Add water to fill slow
cooker three-quarters full.
2. Cover. Cook on Low 8-
10 hours.
3. Top individual servings
with sour cream.

Exchange List Values:
Starch 1.0, Vegetable 3.0,
Meat, lean 1.0

Basic Nutritional Values: Calories
185 (Calories from Fat 25), Total Fat
3 gm (Saturated Fat 0.7 gm,
Polyunsat Fat 0.4 gm, Monounsat Fat
1.1 gm, Cholesterol 28 mg), Sodium
434 mg, Total Carbohydrate 29 gm,
Dietary Fiber 6 gm, Sugars 10 gm,
Protein 14 gm

*Variation: Add 1 cup diced
cooked red beets during the last
half hour of cooking.*

Instead of getting
frustrated looking for
the closest parking spot
at the mall, park
farther away and walk.

Southwestern Bean Soup with Cornmeal Dumplings

Melba Eshleman
Manheim, PA

Makes 8 servings
(Ideal slow cooker size: 4-5-quart)

15½-oz. can red kidney beans, rinsed and drained
15½-oz. can black beans, pinto beans, or Great Northern beans, rinsed and drained
3 cups water
14½-oz. can Mexican-style stewed tomatoes
10-oz. pkg. frozen whole-kernel corn, thawed
1 cup sliced carrots
1 cup chopped onions
4-oz. can chopped green chilies
3 tsp. sodium-free instant bouillon powder (any flavor)
1-2 tsp. chili powder
2 cloves garlic, minced

Dumplings:
⅓ cup flour
¼ cup yellow cornmeal
1 tsp. baking powder
dash of salt
dash of pepper
1 egg white, beaten
2 Tbsp. milk
1 Tbsp. oil

1. Combine all soup ingredients in slow cooker.

2. Cover. Cook on Low 10-12 hours or High 4-5 hours.

3. Make dumplings by mixing together flour, cornmeal, baking powder, salt, and pepper.

4. Combine egg white, milk, and oil. Add to flour mixture. Stir with fork until just combined.

5. At the end of the soup's cooking time, turn slow cooker to High. Drop dumpling mixture by rounded teaspoonfuls to make 8 mounds atop the soup.

6. Cover. Cook for 30 minutes (do not lift lid).

Exchange List Values:
Starch 2.0, Vegetable 2.0

Basic Nutritional Values: Calories 197 (Calories from Fat 13), Total Fat 1 gm (Saturated Fat 0.2 gm, Polyunsat Fat 0.6 gm, Monounsat Fat 0.5 gm, Cholesterol 0 mg), Sodium 367 mg, Total Carbohydrate 39 gm, Dietary Fiber 8 gm, Sugars 6 gm, Protein 9 gm

Beef Dumpling Soup

Barbara Walker, Sturgis, SD

Makes 6 servings
(Ideal slow cooker size: 4-quart)

1 lb. beef stewing meat, trimmed of visible fat, cubed
dry onion soup mix (see recipe on page 254)
6 cups hot water
2 carrots, peeled and shredded
1 celery rib, finely chopped
1 tomato, peeled and chopped
2 cloves garlic
½ tsp. dried basil
¼ tsp. dill weed
1 cup buttermilk biscuit mix
1 Tbsp. finely chopped parsley
6 Tbsp. fat-free milk

1. Place meat in slow cooker. Sprinkle with onion soup mix. Pour water over meat.

2. Add carrots, celery, tomato, garlic, basil, and dill weed.

3. Cover. Cook on Low 4-6 hours, or until meat is tender.

4. Combine biscuit mix and parsley. Stir in milk with fork until moistened. Drop dumplings by teaspoonfuls into pot.

5. Cover. Cook on High 30 minutes.

Exchange List Values:
Starch 1.0, Vegetable 1.0, Meat, lean 1.0, Fat 0.5

Basic Nutritional Values: Calories 206 (Calories from Fat 57), Total Fat 6 gm (Saturated Fat 0.9 gm, Polyunsat Fat 1.4 gm, Monounsat Fat 2.6 gm, Cholesterol 38 mg), Sodium 329 mg, Total Carbohydrate 22 gm, Dietary Fiber 2 gm, Sugars 6 gm, Protein 15 gm

Winter's Night Beef Soup

Kimberly Jensen
Bailey, CO

*Makes 12 servings
(Ideal slow cooker size: 5-quart)*

**1 lb. boneless chuck, cut in
  1/2-inch cubes
1-2 Tbsp. oil
28-oz. can tomatoes
2 tsp. garlic powder
2 carrots, sliced
2 ribs celery, sliced
4 cups water
1/2 cup red wine
1 small onion, coarsely
  chopped
4 beef bouillon cubes
1 tsp. pepper
1 tsp. dry oregano
1/2 tsp. dry thyme
1 bay leaf
1/4-1/2 cup couscous**

1. Brown beef cubes in oil in skillet.
2. Place vegetables in bottom of slow cooker. Add beef.
3. Combine all other ingredients in separate bowl except couscous. Pour over ingredients in slow cooker.
4. Cover. Cook on Low 6 hours. Stir in couscous. Cover and cook 30 minutes.

Exchange List Values:
Vegetable 2.0, Meat, lean 1.0

Basic Nutritional Values: Calories 88 (Calories from Fat 25), Total Fat 3 gm (Saturated Fat 0.5 gm, Polyunsat

Fat 0.5 gm, Monounsat Fat 1.4 gm, Cholesterol 19 mg), Sodium 461 mg, Total Carbohydrate 9 gm, Dietary Fiber 2 gm, Sugars 4 gm, Protein 8 gm

Variation: Add zucchini or mushrooms to the rest of the vegetables before cooking.

Old-Fashioned Vegetable Beef Soup

Pam Hochstedler
Kalona, IA

*Makes 8-10 servings
(Ideal slow cooker size: 4-quart)*

**1 lb. beef short ribs,
  trimmed of all visible
  fat
2 qts. water
1 tsp. salt
1/2 tsp. celery salt
1 small onion, chopped
1 cup diced carrots
1/2 cup diced celery
2 cups diced potatoes
1 lb. can whole-kernel
  corn, undrained
1 lb. can diced tomatoes
  and juice**

1. Combine meat, water, salt, celery salt, onion, carrots, and celery in slow cooker.
2. Cover. Cook on Low 4-6 hours.
3. Debone meat, cut into bite-sized pieces, and return to pot.
4. Add potatoes, corn, and tomatoes.
5. Cover and cook on High 2-3 hours.

Exchange List Values:
Starch 0.5, Vegetable 1.0, Fat 0.5

Basic Nutritional Values: Calories 99 (Calories from Fat 24), Total Fat 3 gm (Saturated Fat 1.0 gm, Polyunsat Fat 0.3 gm, Monounsat Fat 1.0 gm, Cholesterol 11 mg), Sodium 413 mg, Total Carbohydrate 13 gm, Dietary Fiber 3 gm, Sugars 6 gm, Protein 6 gm

Lifting light weights (start with 1 to 5 pounds) builds muscle and strength, whether you're age 9 or age 95.

Green Chile
Corn Chowder

Kelly Evenson, Pittsboro, NC

Makes 8 servings
(Ideal slow cooker size: 4-quart)

16-oz. can cream-style corn
3 potatoes, peeled and diced
2 Tbsp. chopped fresh
   chives
4-oz. can diced green chilies,
   drained
2-oz. jar chopped pimentos,
   drained
1/2 cup chopped cooked ham
2 10 1/2-oz. cans 100%-fat-
   free, lower-sodium
   chicken broth
salt to taste
pepper to taste
Tabasco sauce to taste
1 cup milk

1. Combine all ingredients
except milk in slow cooker.
2. Cover. Cook on Low 7-8
hours or until potatoes are
tender.
3. Stir in milk. Heat until
hot.
4. Serve with homemade
bread.

Exchange List Values:
Starch 1.5

Basic Nutritional Values: Calories
124 (Calories from Fat 16), Total Fat 2
gm (Saturated Fat 0.5 gm, Polyunsat Fat
0.3 gm, Monounsat Fat 0.7 gm,
Cholesterol 7 mg), Sodium 563 mg, Total
Carbohydrate 21 gm, Dietary Fiber 2
gm, Sugars 7 gm, Protein 6 gm

Three-Bean Chili

Chris Kaczynski
Schenectady, NY

Makes 12 servings
(Ideal slow cooker size: 6-quart)

2 lbs. ground beef
2 medium onions, diced
16-oz. jar medium salsa
2 pkgs. dry chili seasoning
2 16-oz. cans red kidney
   beans, drained
2 16-oz. cans black beans,
   drained
2 16-oz. cans white kidney,
   or garbanzo, beans
   drained
28-oz. can crushed
   tomatoes
16-oz. can diced tomatoes
2 tsp. sugar

1. Brown beef and onions
in skillet.
2. Combine all ingredients
in 6-qt. slow cooker, or in 2 4-
or 5-qt. cookers.
3. Cover. Cook on Low 8-
10 hours.
4. Serve with chopped raw
onions.

Exchange List Values:
Starch 2.5, Vegetable 2.0,
Meat, lean 2.0, Fat 0.5

Make exercise fun!

Basic Nutritional Values: Calories
381 (Calories from Fat 80), Total Fat
9 gm (Saturated Fat 3.1 gm,
Polyunsat Fat 0.7 gm, Monounsat Fat
3.4 gm, Cholesterol 45 mg), Sodium
717 mg, Total Carbohydrate 47 gm,
Dietary Fiber 14 gm, Sugars 9 gm,
Protein 29 gm

*Note: This recipe can be cut in
half without injuring the flavor, if
you don't have a cooker large
enough to handle the full amount.*

Country Auction
Chili Soup

Clara Newswanger
Gordonville, PA

Makes 20 servings
(Ideal slow cooker size: 6-quart)

1 1/2 lbs. ground beef
1/4 cup chopped onions
1/2 cup flour
1 Tbsp. chili powder
1 tsp. salt
6 cups water
2 cups ketchup
1/3 cup brown sugar
3 15 1/2-oz. cans kidney
   beans, undrained

1. Brown ground beef and
onions in skillet. Drain.
Spoon meat mixture into slow
cooker.
2. Stir flour into meat and
onions. Add seasonings.
3. Slowly stir in water. Add
ketchup, brown sugar, and
beans.
4. Cover. Cook on High
4 hours or on Low 8 hours.

Basic Nutritional Values: Calories 163 (Calories from Fat 35), Total Fat 4 gm (Saturated Fat 1.4 gm, Polyunsat Fat 0.3 gm, Monounsat Fat 1.5 gm, Cholesterol 20 mg), Sodium 655 mg, Total Carbohydrate 23 gm, Dietary Fiber 3 gm, Sugars 8 gm, Protein 10 gm

Spicy Chili

Deborah Swartz
Grottoes, VA

Makes 4-6 servings
(Ideal slow cooker size: 3-4-quart)

½ lb. sausage, either cut in thin slices or removed from casings
½ lb. ground beef
½ cup chopped onions
½ lb. fresh mushrooms, sliced
⅛ cup chopped celery
⅛ cup chopped green peppers
1 cup salsa
16-oz. can salt-free tomato juice
6-oz. can tomato paste
½ tsp. sugar
¼ tsp. salt
½ tsp. dried oregano
½ tsp. Worcestershire sauce
¼ tsp. dried basil
¼ tsp. pepper

1. Brown sausage, ground beef, and onion in deep skillet. During last 3 minutes of browning, add mushrooms, celery, and green peppers. Continue cooking; then drain.

2. Add remaining ingredients. Pour into slow cooker.

3. Cover. Cook on High 2-3 hours.

Basic Nutritional Values: Calories 195 (Calories from Fat 89), Total Fat 10 gm (Saturated Fat 3.5 gm, Polyunsat Fat 1.1 gm, Monounsat Fat 4.2 gm, Cholesterol 37 mg), Sodium 499 mg, Total Carbohydrate 15 gm, Dietary Fiber 3 gm, Sugars 6 gm, Protein 14 gm

Variations: Add any or all of the following to Step 2:
1 tsp. chili powder
1 tsp. ground cumin
15-oz. can black beans, undrained
15-oz. can whole-kernel corn, undrained

Texican Chili

Becky Oswald, Broadway, VA

Makes 15 servings
(Ideal slow cooker size: 5-6-quart)

8 bacon strips, diced
2½ lbs. beef stewing meat, cubed
28-oz. can stewed tomatoes
14½-oz. can stewed tomatoes
8-oz. can tomato sauce
8-oz. can no-added-salt tomato sauce
16-oz. can kidney beans, rinsed and drained
2 cups sliced carrots
1 medium onion, chopped
1 cup chopped celery
½ cup chopped green pepper
¼ cup minced fresh parsley
1 Tbsp. chili powder
½ tsp. ground cumin
¼ tsp. pepper

1. Cook bacon in skillet until crisp. Drain on paper towel.

2. Brown beef in bacon drippings in skillet.

3. Combine all ingredients in slow cooker.

4. Cover. Cook on Low 9-10 hours, or until meat is tender. Stir occasionally.

Basic Nutritional Values: Calories 165 (Calories from Fat 44), Total Fat 5 gm (Saturated Fat 1.5 gm, Polyunsat Fat 0.5 gm, Monounsat Fat 2.2 gm, Cholesterol 40 mg), Sodium 434 mg, Total Carbohydrate 15 gm, Dietary Fiber 3 gm, Sugars 6 gm, Protein 16 gm

Cassoulet Chowder

Miriam Friesen
Staunton, VA

Makes 8-10 servings
(Ideal slow cooker size: 4-5-quart)

1¼ cups dry pinto beans
4 cups water
8-oz. pkg. brown-and-serve sausage links, cooked and drained
2 cups cubed cooked chicken
2 cups cubed extra-lean, lower-sodium cooked ham
1½ cups sliced carrots
8-oz. can tomato sauce
¾ cup dry red wine
½ cup chopped onions
½ tsp. garlic powder
1 bay leaf

1. Combine beans and water in large saucepan. Bring to boil. Reduce heat and simmer 1½ hours. Refrigerate beans and liquid 4-8 hours.
2. Combine all ingredients in slow cooker.
3. Cover. Cook on Low 8-10 hours or on High 4 hours. If the chowder seems too thin, remove lid during last 30 minutes of cooking time to allow it to thicken.
4. Remove bay leaf before serving.

Exchange List Values:
Starch 1.0, Meat, lean 3.0

Basic Nutritional Values: Calories 249 (Calories from Fat 90), Total Fat 10 gm (Saturated Fat 3.4 gm, Polyunsat Fat 1.6 gm, Monounsat Fat 3.8 gm, Cholesterol 46 mg), Sodium 554 mg, Total Carbohydrate 18 gm, Dietary Fiber 5 gm, Sugars 5 gm, Protein 21 gm

Forgotten Minestrone

Phyllis Attig, Reynolds, IL

Makes 8 servings
(Ideal slow cooker size: 4-5-quart)

1 lb. beef stewing meat, all visible fat removed
6 cups water
28-oz. can tomatoes, diced, undrained
1 beef bouillon cube
1 medium onion, chopped
2 Tbsp. minced dried parsley
¼ tsp. salt
1½ tsp. dried thyme
½ tsp. pepper
1 medium zucchini, thinly sliced
2 cups finely chopped cabbage
16-oz. can garbanzo beans, drained
1 cup uncooked small elbow, or shell, macaroni
3 Tbsp. freshly grated Parmesan cheese

1. Combine beef, water, tomatoes, bouillon, onion, parsley, salt, thyme, and pepper.

2. Cover. Cook on Low 7-9 hours, or until meat is tender.
3. Stir in zucchini, cabbage, beans, and macaroni. Cover and cook on High 30-45 minutes, or until vegetables are tender.
4. Sprinkle individual servings with Parmesan cheese.

Exchange List Values:
Starch 1.0, Vegetable 2.0, Meat, lean 2.0

Basic Nutritional Values: Calories 235 (Calories from Fat 47), Total Fat 5 gm (Saturated Fat 1.5 gm, Polyunsat Fat 0.8 gm, Monounsat Fat 2.0 gm, Cholesterol 44 mg), Sodium 489 mg, Total Carbohydrate 27 gm, Dietary Fiber 5 gm, Sugars 8 gm, Protein 20 gm

Slow-Cooker Minestrone

Dorothy Shank, Sterling, IL

Makes 8 servings
(Ideal slow cooker size: 4-quart)

3 cups water
1½ lbs. stewing meat, cut into bite-sized pieces, all visible fat removed
1 medium onion, diced
4 carrots, diced
14½-oz. can tomatoes
¾ tsp. salt
10-oz. pkg. frozen mixed vegetables, or your choice of frozen vegetables
1 Tbsp. dried basil
½ cup dry vermicelli

1 tsp. dried oregano
grated Parmesan cheese

1. Combine all ingredients except cheese in slow cooker. Stir well.
2. Cover. Cook on Low 10-12 hours, or on High 4-5 hours.
3. Top individual servings with Parmesan cheese.

Exchange List Values:
Starch 1.0, Vegetable 2.0, Meat, lean 1.0

Basic Nutritional Values: Calories 183 (Calories from Fat 33), Total Fat 4 gm (Saturated Fat 1.0 gm, Polyunsat Fat 0.4 gm, Monounsat Fat 1.6 gm, Cholesterol 42 mg), Sodium 413 mg, Total Carbohydrate 21 gm, Dietary Fiber 4 gm, Sugars 7 gm, Protein 17 gm

Hamburger Vegetable Soup
Donna Conto
Saylorsburg, PA

*Makes 8 servings
(Ideal slow cooker size: 4-quart)*

1/2 lb. ground beef, browned, drained, and patted dry with paper toweling
1 beef bouillon cube, crushed
5 tsp. salt-free beef bouillon powder
16-oz. can tomatoes
1 large onion, diced
3/4 cup sliced celery

1 medium carrot, diced
1 garlic clove, minced
1 bay leaf
1/2 tsp. salt
1/8 tsp. pepper
10-oz. pkg. frozen peas
3 Tbsp. chopped parsley

1. Combine all ingredients except peas and parsley in slow cooker.
2. Cover. Cook on Low 5 hours.
3. Stir in peas during last hour.
4. Garnish with parsley before serving.

Exchange List Values:
Vegetable 2.0, Meat, lean 1.0

Basic Nutritional Values: Calories 107 (Calories from Fat 28), Total Fat 3 gm (Saturated Fat 1.1 gm, Polyunsat Fat 0.2 gm, Monounsat Fat 1.3 gm, Cholesterol 17 mg), Sodium 431 mg, Total Carbohydrate 12 gm, Dietary Fiber 3 gm, Sugars 7 gm, Protein 8 gm

Stretching keeps the body younger. As people age, they lose flexibility and balance. Stretching gives it back.

Hearty Alphabet Soup
Maryann Markano,
Wilmington, DE

*Makes 6 servings
(Ideal slow cooker size: 4-quart)*

1/2 lb. beef stewing meat or round steak, all visible fat removed, cubed
14 1/2-oz. can stewed tomatoes
8-oz. can tomato sauce
1 cup water
dry onion soup mix (see recipe on page 254)
10-oz. pkg. frozen vegetables, partially thawed
1/2 cup uncooked alphabet noodles

1. Combine meat, tomatoes, tomato sauce, water, and soup mix in slow cooker.
2. Cover. Cook on Low 6-8 hours. Turn to High.
3. Stir in vegetables and noodles. Add more water if mixture is too dry and thick.
4. Cover. Cook on High 30 minutes, or until vegetables are tender.

Exchange List Values:
Starch 1.0, Vegetable 2.0, Meat, lean 1.0

Basic Nutritional Values: Calories 165 (Calories from Fat 17), Total Fat 2 gm (Saturated Fat 0.5 gm, Polyunsat Fat 0.3 gm, Monounsat Fat 0.8 gm, Cholesterol 19 mg), Sodium 443 mg, Total Carbohydrate 28 gm, Dietary Fiber 3 gm, Sugars 8 gm, Protein 10 gm

Quick and Easy Italian Vegetable Beef Soup

Lisa Warren, Parkesburg, PA

Makes 10 servings
(Ideal slow cooker size: 4-quart)

3/4 lb. 85%-lean ground beef, or turkey, browned and drained
3 carrots, sliced
4 potatoes, peeled and cubed
1 small onion, diced
1 tsp. garlic powder
1 tsp. Italian seasoning
1/2 tsp. salt
1/4 tsp. pepper
15-oz. can diced Italian tomatoes, or 2 fresh tomatoes, chopped
6-oz. can Italian-flavored tomato paste
4 1/2 cups water
1 quart 99%-fat-free, lower-sodium beef broth

1. Combine all ingredients in slow cooker.
2. Cover. Cook on High 6-8 hours, or until potatoes and carrots are tender.

Exchange List Values:
Starch 0.5, Vegetable 2.0, Meat, lean 1.0

Basic Nutritional Values: Calories 138 (Calories from Fat 34), Total Fat 4 gm (Saturated Fat 1.4 gm, Polyunsat Fat 0.3 gm, Monounsat Fat 1.5 gm, Cholesterol 20 mg), Sodium 423 mg, Total Carbohydrate 17 gm, Dietary Fiber 3 gm, Sugars 4 gm, Protein 9 gm

Spicy Beef Vegetable Stew

Melissa Raber
Millersburg, OH

Makes 12 servings
(Ideal slow cooker size: 4-quart)

3/4 lb. ground beef
1 cup chopped onions
30-oz. jar meatless spaghetti sauce
3 1/2 cups water
1 lb. frozen mixed vegetables
10-oz. can diced tomatoes with green chilies
1 cup sliced celery
1 tsp. salt-free beef bouillon powder
1 tsp. pepper

1. Cook beef and onions in skillet until meat is no longer pink. Drain. Transfer to slow cooker.
2. Stir in remaining ingredients.
3. Cover. Cook on Low 8 hours.

Exchange List Values:
Starch 0.5, Vegetable 2.0, Meat, lean 1.0

Basic Nutritional Values: Calories 150 (Calories from Fat 44), Total Fat 5 gm (Saturated Fat 1.4 gm, Polyunsat Fat 0.7 gm, Monounsat Fat 1.9 gm, Cholesterol 17 mg), Sodium 489 mg, Total Carbohydrate 17 gm, Dietary Fiber 3 gm, Sugars 10 gm, Protein 8 gm

Hearty Beef and Cabbage Soup

Carolyn Mathias
Williamsville, NY

Makes 8 servings
(Ideal slow cooker size: 4-quart)

2/3 lb. (about 11 ozs.) ground beef
1 medium onion, chopped
40-oz. can tomatoes
2 cups water
15-oz. can kidney beans
1/2 tsp. pepper
1 Tbsp. chili powder
1/2 cup chopped celery
2 cups thinly sliced cabbage

1. Saute beef in skillet. Drain.
2. Combine all ingredients except cabbage in slow cooker.
3. Cover. Cook on Low 3 hours. Add cabbage. Cook on High 30-60 minutes longer.

Exchange List Values:
Starch 0.5, Vegetable 2.0, Meat, lean 1.0

Basic Nutritional Values: Calories 150 (Calories from Fat 40), Total Fat 4 gm (Saturated Fat 1.5 gm, Polyunsat Fat 0.4 gm, Monounsat Fat 1.7 gm, Cholesterol 22 mg), Sodium 507 mg, Total Carbohydrate 18 gm, Dietary Fiber 5 gm, Sugars 8 gm, Protein 12 gm

Hamburger Soup with Barley

Becky Oswald
Broadway, VA

*Makes 10 servings
(Ideal slow cooker size: 4-quart)*

3/4 lb. 85%-lean ground
   beef
1 medium onion, chopped
2 14½-oz. cans beef
   consomme
1¾ cups water
2 tsp. sodium-free beef
   bouillon powder
28-oz. can no-added-salt
   diced, or crushed,
   tomatoes
3 carrots, sliced
3 celery ribs, sliced
8 Tbsp. barley
1 bay leaf
1 tsp. dried thyme
1 Tbsp. dried parsley
½ tsp. pepper

1. Brown beef and onion in skillet. Drain.
2. Combine all ingredients in slow cooker.
3. Cover. Cook on High 3 hours, or Low 6-8 hours.

Exchange List Values:
Starch 1.0, Vegetable 1.0, Meat, lean 1.0

Basic Nutritional Values: Calories 154 (Calories from Fat 34), Total Fat 4 gm (Saturated Fat 1.4 gm, Polyunsat Fat 0.3 gm, Monounsat Fat 1.5 gm, Cholesterol 22 mg), Sodium 623 mg, Total Carbohydrate 20 gm, Dietary Fiber 4 gm, Sugars 6 gm, Protein 11 gm

Vegetable Soup with Potatoes

Annabelle Unternahrer
Shipshewana, IN

*Makes 8 servings
(Ideal slow cooker size: 4-quart)*

2/3 lb. 85%-lean ground
   beef, browned and
   drained
2 15-oz. cans diced
   tomatoes
2 carrots, sliced or cubed
2 onions, sliced or cubed
2 potatoes, diced
1-2 garlic cloves, minced
12-oz. can V-8 vegetable
   juice
1½-2 cups sliced celery
2 tsp. salt-free beef
   bouillon powder
2-3 cups vegetables
   (cauliflower, peas, corn,
   limas, or your choice of
   leftovers from your
   freezer)

1. Combine all ingredients in slow cooker.
2. Cover. Cook on Low 12 hours, or High 4-6 hours.

Exchange List Values:
Starch 1.0, Vegetable 2.0, Meat, lean 1.0

Basic Nutritional Values: Calories 179 (Calories from Fat 38), Total Fat 4 gm (Saturated Fat 1.5 gm, Polyunsat Fat 0.4 gm, Monounsat Fat 1.7 gm, Cholesterol 22 mg), Sodium 407 mg, Total Carbohydrate 26 gm, Dietary Fiber 5 gm, Sugars 11 gm, Protein 11 gm

Note: If you are using leftover vegetables that are precooked, add during last hour if cooking on Low, or during last half hour if cooking on High.

Variation: Use 3 cups pre-cooked dried beans or lentils instead of hamburger.

Have a plan in place in case you get sick—whom to call and when. Don't hesitate to call your doctor if you have questions.

Hamburger Lentil Soup

Juanita Marner
Shipshewana, IN

Makes 8 servings
(Ideal slow cooker size: 4-quart)

1/2 lb. 85%-lean ground beef
1/2 cup chopped onions
4 carrots, diced
3 ribs celery, diced
1 garlic clove, minced, or 1 tsp. garlic powder
1 qt. no-salt-added tomato juice
1 1/2 tsp. salt
2 cups dry lentils, washed with stones removed
1 qt. water
1/2 tsp. dried marjoram
1 Tbsp. brown sugar

1. Brown ground beef and onions in skillet. Drain.
2. Combine all ingredients in slow cooker.
3. Cover. Cook on Low 8-10 hours, or High 4-6 hours.

Exchange List Values:
Starch 2.0, Vegetable 2.0, Meat, lean 1.0

Basic Nutritional Values: Calories 247 (Calories from Fat 32), Total Fat 4 gm (Saturated Fat 1.2 gm, Polyunsat Fat 0.4 gm, Monounsat Fat 1.4 gm, Cholesterol 17 mg), Sodium 508 mg, Total Carbohydrate 38 gm, Dietary Fiber 12 gm, Sugars 10 gm, Protein 18 gm

Russian Red Lentil Soup

Naomi E. Fast, Hesston, KS

Makes 8 servings
(Ideal slow cooker size: 5-6-quart)

1 Tbsp. canola oil
1 large onion, chopped
3 cloves garlic, minced
1/2 cup diced, dried apricots
1 1/2 cups dried red lentils
1/2 tsp. cumin
1/2 tsp. dried thyme
3 cups water
2 14 1/2-oz. cans chicken or vegetable broth
14 1/2-oz. can diced tomatoes
1 Tbsp. honey
1/2 tsp. coarsely ground black pepper
2 Tbsp. chopped fresh mint
1 1/2 cups plain yogurt

1. Combine all ingredients except mint and yogurt in slow cooker.
2. Cover. Heat on High until soup starts to simmer, then turn to Low and cook 3-4 hours.
3. Add mint and dollop of yogurt to each bowl of soup.

Exchange List Values:
Starch 1.5, Fruit 1.0, Vegetable 1.0, Meat, very lean 1.0

Basic Nutritional Values: Calories 244 (Calories from Fat 37), Total Fat 4 gm (Saturated Fat 1.2 gm, Polyunsat Fat 0.8 gm, Monounsat Fat 1.5 gm, Cholesterol 8 mg), Sodium 587 mg, Total Carbohydrate 42 gm, Dietary Fiber 10 gm, Sugars 21 gm, Protein 13 gm

Vegetable Soup with Noodles

Glenda S. Weaver
New Holland, PA

Makes 8 servings
(Ideal slow cooker size: 4-quart)

1 pint water
2 tsp. sodium-free beef bouillon powder
1 onion, chopped
2/3 lb. 85%-lean ground beef
1/4 cup ketchup
1/8 tsp. celery salt
1/2 cup uncooked noodles
16-oz. pkg. frozen mixed vegetables, or vegetables of your choice
2 cups tomato juice

1. Dissolve bouillon cubes in water.
2. Brown onion and beef in skillet. Drain.
3. Combine all ingredients in slow cooker.
4. Cover. Cook on Low 6 hours, or on High 2-3 hours, until vegetables are tender.

Exchange List Values:
Starch 0.5, Vegetable 2.0, Meat, lean 1.0

Basic Nutritional Values: Calories 135 (Calories from Fat 37), Total Fat 4 gm (Saturated Fat 1.5 gm, Polyunsat Fat 0.2 gm, Monounsat Fat 1.7 gm, Cholesterol 25 mg), Sodium 374 mg, Total Carbohydrate 16 gm, Dietary Fiber 2 gm, Sugars 7 gm, Protein 10 gm

Dottie's Creamy Steak Soup

Debbie Zeida
Mashpee, MA

Makes 8 main dish servings
(Ideal slow cooker size: 4-quart)

1/2 lb. 85%-lean ground beef
half a large onion, chopped
12-oz. can Low sodium V-8 vegetable juice
3 medium potatoes, diced
10 3/4-oz. can 98%-fat-free, reduced-sodium cream of mushroom soup
10 3/4-oz. can cream of celery soup
16-oz. pkg. frozen mixed vegetables, or your choice of frozen vegetables
1/2-3/4 tsp. pepper

1. Saute beef and onions in skillet. Drain.
2. Combine all ingredients in slow cooker.
3. Cover. Cook on Low 8-10 hours.

Basic Nutritional Values: Calories 202 (Calories from Fat 54), Total Fat 6 gm (Saturated Fat 2.2 gm, Polyunsat Fat 1.2 gm, Monounsat Fat 1.8 gm, Cholesterol 19 mg), Sodium 506 mg, Total Carbohydrate 28 gm, Dietary Fiber 4 gm, Sugars 7 gm, Protein 10 gm

Sausage Bean Soup

Janie Steele
Moore, OK

Makes 10 servings
(Ideal slow cooker size: 5-6-quart)

1 lb. pkg. dried Great Northern beans
28-oz. can whole tomatoes
2 8-oz. cans no-salt-added tomato sauce
2 large onions, chopped
3 cloves garlic, minced
1/4-1/2 tsp. pepper, according to your taste preference
3 celery ribs, sliced
bell pepper, sliced
large ham bone, all skin and visible fat removed (to yield 6 ozs. ham)
1-2 lbs. Low-fat smoked sausage links, sliced

1. Cover beans with water and soak for 8 hours. Rinse and drain.
2. Place beans in 6-qt. cooker and cover with water.

3. Combine all other ingredients, except sausage, in large bowl. Stir into beans in slow cooker.
4. Cover. Cook on High 1-1 1/2 hours. Reduce to Low. Cook 7 hours.
5. Remove ham bone or hock and debone. Stir ham pieces back into soup.
6. Add sausage links.
7. Cover. Cook on Low 1 hour.

Basic Nutritional Values: Calories 276 (Calories from Fat 34), Total Fat 4 gm (Saturated Fat 1.3 gm, Polyunsat Fat 1.2 gm, Monounsat Fat 1.0 gm, Cholesterol 29 mg), Sodium 760 mg, Total Carbohydrate 41 gm, Dietary Fiber 11 gm, Sugars 12 gm, Protein 21 gm

Note: For enhanced flavor, brown sausage before adding to soup.

If you're angry or tense after a stressful day, you need to get moving to get past it!

Black Bean Soup

Janie Steele
Moore, OK

Makes 5-6 quarts,
or about 18 servings
(Ideal slow cooker size:
2 cookers, each 4-5-quart)

4 cups dry black beans
5 qts. water
ham bone, ham pieces, or
    ham hocks
3 bunches of green onions,
    sliced thin
4 bay leaves
1 tsp. salt
1/4-1/2 tsp. pepper
3 cloves minced garlic
4 celery ribs, chopped
3 large onions, chopped
10 1/2-oz. can consomme
2 1/2 Tbsp. margarine
2 1/2 Tbsp. flour
1/2 cup minced parsley
1 cup Madeira wine,
    optional
chopped parsley

1. In each slow cooker,
soak half the beans in 2 1/2 qts.
water for 8 hours. Rinse.
Drain. Pour beans back into
slow cookers.
2. Add ham, green onions,
bay, salt, pepper, garlic,
celery, and onions. Pour in
consomme. Add water to
cover vegetables and meat.
3. Cover. Cook on High
1 1/2-2 hours. Reduce heat to
Low and cook for 6-8 hours.
4. Remove ham bones and
bay leaves. Cut ham off
bones and set meat aside.
5. Force vegetable mixture

through sieve, if you wish.
6. Return cooked
ingredients and cut-up ham
to cookers.
7. In saucepan, melt
margarine. Stir in flour until
smooth. Stir into soup to
thicken and enrich.
8. Prior to serving, add
wine to heated soup mixture.
Garnish with chopped
parsley.

Exchange List Values:
Starch 2.0, Meat, lean 1.0

Basic Nutritional Values: Calories
202 (Calories from Fat 26), Total Fat
3 gm (Saturated Fat 0.6 gm,
Polyunsat Fat 0.9 gm, Monounsat Fat
1.0 gm, Cholesterol 6 mg), Sodium
399 mg, Total Carbohydrate 32 gm,
Dietary Fiber 11 gm, Sugars 6 gm,
Protein 14 gm

Taco Soup with Black Beans

Alexa Slonin
Harrisonburg, VA

Makes 6-8 servings
(Ideal slow cooker size: 4-quart)

3/4 lb. 90%-lean ground
    beef, browned and
    drained
28-oz. can crushed
    tomatoes
1/4-1/2 cup water
15 1/4-oz. can corn, drained
    and rinsed
15-oz. can no-salt-added
    black beans, undrained
15 1/2-oz. can no-salt-added

red kidney beans,
    undrained
1 envelope dry Hidden
    Valley Ranch Dressing
    mix
2 Tbsp. Low-Sodium
    Seasoning Mix (see
    recipe on page 254)
1 small onion

1. Combine all ingredients
in slow cooker.
2. Cover. Cook on Low 4-6
hours.

Exchange List Values:
Starch 1.5, Vegetable 2.0,
Meat, very lean 2.0

Basic Nutritional Values: Calories
247 (Calories from Fat 41), Total Fat
5 gm (Saturated Fat 1.5 gm,
Polyunsat Fat 0.6 gm, Monounsat Fat
1.7 gm, Cholesterol 26 mg), Sodium
652 mg, Total Carbohydrate 35 gm,
Dietary Fiber 9 gm, Sugars 9 gm,
Protein 17 gm

Suggested garnishes:
    broken tortilla,
        or corn, chips
    fat-free shredded cheese
    fat-free sour cream

Sante Fe Soup

Carla Koslowsky
Hillsboro, KS

Makes 8 servings
(Ideal slow cooker size: 4-quart)

8 ozs. sharp fat-free
   cheddar cheese, cubed
3/4 lb. 90%-lean ground
   beef, browned and
   drained
15 1/4-oz. can corn,
   undrained
15-oz. can no-added-salt
   kidney beans,
   undrained
14 1/2-oz. can diced
   tomatoes with green
   chilies
14 1/2-oz. can no-added-salt
   stewed tomatoes
2 Tbsp. Low-Sodium Taco
   Seasoning Mix (recipe
   on page 254)

1. Combine all ingredients
in slow cooker.
2. Cover. Cook on High 3
hours.
3. Serve with corn chips as
a side, or dip soft tortillas in
in soup bowls if your diet
allows.

Exchange List Values:
Starch 1.0, Vegetable 1.0,
Meat, lean 2.0

Basic Nutritional Values: Calories
215 (Calories from Fat 40), Total Fat
4 gm (Saturated Fat 1.5 gm,
Polyunsat Fat 0.5 gm, Monounsat Fat
1.7 gm, Cholesterol 29 mg), Sodium
617 mg, Total Carbohydrate 22 gm,
Dietary Fiber 5 gm, Sugars 8 gm,
Protein 22 gm

Taco Soup with Whole Tomatoes

Marla Folkerts
Holland, OH

Makes 6-8 servings
(Ideal slow cooker size: 4-quart)

2/3 lb. 85%-lean ground
   beef
1/2 cup chopped onions
28-oz. can whole tomatoes
   with juice
14-oz. can kidney beans
   with juice
1 7-oz. can corn with juice
8-oz. can no-salt-added
   tomato sauce
2 Tbsp. Low-Sodium Taco
   Seasoning Mix (recipe
   on page 254)
1-2 cups water
salt to taste
pepper to taste
1 cup fat-free grated
   cheddar cheese

1. Brown beef and onions
in skillet. Drain.
2. Combine all ingredients
except cheese in slow cooker.
3. Cover. Cook on Low 4-6
hours.
4. Ladle into bowls. Top
with cheese and serve with
taco/corn chips if your diet
allows.

Exchange List Values:
Starch 1.0, Vegetable 1.0,
Meat, lean 1.0, Fat 0.5

Basic Nutritional Values: Calories
191 (Calories from Fat 44), Total Fat
5 gm (Saturated Fat 1.6 gm,
Polyunsat Fat 0.5 gm, Monounsat Fat
1.9 gm, Cholesterol 24 mg), Sodium
612 mg, Total Carbohydrate 22 gm,
Dietary Fiber 5 gm, Sugars 10 gm,
Protein 16 gm

You can reduce your
risk of eye disease by
keeping your blood
sugars near normal and
getting a regular exam
by an eye doctor who
specializes in diabetes.

Norma's Vegetarian Chili

Kathy Hertzler
Lancaster, PA

Makes 8-10 servings
(Ideal slow cooker size: 5-6-quart)

2 Tbsp. canola oil
2 cups minced celery
1½ cups chopped green pepper
1 cup minced onions
4 garlic cloves, minced
5½ cups no-salt-added stewed tomatoes
2 1 lb. cans kidney beans, undrained
1½ cups raisins
¼ cup wine vinegar
1 Tbsp. chopped parsley
1 tsp. salt
1½ tsp. dried oregano
1½ tsp. cumin
¼ tsp. pepper
¼ tsp. Tabasco sauce
1 bay leaf
¾ cup unsalted cashews
1 cup grated cheese, optional

1. Combine all ingredients except cashews and cheese in slow cooker.
2. Cover. Simmer on Low for 8 hours. Add cashews and simmer 30 minutes.
3. Garnish individual servings with grated cheese.

Exchange List Values:
Starch 1.0, Fruit 1.0, Vegetable 3.0, Fat 1.5

Basic Nutritional Values: Calories 279 (Calories from Fat 77), Total Fat 9 gm (Saturated Fat 1.4 gm, Polyunsat Fat 2.0 gm, Monounsat Fat 4.7 gm, Cholesterol 0 mg), Sodium 603 mg, Total Carbohydrate 47 gm, Dietary Fiber 7 gm, Sugars 22 gm, Protein 9 gm

Easy Chili

Sheryl Shenk
Harrisonburg, VA

Makes 10-12 servings
(Ideal slow cooker size: 5-quart)

1 lb. ground beef
1 onion, chopped
1 medium green pepper, chopped
½ tsp. salt
1 Tbsp. chili powder
2 tsp. Worcestershire sauce
29-oz. can no-added-salt tomato sauce
3 16-oz. cans kidney beans, drained
14½-oz. can crushed, or stewed, tomatoes
6-oz. can tomato paste
4 ozs. fat-free grated cheddar cheese

1. Brown meat in skillet. Add onion and green pepper halfway through browning process. Drain. Pour into slow cooker.
2. Stir in remaining ingredients except cheese.
3. Cover. Cook on High 3 hours, or Low 7-8 hours.
4. Serve in bowls topped with cheddar cheese.

Exchange List Values:
Starch 1.0, Vegetable 3.0, Meat, lean 1.0, Fat 0.5

Basic Nutritional Values: Calories 232 (Calories from Fat 41), Total Fat 5 gm (Saturated Fat 1.5 gm, Polyunsat Fat 0.5 gm, Monounsat Fat 1.8 gm, Cholesterol 23 mg), Sodium 456 mg, Total Carboh....

Slow-Cooker Chili

Wanda S. Curtin
Bradenton, FL
Ann Sunday McDowell
Newtown, PA

Makes 10 servings
(Ideal slow cooker size: 4-5-quart)

2 lbs. ground beef, browned and drained
2 16-oz. cans red kidney beans, drained
2 14½-ozs. cans diced tomatoes, drained
2 medium onions, chopped
2 garlic cloves, crushed
2 Tbsp. chili powder
1 tsp. ground cumin
1 tsp. black pepper
1 tsp. salt

1. Combine all ingredients in slow cooker.
2. Cover. Cook on Low 8-10 hours.

Exchange List Values:
Starch 1.0, Vegetable 1.0,
Meat, lean 3.0

Basic Nutritional Values: Calories 265 (Calories from Fat 89), Total Fat 10 gm (Saturated Fat 3.6 gm, Polyunsat Fat 0.7 gm, Monounsat Fat 4.1 gm, Cholesterol 54 mg), Sodium 568 mg, Total Carbohydrate 21 gm, Dietary Fiber 6 gm, Sugars 6 gm, Protein 23 gm

Note: Use leftovers over lettuce and other fresh garden vegetables to make a taco salad.

Variations:
1. For more flavor, add cayenne pepper or a jalapeno pepper before cooking.
Dorothy Shank
Sterling, IL

2. Add 1 cup chopped green peppers before cooking.
Mary V. Warye
West Liberty, OH

Colleen's Favorite Chili
Colleen Heatwole
Burton, MI

Makes 8 servings
(Ideal slow cooker size: 4-quart)

2 medium onions, coarsely chopped
1-1½ lbs. 85%-lean ground beef, browned and drained
2 garlic cloves, minced fine, or ½ tsp. garlic

powder
¾ cup finely diced green peppers
2 14½-oz. cans diced tomatoes, or 1 quart home-canned tomatoes
30-32 ozs. beans—kidney, or pinto, or mixture of the two, drained and rinsed
¼-½ cup water
8-oz. can no-salt-added tomato sauce
1 tsp. ground cumin
½ tsp. pepper
1 tsp. seasoned salt
1 Tbsp., or more, chili powder
1 tsp. dried basil

1. Combine all ingredients in slow cooker.
2. Cover. Cook on Low 8-12 hours, or High 5-6 hours.

Exchange List Values:
Starch 1.0, Vegetable 3.0,
Meat, lean 2.0, Fat 0.5

Basic Nutritional Values: Calories 296 (Calories from Fat 86), Total Fat 10 gm (Saturated Fat 3.4 gm, Polyunsat Fat 0.7 gm, Monounsat Fat 4.0 gm, Cholesterol 54 mg), Sodium 581 mg, Total Carbohydrate 30 gm, Dietary Fiber 9 gm, Sugars 10 gm, Protein 24 gm

Variations:
1. Add 1 Tbsp. brown sugar to mixture before cooking.
2. Put in another 1 lb. beans and then decrease ground beef to 1 lb.

Trail Chili
Jeanne Allen, Rye, CO

Makes 10 servings
(Ideal slow cooker size: 4-5-quart)

1½ lbs. 90%-lean ground beef
1 large onion, diced
28-oz. can diced tomatoes
2 8-oz. cans tomato puree
16-oz. cans kidney beans, undrained
4-oz. can diced green chilies
1 cup water
2 garlic cloves, minced
2 Tbsp. mild chili powder
½ tsp. salt
2 tsp. ground cumin
1 tsp. pepper

1. Brown beef and onion in skillet. Drain. Place in slow cooker on High.
2. Stir in remaining ingredients. Cook on High 30 minutes.
3. Reduce heat to Low. Cook 4-6 hours.

Exchange List Values:
Starch 0.5, Vegetable 2.0,
Meat, lean 2.0

Basic Nutritional Values: Calories 195 (Calories from Fat 57), Total Fat 6 gm (Saturated Fat 2.3 gm, Polyunsat Fat 0.5 gm, Monounsat Fat 2.6 gm, Cholesterol 41 mg), Sodium 545 mg, Total Carbohydrate 17 gm, Dietary Fiber 4 gm, Sugars 8 gm, Protein 18 gm

Note: Top individual servings with shredded cheese. Serve with taco chips if your diet allows.

Soups

Quick and Easy Chili

Nan Decker
Albuquerque, NM

Makes 6 servings
(Ideal slow cooker size: 3-4-quart)

1 lb. ground beef
1 onion, chopped
16-oz. can stewed tomatoes
11¹/₂-oz. can Hot V-8 juice
2 15-oz. cans pinto beans, drained and rinsed
¹/₄-¹/₂ cup water
¹/₄ tsp. cayenne pepper
1 Tbsp. chili powder

1. Crumble ground beef in microwave-safe casserole. Add onion. Microwave, covered, on High 15 minutes. Drain. Break meat into pieces.
2. Combine all ingredients in slow cooker.
3. Cook on Low 4-5 hours.
4. Garnish with sour cream, chopped green onions, grated cheese, and sliced ripe olives if your diet allows.

Exchange List Values:
Starch 1.5, Vegetable 2.0, Meat, lean 2.0, Fat 0.5

Basic Nutritional Values: Calories 302 (Calories from Fat 76), Total Fat 8 gm (Saturated Fat 3.0 gm, Polyunsat Fat 0.7 gm, Monounsat Fat 3.5 gm, Cholesterol 45 mg), Sodium 539 mg, Total Carbohydrate 34 gm, Dietary Fiber 10 gm, Sugars 7 gm, Protein 23 gm

Suggested garnishes:
sour cream
chopped green onions
grated cheese
sliced ripe olives

Pirate Stew

Nancy Graves, Manhattan, KS

Makes 4-6 servings
(Ideal slow cooker size: 4-quart)

³/₄ cup sliced onion
1 lb. ground beef
¹/₄ cup uncooked, long grain rice
3 cups diced raw potatoes
1 cup diced celery
2 cups canned kidney beans, drained
¹/₂ tsp. salt
¹/₈ tsp. pepper
¹/₄ tsp. chili powder
¹/₄ tsp. Worcestershire sauce
1 cup tomato sauce
¹/₂ cup water

1. Brown onions and ground beef in skillet. Drain.
2. Layer ingredients in slow cooker in order given.
3. Cover. Cook on Low 6 hours, or until potatoes and rice are cooked.

Exchange List Values:
Starch 2.0, Vegetable 1.0, Meat, lean 2.0, Fat 0.5

Basic Nutritional Values: Calories 310 (Calories from Fat 73), Total Fat 8 gm (Saturated Fat 3.0 gm, Polyunsat Fat 0.5 gm, Monounsat Fat

3.4 gm, Cholesterol 45 mg), Sodium 611 mg, Total Carbohydrate 38 gm, Dietary Fiber 7 gm, Sugars 6 gm, Protein 22 gm

Variation: Add a layer of 2 cups sliced carrots between potatoes and celery.
Katrine Rose
Woodbridge, VA

Corn Chili

Gladys Longacre
Susquehanna, PA

Makes 4-6 servings
(Ideal slow cooker size: 4-quart)

1 lb. ground beef
¹/₂ cup chopped onions
¹/₂ cup chopped green peppers
¹/₄ tsp. salt
¹/₈ tsp. pepper
¹/₄ tsp. dried thyme
14¹/₂-oz. can diced tomatoes with Italian herbs
6-oz. can tomato paste, diluted with 1 can water
2 cups frozen whole-kernel corn
16-oz. can kidney beans
1 Tbsp. chili powder
sour cream, optional
shredded cheese, optional

1. Saute ground beef, onions, and green peppers in deep saucepan. Drain and season with salt, pepper, and thyme.
2. Stir in tomatoes, tomato paste, water, and corn. Heat

until corn is thawed. Add kidney beans and chili powder. Pour into slow cooker.

3. Cover. Cook on Low 5-6 hours.

4. Top individual servings with dollops of sour cream, or sprinkle with shredded cheese if your diet allows.

Exchange List Values:
Starch 1.5, Vegetable 2.0, Meat, lean 2.0

Basic Nutritional Values: Calories 281 (Calories from Fat 78), Total Fat 9 gm (Saturated Fat 3.1 gm, Polyunsat Fat 0.7 gm, Monounsat Fat 3.5 gm, Cholesterol 45 mg), Sodium 574 mg, Total Carbohydrate 33 gm, Dietary Fiber 7 gm, Sugars 7 gm, Protein 21 gm

White Bean Chili
Tracey Stenger
Gretna, LA

Makes 12 servings
(Ideal slow cooker size: 6-quart)

1 lb. ground beef, browned and drained
1 lb. ground turkey, browned and drained
3 bell peppers, chopped
2 onions, chopped
4 garlic cloves, minced
2 14½-oz. cans 98%-fat-free, lower-sodium chicken, or vegetable, broth
15½-oz. can butter beans, rinsed and drained

15-oz. can black-eyed peas, rinsed and drained
15-oz. can garbanzo beans, rinsed and drained
15-oz. can navy beans, rinsed and drained
4-oz. can chopped green chilies
2 Tbsp. chili powder
3 tsp. ground cumin
2 tsp. dried oregano
2 tsp. paprika
½ tsp. salt
½ tsp. pepper

1. Combine all ingredients in slow cooker.

2. Cover. Cook on Low 8-10 hours.

Exchange List Values:
Starch 1.5, Vegetable 1.0, Meat, lean 2.0, Fat 0.5

Basic Nutritional Values: Calories 282 (Calories from Fat 79), Total Fat 9 gm (Saturated Fat 2.5 gm, Polyunsat Fat 1.6 gm, Monounsat Fat 3.3 gm, Cholesterol 50 mg), Sodium 570 mg, Total Carbohydrate 28 gm, Dietary Fiber 8 gm, Sugars 6 gm, Protein 24 gm

Dorothea's Slow-Cooker Chili
Dorothea K. Ladd
Ballston Lake, NY

Makes 8 servings
(Ideal slow cooker size: 4-quart)

1 lb. ground beef
¼ lb. bulk pork sausage
1 large onion, chopped

1 large green pepper, chopped
2-3 ribs celery, chopped
2 15½-oz. cans kidney beans, drained and rinsed
¼-½ cup water
29-oz. can no-added-salt tomato puree
6-oz. can tomato paste
2 cloves garlic, minced
2 Tbsp. chili powder
½ tsp. salt

1. Brown ground beef and sausage in skillet. Drain.

2. Combine all ingredients in slow cooker.

3. Cover. Cook on Low 8-10 hours.

Exchange List Values:
Starch 1.5, Vegetable 3.0, Meat, lean 2.0

Basic Nutritional Values: Calories 298 (Calories from Fat 80), Total Fat 9 gm (Saturated Fat 3.0 gm, Polyunsat Fat 1.0 gm, Monounsat Fat 3.6 gm, Cholesterol 39 mg), Sodium 453 mg, Total Carbohydrate 35 gm, Dietary Fiber 9 gm, Sugars 10 gm, Protein 22 gm

Variations:
1. For extra flavor, add 1 tsp. cayenne pepper.
2. For more zest, use mild or hot Italian sausage instead of regular pork sausage.
3. Top individual servings with shredded sharp cheddar cheese if diets permit.

Chili for Twenty

Janie Steele
Moore, OK

Makes 20 servings
(Ideal slow cooker size: use 2 slow cookers approx. 4-5-quarts each)

3 lbs. 85%-lean ground beef
3 onions, finely chopped
3 green peppers, finely chopped
2 garlic cloves, minced
4 16-oz. cans Italian-style tomatoes
4 16-oz. cans kidney beans, drained
10-oz. can diced tomatoes and chilies
2 6-oz. cans tomato paste
1 cup water
1¼ tsp. salt
1 tsp. pepper
3 whole cloves
2 bay leaves
2 Tbsp. chili powder

1. Brown meat, onions, and peppers in soup pot on top of stove. Drain.
2. Combine all ingredients in large bowl. Divide among several medium-sized slow cookers.
3. Cover. Cook on Low 3-4 hours.

Exchange List Values:
Starch 1.0, Vegetable 2.0, Meat, lean 2.0

Basic Nutritional Values: Calories 243 (Calories from Fat 69), Total Fat 8 gm (Saturated Fat 2.7 gm, Polyunsat Fat 0.6 gm, Monounsat Fat 3.1 gm, Cholesterol 40 mg), Sodium 547 mg, Total Carbohydrate 25 gm, Dietary Fiber 7 gm, Sugars 7 gm, Protein 20 gm

Crab Soup

Susan Alexander, Baltimore, MD

Makes 10 servings
(Ideal slow cooker size: 5-quart)

1 lb. carrots, sliced
½ bunch celery, sliced
1 large onion, diced
2 10-oz. bags frozen mixed vegetables, or your choice of frozen vegetables
12-oz. can no-added-salt tomato juice
8 ozs. extra-lean, lower-sodium ham
1 lb. beef, cubed
6 slices bacon, chopped
¼ tsp. pepper
1 Tbsp. Old Bay seasoning
1 lb. claw crabmeat

1. Combine all ingredients except seasonings and crab-meat in large slow cooker. Pour in water until cooker is half-full.
2. Add spices. Stir in thoroughly. Put crab on top.
3. Cover. Cook on Low 8-10 hours.
4. Stir well and serve.

Exchange List Values:
Starch 0.5, Vegetable 2.0, Meat, lean 2.0

Basic Nutritional Values: Calories 199 (Calories from Fat 44), Total Fat 5 gm (Saturated Fat 1.5 gm, Polyunsat Fat 0.7 gm, Monounsat Fat 2.0 gm, Cholesterol 74 mg), Sodium 649 mg, Total Carbohydrate 17 gm, Dietary Fiber 4 gm, Sugars 8 gm, Protein 23 gm

Corn and Shrimp Chowder

Naomi E. Fast
Hesston, KS

Makes 6 servings
(Ideal slow cooker size: 4-5-quart)

4 slices bacon, diced
1 cup chopped onions
2 cups diced, unpeeled red potatoes
2 10-oz. pkgs. frozen corn
1 tsp. Worcestershire sauce
½ tsp. paprika
½ tsp. salt
⅛ tsp. pepper
2 6-oz. cans shrimp
2 cups water
2 Tbsp. light, soft tub margarine
12-oz. can fat-free evaporated milk
chopped chives

1. Fry bacon in skillet until lightly crisp. Add onions to drippings and saute until transparent. Using slotted spoon, transfer bacon and onions to slow cooker.
2. Add remaining ingredients to cooker except milk and chives.
3. Cover. Cook on Low 3-4 hours, adding milk and

chives 30 minutes before end of cooking time.

4. Serve with broccoli salad for a tasty meal.

Exchange List Values:
Starch 3.0, Milk, fat-free 0.5, Meat, very lean 1.0, Fat 0.5

Basic Nutritional Values: Calories 331 (Calories from Fat 50), Total Fat 6 gm (Saturated Fat 0.9 gm, Polyunsat Fat 1.2 gm, Monounsat Fat 2.1 gm, Cholesterol 102 mg), Sodium 488 mg, Total Carbohydrate 49 gm, Dietary Fiber 5 gm, Sugars 11 gm, Protein 24 gm

---

I learned to make this recipe in a 7th grade home economics class. It made an impression on my father who liked seafood very much. The recipe calls only for canned shrimp, but I often increase the taste appeal with extra cooked shrimp.

I frequently use frozen hash brown potatoes for speedy preparation. There is no difference in the taste.

You might put on weight when you first go on insulin because you're no longer losing calories in your urine, but the benefits of lower blood sugars outweigh the risk of a small weight gain.

Special Seafood Chowder

Dorothea K. Ladd
Ballston Lake, NY

Makes 8-10 servings
(Ideal slow cooker size: 4-quart)

½ cup chopped onions
1 Tbsp. canola oil
1 lb. fresh or frozen cod, or haddock
4 cups diced potatoes
15-oz. can creamed corn
½ tsp. salt
dash pepper
2 cups water
1 pint fat-free half-and-half

1. Saute onions in oil in skillet until transparent but not brown.

2. Cut fish into ¾-inch cubes. Combine fish, onions, potatoes, corn, seasonings, and water in slow cooker.

3. Cover. Cook on Low 6 hours, until potatoes are tender.

4. Add half-and-half during last hour.

Exchange List Values:
Carbohydrate 1.5, Meat, lean 1.0

Basic Nutritional Values: Calories 172 (Calories from Fat 25), Total Fat 3 gm (Saturated Fat 0.5 gm, Polyunsat Fat 0.6 gm, Monounsat Fat 0.9 gm, Cholesterol 29 mg), Sodium 381 mg, Total Carbohydrate 24 gm, Dietary Fiber 2 gm, Sugars 8 gm, Protein 12 gm

Clam Chowder

Ruth Shank, Gridley, IL

Makes 8-12 servings
(Ideal slow cooker size: 5-quart)

2 10¾-oz. cans cream of potato soup
10¾-oz. can cream of celery soup
2 6½-oz. cans minced clams, drained
2 slices bacon, diced and fried
1 soup can of water
1 small onion, minced
1 Tbsp. fresh parsley
dash of dried marjoram
1 Tbsp. Worcestershire sauce
pepper to taste
1½ cups fat-free milk
1 cup fat-free half-and-half

1. Combine all ingredients, except milk and half-and-half, in slow cooker.

2. Cover. Cook on Low 6-8 hours.

3. Twenty minutes before end of cooking time, stir in milk and half-and-half. Continue cooking until heated through.

Exchange List Values:
Carbohydrate 1.0, Meat, very lean 1.0, Fat 0.5

Basic Nutritional Values: Calories 114 (Calories from Fat 34), Total Fat 4 gm (Saturated Fat 1.5 gm, Polyunsat Fat 0.9 gm, Monounsat Fat 0.8 gm, Cholesterol 17 mg), Sodium 634 mg, Total Carbohydrate 13 gm, Dietary Fiber 1 gm, Sugars 5 gm, Protein 7 gm

Manhattan Clam Chowder

Joyce Slaymaker
Strasburg, PA
Louise Stackhouse
Benton, PA

Makes 8 servings
(Ideal slow cooker size: 4-quart)

1/4 lb. bacon, diced and fried
1 large onion, chopped
2 carrots, thinly sliced
3 ribs celery, sliced
1 Tbsp. dried parsley flakes
1 lb. 12-oz. can tomatoes
1/8 tsp. salt
2 8-oz. cans clams with liquid
2 whole peppercorns
1 bay leaf
1 1/2 tsp. dried crushed thyme
3 medium potatoes, cubed

1. Combine all ingredients in slow cooker.
2. Cover. Cook on Low 8-10 hours.

Exchange List Values:
Starch 0.5, Vegetable 2.0, Meat, lean 1.0

Basic Nutritional Values: Calories 151 (Calories from Fat 25), Total Fat 3 gm (Saturated Fat 0.8 gm, Polyunsat Fat 0.6 gm, Monounsat Fat 0.9 gm, Cholesterol 21 mg), Sodium 427 mg, Total Carbohydrate 22 gm, Dietary Fiber 4 gm, Sugars 8 gm, Protein 11 gm

Chicken Clam Chowder

Irene Klaeger, Inverness, Fl

Makes 12 servings
(Ideal slow cooker size: 6-quart)

1/4 lb. bacon, diced
1/4 lb. extra-lean, lower-sodium ham, cubed
2 cups chopped onions
2 cups diced celery
1/4 tsp. pepper
2 cups diced potatoes
2 cups cooked, diced chicken
4 tsp. sodium-free chicken bouillon powder mixed with 4 cups water
2 bottles clam juice, or 2 cans clams with juice
1 lb. can whole-kernel corn, drained and rinsed
1/4-1/2 cup water
3/4 cup flour
3 cups fat-free milk
1 1/2 cups fat-free half-and-half
4 cups shredded cheddar, or Jack, cheese
1/2 cup whipping cream (not whipped)
2 Tbsp. fresh parsley

1. Saute bacon, ham, onions, and celery in skillet until bacon is crisp and onions and celery are limp. Add pepper.
2. Combine all ingredients in slow cooker except flour, milk, half-and-half, cheese, cream, and parsley.
3. Cover. Cook on Low 6-8 hours, or on High 3-4 hours.
4. Whisk flour into milk and half-and-half. Stir into soup, along with cheese, whipping cream, and parsley. Cook one more hour on High.

Exchange List Values:
Carbohydrate 1.5, Meat, lean 2.0

Basic Nutritional Values: Calories 225 (Calories from Fat 37), Total Fat 4 gm (Saturated Fat 1.3 gm, Polyunsat Fat 0.8 gm, Monounsat Fat 1.4 gm, Cholesterol 34 mg), Sodium 517 mg, Total Carbohydrate 26 gm, Dietary Fiber 2 gm, Sugars 9 gm, Protein 21 gm

Get all your prescriptions on the same schedule so that you do not have to go to the pharmacy several times a month.

Chicken Broth

Ruth Conrad Liechty
Goshen IN

Makes about 6 1-cup servings
(Ideal slow cooker size: 4-quart)

bony chicken pieces from 2
  chickens, skin and
  visible fat removed
1 onion, quartered
3 whole cloves, optional
3 ribs celery, cut up
1 carrot, quartered
1/2 tsp. salt
1/4 tsp. pepper
4 cups water

1. Place chicken in slow
cooker.
2. Stud onion with cloves.
Add to slow cooker with
other ingredients.
3. Cover. Cook on High 4-5
hours.
4. Remove chicken and
vegetables. Discard vegetables. Debone chicken. Cut up
meat to equal about 1 cup
and add to broth.
5. Place broth in the
refrigerator. After broth is
cooled, skim fat from the
surface. Use as stock for
soups.

Exchange List Values:
Meat, lean 1.0

Basic Nutritional Values: Calories
42 (Calories from Fat 14), Total Fat 2
gm (Saturated Fat 0.4 gm, Polyunsat
Fat 0.4 gm, Monounsat Fat 0.6 gm,
Cholesterol 19 mg), Sodium 211
mg, Total Carbohydrate 0 gm, Dietary
Fiber 0 gm, Sugars 0 gm, Protein 6 gm

Chicken Noodle Soup

Beth Shank
Wellman, IA

Makes 6-8 servings
(Ideal slow cooker size: 4-quart)

5 cups hot water
2 tsp. sodium-free chicken
  bouillon powder
46-oz. can 100%-fat-free,
  lower-sodium chicken
  broth
2 cups cooked chicken
4 cups "homestyle"
  noodles, uncooked
1/3 cup thinly sliced celery,
  lightly pre-cooked in
  microwave
1/3 cup shredded, or
  chopped, carrots

1. Dissolve bouillon in
water. Pour into slow cooker.
2. Add remaining ingredi-
ents. Mix well.
3. Cover. Cook on Low 4-6
hours.

Exchange List Values:
Starch 1.0, Meat, lean 1.0

Basic Nutritional Values: Calories
155 (Calories from Fat 31), Total Fat
3 gm (Saturated Fat 1.0 gm,
Polyunsat Fat 0.8 gm, Monounsat Fat
1.2 gm, Cholesterol 49 mg), Sodium
382 mg, Total Carbohydrate 15 gm,
Dietary Fiber 1 gm, Sugars 2 gm,
Protein 14 gm

Brown Jug Soup

Dorothy Shank
Sterling, IL

Makes 10-12 servings
(Ideal slow cooker size: 6-quart)

10 1/2-oz. can chicken broth
4 tsp. sodium-free chicken
  bouillon powder
1 qt. water
2 cups (3-4 ribs) diced
  celery
2 cups (2 medium-sized)
  diced onions
4 cups diced potatoes
3 cups diced carrots
10-oz. pkg. frozen whole-
  kernel corn
2 10 3/4-oz. cans 98%-fat-
  free, reduced-sodium
  cream of chicken soup
4 ozs. shredded sharp
  cheddar cheese

1. Combine all ingredients
except cheese in slow cooker.
2. Cover. Cook on Low 10-
12 hours, or until vegetables
are tender.
3. Just before serving, add
cheese. Stir until cheese is
melted. Serve.

Exchange List Values:
Starch 1.5, Vegetable 1.0

Basic Nutritional Values: Calories
138 (Calories from Fat 13), Total Fat
1 gm (Saturated Fat 0.4 gm,
Polyunsat Fat 0.6 gm, Monounsat Fat
0.3 gm, Cholesterol 6 mg), Sodium
464 mg, Total Carbohydrate 25 gm,
Dietary Fiber 3 gm, Sugars 6 gm,
Protein 7 gm

Chicken Corn Soup

Eleanor Larson, Glen Lyon, PA

Makes 4-6 servings
(Ideal slow cooker size: 4-quart)

2 whole boneless skinless
  chicken breasts, cubed
1 onion, chopped
1 garlic clove, minced
2 carrots, sliced
2 ribs celery, chopped
2 medium potatoes, cubed
1 tsp. mixed dried herbs
1/3 cup tomato sauce
12-oz. can cream-style corn
14-oz. can whole-kernel
  corn
3 tsp. sodium-free chicken
  bouillon powder
3 cups water
1/4 cup chopped Italian
  parsley
1/4 tsp. pepper

1. Combine all ingredients
except parsley and pepper in
slow cooker.
2. Cover. Cook on Low 8-9
hours, or until chicken is tender.
3. Add parsley and seasoning 30 minutes before serving.

Exchange List Values:
Starch 2.0, Vegetable 1.0,
Meat, very lean 3.0

Basic Nutritional Values: Calories
251 (Calories from Fat 28), Total Fat
3 gm (Saturated Fat 0.6 gm,
Polyunsat Fat 0.8 gm, Monounsat Fat
0.9 gm, Cholesterol 49 mg), Sodium
534 mg, Total Carbohydrate 33 gm,
Dietary Fiber 5 gm, Sugars 13 gm,
Protein 23 gm

Chili, Chicken, Corn Chowder

Jeanne Allen
Rye, CO

Makes 6-8 servings
(Ideal slow cooker size: 4-quart)

2 Tbsp. canola oil
1 large onion, diced
1 garlic clove, minced
1 rib celery, finely chopped
2 cups frozen, or canned,
  corn
2 cups cooked, deboned,
  diced chicken
4-oz. can diced green
  chilies
1/2 tsp. black pepper
2 cups 100%-fat-free,
  lower-sodium chicken
  broth
1/4 tsp. salt
1 cup fat-free half-and-half

1. In saucepan, saute
onion, garlic, and celery in oil
until limp.
2. Stir in corn, chicken,
and chilies. Saute for 2-3 minutes.
3. Combine all ingredients
except half-and-half in slow
cooker.
4. Cover. Heat on Low 4
hours.
5. Stir in half-and-half
before serving. Do not boil,
but be sure cream is heated
through.

Exchange List Values:
Starch 0.5, Vegetable 1.0,
Meat, lean 1.0, Fat 1.0

Basic Nutritional Values: Calories
169 (Calories from Fat 60), Total Fat
7 gm (Saturated Fat 1.2 gm,
Polyunsat Fat 1.7 gm, Monounsat Fat
3.0 gm, Cholesterol 33 mg), Sodium
343 mg, Total Carbohydrate 14 gm,
Dietary Fiber 2 gm, Sugars 4 gm,
Protein 13 gm

White Chili

Esther Martin
Ephrata, PA

Makes 8 servings
(Ideal slow cooker size: 5-quart)

3 15-oz. cans Great
  Northern beans, drained
8 ozs. cooked and
  shredded chicken
  breasts
1 cup chopped onions
1 1/2 cups chopped yellow,
  red, or green bell
  peppers
2 garlic cloves, minced
2 tsp. ground cumin
1/2 tsp. salt
1/2 tsp. dried oregano
3 1/2 cups chicken broth

1. Combine all ingredients
in slow cooker.
2. Cover. Cook on Low 8-
10 hours, or High 4-5 hours.
3. Ladle into bowls and
top individual servings with
reduced-fat sour cream,
reduced-fat cheddar cheese,
and baked tortilla chips, if
diets allow.

Exchange List Values:
Starch 1.5, Vegetable 1.0,
Meat, very lean 1.0

Basic Nutritional Values: Calories 189 (Calories from Fat 15), Total Fat 2 gm (Saturated Fat 0.4 gm, Polyunsat Fat 0.5 gm, Monounsat Fat 0.5 gm, Cholesterol 24 mg), Sodium 561 mg, Total Carbohydrate 25 gm, Dietary Fiber 8 gm, Sugars 5 gm, Protein 19 gm

Suggested garnishes:
reduced-fat sour cream
reduced-fat cheddar cheese
baked tortilla chips

White Chili Speciality

Barbara McGinnis, Jupiter, FL

*Makes 10 servings
(Ideal slow cooker size: 5-quart)*

1 lb. large Great Northern beans, soaked overnight
2 lbs. boneless, skinless chicken breasts, cut up
1 medium onion, chopped
2 4½-oz. cans chopped green chilies
2 tsp. cumin
½ tsp. salt
14½-oz. can chicken broth
1 cup water

1. Put soaked beans in medium-sized saucepan and cover with water. Bring to boil and simmer 20 minutes. Discard water.
2. Brown chicken in fat-free cooking spray, in skillet.

3. Combine pre-cooked and drained beans, chicken, and all remaining ingredients in slow cooker.
4. Cover. Cook on Low 10-12 hours, or High 5-6 hours.

Exchange List Values:
Starch 2.0, Meat, very lean 3.0

Basic Nutritional Values: Calories 258 (Calories from Fat 28), Total Fat 3 gm (Saturated Fat 0.9 gm, Polyunsat Fat 0.8 gm, Monounsat Fat 1.0 gm, Cholesterol 55 mg), Sodium 571 mg, Total Carbohydrate 26 gm, Dietary Fiber 9 gm, Sugars 4 gm, Protein 30 gm

Mexican Rice and Bean Soup

Esther J. Mast,
East Petersburg, PA

*Makes 6 servings
(Ideal slow cooker size: 4-quart)*

½ cup chopped onions
⅓ cup chopped green peppers
1 garlic clove, minced
1 Tbsp. oil
4-oz. pkg. sliced or chipped dried beef
18-oz. can no-added-salt tomato juice
15½-oz. can red kidney beans, undrained
1½ cups water
½ cup long grain rice, uncooked
1 tsp. paprika
½-1 tsp. chili powder
dash of pepper

1. Cook onions, green peppers, and garlic in oil in skillet until vegetables are tender but not brown. Transfer to slow cooker.
2. Tear beef into small pieces and add to slow cooker.
3. Add remaining ingredients. Mix well.
4. Cover. Cook on Low 6 hours. Stir before serving.
5. Serve with relish tray and corn bread, home-canned fruit, and cookies.

Exchange List Values:
Starch 1.5, Vegetable 2.0, Fat 0.5

Basic Nutritional Values: Calories 190 (Calories from Fat 28), Total Fat 3 gm (Saturated Fat 0.4 gm, Polyunsat Fat 0.9 gm, Monounsat Fat 1.6 gm, Cholesterol 15 mg), Sodium 796 mg, Total Carbohydrate 30 gm, Dietary Fiber 4 gm, Sugars 7 gm, Protein 12 gm

This is a recipe I fixed often when our sons were growing up. We have all enjoyed it in any season of the year.

Try not to think of exercise as a chore, but as play. Get in touch with your inner kid!

Chicken Tortilla Soup

Becky Harder
Monument, CO

Makes 6-8 servings
(Ideal slow cooker size: 4-5-quart)

4 chicken breast halves
2 15-oz. cans no-salt-added black beans, undrained
2 15-oz. cans Mexican stewed tomatoes, or Rotel tomatoes
1 cup salsa (mild, medium, or hot, whichever you prefer)
4-oz. can chopped green chilies
14½-oz. can no-added-salt tomato sauce
2ozs. (about 24 chips) tortilla chips
1 cup fat-free cheddar cheese

1. Combine all ingredients except chips and cheese in large slow cooker.
2. Cover. Cook on Low 8 hours.
3. Just before serving, remove chicken breasts and slice into bite-sized pieces. Stir into soup.
4. To serve, put a handful of chips in each individual soup bowl. Ladle soup over chips. Top with cheese.

Exchange List Values:
Starch 1.0, Vegetable 2.0, Meat, very lean 3.0, Fat 0.5

Basic Nutritional Values: Calories 263 (Calories from Fat 36), Total Fat 4 gm (Saturated Fat 0.9 gm, Polyunsat Fat 0.8 gm, Monounsat Fat 1.7 gm, Cholesterol 43 mg), Sodium 793 mg, Total Carbohydrate 29 gm, Dietary Fiber 7 gm, Sugars 9 gm, Protein 28 gm

Tortilla Soup

Joy Mintzer
Newark, DE

Makes 6 servings
(Ideal slow cooker size: 4-quart)

4 chicken breast halves
1 garlic clove, minced
1½ tsp. canola oil
2 14½-oz. cans 100%-fat-free reduced-sodium chicken broth
2 14½-oz. cans no-added-salt, chopped, stewed tomatoes
1 cup salsa (mild, medium, or hot, whichever you prefer)
½ cup chopped cilantro
1 Tbsp., or more, ground cumin
8 ozs. reduced-fat Monterey Jack cheese, cubed

1. Cook, debone, and shred chicken.
2. Add minced garlic to oil in slow cooker. Saute.
3. Combine all ingredients except cheese.
4. Cover. Cook on Low 8-10 hours.
5. Divide cubed cheese among 6 individual soup bowls. Ladle soup over cheese. Sprinkle with chips and top each bowl with a dollop of sour cream if diets allow.

Exchange List Values:
Vegetable 3.0, Meat, lean 3.0

Basic Nutritional Values: Calories 234 (Calories from Fat 65), Total Fat 7 gm (Saturated Fat 3.4 gm, Polyunsat Fat 1.1 gm, Monounsat Fat 2.6 gm, Cholesterol 69 mg), Sodium 669 mg, Total Carbohydrate 12 gm, Dietary Fiber 2 gm, Sugars 5 gm, Protein 31 gm

---

Suggested garnishes
fat-free sour cream
tortilla chips

Tex-Mex Chicken Chowder

Janie Steele, Moore, OK

*Makes 8-10 servings
(Ideal slow cooker size: 5-quart
or larger)*

1 cup chopped onions
1 cup thinly sliced celery
2 garlic cloves, minced
1 Tbsp. canola oil
1½ lbs. boneless, skinless
   chicken breasts, cubed
4 tsp. sodium-free chicken
   bouillon powder
4 cups water
1 pkg. country gravy mix
2 cups fat-free milk
16-oz. jar chunky salsa
32-oz. bag frozen hash
   brown potatoes
4½-oz. can chopped green
   chilies
4 ozs. fat-free American
   cheese

1. Combine onions, celery, garlic, oil, chicken, and bouillon mixed with water in 5-quart or larger slow cooker.
2. Cover. Cook on Low 2½ hours, until chicken is no longer pink.
3. In separate bowl, dissolve gravy mix in milk. Stir into chicken mixture. Add salsa, potatoes, chilies, and cheese and combine well. Cook on Low 2-4 hours, or until potatoes are fully cooked.

Ham and Potato Chowder

Penny Blosser
Beavercreek, OH

*Makes 5 servings
(Ideal slow cooker size: 4-quart)*

5-oz. pkg. scalloped
   potatoes
sauce mix from potato
   pkg.
1 cup extra-lean, reduced-
   sodium, cooked ham,
   cut into narrow strips
4 tsp. sodium-free bouillon
   powder
4 cups water
1 cup chopped celery
⅓ cup chopped onions
salt to taste
pepper to taste
2 cups fat-free half-and-
   half
⅓ cup flour

1. Combine potatoes, sauce mix, ham, bouillon powder, water, celery, onions, salt, and pepper in slow cooker.
2. Cover. Cook on Low 7 hours.
3. Combine half-and-half and flour. Gradually add to slow cooker, blending well.
4. Cover. Cook on Low up to 1 hour, stirring occasionally until thickened.

Drink plenty of water. You should try to drink eight 8-oz. glasses each day.

Chicken and Ham Gumbo

Barbara Tenney
Delta, PA

Makes 6 servings
(Ideal slow cooker size: 4-quart)

1½ lbs. boneless, skinless chicken thighs
1 Tbsp. oil
10-oz. pkg. frozen okra
½ lb. extra-lean, lower-sodium ham, cut into small chunks
1½ cups coarsely chopped onions
1½ cups coarsely chopped green peppers
2 10-oz. cans no-added-salt cannellini beans, drained
6 cups low-sodium chicken broth
2 10-oz. cans diced tomatoes with green chilies
2 Tbsp. chopped fresh cilantro

1. Cut chicken into bite-sized pieces. Cook in oil in skillet until no longer pink.
2. Run hot water over okra until pieces separate easily.
3. Combine all ingredients but cilantro in slow cooker.
4. Cover. Cook on Low 6-8 hours. Stir in cilantro before serving.

Exchange List Values:
Starch 1.0, Vegetable 3.0, Meat, lean 4.0

Basic Nutritional Values: Calories 385 (Calories from Fat 120), Total Fat 13 gm (Saturated Fat 3.1 gm, Polyunsat Fat 3.4 gm, Monounsat Fat 5.2 gm, Cholesterol 96 mg), Sodium 879 mg, Total Carbohydrate 28 gm, Dietary Fiber 7 gm, Sugars 10 gm, Protein 38 gm

Variations:
1. Stir in ½ cup long grain, dry rice with rest of ingredients.
2. Add ¼ tsp. pepper with other ingredients.

Easy Southern Brunswick Stew

Barbara Sparks
Glen Burnie, MD

Makes 12 servings
(Ideal slow cooker size: 4-quart)

2 lbs. pork butt, visible fat removed
17-oz. can white corn
1¼ cup ketchup
2 cups diced, cooked potatoes
10-oz. pkg. frozen peas
2 10¾-oz. cans reduced-sodium tomato soup

1. Place pork in slow cooker.
2. Cover. Cook on Low 6-8 hours. Remove meat from bone and shred, removing and discarding all visible fat.
3. Combine all ingredients in slow cooker.
4. Cover. Bring to boil on High. Reduce heat to Low and simmer 30 minutes.

Exchange List Values:
Starch 1.0, Vegetable 2.0, Meat, lean 1.0, Fat 0.5

Basic Nutritional Values: Calories 213 (Calories from Fat 61), Total Fat 7 gm (Saturated Fat 2.3 gm, Polyunsat Fat 0.9 gm, Monounsat Fat 2.6 gm, Cholesterol 34 mg), Sodium 584 mg, Total Carbohydrate 27 gm, Dietary Fiber 3 gm, Sugars 9 gm, Protein 13 gm

Optional ingredients:
hot sauce to taste
salt to taste
pepper to taste

Oriental Pork Soup

Judi Manos
West Islip, NY

Makes 8 servings
(Ideal slow cooker size: 5-quart)

¹/₂ lb. ground pork
1 garlic clove, minced
2 medium carrots, cut into
   julienne strips
4 medium green onions,
   cut into 1" pieces
1 garlic clove, minced
2 Tbsp. light soy sauce
¹/₂ tsp. gingerroot, chopped
¹/₈ tsp. pepper
2 14¹/₂-oz. cans chicken
   broth
2¹/₂ tsp. sodium free
   chicken bouillon powder
2¹/₂ cups water
1 cup sliced mushrooms
1 cup bean sprouts

1. Cook meat with garlic
in skillet until brown. Drain.
2. Combine all ingredients
except mushrooms and
sprouts in slow cooker.
3. Cover. Cook on Low 7-9
hours or High 3-4 hours.
4. Stir in mushrooms and
bean sprouts.
5. Cover. Cook on Low 1
hour.

Exchange List Values:
Vegetable 1.0, Meat,
medium fat 1.0

Basic Nutritional Values: Calories
97 (Calories from Fat 39), Total Fat 4
gm (Saturated Fat 1.5 gm, Polyunsat
Fat 0.4 gm, Monounsat Fat 1.8 gm,
Cholesterol 19 mg), Sodium 486

mg, Total Carbohydrate 6 gm, Dietary
Fiber 2 gm, Sugars 3 gm, Protein 8
gm

---

*Variation: To add flavor to the
pork, add ¹/₈ tsp. five-spice
blend to Step 1.*

Joy's Brunswick Stew

Joy Sutter
Iowa City, IA

Makes 8 servings
(Ideal slow cooker size: 4-quart)

1 lb. skinless, boneless
   chicken breasts, cut into
   bite-sized pieces
2 potatoes, thinly sliced
10³/₄-oz. can tomato soup
16-oz. can stewed tomatoes
10-oz. pkg. frozen corn
10-oz. pkg. frozen lima
   beans
3 Tbsp. onion flakes
¹/₄ tsp. salt
¹/₈ tsp. pepper

1. Combine all ingredients
in slow cooker.
2. Cover. Cook on High 2
hours. Reduce to Low and
cook 2 hours.

Exchange List Values:
Starch 2.0, Vegetable 1.0,
Meat, very lean 1.0

Basic Nutritional Values: Calories
220 (Calories from Fat 21), Total Fat
2 gm (Saturated Fat 0.6 gm,
Polyunsat Fat 0.8 gm, Monounsat Fat
0.6 gm, Cholesterol 34 mg), Sodium
480 mg, Total Carbohydrate 33 gm,
Dietary Fiber 5 gm, Sugars 8 gm,
Protein 18 gm

---

*Variation: For more flavor,
add 1 or 2 bay leaves during
cooking.*

For exercise that lasts
longer than an hour
and is fairly intense,
try sports drinks,
which are convenient
and easy to digest.

Brunswick Soup Mix

Joyce B. Suiter
Garysburg, NC

Makes 14 servings
(Ideal slow cooker size: 5-quart)

1 large onion, chopped
4 cups frozen, cubed, hash browns, thawed
4 cups chopped cooked chicken, or 2 20-oz. cans canned chicken
14½-oz. can diced tomatoes
15-oz. can tomato sauce
15¼-oz. can corn
15¼-oz. can lima beans, drained
2 cups 100%-fat-free, lower-sodium chicken broth
¼ tsp. salt
½ tsp. pepper
¼ tsp. Worcestershire sauce
¼ cup sugar

1. Combine all ingredients in large slow cooker.
2. Cover. Cook on High 7 hours.
3. Cool and freeze in 2-cup portions.
4. To use, empty 1 frozen portion into saucepan with small amount of liquid: tomato juice, V-8 juice, or broth. Cook slowly until soup mixture thaws. Stir frequently, adding more liquid until of desired consistency.

Exchange List Values:
Starch 1.5, Vegetable 1.0, Meat, lean 1.0

Basic Nutritional Values: Calories 206 (Calories from Fat 34), Total Fat 4 gm (Saturated Fat 1.0 gm, Polyunsat Fat 1.0 gm, Monounsat Fat 1.1 gm, Cholesterol 36 gm), Sodium 578 mg, Total Carbohydrate 28 gm, Dietary Fiber 5 gm, Sugars 10 gm, Protein 16 gm

Oriental Turkey Chili

Kimberly Jensen, Bailey, CO

Makes 6 servings
(Ideal slow cooker size: 4-quart)

2 cups yellow onions, diced
1 small red bell pepper, diced
1 lb. ground turkey, browned
2 Tbsp. minced gingerroot
3 cloves garlic, minced
¼ cup dry sherry
¼ cup hoisin sauce
2 Tbsp. chili powder
1 Tbsp. corn oil
2 Tbsp. light soy sauce
1 tsp. sugar
2 cups canned whole tomatoes
16-oz. can no-salt-added dark red kidney beans, undrained

1. Combine all ingredients in slow cooker.
2. Cover. Cook on Low 6 hours.

3. Serve topped with chow mein noodles or over cooked white rice.

Exchange List Values:
Starch 1.0, Vegetable 2.0, Meat, lean 2.0, Fat 1.0

Basic Nutritional Values: Calories 279 (Calories from Fat 93), Total Fat 10 gm (Saturated Fat 2.4 gm, Polyunsat Fat 3.5 gm, Monounsat Fat 3.4 gm, Cholesterol 56 mg), Sodium 612 mg, Total Carbohydrate 26 gm, Dietary Fiber 8 gm, Sugars 12 gm, Protein 22 gm

Note: If you serve this chili over rice, this recipe will yield 10-12 servings.

Pumpkin Black-Bean Turkey Chili

Rhoda Atzeff
Harrisburg, PA

Makes 10 servings
(Ideal slow cooker size: 4-5-quart)

1 cup chopped onions
1 cup chopped yellow bell pepper
3 garlic cloves, minced
2 Tbsp. canola oil
1½ tsp. dried oregano
1½-2 tsp. ground cumin
2 tsp. chili powder
2 15-oz. cans black beans, rinsed and drained
2½ cups chopped cooked turkey
16-oz. can pumpkin

14½-oz. can diced
   tomatoes
3 cups 98%-fat-free, lower-
   sodium chicken broth

1. Saute onions, yellow
pepper, and garlic in oil for 8
minutes, or until soft.
2. Stir in oregano, cumin,
and chili powder. Cook 1
minute. Transfer to slow
cooker.
3. Add remaining
ingredients.
4. Cover. Cook on Low 7-8
hours.

Exchange List Values:
Starch 1.0, Vegetable 1.0,
Meat, lean 1.0, Fat 0.5

Basic Nutritional Values: Calories
189 (Calories from Fat 46), Total Fat
5 gm (Saturated Fat 0.9 gm,
Polyunsat Fat 1.5 gm, Monounsat Fat
2.1 gm, Cholesterol 27 mg), Sodium
327 mg, Total Carbohydrate 20 gm,
Dietary Fiber 7 gm, Sugars 6 gm,
Protein 17 gm

Be sure to tell your
doctor right away if you
have symptoms such as
a change in vision,
swelling of the ankles or
pain in the feet, or
chest pain.

Turkey Chili
Reita F. Yoder
Carlsbad, NM

Makes 6-8 servings
(Ideal slow cooker size: 4-quart)

2 lbs. ground turkey,
   browned and drained
16-oz. can pinto, or kidney,
   beans
2 cups fresh tomatoes,
   chopped
2 cups no-salt-added
   tomato sauce
1 garlic clove, minced
1 small onion, chopped
16-oz. can rotel tomatoes
1-oz. pkg. Williams chili
   seasoning

1. Crumble ground turkey
in bottom of slow cooker.
2. Add remaining
ingredients. Mix well.
3. Cover. Cook on Low 6-8
hours.

Exchange List Values:
Starch 0.5, Vegetable 2.0,
Meat, lean 3.0, Fat 0.5

Basic Nutritional Values: Calories
294 (Calories from Fat 106), Total Fat
12 gm (Saturated Fat 2.8 gm,
Polyunsat Fat 2.9 gm, Monounsat Fat
4.2 gm, Cholesterol 84 mg), Sodium
633 mg, Total Carbohydrate 19 gm,
Dietary Fiber 5 gm, Sugars 9 gm,
Protein 27 gm

Joyce's Slow-Cooked Chili
Joyce Slaymaker
Strasburg, PA

Makes 10 servings
(Ideal slow cooker size: 4-quart)

2 lbs. ground turkey
2 16-oz. cans kidney beans,
   rinsed and drained
2 14½-oz. cans diced
   tomatoes, undrained
8-oz. can tomato sauce
2 medium onions, chopped
1 green pepper, chopped
2 cloves garlic, minced
2 Tbsp. chili powder
1 tsp. pepper

1. Brown ground turkey in
skillet. Drain. Transfer to
slow cooker.
2. Stir in remaining ingredients.
3. Cover. Cook on Low 8-
10 hours, or on High 4 hours.
4. Garnish individual servings with cheese.

Exchange List Values:
Starch 1.0, Vegetable 2.0,
Meat, lean 2.0, Fat 0.5

Basic Nutritional Values: Calories
276 (Calories from Fat 85), Total Fat
9 gm (Saturated Fat 2.2 gm,
Polyunsat Fat 2.5 gm, Monounsat Fat
3.3 gm, Cholesterol 67 mg), Sodium
490 mg, Total Carbohydrate 24 gm,
Dietary Fiber 6 gm, Sugars 8 gm,
Protein 25 gm

Turkey Chili

Dawn Day
Westminster, CA

Makes 8 servings
(Ideal slow cooker size: 4-quart)

1 large chopped onion
2 Tbsp. oil
1 lb. ground turkey
3 Tbsp. chili powder
6-oz. can tomato paste
3 1 lb. cans small red
  beans with liquid
1 cup frozen corn

1. Saute onion in oil in skillet until transparent. Add turkey and brown lightly in skillet.
2. Combine all ingredients in slow cooker. Mix well.
3. Cover. Cook on Low 8-9 hours.

Exchange List Values:
Starch 2.0, Vegetable 1.0,
Meat, lean 2.0, Fat 0.5

Basic Nutritional Values: Calories 319 (Calories from Fat 91), Total Fat 10 gm (Saturated Fat 1.7 gm, Polyunsat Fat 3.0 gm, Monounsat Fat 4.3 gm, Cholesterol 42 mg), Sodium 678 mg, Total Carbohydrate 37 gm, Dietary Fiber 9 gm, Sugars 7 gm, Protein 22 gm

Note: Ground beef can be used in place of turkey.

Variation: Serve over rice, topped with fat-free shredded cheddar cheese and fat-free sour cream.

Chili Sans Cholesterol

Dolores S. Kratz
Souderton, PA

Makes 4 servings
(Ideal slow cooker size: 4-quart)

1 lb. ground turkey
1/2 cup chopped celery
1/2 cup chopped onions
8-oz. can tomatoes
15-oz. can no-salt-added
  pinto beans
14 1/2-oz. can diced
  tomatoes
1/2 tsp., or more, chili
  powder
1/4 tsp. salt
dash pepper

1. Saute turkey in skillet until browned. Drain.
2. Combine all ingredients in slow cooker.
3. Cover. Cook on Low 6 hours.

Exchange List Values:
Starch 1.0, Vegetable 2.0,
Meat, lean 3.0, Fat 0.5

Basic Nutritional Values: Calories 317 (Calories from Fat 104), Total Fat 12 gm (Saturated Fat 2.9 gm, Polyunsat Fat 3.0 gm, Monounsat Fat 4.1 gm, Cholesterol 84 mg), Sodium 578 mg, Total Carbohydrate 24 gm, Dietary Fiber 7 gm, Sugars 8 gm, Protein 29 gm

**More vegetables =
Fewer heart attacks**

Italian Vegetable Soup

Patti Boston, Newark, OH

Makes 4-6 servings
(Ideal slow cooker size: 4-quart)

3 small carrots, sliced
1 small onion, chopped
2 small potatoes, diced
2 Tbsp. chopped parsley
1 garlic clove, minced
3 tsp. sodium-free beef
  bouillon powder
1 1/4 tsp. dried basil
1/4 tsp. pepper
16-oz. can red kidney
  beans, undrained
3 cups water
14 1/2-oz. can stewed
  tomatoes, with juice
1 cup diced, extra-lean,
  lower-sodium cooked
  ham

1. Layer carrots, onions, potatoes, parsley, garlic, beef bouillon, basil, pepper, and kidney beans in slow cooker. Do not stir. Add water.
2. Cover. Cook on Low 8-9 hours, or on High 4 1/2-5 1/2 hours, until vegetables are tender.
3. Stir in tomatoes and ham. Cover and cook on High 10-15 minutes.

Exchange List Values:
Starch 1.5, Vegetable 2.0

Basic Nutritional Values: Calories 156 (Calories from Fat 7), Total Fat 1 gm (Saturated Fat 0.2 gm, Polyunsat Fat 0.3 gm, Monounsat Fat 0.2 gm,

Cholesterol 9 mg), Sodium 614 mg,Total Carbohydrate 29 gm, Dietary Fiber 5 gm, Sugars 8 gm, Protein 9 gm

708 mg,Total Carbohydrate 46 gm, Dietary Fiber 9 gm, Sugars 21 gm, Protein 20 gm

Sauerkraut Soup

Barbara Tenny
Delta, PA

Makes 10 servings
(Ideal slow cooker size: 5-quart)

low-fat kielbasa, cut into
  1/2-inch pieces
5 medium potatoes, cubed
2 large onions, chopped
2 large carrots, cut into
  1/4-inch slices
4 tsp. sodium-free chicken
  bouillon powder
4 cups water
32-oz. can or bag
  sauerkraut, rinsed and
  drained
6-oz. can tomato paste

1. Combine all ingredients in large slow cooker. Stir to combine.
2. Cover. Cook on High 2 hours, and then on Low 6-8 hours.
3. Delicious served with rye bread.

Exchange List Values:
Starch 1.0, Vegetable 3.0, Meat, lean 1.0

Basic Nutritional Values: Calories 188 (Calories from Fat 22), Total Fat 2 gm (Saturated Fat 0.8 gm, Polyunsat Fat 0.4 gm, Monounsat Fat 1.2 gm, Cholesterol 21 mg), Sodium 772 mg,Total Carbohydrate 33 gm, Dietary Fiber 6 gm, Sugars 9 gm, Protein 10 gm

Chet's Trucker Stew

Janice Muller, Derwood, MD

Makes 12 servings
(Ideal slow cooker size: 4-5-quart)

1 lb. bulk pork sausage,
  cooked and drained
1 lb. ground beef, cooked
  and drained
31-oz. can pork and beans
2 15-oz. cans no-salt-added
  kidney beans, drained
14 1/2-oz. can waxed beans,
  drained
14 1/2-oz. can lima beans,
  drained
1 cup no-added-salt
  ketchup
1/2 cup brown sugar
brown sugar substitute to
  equal 1/4 cup
1 Tbsp. spicy prepared
  mustard

1. Combine all ingredients in slow cooker.
2. Cover. Simmer on High 2-3 hours.

Exchange List Values:
Starch 2.0, Carbohydrate 1.0, Meat, medium fat 2.0

Basic Nutritional Values: Calories 363 (Calories from Fat 100), Total Fat 11 gm (Saturated Fat 3.5 gm, Polyunsat Fat 1.3 gm, Monounsat Fat 4.8 gm, Cholesterol 40 mg), Sodium

Spicy Potato Soup

Sharon Kauffman
Harrisonburg, VA

Makes 8 servings
(Ideal slow cooker size: 4-quart)

3/4 lb. 90%-lean ground
  beef, browned
4 cups cubed peeled
  potatoes
1 small onion, chopped
3 8-oz. cans no-added-salt
  tomato sauce
1 tsp. salt
1 1/2 tsp. pepper
1/2-1 tsp. hot pepper sauce
water

1. Combine all ingredients except water in slow cooker. Add enough water to cover ingredients.
2. Cover. Cook on Low 8-10 hours, or High 5 hours, until potatoes are tender.

Exchange List Values:
Starch 1.0, Vegetable 1.0, Meat, lean 1.0

Basic Nutritional Values: Calories 152 (Calories from Fat 32), Total Fat 4 gm (Saturated Fat 1.4 gm, Polyunsat Fat 0.2 gm, Monounsat Fat 1.5 gm, Cholesterol 26 mg), Sodium 346 mg,Total Carbohydrate 19 gm, Dietary Fiber 2 gm, Sugars 7 gm, Protein 10 gm

Hearty Potato Sauerkraut Soup

Kathy Hertzler
Lancaster, PA

Makes 6-8 servings
(Ideal slow cooker size: 4-quart)

4 tsp. sodium-free chicken
  bouillon powder
4 cups water
10³/₄-oz. can 98%-fat-free,
  reduced-sodium cream
  of mushroom soup
16-oz. can sauerkraut,
  rinsed and drained
8 ozs. fresh mushrooms,
  sliced
1 medium potato, cubed
2 medium carrots, peeled
  and sliced
2 ribs celery, chopped
8 ozs. low-fat Polish
  kielbasa (smoked),
  cubed
2 cups chopped cooked
  chicken
2 Tbsp. vinegar
2 tsp. dried dill weed
1¹/₂ tsp. pepper

1. Mix together bouillon
powder and water. Pour into
slow cooker.
2. Combine remaining
ingredients in large slow
cooker.
3. Cover. Cook on Low 10-
12 hours.
4. If necessary, skim fat
before serving.

Exchange List Values:
Carbohydrate 1.0,
Vegetable 1.0, Meat, lean
1.0, Fat 0.5

Basic Nutritional Values: Calories
178 (Calories from Fat 44), Total Fat
5 gm (Saturated Fat 1.5 gm,
Polyunsat Fat 1.0 gm, Monounsat Fat
1.8 gm, Cholesterol 45 mg), Sodium
664 mg, Total Carbohydrate 17 gm,
Dietary Fiber 3 gm, Sugars 5 gm,
Protein 16 gm

Kielbasa Soup

Bernice M. Gnidovec
Streator, IL

Makes 8 servings
(Ideal slow cooker size: 4-quart)

16-oz. pkg. frozen mixed
  vegetables, or your
  choice of vegetables
6-oz. can tomato paste
1 medium onion, chopped
3 medium potatoes, diced
12 ozs. low-fat kielbasa,
  cut into ¹/₄-inch pieces
4 qts. water
fresh parsley

1. Combine all ingredients
except parsley in large slow
cooker.
2. Cover. Cook on Low 12
hours.
3. Garnish individual servings with fresh parsley.

Exchange List Values:
Starch 1.5, Vegetable 1.0,
Meat, very lean 1.0

Basic Nutritional Values: Calories
167 (Calories from Fat 20), Total Fat
2 gm (Saturated Fat 0.7 gm,
Polyunsat Fat 0.3 gm, Monounsat Fat
1.1 gm, Cholesterol 19 mg), Sodium
412 mg, Total Carbohydrate 29 gm,
Dietary Fiber 4 gm, Sugars 6 gm,
Protein 9 gm

Curried Carrot Soup

Ann Bender, Ft. Defiance, VA

Makes 6-8 servings
(Ideal slow cooker size: 4-quart)

1 garlic clove, minced
1 large onion, chopped
2 Tbsp. oil
1 Tbsp. butter
1 tsp. curry powder
1 Tbsp. flour
4 cups 100%-fat-free,
  lower-sodium chicken
  broth
6 large carrots, sliced
¹/₄ tsp. salt
¹/₄ tsp. ground red pepper,
  optional
1¹/₂ cups plain yogurt, or
  light sour cream

1. In skillet cook minced
garlic and onion in oil and
butter until limp but not
brown.
2. Add curry and flour.
Cook 30 seconds. Pour into
slow cooker.
3. Add chicken broth and
carrots.
4. Cover. Cook on High for
about 2 hours, or until carrots
are soft.

5. Puree mixture in blender. Season with salt and pepper. Return to slow cooker and keep warm until ready to serve.

6. Add a dollop of yogurt or sour cream to each serving.

Exchange List Values:
Vegetable 2.0, Fat 1.0

Basic Nutritional Values: Calories 113 (Calories from Fat 46), Total Fat 5 gm (Saturated Fat 1.2 gm, Polyunsat Fat 1.1 gm, Monounsat Fat 2.5 gm, Cholesterol 5 mg), Sodium 414 mg, Total Carbohydrate 13 gm, Dietary Fiber 2 gm, Sugars 7 gm, Protein 5 gm

Curried Pork and Pea Soup

Kathy Hertzler
Lancaster, PA

Makes 8 servings
(Ideal slow cooker size: 4-quart)

1¹/₂ lbs. boneless pork shoulder roast
1 cup yellow, or green, split peas, rinsed and drained
¹/₂ cup finely chopped carrots
¹/₂ cup finely chopped celery
¹/₂ cup finely chopped onions
49¹/₂-oz. can (approximately 6 cups) reduced-sodium chicken broth
2 tsp. curry powder
¹/₂ tsp. paprika

¹/₄ tsp. ground cumin
¹/₄ tsp. pepper
2 cups torn fresh spinach

1. Trim fat from pork and cut pork into ¹/₂-inch pieces.
2. Combine split peas, carrots, celery, and onions in slow cooker.
3. Stir in broth, curry powder, paprika, cumin, and pepper. Stir in pork.
4. Cover. Cook on Low 10-12 hours, or on High 4 hours.
5. Stir in spinach. Serve immediately.

Exchange List Values:
Starch 1.0, Meat, very lean 3.0, Fat 0.5

Basic Nutritional Values: Calories 206 (Calories from Fat 41), Total Fat 5 gm (Saturated Fat 1.5 gm, Polyunsat Fat 0.6 gm, Monounsat Fat 1.9 gm, Cholesterol 43 mg), Sodium 480 mg, Total Carbohydrate 16 gm, Dietary Fiber 6 gm, Sugars 3 gm, Protein 24 gm

Control the diabetes so it doesn't control you.

Ruth's Split Pea Soup

Ruth Conrad Liechty
Goshen, IN

Makes 8 servings
(Ideal slow cooker size: 4-quart)

¹/₂ lb. bulk sausage, browned and drained
6 cups water
1 bag (2¹/₄ cups) dry split peas
2 medium potatoes, diced
1 onion, chopped
¹/₂ tsp. dried marjoram, or thyme
¹/₂ tsp. pepper

1. Wash and sort dried peas, removing any stones. Then combine all ingredients in slow cooker.
2. Cover. Cook on Low 12 hours.

Exchange List Values:
Starch 2.5, Meat, medium fat 1.0

Basic Nutritional Values: Calories 257 (Calories from Fat 43), Total Fat 5 gm (Saturated Fat 1.5 gm, Polyunsat Fat 0.8 gm, Monounsat Fat 2.0 gm, Cholesterol 11 mg), Sodium 179 mg, Total Carbohydrate 39 gm, Dietary Fiber 13 gm, Sugars 6 gm, Protein 16 gm

Kelly's Split Pea Soup

Kelly Evenson
Pittsboro, NC

Makes 8 servings
(Ideal slow cooker size: 4-quart)

2 cups dry split peas
2 quarts water
2 onions, chopped
2 carrots, peeled and sliced
4 slices Canadian bacon, chopped
2 Tbsp. sodium-free chicken bouillon powder
3/4 tsp. salt
1/4-1/2 tsp. pepper

1. Combine all ingredients in slow cooker.
2. Cover. Cook on Low 8-9 hours.

Exchange List Values:
Starch 2.0, Meat, very lean 1.0

Basic Nutritional Values: Calories 195 (Calories from Fat 14), Total Fat 2 gm (Saturated Fat 0.4 gm, Polyunsat Fat 0.3 gm, Monounsat Fat 0.6 gm, Cholesterol 7 mg), Sodium 411 mg, Total Carbohydrate 32 gm, Dietary Fiber 11 gm, Sugars 7 gm, Protein 14 gm

Variation: For a creamier soup, remove half of soup when done and puree. Stir back into rest of soup.

Karen's Split Pea Soup

Karen Stoltzfus
Alto, MI

Makes 6 servings
(Ideal slow cooker size: 4-5-quart)

2 carrots
2 ribs celery
1 onion
1 parsnip
1 leek (do not use top 3 inches of green)
1 ripe tomato
6 ozs. extra-lean lower-sodium ham, cubed
1 3/4 cups (1 lb.) dried split peas, washed, with stones removed
2 Tbsp. olive oil
1 bay leaf
1 tsp. dried thyme
4 cups chicken broth
4 cups water
1 tsp. salt
1/4 tsp. pepper
2 tsp. chopped fresh parsley

1. Cut all vegetables into 1/4-inch pieces and place in slow cooker. Add remaining ingredients except salt, pepper, and parsley.
2. Cover. Cook on High 7 hours.
3. Season soup with salt and pepper. Stir in parsley. Serve immediately.

Exchange List Values:
Starch 2.0, Vegetable 2.0, Meat, lean 1.0

Basic Nutritional Values: Calories 275 (Calories from Fat 41), Total Fat 5 gm (Saturated Fat 0.7 gm, Polyunsat Fat 0.7 gm, Monounsat Fat 2.8 gm, Cholesterol 10 mg), Sodium 453 mg, Total Carbohydrate 41 gm, Dietary Fiber 14 gm, Sugars 7 gm, Protein 20 gm

Dorothy's Split Pea Soup

Dorothy M. Van Deest
Memphis, TN

Makes 8 servings
(Ideal slow cooker size: 5-quart)

2 Tbsp. canola oil
1 cup minced onions
8 cups water
2 cups (1 lb.) green split peas, washed and stones removed
4 whole cloves
1 bay leaf
1/4 tsp. pepper
6 ozs. extra-lean lower-sodium ham, cubed
1 cup finely minced celery
1 cup diced carrots
1/8 tsp. dried marjoram
3/4 tsp. salt
1/8 tsp. dried savory

1. Combine all ingredients in slow cooker.
2. Cover. Cook on Low 8-10 hours.

Exchange List Values:
Starch 2.0, Vegetable 1.0, Meat, lean 1.0

Basic Nutritional Values: Calories 239 (Calories from Fat 40), Total Fat 4 gm (Saturated Fat 0.5 gm, Polyunsat Fat 1.4 gm, Monounsat Fat 2.3 gm, Cholesterol 10 mg), Sodium 419 mg, Total Carbohydrate 35 gm, Dietary Fiber 13 gm, Sugars 7 gm, Protein 16 gm

---

Variation: For a thick soup, uncover soup after 8-10 hours and turn heat to High. Simmer, stirring occasionally, until the desired consistency is reached.

Skipping meals only makes you hungrier and can cause you to overeat at the next meal.

Rosemarie's Pea Soup

Rosemarie Fitzgerald, Gibsonia, PA
Shirley Sears, Tiskilwa, IL

---

*Makes 6 servings
(Ideal slow cooker size: 4-quart)*

2 cups dried split peas
4 cups water
1 rib celery, chopped
1 cup chopped potatoes
1 large carrot, chopped
1 medium onion, chopped
1/4 tsp. dried thyme, or marjoram
1 bay leaf
1/2 tsp. salt
1 garlic clove
1/2 tsp. dried basil

1. Combine all ingredients in slow cooker.
2. Cover. Cook on Low 8-12 hours, or on High 6 hours, until peas are tender.

Exchange List Values:
Starch 2.5, Vegetable 1.0

Basic Nutritional Values: Calories 230 (Calories from Fat 7), Total Fat 1 gm (Saturated Fat 0.1 gm, Polyunsat Fat 0.3 gm, Monounsat Fat 0.1 gm, Cholesterol 0 mg), Sodium 216 mg, Total Carbohydrate 43 gm, Dietary Fiber 15 gm, Sugars 7 gm, Protein 15 gm

---

Variations: For increased flavor, use chicken broth instead of water. Stir in curry powder, coriander, or red pepper flakes to taste.

French Market Soup

Ethel Mumaw
Berlin, OH

---

*Makes about 2 1/2 quarts total
(Ideal slow cooker size: 4-quart)*

2 cups dry bean mix, washed with stones removed
2 quarts water
1 ham hock, all visible fat removed
1 tsp. salt
1/4 tsp. pepper
16-oz. can tomatoes
1 large onion, chopped
1 garlic clove, minced
1 chili pepper, chopped, or 1 tsp. chili powder
1/4 cup lemon juice

1. Combine all ingredients in slow cooker.
2. Cover. Cook on Low 8 hours. Turn to High and cook an additional 2 hours, or until beans are tender.
3. Debone ham, cut meat into bite-sized pieces, and stir back into soup.

Exchange List Values:
Starch 1.5, Vegetable 1.0, Meat, lean 1.0

Basic Nutritional Values: Calories 191 (Calories from Fat 34), Total Fat 4 gm (Saturated Fat 1.3 gm, Polyunsat Fat 0.6 gm, Monounsat Fat 1.5 gm, Cholesterol 9 mg), Sodium 488 mg, Total Carbohydrate 29 gm, Dietary Fiber 7 gm, Sugars 5 gm, Protein 12 gm

Nine Bean Soup with Tomatoes

Violette Harris Denney
Carrollton, GA

Makes 8 servings
(Ideal slow cooker size: 5-quart)

2 cups dry nine-bean soup
 mix
12 ozs. extra-lean, lower-
 sodium ham, diced
1 large onion, chopped
1 garlic clove, minced
2 qts. water
16-oz. can no-added-salt
 tomatoes, undrained
 and chopped
10-oz. can tomatoes with
 green chilies, undrained

1. Sort and wash bean mix. Place in slow cooker. Cover with water 2 inches above beans. Let soak overnight. Drain.
2. Add ham, onion, garlic, and 2 quarts fresh water.
3. Cover. Cook on Low 7 hours.
4. Add remaining ingredients and continue cooking on Low another hour. Stir occasionally.

Exchange List Values:
Starch 2.0, Vegetable 1.0,
Meat, very lean 1.0

Basic Nutritional Values: Calories 231 (Calories from Fat 14), Total Fat 2 gm (Saturated Fat 0.4 gm, Polyunsat Fat 0.5 gm, Monounsat Fat 0.4 gm, Cholesterol 20 mg), Sodium 518 mg, Total Carbohydrate 37 gm, Dietary Fiber 9 gm, Sugars 9 gm, Protein 19 gm

Note: Bean Soup mix is a mix of barley pearls, black beans, red beans, pinto beans, navy beans, Great Northern beans, lentils, split peas, and black-eyed peas.

Lentil Soup with Ham Bone

Rhoda Atzeff
Harrisburg, PA

Makes 6-8 servings
(Ideal slow cooker size: 5-quart)

1 lb. lentils, washed and
 drained
1 celery rib, chopped
1 large carrot, grated
1/2 cup chopped onions
1 bay leaf
1/4 tsp. dried thyme
7-8 cups water
1 ham bone, skin and
 visible fat removed
1/4-1/2 tsp. crushed red hot
 pepper flakes
pepper to taste
salt to taste

1. Combine all ingredients except pepper and salt in slow cooker.
2. Cover. Cook on Low 8-9 hours. Remove bay leaf and ham bone. Dice meat from bone and return to cooker.
3. Season to taste with pepper and salt.
4. Serve alone, or over rice with grated cheese on top.

Exchange List Values:
Starch 2.0, Meat, lean 1.0

Basic Nutritional Values: Calories 220 (Calories from Fat 17), Total Fat 2 gm (Saturated Fat 0.5 gm, Polyunsat Fat 0.4 gm, Monounsat Fat 0.6 gm, Cholesterol 12 mg), Sodium 298 mg, Total Carbohydrate 33 gm, Dietary Fiber 13 gm, Sugars 4 gm, Protein 19 gm

Calico Ham and Bean Soup

Esther Martin, Ephrata, PA

Makes 8 servings
(Ideal slow cooker size: 5-6-quart)

1 lb. dry bean mix, rinsed
 and drained, with
 stones removed
6 cups water
2 cups extra-lean, lower-
 sodium, cubed, cooked
 ham
1 cup chopped onions
1 cup chopped carrots
1 tsp. dried basil
1 tsp. dried oregano
3/4 tsp. salt
1/4 tsp. pepper
2 bay leaves
6 cups water
1 tsp. liquid smoke,
 optional

1. Combine beans and 6 cups water in large saucepan. Bring to boil, reduce heat, and simmer uncovered for 10 minutes. Drain, discarding cooking water, and rinse beans.

2. Combine all ingredients in slow cooker.

3. Cover. Cook on Low 8-10 hours, or High 4-5 hours. Discard bay leaves before serving.

Exchange List Values:
Starch 2.0, Vegetable 1.0, Meat, very lean 1.0

Basic Nutritional Values: Calories 228 (Calories from Fat 12), Total Fat 1 gm (Saturated Fat 0.4 gm, Polyunsat Fat 0.5 gm, Monounsat Fat 0.3 gm, Cholesterol 13 mg), Sodium 462 mg, Total Carbohydrate 38 gm, Dietary Fiber 10 gm, Sugars 6 gm, Protein 17 gm

Bean and Herb Soup
LaVerne A. Olson,
Willow Street, PA

Makes 6 servings
(Ideal slow cooker size: 5-6-quart)

1½ cups dry mixed beans
5 cups water
6 ozs. extra-lean, lower-sodium ham
1 cup chopped onions
1 cup chopped celery
1 cup chopped carrots
2-3 cups water
½ tsp. salt
¼-½ tsp. pepper
1-2 tsp. fresh basil, or
  ½ tsp. dried basil
1-2 tsp. fresh oregano, or
  ½ tsp. dried oregano
1-2 tsp. fresh thyme, or
  ½ tsp. dried thyme

2 cups fresh tomatoes, crushed

1. Combine beans, water, and ham in saucepan. Bring to boil. Turn off heat and let stand 1 hour.

2. Combine onions, celery, and carrots in 2-3 cups water in another saucepan. Cook until soft. Mash slightly.

3. Combine all ingredients in slow cooker.

4. Cover. Cook on High 2 hours, and then on Low 2 hours.

Exchange List Values:
Starch 2.0, Vegetable 1.0, Meat, very lean 1.0

Basic Nutritional Values: Calories 222 (Calories from Fat 13), Total Fat 1 gm (Saturated Fat 0.3 gm, Polyunsat Fat 0.5 gm, Monounsat Fat 0.3 gm, Cholesterol 13 mg), Sodium 465 mg, Total Carbohydrate 38 gm, Dietary Fiber 10 gm, Sugars 8 gm, Protein 16 gm

If you plan to drink alcohol, be sure you will be eating too.

Northern Bean Soup
Patricia Howard
Albuquerque, NM

Makes 6-8 servings
(Ideal slow cooker size: 4-quart)

1 lb. dry Northern beans
1 lb. extra-lean, lower-sodium ham
2 medium onions, chopped
half a green pepper, chopped
1 cup chopped celery
16-oz. can diced tomatoes
4 carrots, peeled and chopped
4-oz. can green chili peppers
1 tsp. garlic powder
1-2 qts. water

1. Wash beans. Cover with water and soak overnight. Drain. Pour into slow cooker.

2. Dice ham into 1-inch pieces. Add to beans.

3. Stir in remaining ingredients.

4. Cover. Cook on High 2 hours, then on Low 10-12 hours, or until beans are tender.

Exchange List Values:
Starch 2.0, Vegetable 2.0, Meat, very lean 2.0

Basic Nutritional Values: Calories 272 (Calories from Fat 17), Total Fat 2 gm (Saturated Fat 0.6 gm, Polyunsat Fat 0.6 gm, Monounsat Fat 0.4 gm, Cholesterol 26 mg), Sodium 674 mg, Total Carbohydrate 42 gm, Dietary Fiber 13 gm, Sugars 11 gm, Protein 23 gm

Soups

Easy Lima Bean Soup
Barbara Tenney, Delta, PA

Makes 8-10 servings
(Ideal slow cooker size: 5-6-quart)

1 lb. bag large dry lima beans
1 large onion, chopped
6 ribs celery, chopped
3 large potatoes, cut in
 ½-inch cubes
2 large carrots, cut in
 ¼-inch rounds
2 cups extra-lean, lower-sodium ham
1 tsp. salt
1 tsp. pepper
2 bay leaves
3 quarts water, or combination water and beef broth

1. Sort beans. Soak overnight. Drain.
2. Combine all ingredients in slow cooker.
3. Cover. Cook on Low 8-10 hours.

Exchange List Values:
Starch 2.5, Vegetable 1.0,
Meat, very lean 1.0

Basic Nutritional Values: Calories 258 (Calories from Fat 12), Total Fat 1 gm (Saturated Fat 0.4 gm, Polyunsat Fat 0.5 gm, Monounsat Fat 0.4 gm, Cholesterol 21 mg), Sodium 648 mg, Total Carbohydrate 43 gm, Dietary Fiber 11 gm, Sugars 9 gm, Protein 19 gm

Variation: For extra flavor, add 1 tsp. dried oregano before cooking.

Navy Bean and Bacon Chowder
Ruth A. Feister, Narvon, PA

Makes 6 servings
(Ideal slow cooker size: 4-quart)

1½ cups dried navy beans
2 cups cold water
5 slices bacon, cooked and crumbled
2 medium carrots, sliced
1 rib celery, sliced
1 medium onion, chopped
1 tsp. dried Italian seasoning
⅛ tsp. pepper
46-oz. can 100%-fat-free, 30-50%-less-sodium chicken broth
1 cup milk

1. Soak beans in 2 cups cold water for 8 hours.
2. After beans have soaked, drain, if necessary, and place in slow cooker.
3. Add all remaining ingredients, except milk, to slow cooker.
4. Cover. Cook on Low 7-9 hours, or until beans are crisp-tender.
5. Place 2 cups cooked bean mixture into blender. Process until smooth. Return to slow cooker.
6. Add milk. Cover and heat on High 10 minutes.
7. Serve with crusty French bread and additional herbs and seasonings for diners to add as they wish.

Exchange List Values:
Starch 2.5, Vegetable 1.0,
Meat, very lean 1.0, Fat 0.5

Basic Nutritional Values: Calories 263 (Calories from Fat 37), Total Fat 4 gm (Saturated Fat 1.4 gm, Polyunsat Fat 0.6 gm, Monounsat Fat 1.6 gm, Cholesterol 7 mg), Sodium 623 mg, Total Carbohydrate 41 gm, Dietary Fiber 9 gm, Sugars 8 gm, Protein 17 gm

Slow Cooked Navy Beans with Ham
Julia Lapp
New Holland, PA

Makes 10 servings
(Ideal slow cooker size: 4-quart)

1 lb. dry navy beans
 (2½ cups)
5 cups water
1 garlic clove, minced
1 ham hock, skin and all visible fat removed
1 tsp. salt

1. Soak beans in water at least 4 hours in slow cooker.
2. Add garlic and ham hock.
3. Cover. Cook on Low 7-8 hours, or High 4 hours. Add salt during last hour of cooking time.
4. Remove ham hock from cooker. Allow to cool. Cut ham from hock and stir back into bean mixture. Correct seasonings and serve in soup bowls with hot corn bread.

Basic Nutritional Values: Calories 199 (Calories from Fat 34), Total Fat 4 gm (Saturated Fat 1.3 gm, Polyunsat Fat 0.6 gm, Monounsat Fat 1.4 gm, Cholesterol 9 mg), Sodium 418 mg, Total Carbohydrate 30 gm, Dietary Fiber 7 gm, Sugars 3 gm, Protein 12 gm

Variation: For added flavor, stir 1 chopped onion, 2-3 chopped celery stalks, 2-3 sliced carrots, and 3-4 cups canned tomatoes into cooker with garlic and ham hock.

Navy Bean Soup
Joyce Bowman
Lady Lake, FL

Makes 8 servings
(Ideal slow cooker size: 4-quart)

1 lb. dry navy beans
8 cups water
1 onion, finely chopped
2 bay leaves
1/2 tsp. ground thyme
1/2 tsp. nutmeg
1/2 tsp. salt
1/2 tsp. lemon pepper
3 garlic cloves, minced
1 lb. extra-lean, lower-
    sodium ham pieces

1. Soak beans in water overnight. Strain out stones but reserve liquid.
2. Combine all ingredients in slow cooker.
3. Cover. Cook on Low 8-10 hours. Debone meat and cut into bite-sized pieces. Set ham aside.
4. Puree three-fourths of soup in blender in small batches. When finished blending, stir in meat.

Basic Nutritional Values: Calories 264 (Calories from Fat 17), Total Fat 2 gm (Saturated Fat 0.6 gm, Polyunsat Fat 0.5 gm, Monounsat Fat 0.5 gm, Cholesterol 26 mg), Sodium 631 mg, Total Carbohydrate 40 gm, Dietary Fiber 9 gm, Sugars 7 gm, Protein 22 gm

Variation: Add small chunks of cooked potatoes when stirring in ham pieces after blending.

Don't be afraid to use insulin if the doctor says you need it.

Old-Fashioned Bean Soup
Gladys M. High
Ephrata, PA

Makes 7 servings
(Ideal slow cooker size: 4-quart)

1 lb. dry navy beans, or
    dry green split peas
1 lb. extra-lean, lower-
    sodium ham pieces
1/8 tsp. salt
1/4 tsp. ground pepper
1/2 cup chopped celery
    leaves
2 qts. water
1 medium onion, chopped
1 bay leaf, optional

1. Soak beans or peas overnight. Drain, discarding soaking water.
2. Combine all ingredients in slow cooker.
3. Cover. Cook on High 8-9 hours.

Basic Nutritional Values: Calories 300 (Calories from Fat 19), Total Fat 2 gm (Saturated Fat 0.7 gm, Polyunsat Fat 0.6 gm, Monounsat Fat 0.5 gm, Cholesterol 30 mg), Sodium 576 mg, Total Carbohydrate 46 gm, Dietary Fiber 11 gm, Sugars 7 gm, Protein 25 gm

Black Bean Chili Con Carne

Janie Steele
Moore, OK

Makes 18 1-cup servings
(Ideal slow cooker size:
2 cookers, each 4-5-quarts)

1 lb. black beans
3 lbs. ground beef
2 large onions, chopped
1 green pepper, chopped
3 cloves garlic, minced
2 tsp. salt
1 tsp. pepper
6-oz. can tomato paste
3 cups tomato juice, or
   more
1 tsp. celery salt
1 Tbsp. Worcestershire
   sauce
1 tsp. dry mustard
cayenne pepper to taste
cumin to taste
3 Tbsp. chili powder

1. Cover beans with water and soak 8 hours or overnight. Rinse and drain.
2. Brown ground beef in batches in large skillet. Drain.
3. Combine all ingredients and then divide between 2 cookers.
4. Cover. Cook on Low 8 hours.
5. Serve over salad greens or wrapped in tortillas, topped with lettuce and grated cheese.

Exchange List Values:
Starch 1.0, Vegetable 1.0,
Meat, lean 2.0, Fat 0.5

Basic Nutritional Values: Calories 237 (Calories from Fat 76), Total Fat 8 gm (Saturated Fat 3.1 gm, Polyunsat Fat 0.5 gm, Monounsat Fat 3.4 gm, Cholesterol 45 mg), Sodium 510 mg, Total Carbohydrate 21 gm, Dietary Fiber 7 gm, Sugars 5 gm, Protein 20 gm

Caribbean-Style Black Bean Soup

Sheryl Shenk
Harrisonburg, VA

Makes 8-10 servings
(Ideal slow cooker size: 4-quart)

1 lb. dried black beans,
   washed and stones
   removed
4 qts. water
3 medium onions, chopped
1 medium green pepper,
   chopped
4 cloves garlic, minced
3/4 cup cubed ham
1 Tbsp. canola oil
1 Tbsp. ground cumin
2 tsp. dried oregano
1 tsp. dried thyme
2 tsp. salt
1/2 tsp. pepper
3 cups water
2 Tbsp. vinegar
fresh chopped cilantro

1. Soak beans overnight in 4 quarts water. Drain.
2. Combine beans, onions, green pepper, garlic, ham, oil,

cumin, oregano, thyme, salt, pepper, and 3 cups fresh water. Stir well.
3. Cover. Cook on Low 8-10 hours, or on High 4-5 hours.
4. For a thick soup, remove half of cooked bean mixture and puree until smooth in blender or mash with potato masher. Return to cooker. If you like a soupier soup, leave as is.
5. Add vinegar and stir well.
6. Serve in soup bowls topped with fresh cilantro.

Exchange List Values:
Starch 1.5, Vegetable 1.0,
Meat, very lean 1.0

Basic Nutritional Values: Calories 188 (Calories from Fat 24), Total Fat 3 gm (Saturated Fat 0.4 gm, Polyunsat Fat 0.8 gm, Monounsat Fat 1.2 gm, Cholesterol 5 mg), Sodium 582 mg, Total Carbohydrate 30 gm, Dietary Fiber 10 gm, Sugars 6 gm, Protein 12 gm

Katelyn's Black Bean Soup

Katelyn Bailey
Mechanicsburg, PA

Makes 4-6 servings
(Ideal slow cooker size: 4-quart)

1/3 cup chopped onions
1 garlic clove, minced
1-2 Tbsp. oil
2 15 1/2-oz. cans black
   beans, undrained

1 cup water
1 tsp. sodium-free chicken
  bouillon powder
1/2 cup diced, cooked,
  smoked ham
1/2 cup diced carrots
1 dash, or more, cayenne
  pepper
1-2 drops, or more,
  Tabasco sauce
sour cream

1. Saute onion and garlic in oil in saucepan.
2. Puree or mash contents of one can of black beans. Add to sauteed ingredients.
3. Combine all ingredients except sour cream in slow cooker.
4. Cover. Cook on Low 6-8 hours.
5. Add dollop of sour cream to each individual bowl before serving.

Exchange List Values: Starch 1.5, Meat, very lean 1.0

Basic Nutritional Values: Calories 161 (Calories from Fat 29), Total Fat 3 gm (Saturated Fat 0.4 gm, Polyunsat Fat 0.9 gm, Monounsat Fat 1.6 gm, Cholesterol 5 mg), Sodium 540 mg, Total Carbohydrate 22 gm, Dietary Fiber 6 gm, Sugars 3 gm,

A registered dietitian can help you create the right meal plan for you, and your health insurance company may even cover the sessions!

Vegetable Bean Soup

Kathi Rogge
Alexandria, IN

Makes 8 servings
(Ideal slow cooker size: 4-quart)

6 cups cooked beans: navy,
  pinto, Great Northern
1 meaty ham bone (about
  6 ozs. ham), visible fat
  and skin removed
1 cup cooked ham, diced
1/4 tsp. garlic powder
1 small bay leaf
1 cup cubed potatoes
1 cup chopped onions
1 cup chopped celery
1 cup chopped carrots
water

1. Combine all ingredients except water in 4-quart slow cooker. Add water to about 1 inch from top.
2. Cover. Cook on Low 5-8 hours.
3. Remove bay leaf before serving.

Exchange List Values:
Starch 2.0, Vegetable 1.0,
Meat, very lean 2.0

Basic Nutritional Values: Calories 261 (Calories from Fat 25), Total Fat 3 gm (Saturated Fat 0.8 gm, Polyunsat Fat 0.6 gm, Monounsat Fat 1.0 gm, Cholesterol 20 mg), Sodium 499 mg, Total Carbohydrate 39 gm, Dietary Fiber 11 gm, Sugars 5 gm, Protein 21 gm

Slow-Cooker Black Bean Chili

Mary Seielstad
Sparks, NV

Makes 8 servings
(Ideal slow cooker size: 4-quart)

1 lb. pork tenderloin, cut
  into 1-inch chunks
16-oz. jar thick chunky
  salsa
3 15-oz. cans black beans,
  rinsed and drained
1/2 cup chicken broth
1 medium red bell pepper,
  chopped
1 medium onion, chopped
1 tsp. ground cumin
2 tsp. chili powder
1-1 1/2 tsp. dried oregano
1/4 cup sour cream

1. Combine all ingredients except sour cream in slow cooker.
2. Cover. Cook on Low 6-8 hours, or until pork is tender.
3. Garnish individual servings with sour cream.

Exchange List Values:
Starch 1.5, Vegetable 1.0,
Meat, very lean 2.0, Fat 0.5

Basic Nutritional Values: Calories 231 (Calories from Fat 38), Total Fat 4 gm (Saturated Fat 1.6 gm, Polyunsat Fat 0.6 gm, Monounsat Fat 1.4 gm, Cholesterol 36 mg), Sodium 389 mg, Total Carbohydrate 28 gm, Dietary Fiber 9 gm, Sugars 6 gm, Protein 21 gm

Mjeddrah or Esau's Lentil Soup

Dianna Milhizer
Springfield, VA

Makes 12 servings
(Ideal slow cooker size: 4-quart)

1 cup chopped carrots
1 cup diced celery
2 cups chopped onions
1 Tbsp. olive oil, or butter
2 cups brown rice
1 Tbsp. olive oil, or butter
6 cups water
1 lb. lentils, washed and
    drained
garden salad
vinaigrette

1. Saute carrots, celery, and onions in 1 Tbsp. oil in skillet. When soft and translucent place in slow cooker.

2. Brown rice in 1 Tbsp. oil until dry. Add to slow cooker.

3. Stir in water and lentils.

4. Cover. Cook on High 6-8 hours.

5. When thoroughly cooked, serve in individual soup bowls. Cover each with a serving of fresh garden salad (lettuce, spinach leaves, chopped tomatoes, minced onions, chopped bell peppers, sliced olives, sliced radishes). Pour favorite vinaigrette over all.

Exchange List Values:
Starch 3.0, Meat, very lean 1.0

Basic Nutritional Values: Calories 269 (Calories from Fat 33), Total Fat 4 gm (Saturated Fat 0.5 gm, Polyunsat Fat 0.7 gm, Monounsat Fat 2.1 gm, Cholesterol 0 mg), Sodium 21 mg, Total Carbohydrate 48 gm, Dietary Fiber 10 gm, Sugars 4 gm, Protein 12 gm

French Onion Soup

Jenny R. Unternahrer
Wayland, IA
Janice Yoskovich
Carmichaels, PA

Makes 10 servings
(Ideal slow cooker size: 4-quart)

8-10 large onions, sliced
1/2 cup light, soft tub
    margarine
3 14-oz. cans 98%-fat-free,
    lower-sodium beef broth
2 1/2 cups water
3 tsp. sodium free chicken
    bouillon powder
1 1/2 tsp. Worcestershire
    sauce
3 bay leaves
10 (1-oz.) slices French
    bread, toasted

1. Saute onions in margarine until crisp-tender. Transfer to slow cooker.

2. Add beef broth, water and bouillon powder. Mix well. Add Worcestershire sauce and bay leaves.

3. Cover. Cook on Low 5-7 hours, or until onions are tender. Discard bay leaves.

4. Ladle into bowls. Top each with a slice of bread.

Exchange List Values:
Starch 1.0, Vegetable 3.0, Fat 0.5

Basic Nutritional Values: Calories 178 (Calories from Fat 35), Total Fat 4 gm (Saturated Fat 0.3 gm, Polyunsat Fat 0.9 gm, Monounsat Fat 2.0 gm, Cholesterol 0 mg), Sodium 476 mg, Total Carbohydrate 31 gm, Dietary Fiber 4 gm, Sugars 12 gm, Protein 6 gm

Note: For a more intense beef flavor, add one beef bouillon cube, or use home-cooked beef broth instead of canned broth.

Ask your doctor if you should take an aspirin every day—it may prevent a heart attack.

Potato Soup

Jeanne Hertzog, Bethlehem, PA
Marcia S. Myer, Manheim, PA
Rhonda Lee Schmidt, Scranton, PA
Mitzi McGlynchey,
Downingtown, PA
Vera Schmucker, Goshen, IN
Kaye Schnell, Falmouth, MA
Elizabeth Yoder, Millersburg, OH

Makes 10 servings
(Ideal slow cooker size: 4-quart)

**6 potatoes, peeled and
cubed
2 leeks, chopped
2 onions, chopped
1 rib celery, sliced
4 chicken bouillon cubes
1 Tbsp. dried parsley
flakes
5 cups water
pepper to taste
3 Tbsp. light, soft tub
margarine
12-oz. can fat-free
evaporated milk
chopped chives**

1. Combine all ingredients except milk and chives in slow cooker.
2. Cover. Cook on Low 10-12 hours, or High 3-4 hours. Stir in milk during last hour.
3. If desired, mash potatoes before serving.
4. Garnish with chives.

Exchange List Values:
Carbohydrate 1.5

Basic Nutritional Values: Calories 123 (Calories from Fat 14), Total Fat 2 gm (Saturated Fat 0.1 gm, Polyunsat Fat 0.4 gm, Monounsat Fat 0.8 gm, Cholesterol 0 mg), Sodium 447 mg,Total Carbohydrate 23 gm, Dietary Fiber 2 gm, Sugars 7 gm, Protein 5 gm

Variations:
1. Add one carrot, sliced, to vegetables before cooking.
2. Instead of water and bouillon cubes, use 4-5 cups chicken stock.

No-Fuss Potato Soup

Lucille Amos, Greensboro, NC
Lavina Hochstedler,
Grand Blanc, MI
Betty Moore, Plano, IL

Makes 8-10 servings
(Ideal slow cooker size: 5-6-quart)

**6 cups diced, peeled
potatoes
5 cups water
2 cups diced onions
1/2 cup diced celery
1/2 cup chopped carrots
1/4 cup light, soft tub
margarine
4 tsp. sodium free chicken
bouillon powder
1 tsp. salt
1/4 tsp. pepper
12-oz. can fat-free
evaporated milk
3 Tbsp. chopped fresh
parsley
8 ozs. fat-free cheddar,
shredded**

1. Combine all ingredients except milk, parsley, and cheese in slow cooker.
2. Cover. Cook on High 7-8 hours, or until vegetables are tender.
3. Stir in milk and parsley. Stir in cheese until it melts. Heat thoroughly.

Exchange List Values:
Starch 1.5, Vegetable 1.0, Meat, very lean 1.0

Basic Nutritional Values: Calories 173 (Calories from Fat 19), Total Fat 2 gm (Saturated Fat 0.2 gm, Polyunsat Fat 0.5 gm, Monounsat Fat 1.0 gm, Cholesterol 2 mg), Sodium 493 mg,Total Carbohydrate 27 gm, Dietary Fiber 2 gm, Sugars 8 gm, Protein 12 gm

Variations:
1. For added flavor, stir in 3 slices bacon, browned until crisp, and crumbled.
2. Top individual servings with chopped chives.

Baked Potato Soup

Kristina Shuil
Timberville, VA

Makes 6-8 servings
(Ideal slow cooker size: 4-quart)

4 large baked potatoes
3 Tbsp. light, soft tub
margarine
2/3 cup flour
3 cups fat-free milk
3 cups fat-free half-and-
half
1/4 tsp. salt
1/2 tsp. pepper
4 green onions, chopped
4 slices bacon, fried,
patted dry, and
crumbled
1 1/2 cups fat-free shredded
cheddar cheese
3/4 cup fat-free sour cream

1. Cut potatoes in half. Scoop out pulp and put in small bowl.
2. Melt margarine in large kettle. Add flour. Gradually stir in milk and half-and-half. Continue to stir until smooth, thickened, and bubbly.
3. Stir in potato pulp, salt, pepper, and three-quarters of the onions, bacon, and cheese. Cook until heated. Stir in sour cream.
4. Transfer to slow cooker set on Low. Top with remaining onions, bacon, and cheese. Take to a potluck, or serve on a buffet table, straight from the cooker.

Exchange List Values:
Carbohydrate 3.0, Meat, very lean 1.0, Fat 1.0

Basic Nutritional Values: Calories 307 (Calories from Fat 57), Total Fat 6 gm (Saturated Fat 1.5 gm, Polyunsat Fat 1.0 gm, Monounsat Fat 2.6 gm, Cholesterol 14 mg), Sodium 541 mg, Total Carbohydrate 45 gm, Dietary Fiber 2 gm, Sugars 14 gm, Protein 17 gm

Variation: Add several slices of Velveeta cheese to make soup extra cheesy and creamy.

German Potato Soup

Lee Ann Hazlett
Freeport, IL

Makes 8 servings
(Ideal slow cooker size: 4-quart)

1 onion, chopped
1 leek, trimmed and diced
2 carrots, diced
1 cup chopped cabbage
1/4 cup chopped fresh
parsley
4 cups 99%-fat-free, lower-
sodium beef broth
1 lb. potatoes, diced
1 bay leaf
1-2 tsp. black pepper
1 tsp. salt, optional
1/2 tsp. caraway seeds,
optional
1/4 tsp. nutmeg
1/2 lb. bacon, cooked and
crumbled
1/2 cup fat-free sour cream

1. Combine all ingredients except bacon and sour cream.
2. Cover. Cook on Low 8-10 hours, or High 4-5 hours.
3. Remove bay leaf. Use a slotted spoon to remove potatoes. Mash potatoes and mix with sour cream. Return to slow cooker. Stir in. Add bacon and mix together thoroughly.

Exchange List Values:
Starch 1.0, Vegetable 1.0, Fat 0.5

Basic Nutritional Values: Calories 130 (Calories from Fat 37), Total Fat 4 gm (Saturated Fat 1.3 gm, Polyunsat Fat 0.5 gm, Monounsat Fat 1.9 gm, Cholesterol 8 mg), Sodium 384 mg, Total Carbohydrate 17 gm, Dietary Fiber 2 gm, Sugars 4 gm, Protein 6 gm

Black-Eye and Vegetable Chili

Julie Weaver, Reinholds, PA

Makes 4-6 servings
(Ideal slow cooker size: 4-quart)

1 cup finely chopped
onions
1 cup finely chopped
carrots
1 cup finely chopped red
or green pepper, or
mixture of two
1 garlic clove, minced
4 tsp. chili powder
1 tsp. ground cumin
2 Tbsp. chopped cilantro
14 1/2-oz. can diced
tomatoes

3 cups cooked black-eyed beans, or 2 15-oz. cans black-eyed beans, drained
4-oz. can chopped green chilies
3/4 cup orange juice
3/4 cup water, or broth
1 Tbsp. cornstarch
2 Tbsp. water
1/2 cup shredded cheddar cheese
2 Tbsp. chopped cilantro

1. Combine all ingredients except cornstarch, 2 Tbsp. water, cheese, and cilantro.
2. Cover. Cook on Low 6-8 hours, or High 4 hours.
3. Dissolve cornstarch in water. Stir into soup mixture 30 minutes before serving.
4. Garnish individual servings with cheese and cilantro.

Exchange List Values:
Starch 1.5, Vegetable 2.0, Fat 0.5

Basic Nutritional Values: Calories 205 (Calories from Fat 38), Total Fat 4 gm (Saturated Fat 2.1 gm, Polyunsat Fat 0.6 gm, Monounsat Fat 1.1 gm, Cholesterol 10 mg), Sodium 317 mg, Total Carbohydrate 33 gm, Dietary Fiber 9 gm, Sugars 12 gm, Protein 11 gm

Note: Black-eyed beans are also known as black-eyed peas or crowder peas.

> **Walking keeps you younger in mind and body.**

Veggie Chili
Wanda Roth
Napoleon, OH

Makes 6 servings
(Ideal slow cooker size: 4-quart)

2 qts. no-added-salt whole or diced tomatoes, undrained
6-oz. can tomato paste
1/2 cup chopped onions
1/2 cup chopped celery
1/2 cup chopped green peppers
2 garlic cloves, minced
1/2 tsp. salt
1 1/2 tsp. ground cumin
1 tsp. dried oregano
1/4 tsp. cayenne pepper
3 Tbsp. brown sugar
15-oz. can garbanzo beans

1. Combine all ingredients except beans in slow cooker.
2. Cook on Low 6-8 hours, or High 3-4 hours. Add beans one hour before serving.

Exchange List Values:
Starch 1.0, Carbohydrate 0.5, Vegetable 4.0

Basic Nutritional Values: Calories 214 (Calories from Fat 16), Total Fat 2 gm (Saturated Fat 0.1 gm, Polyunsat Fat 0.8 gm, Monounsat Fat 0.4 gm, Cholesterol 0 mg), Sodium 571 mg, Total Carbohydrate 47 gm, Dietary Fiber 11 gm, Sugars 22 gm, Protein 8 gm

Variation: If you prefer a less tomatoey taste, substitute 2 vegetable bouillon cubes and 1 cup water for tomato paste.

Vegetarian Chili
Connie Johnson
Loudon, NH

Makes 6 servings
(Ideal slow cooker size: 4-quart)

3 garlic cloves, minced
2 onions, chopped
1 cup textured vegetable protein (T.V.P.)
1 lb. can beans of your choice, drained
1 green bell pepper, chopped
1 jalapeno pepper, seeds removed, chopped
28-oz. can diced Italian tomatoes
1 bay leaf
1 Tbsp. dried oregano
1/2 tsp. salt
1/4 tsp. pepper

1. Combine all ingredients in slow cooker.
2. Cover. Cook on Low 6-8 hours.

Exchange List Values:
Starch 1.0, Vegetable 2.0, Meat, very lean 1.0

Basic Nutritional Values: Calories 157 (Calories from Fat 6), Total Fat 1 gm (Saturated Fat 0.1 gm, Polyunsat Fat 0.3 gm, Monounsat Fat 0.1 gm, Cholesterol 0 mg), Sodium 518 mg, Total Carbohydrate 28 gm, Dietary Fiber 9 gm, Sugars 11 gm, Protein 14 gm

Hearty Black Bean Soup

Della Yoder, Kalona, IA

Makes 6-8 servings
(Ideal slow cooker size: 4-quart)

3 medium carrots, halved and thinly sliced
2 celery ribs, thinly sliced
1 medium onion, chopped
4 cloves garlic, minced
20-oz. can black beans, drained and rinsed
2 14½-oz. cans 98%-fat-free, lower-sodium chicken broth
15-oz. can crushed tomatoes
1½ tsp. dried basil
½ tsp. dried oregano
½ tsp. ground cumin
½ tsp. chili powder
½ tsp. hot pepper sauce

1. Combine all ingredients in slow cooker.
2. Cover. Cook on Low 9-10 hours.

Exchange List Values:
Starch 0.5, Vegetable 2.0

Basic Nutritional Values: Calories 104 (Calories from Fat 4), Total Fat 0 gm (Saturated Fat 0.1 gm, Polyunsat Fat 0.2 gm, Monounsat Fat 0.1 gm, Cholesterol 0 mg), Sodium 481 mg, Total Carbohydrate 19 gm, Dietary Fiber 6 gm, Sugars 7 gm, Protein 6 gm

Note: May be served over cooked rice.

Variation: If you prefer a thicker soup, use only 1 can chicken broth.

Black Bean and Corn Soup

Joy Sutter
Iowa City, IA

Makes 6-8 servings
(Ideal slow cooker size: 4-quart)

2 15-oz. cans black beans, drained and rinsed
14½-oz. can Mexican stewed tomatoes, undrained
14½-oz. can diced tomatoes, undrained
11-oz. can whole-kernel corn, drained
4 green onions, sliced
2 Tbsp. chili powder
1 tsp. ground cumin
½ tsp. dried minced garlic

1. Combine all ingredients in slow cooker.
2. Cover. Cook on ~~High~~ *Low* 5-6 hours.

Exchange List Values:
Starch 1.5, Vegetable 1.0

Basic Nutritional Values: Calories 134 (Calories from Fat 10), Total Fat 1 gm (Saturated Fat 0.1 gm, Polyunsat Fat 0.5 gm, Monounsat Fat 0.2 gm, Cholesterol 0 mg), Sodium 366 mg, Total Carbohydrate 26 gm, Dietary Fiber 8 gm, Sugars 7 gm, Protein 7 gm

Variations:
1. Use 2 cloves fresh garlic, minced, instead of dried garlic.
2. Add 1 large rib celery, sliced thinly, and 1 small green pepper, chopped.

Tuscan Garlicky Bean Soup

Sara Harter Fredette
Williamsburg, MA

Makes 8-10 servings
(Ideal slow cooker size: 4-quart)

1 lb. dry Great Northern, or other dry white, beans
1 qt. water
1 qt. 99%-fat-free, lower-sodium beef broth
3 Tbsp. olive oil
2 garlic cloves, minced
4 Tbsp. chopped parsley
1¼ tsp. salt
½ tsp. pepper

1. Place beans in large soup pot. Cover with water and bring to boil. Cook 2 minutes. Remove from heat. Cover pot and allow to stand for 1 hour. Drain, discarding water.
2. Combine beans, 1 quart fresh water, and beef broth in slow cooker.
3. Saute garlic and parsley in olive oil in skillet. Stir into slow cooker. Add salt and pepper.
4. Cover. Cook on Low 8-10 hours, or until beans are tender.

Exchange List Values:
Starch 1.5, Meat, very lean 1.0, Fat 0.5

Basic Nutritional Values: Calories 174 (Calories from Fat 41), Total Fat 5 gm (Saturated Fat 0.7 gm, Polyunsat Fat 0.5 gm, Monounsat Fat 3.0 gm, Cholesterol 0 mg), Sodium 470 mg, Total Carbohydrate 24 gm, Dietary Fiber 8 gm, Sugars 3 gm, Protein 10 gm

Green Bean Soup

Loretta Krahn
Mountain Lake, MN

Makes 6 servings
(Ideal slow cooker size: 4-quart)

2 cups cubed, extra-lean, lower-sodium ham
1½ qts. water
1 large onion, chopped
2-3 cups cut-up green beans
3 large carrots, sliced
2 large potatoes, peeled and cubed
1 Tbsp. parsley
1 Tbsp. summer savory
¼ tsp. pepper
1 cup fat-free half-and-half

1. Combine all ingredients except half-and-half in slow cooker.
2. Cover. Cook on High 4-6 hours.
3. Turn to Low. Stir in half-and-half. Heat through and serve.

Exchange List Values:
Starch 1.0, Vegetable 2.0, Meat, lean 1.0

Basic Nutritional Values: Calories 170 (Calories from Fat 15), Total Fat 2 gm (Saturated Fat 0.6 gm, Polyunsat Fat 0.3 gm, Monounsat Fat 0.4 gm, Cholesterol 24 mg), Sodium 468 mg, Total Carbohydrate 27 gm, Dietary Fiber 4 gm, Sugars 10 gm, Protein 12 gm

Bean Soup

Joyce Cox
Port Angeles, WA

Makes 10-12 servings
(Ideal slow cooker size: 4-quart)

1 cup dry Great Northern beans
1 cup dry red beans, or pinto beans
4 cups water
28-oz. can diced tomatoes
1 medium onion, chopped
2 Tbsp. vegetable bouillon granules, or 4 bouillon cubes
2 garlic cloves, minced
2 tsp. Italian seasoning, crushed
9-oz. pkg. frozen green beans, thawed

1. Soak and rinse dried beans. Drain.
2. Combine all ingredients except green beans in slow cooker.
3. Cover. Cook on High 5½-6½ hours, or on Low 11-13 hours.
4. Stir green beans into soup during last 2 hours.

Exchange List Values:
Starch 1.0, Vegetable 1.0

Basic Nutritional Values: Calories 114 (Calories from Fat 5), Total Fat 1 gm (Saturated Fat 0.1 gm, Polyunsat Fat 0.2 gm, Monounsat Fat 0.0 gm, Cholesterol 0 mg), Sodium 435 mg, Total Carbohydrate 22 gm, Dietary Fiber 7 gm, Sugars 5 gm, Protein 7 gm

Invite a friend or family member to do any 10 of the tips in this book with you. It's easier when you have company!

Vegetarian Minestrone Soup

Connie Johnson
Loudon, NH

Makes 8 servings
(Ideal slow cooker size: 4-quart)

6 cups fat-free, 60%-less-sodium, vegetable broth
2 carrots, chopped
2 large onions, chopped
3 ribs celery, chopped
2 garlic cloves, minced
1 small zucchini, cubed
1 handful fresh kale, chopped
1/2 cup dry barley
1 can chickpeas, or white kidney beans, drained
1 Tbsp. parsley
1/2 tsp. dried thyme
1 tsp. dried oregano
28-oz. can crushed Italian tomatoes
1/4 tsp. pepper

1. Combine all ingredients in slow cooker.
2. Cover. Cook on Low 6-8 hours, or until vegetables are tender.

Exchange List Values:
Starch 1.5, Vegetable 4.0

Basic Nutritional Values: Calories 200 (Calories from Fat 13), Total Fat 1 gm (Saturated Fat 0.1 gm, Polyunsat Fat 0.6 gm, Monounsat Fat 0.3 gm, Cholesterol 0 mg), Sodium 641 mg, Total Carbohydrate 41 gm, Dietary Fiber 9 gm, Sugars 12 gm, Protein 7 gm

Joyce's Minestrone

Joyce Shackelford
Green Bay, Wisconsin

Makes 6 servings
(Ideal slow cooker size: 4-5-quart)

3 1/2 cups 99%-fat-free, lower-sodium beef broth
28-oz. can crushed tomatoes
2 medium carrots, thinly sliced
1/2 cup chopped onion
1/2 cup chopped celery
2 medium potatoes, thinly sliced
1-2 garlic cloves, minced
15-oz. can no-added-salt red kidney beans, drained
2 ozs. thin spaghetti, broken into 2-inch pieces
2 Tbsp. parsley flakes
2-3 tsp. dried basil
1-2 tsp. dried oregano
1 bay leaf

1. Combine all ingredients in slow cooker.
2. Cover. Cook on Low 10-16 hours, or on High 4-6 hours.
3. Remove bay leaf. Serve.

Exchange List Values:
Starch 2.0, Vegetable 2.0

Basic Nutritional Values: Calories 213 (Calories from Fat 7), Total Fat 1 gm (Saturated Fat 0.0 gm, Polyunsat Fat 0.4 gm, Monounsat Fat 0.1 gm, Cholesterol 0 mg), Sodium 655 mg, Total Carbohydrate 42 gm, Dietary Fiber 9 gm, Sugars 11 gm, Protein 10 gm

Grace's Minestrone Soup

Grace Ketcham, Marietta, GA

Makes 8 servings
(Ideal slow cooker size: 4-5-quart)

3/4 cup dry elbow macaroni
2 qts. 98%-fat-free, lower-sodium chicken stock
2 large onions, diced
2 carrots, sliced
half a head of cabbage, shredded
1/2 cup celery, diced
1 lb. can no-salt-added tomatoes
1/2 tsp. dried oregano
1 Tbsp. minced parsley
1/4 cup each frozen corn, peas, and lima beans
1/4 tsp. pepper

1. Cook macaroni according to package directions. Set aside.
2. Combine all ingredients except macaroni in large slow cooker.
3. Cover. Cook on Low 8 hours. Add macaroni during last 30 minutes of cooking time.

Exchange List Values:
Starch 1.0, Vegetable 2.0

Basic Nutritional Values: Calories 112 (Calories from Fat 5), Total Fat 1 gm (Saturated Fat 0.0 gm, Polyunsat Fat 0.3 gm, Monounsat Fat 0.1 gm, Cholesterol 0 mg), Sodium 559 mg, Total Carbohydrate 22 gm, Dietary Fiber 4 gm, Sugars 8 gm, Protein 6 gm

Winter Squash and White Bean Stew

Mary E. Herr, Three Rivers, MI

Makes 6 servings
(Ideal slow cooker size: 4-quart)

1 cup chopped onions
1 Tbsp. olive oil
1/2 tsp. ground cumin
1/4 tsp. cinnamon
1 garlic clove, minced
3 cups peeled, butternut squash, cut into 3/4-inch cubes
1 1/2 cups chicken broth
19-oz. can cannellini beans, drained
14 1/2-oz. can diced tomatoes, undrained
1 Tbsp. chopped fresh cilantro

1. Combine all ingredients in slow cooker.
2. Cover. Cook on High 1 hour. Reduce heat to Low and cook 2-3 hours.

Exchange List Values:
Starch 1.5, Vegetable 1.0, Fat 0.5

Basic Nutritional Values: Calories 164 (Calories from Fat 30), Total Fat 3 gm (Saturated Fat 0.5 gm, Polyunsat Fat 0.6 gm, Monounsat Fat 1.9 gm, Cholesterol 1 mg), Sodium 586 mg, Total Carbohydrate 28 gm, Dietary Fiber 7 gm, Sugars 6 gm, Protein 8 gm

Variations:
1. Beans can be pureed in blender and added during the last hour.

2. Eight ounces dried beans can be soaked overnight, cooked until soft, and used in place of canned beans.

Cabbage Soup
Margaret Jarrett
Anderson, IN

Makes 8 servings
(Ideal slow cooker size: 4-quart)

half a head of cabbage, sliced thin
2 ribs celery, sliced thin
2-3 carrots, sliced thin
1 onion, chopped
2 tsp. sodium-free chicken bouillon powder
2 garlic cloves, minced
1 qt. tomato juice
1/4 tsp. pepper
water

1. Combine all ingredients except water in slow cooker. Add water to within 3 inches of top of slow cooker.
2. Cover. Cook on High 3 1/2-4 hours, or until vegetables are tender.

Exchange List Values:
Vegetable 2.0

Basic Nutritional Values: Calories 55 (Calories from Fat 3), Total Fat 0 gm (Saturated Fat 0.0 gm, Polyunsat Fat 0.1 gm, Monounsat Fat 0.0 gm, Cholesterol 0 mg), Sodium 474 mg, Total Carbohydrate 13 gm, Dietary Fiber 3 gm, Sugars 8 gm, Protein 2 gm

Cheese and Corn Chowder

Loretta Krahn, Mt. Lake, MN

Makes 8 servings
(Ideal slow cooker size: 4-quart)

3/4 cup water
1/2 cup chopped onions
1 1/2 cups sliced carrots
1 1/2 cups chopped celery
1/4 tsp. salt
1/2 tsp. pepper
15 1/4-oz. can whole-kernel corn, drained
15-oz. can no-added-salt cream-style corn
1 1/2 cups fat-free milk
1 1/2 cups fat-free half-and-half
1 cup grated fat-free cheddar cheese

1. Combine water, onions, carrots, celery, salt, and pepper in slow cooker.
2. Cover. Cook on High 4-6 hours.
3. Add corn, milk, half-and-half, and cheese. Heat on High 1 hour, and then turn to Low until you are ready to eat.

Exchange List Values:
Starch 1.0, Milk, fat-free 1.0

Basic Nutritional Values: Calories 168 (Calories from Fat 29), Total Fat 3 gm (Saturated Fat 1.3 gm, Polyunsat Fat 0.4 gm, Monounsat Fat 0.9 gm, Cholesterol 12 mg), Sodium 391 mg, Total Carbohydrate 26 gm, Dietary Fiber 3 gm, Sugars 13 gm, Protein 11 gm

Broccoli-Cheese Soup

Darla Sathre, Baxter, MN

Makes 8 servings
(Ideal slow cooker size: 4-quart)

2 16-oz. pkgs. frozen
  chopped broccoli
10³/4-oz. can cheddar
  cheese soup
12-oz. can fat-free
  evaporated milk
2¹/2 cups fat-free half-and-
  half
¹/4 cup finely chopped
  onions
1 Tbsp. dry Italian
  Seasoning Mix (see
  recipe on page 254)
¹/4 tsp. pepper
2-oz. fat-free cheddar
  cheese
sunflower seeds, optional
crumbled bacon, optional

1. Combine all ingredients
except sunflower seeds and
bacon in slow cooker.
2. Cover. Cook on Low 8-
10 hours.
3. Garnish with sunflower
seeds and bacon.

Exchange List Values:
Milk, fat-free 1.0, Vegetable
2.0, Fat 0.5

Basic Nutritional Values: Calories
171 (Calories from Fat 36), Total Fat
4 gm (Saturated Fat 1.6 gm,
Polyunsat Fat 0.9 gm, Monounsat Fat
0.9 gm, Cholesterol 12 mg), Sodium
581 mg, Total Carbohydrate 22 gm,
Dietary Fiber 4 gm, Sugars 12 gm,
Protein 12 gm

Corn Chowder

Mary Rogers
Waseca, MN

Makes 12 servings
(Ideal slow cooker size: 6-quart)

6 ozs. bacon
4 cups diced potatoes
2 cups chopped onions
2 cups fat-free sour cream
1¹/2 cups 2%-reduced-fat
  milk
1 cup fat-free half-and-half
2 10³/4-oz. cans 98%-fat-
  free, lower-sodium
  cream of chicken soup
2 15¹/4-oz. cans corn,
  undrained

1. Cut bacon into 1"
pieces. Cook for 5 minutes in
large skillet.
2. Add potatoes and onions
and a bit of water. Cook 15-
20 minutes, until tender,
stirring occasionally. Drain.
Transfer to slow cooker.
3. Combine sour cream,
milk, half-and-half, chicken
soup, and corn. Place in slow
cooker.
4. Cover. Cook on Low for
2 hours.
5. Serve with homemade
biscuits or a pan of steaming
corn bread fresh from the
oven.

Exchange List Values:
Starch 1.0, Carbohydrate
1.0, Fat 1.0

Basic Nutritional Values: Calories
202 (Calories from Fat 41), Total Fat
5 gm (Saturated Fat 1.5 gm,
Polyunsat Fat 0.9 gm, Monounsat Fat
1.5 gm, Cholesterol 14 mg), Sodium
568 mg, Total Carbohydrate 32 gm,
Dietary Fiber 3 gm, Sugars 13 gm,
Protein 8 gm

> Make your goals
> realistic and specific.
> Instead of thinking, "I'll
> walk more often," you
> might say, "I'm going to
> walk for 30 minutes,
> 5 days a week."

Vegetables

Very Special Spinach

Jeanette Oberholtzer
Manheim, PA

Makes 8 servings
(Ideal slow cooker size: 4-quart)

3 10-oz. boxes frozen spinach, thawed and drained
2 cups low-fat (1%) cottage cheese
1½ cups grated fat-free cheddar cheese
3 eggs
¼ cup flour
4 Tbsp. (¼ cup) light, soft tub margarine, melted

1. Mix together all ingredients.
2. Pour into slow cooker.
3. Cook on High 1 hour. Reduce heat to Low and cook 4 more hours.

Exchange List Values:
Starch 0.5, Vegetable 1.0, Meat, lean 2.0

Basic Nutritional Values: Calories 160 (Calories from Fat 44), Total Fat 5 gm (Saturated Fat 1.3 gm, Polyunsat Fat 0.9 gm, Monounsat Fat 2.1 gm, Cholesterol 84 mg), Sodium 520 mg, Total Carbohydrate 11 gm, Dietary Fiber 3 gm, Sugars 3 gm, Protein 19 gm

Caramelized Onions

Mrs. J.E. Barthold
Bethlehem, PA

Makes 8 servings
(Ideal slow cooker size: 4-quart)

6 large Vidalia or other sweet onions
4 Tbsp. margarine
10-oz. can chicken, or vegetable, broth

1. Peel onions. Remove stems and root ends. Place in slow cooker.
2. Pour margarine and broth over.
3. Cook on Low 12 hours.

Exchange List Values:
Vegetable 3.0, Fat 1.0

Basic Nutritional Values: Calories 123 (Calories from Fat 57), Total Fat 6 gm (Saturated Fat 1.1 gm, Polyunsat Fat 2.0 gm, Monounsat Fat 2.7 gm, Cholesterol 1 mg), Sodium 325 mg, Total Carbohydrate 15 gm, Dietary Fiber 3 gm, Sugars 11 gm, Protein 2 gm

Note: Serve as a side dish, or use onions and liquid to flavor soups or stews, or as topping for pizza.

Barbecued Green Beans

Arlene Wengerd
Millersburg, OH

Makes 6 servings
(Ideal slow cooker size: 3-4-quart)

4 slices bacon
1/4 cup chopped onions
1/2 cup ketchup
2 Tbsp. brown sugar
brown sugar substitute to
    equal 2 Tbsp.
3 tsp. Worcestershire sauce
1/8 tsp. salt
4 cups green beans

1. Brown bacon in skillet until crisp and then break into pieces.
2. Saute onions in non-fat cooking spray in skillet.
3. Combine ketchup, brown sugar, sugar substitute, Worcestershire sauce, and salt. Stir into bacon and onions.
4. Pour mixture over green beans and mix lightly.
5. Pour into slow cooker and cook on High 3-4 hours, or on Low 6-8 hours.

Exchange List Values:
Carbohydrate 0.5,
Vegetable 2.0, Fat 0.5

Basic Nutritional Values: Calories 98 (Calories from Fat 22), Total Fat 2 gm (Saturated Fat 0.7 gm, Polyunsat Fat 0.3 gm, Monounsat Fat 0.9 gm, Cholesterol 3 mg), Sodium 386 mg, Total Carbohydrate 18 gm, Dietary Fiber 3 gm, Sugars 9 gm, Protein 3 gm

Dutch Green Beans

Edwina Stoltzfus
Narvon, PA

Makes 12 servings
(Ideal slow cooker size: 4-5-quart)

6 slices bacon
4 medium onions, sliced
2 Tbsp. canola oil
2 qts. fresh, frozen, or
    canned, green beans
4 cups diced, fresh
    tomatoes
1/2 tsp. salt
1/4 tsp. pepper

1. Brown bacon until crisp in skillet. Drain. Crumble bacon into small pieces.
2. Saute onions in canola oil.
3. Combine all ingredients in slow cooker.
4. Cover. Cook on Low 4 1/2 hours.

Exchange List Values:
Vegetable 3.0, Fat 0.5

Basic Nutritional Values: Calories 99 (Calories from Fat 39), Total Fat 4 gm (Saturated Fat 0.7 gm, Polyunsat Fat 1.1 gm, Monounsat Fat 2.1 gm, Cholesterol 3 mg), Sodium 154 mg, Total Carbohydrate 14 gm, Dietary Fiber 4 gm, Sugars 6 gm, Protein 4 gm

Easy Flavor-Filled Green Beans

Paula Showalter
Weyers Cave, VA

Makes 10 servings
(Ideal slow cooker size: 4-5-quart)

2 qts. green beans, drained
1/3 cup chopped onions
4-oz. can mushrooms,
    drained
1 Tbsp. brown sugar
brown sugar substitute to
    equal 1 1/2 tsp.
3 Tbsp. light, soft tub
    margarine
pepper to taste

1. Combine beans, onions, and mushrooms in slow cooker.
2. Sprinkle with brown sugar and sugar substitute.
3. Dot with margarine.
4. Sprinkle with pepper.
5. Cover. Cook on High 3-4 hours. Stir just before serving.

Exchange List Values:
Vegetable 2.0

Basic Nutritional Values: Calories 47 (Calories from Fat 14), Total Fat 2 gm (Saturated Fat 0.0 gm, Polyunsat Fat 0.4 gm, Monounsat Fat 0.8 gm, Cholesterol 0 mg), Sodium 339 mg, Total Carbohydrate 7 gm, Dietary Fiber 3 gm, Sugars 4 gm, Protein 2 gm

Green Bean Casserole

Vicki Dinkel, Sharon Springs, KS

Makes 9-11 servings
(Ideal slow cooker size: 3-4-quart)

3 10-oz. pkgs. frozen, cut green beans
1½ 10½-oz. cans cheddar cheese soup
½ cup water
¼ cup chopped green onions
4-oz. can sliced mushrooms, drained
8-oz. can water chestnuts, drained and sliced (optional)
½ cup slivered almonds
¼ tsp. pepper

1. Combine all ingredients in lightly greased slow cooker. Mix well.
2. Cover. Cook on Low 8-10 hours or on High 3-4 hours.

Exchange List Values:
Carbohydrate 0.5,
Vegetable 1.0, Fat 1.0

Basic Nutritional Values: Calories 102 (Calories from Fat 51), Total Fat 6 gm (Saturated Fat 1.4 gm, Polyunsat Fat 1.6 gm, Monounsat Fat 2.6 gm, Cholesterol 7 mg), Sodium 407 mg, Total Carbohydrate 10 gm, Dietary Fiber 3 gm, Sugars 3 gm, Protein 4 gm

Creamy Cheesy Bean Casserole

Martha Hershey
Ronks, PA

Makes 5 servings
(Ideal slow cooker size: 3-4-quart)

16-oz. bag frozen green beans, cooked
¾ cup fat-free milk
1 cup grated fat-free American cheese
2 slices bread, crumbled

1. Place beans in slow cooker.
2. Combine milk and cheese in saucepan. Heat, stirring continually, until cheese melts. Fold in bread cubes and pour mixture over beans.
3. Cover. Heat on High 2 hours.

Exchange List Values:
Carbohydrate 0.5,
Vegetable 1.0, Meat, very lean 1.0

Basic Nutritional Values: Calories 94 (Calories from Fat 5), Total Fat 1 gm (Saturated Fat 0.1 gm, Polyunsat Fat 0.3 gm, Monounsat Fat 0.1 gm, Cholesterol 4 mg), Sodium 366 mg, Total Carbohydrate 14 gm, Dietary Fiber 3 gm, Sugars 5 gm, Protein 9 gm

Variation: Use 15-oz. container of Cheez Whiz instead of making cheese sauce. Mix crumbled bread into Cheez Whiz and pour over beans. Proceed with Step 3.

Stewed Tomatoes

Michelle Showalter
Bridgewater, VA

Makes 10-12 servings
(Ideal slow cooker size: 4-quart)

2 qts. canned tomatoes
2½ Tbsp. sugar
sugar substitute to equal 1½ Tbsp.
½ tsp. salt
dash of pepper
1½ Tbsp. light, soft tub margarine
2 cups bread cubes

1. Place tomatoes in slow cooker.
2. Sprinkle with sugar, sugar substitute, salt, and pepper.
3. Lightly toast bread cubes in melted margarine. Spread over tomatoes.
4. Cover. Cook on High 3-4 hours.

Exchange List Values:
Vegetable 2.0

Basic Nutritional Values: Calories 62 (Calories from Fat 9), Total Fat 1 gm (Saturated Fat 0.0 gm, Polyunsat Fat 0.4 gm, Monounsat Fat 0.4 gm, Cholesterol 0 mg), Sodium 377 mg, Total Carbohydrate 13 gm, Dietary Fiber 2 gm, Sugars 7 gm, Protein 2 gm

Variation: If you prefer bread that is less moist and soft, add bread cubes 15 minutes before serving and continue cooking without lid.

Orange Glazed Carrots

Cyndie Marrara
Port Matilda, PA

Makes 8 servings
(Ideal slow cooker size: 4-quart)

32-oz. (2 lbs.) pkg. baby
   carrots
3 Tbsp. brown sugar
brown sugar substitute to
   equal 2 Tbsp.
1/2 cup orange juice
2 Tbsp margarine
3/4 tsp. cinnamon
1/4 tsp. nutmeg
2 Tbsp. cornstarch
1/4 cup water

1. Combine all ingredients
except cornstarch and water
in slow cooker.
2. Cover. Cook on Low 3-4
hours until carrots are tender-
crisp.
3. Put carrots in serving
dish and keep warm, reserving cooking juices. Put
reserved juices in small
saucepan. Bring to boil.
4. Mix cornstarch and
water in small bowl until
blended. Add to juices. Boil
one minute or until thickened, stirring constantly.
5. Pour over carrots and
serve.

Exchange List Values:
Carbohydrate 0.5,
Vegetable 2.0, Fat 0.5

Basic Nutritional Values: Calories
108 (Calories from Fat 29), Total Fat
3 gm (Saturated Fat 0.6 gm,
Polyunsat Fat 1.0 gm, Monounsat Fat
1.3 gm, Cholesterol 0 mg), Sodium
115 mg,Total Carbohydrate 20 gm,
Dietary Fiber 4 gm, Sugars 12 gm,
Protein 1 gm

Glazed Tzimmes

Elaine Vigoda
Rochester, NY

Makes 6-8 servings
(Ideal slow cooker size:
2 4-5-qt. cookers)

1 sweet potato
6 carrots, sliced
1 potato, peeled and diced
1 onion, chopped
2 apples, peeled and sliced
1 medium (about 1 1/2 lbs.)
   butternut squash,
   peeled and sliced
1/4 cup dry white wine or
   apple juice
1/2 lb. dried apricots
1 Tbsp. ground cinnamon
1 Tbsp. apple pie spice
1 Tbsp. maple syrup or
   honey
1 tsp. salt
1 tsp. ground ginger

1. Combine all ingredients
in large slow cooker, or mix
all ingredients in large bowl
and then divide between 2 4-
or 5-qt. cookers.
2. Cover. Cook on Low 10
hours.

Exchange List Values:
Starch 1.0, Fruit 1.5,
Vegetable 1.0

Basic Nutritional Values: Calories
179 (Calories from Fat 5), Total Fat 1
gm (Saturated Fat 0.1 gm, Polyunsat
Fat 0.2 gm, Monounsat Fat 0.1 gm,
Cholesterol 0 mg), Sodium 332
mg,Total Carbohydrate 45 gm,
Dietary Fiber 6 gm, Sugars 27 gm,
Protein 3 gm

---

*This is a special dish served
primarily on Jewish holidays,
such as Rosh Hashana and
Passover. The sweetness of the
vegetables and fruit signifies
wishes for a sweet year.*

**Start liking yourself.
If you're going to lose
weight or make other
changes, you need to be
your own cheerleader.**

Vegetable Medley

Teena Wagner
Waterloo, ON

Makes 8 servings
(Ideal slow cooker size: 4-quart)

2 medium parsnips
4 medium carrots
1 turnip, about 4 1/2 inches
  around
1/2 cup water
1 tsp. salt
3 Tbsp. sugar
2 Tbsp. canola or olive oil
1/2 tsp. salt

1. Clean and peel vegetables. Cut in 1-inch pieces.
2. Dissolve 1 tsp. salt in water in saucepan. Add vegetables and boil for 10 minutes. Drain, reserving 1/2 cup liquid.
3. Place vegetables in slow cooker. Add liquid.
4. Stir in sugar, oil, and 1/2 tsp. salt.
5. Cover. Cook on Low 2-3 hours.
6. Remove vegetables from juice in pot to serve.

Exchange List Values:
Starch 1.0

Basic Nutritional Values: Calories 63 (Calories from Fat 17), Total Fat 2 gm (Saturated Fat 0.1 gm, Polyunsat Fat 0.6 gm, Monounsat Fat 1.0 gm, Cholesterol 0 mg), Sodium 327 mg,Total Carbohydrate 12 gm, Dietary Fiber 2 gm, Sugars 6 gm, Protein 1 gm

Easy Olive Bake

Jean Robinson
Cinnaminson, NJ

Makes 8 servings
(Ideal slow cooker size: 4-quart)

1 cup uncooked rice
2 medium onions, chopped
2 Tbsp. light soft tub
  margarine, melted
2 cups stewed tomatoes
2 cups water
1 cup black olives,
  quartered
1/2 tsp. chili powder
1 Tbsp. Worcestershire
  sauce
4-oz. can mushrooms with
  juice
1/2 cup grated fat-free
  cheese

1. Wash and drain rice. Place in slow cooker.
2. Add remaining ingredients except cheese. Mix well.
3. Cover. Cook on High 1 hour, then on Low 2 hours, or until rice is tender but not mushy.
4. Add cheese before serving.
5. This is a good accompaniment to baked ham.

Exchange List Values:
Starch 1.0, Vegetable 2.0, Fat 0.5

Basic Nutritional Values: Calories 163 (Calories from Fat 28), Total Fat 3 gm (Saturated Fat 0.2 gm, Polyunsat Fat 0.5 gm, Monounsat Fat

1.9 gm, Cholesterol 1 mg), Sodium 492 mg,Total Carbohydrate 29 gm, Dietary Fiber 2 gm, Sugars 5 gm, protein 6 gm

Zucchini Special

Louise Stackhouse
Benten, PA

Makes 8 servings
(Ideal slow cooker size: 4-quart)

1 medium to large
  zucchini, peeled and
  sliced
1 medium onion, sliced
1 qt. stewed, no-added-salt
  tomatoes with juice, or
  2 14 1/2-oz. cans stewed,
  no-added-salt tomatoes
  with juice
1/2 tsp. salt
1 tsp. dried basil
4 ozs. (1 cup) reduced-fat
  mozzarella cheese,
  shredded

1. Layer zucchini, onion, and tomatoes in slow cooker.
2. Sprinkle with salt, basil, and cheese.
3. Cover. Cook on Low 6-8 hours.

Exchange List Values:
Vegetable 2.0, Fat 0.5

Basic Nutritional Values: Calories 79 (Calories from Fat 21), Total Fat 2 gm (Saturated Fat 1.3 gm, Polyunsat Fat 0.3 gm, Monounsat Fat 0.4 gm, Cholesterol 8 mg), Sodium 273 mg,Total Carbohydrate 11 gm, Dietary Fiber 2 gm, Sugars 5 gm, Protein 6 gm

Squash Casserole

Sharon Anders, Alburtis, PA

Makes 9 servings
(Ideal slow cooker size: 4-quart)

2 lbs. yellow summer squash, or zucchini, thinly sliced (about 6 cups)
half a medium onion, chopped
1 cup peeled, shredded carrot
10³/₄-oz. can 98%-fat-free, lower-sodium, condensed cream of chicken soup
1/2 cup fat-free sour cream
2 Tbsp. flour
4 ozs. (1/2 of 8-oz. pkg.) seasoned stuffing crumbs
2 Tbsp. canola oil

1. Combine squash, onion, carrots, and soup.
2. Mix together sour cream and flour. Stir into vegetables.
3. Toss stuffing mix with oil. Spread half in bottom of slow cooker. Add vegetable mixture. Top with remaining crumbs.
4. Cover. Cook on Low 7-9 hours.

Exchange List Values:
Starch 1.0, Vegetable 1.0, Fat 1.0

Basic Nutritional Values: Calories 140 (Calories from Fat 38), Total Fat 4 gm (Saturated Fat 0.5 gm, Polyunsat Fat 1.4 gm, Monounsat Fat 2.1 gm, Cholesterol 4 mg), Sodium 486 mg, Total Carbohydrate 21 gm, Dietary Fiber 3 gm, Sugars 5 gm, Protein 4 gm

Squash Medley

Evelyn Page
Riverton, WY

Makes 8 servings
(Ideal slow cooker size: 4-quart)

8 (up to 8 ozs. total) summer squash, each about 4" long, thinly sliced
1/2 tsp. salt
2 tomatoes, peeled and chopped
1/4 cup sliced green onions
half a small sweet green pepper, chopped
1 chicken bouillon cube
1/4 cup hot water
4 slices bacon, fried and crumbled
1/4 cup fine dry bread crumbs

1. Sprinkle squash with salt.
2. In slow cooker, layer half the squash, tomatoes, onions, and pepper. Repeat layers.
3. Dissolve bouillon in hot water. Pour into slow cooker.
4. Top with bacon. Sprinkle bread crumbs over top.
5. Cover. Cook on Low 4-6 hours.

Exchange List Values:
Vegetable 1.0, Fat 0.5

Basic Nutritional Values: Calories 47 (Calories from Fat 17), Total Fat 2 gm (Saturated Fat 0.5 gm, Polyunsat Fat 0.3 gm, Monounsat Fat 0.8 gm, Cholesterol 3 mg), Sodium 339 mg, Total Carbohydrate 6 gm, Dietary Fiber 1 gm, Sugars 2 gm, Protein 2 gm

Variation: For a sweeter touch, sprinkle 1 Tbsp. brown sugar over half the layered vegetables. Repeat over second half of layered vegetables.

Baked Acorn Squash

Dale Peterson
Rapid City, SD

Makes 4 servings
(Ideal slow cooker size: 3-4-quart)

2 small (1¹/₄ lbs. each) acorn squash
1/2 cup cracker crumbs
1/4 cup coarsely chopped pecans
2 Tbsp. light, soft tub margarine, melted
2 Tbsp. brown sugar brown sugar substitute to equal 1 Tbsp.
1/4 tsp. salt
1/4 tsp. ground nutmeg
2 Tbsp. orange juice

1. Cut squash in half. Remove seeds.
2. Combine remaining ingredients. Spoon into squash halves. Place squash in slow cooker.
3. Cover. Cook on Low 5-6 hours, or until squash is tender.

Exchange List Values:
Starch 2.0, Carbohydrate
0.5, Fat 1.0

Basic Nutritional Values: Calories 229 (Calories from Fat 82), Total Fat 9 gm (Saturated Fat 0.8 gm, Polyunsat Fat 2.3 gm, Monounsat Fat 5.1 gm, Cholesterol 0 mg), Sodium 314 mg, Total Carbohydrate 38 gm, Dietary Fiber 8 gm, Sugars 15 gm, Protein 3 gm

Apple Walnut Squash

Michele Ruvola, Selden, NY

*Makes 4 servings
(Ideal slow cooker size: 3-4-quart)*

1/4 cup water
2 small (1 1/4 lbs. each) acorn squash
2 Tbsp. brown sugar
brown sugar substitute to equal 1 Tbsp.
2 Tbsp. light, soft tub margarine
3 Tbsp. apple juice
1 1/2 tsp. ground cinnamon
1/4 tsp. salt
1 cup toasted walnuts halves
1 medium apple, unpeeled, chopped

1. Pour water into slow cooker.
2. Cut squash crosswise in half. Remove seeds. Place in slow cooker, cut sides up.
3. Combine brown sugar, sugar substitute, margarine, apple juice, cinnamon, and salt. Spoon into squash.
4. Cover. Cook on High 3-4 hours, or until squash is tender.
5. Combine walnuts and chopped apple. Add to center of squash and mix with sauce to serve.
6. Serve with a pork dish.

Exchange List Values:
Starch 1.5, Fruit 1.0, Fat 1.5

Basic Nutritional Values: Calories 244 (Calories from Fat 96), Total Fat 11 gm (Saturated Fat 0.8 gm, Polyunsat Fat 6.5 gm, Monounsat Fat 2.4 gm, Cholesterol 0 mg), Sodium 202 mg, Total Carbohydrate 39 gm, Dietary Fiber 9 gm, Sugars 19 gm, Protein 4 gm

Stuffed Acorn Squash

Jean Butzer, Batavia, NY

*Makes 6 servings
(Ideal slow cooker size: 4-quart)*

3 small (1 1/4 lbs. each) acorn squash
5 Tbsp. dry instant brown rice
3 Tbsp. dried cranberries
3 Tbsp. diced celery
3 Tbsp. minced onion
pinch of ground or dried sage
1 tsp. butter, divided
3 Tbsp. orange juice
1/2 cup water

1. Slice off points on the bottoms of squash so they will stand in slow cooker. Slice off tops and discard. Scoop out seeds. Place squash in slow cooker.
2. Combine rice, cranberries, celery, onion, and sage. Stuff into squash.
3. Dot with butter.
4. Pour 1 Tbsp. orange juice into each squash.
5. Pour water into bottom of slow cooker.
6. Cover. Cook on Low 2 1/2 hours.
7. Serve with cooked turkey breast.

Exchange List Values:
Starch 2.0

Basic Nutritional Values: Calories 131 (Calories from Fat 10), Total Fat 1 gm (Saturated Fat 0.4 gm, Polyunsat Fat 0.2 gm, Monounsat Fat 0.3 gm, Cholesterol 2 mg), Sodium 18 mg, Total Carbohydrate 31 gm, Dietary Fiber 7 gm, Sugars 11 gm, Protein 2 gm

Note: To make squash easier to slice, microwave whole squash on High for 5 minutes to soften skin.

Caponata
Katrine Rose
Woodbridge, VA

Makes 10 servings
(Ideal slow cooker size: 4-quart)

1 medium (1 lb.) eggplant, peeled and cut into ½" cubes
14-oz. can diced tomatoes
1 medium onion, chopped
1 red bell pepper, cut into ½" pieces
¾ cup salsa
¼ cup olive oil
2 Tbsp. capers, drained
3 Tbsp. balsamic vinegar
3 garlic cloves, minced
1¼ tsp. dried oregano
⅓ cup chopped fresh basil, packed in measuring cup

1. Combine all ingredients except basil in slow cooker.
2. Cover. Cook on Low 7-8 hours, or until vegetables are tender.
3. Stir in basil. Serve spread on toasted French bread.

Exchange List Values:
Vegetable 2.0, Fat 1.0

Basic Nutritional Values: Calories 84 (Calories from Fat 51), Total Fat 6 gm (Saturated Fat 0.7 gm, Polyunsat Fat 0.6 gm, Monounsat Fat 4.0 gm, Cholesterol 0 mg), Sodium 182 mg, Total Carbohydrate 9 gm, Dietary Fiber 2 gm, Sugars 5 gm, Protein 1 gm

Julia's Broccoli and Cauliflower with Cheese
Julia Lapp, New Holland, PA

Makes 6 servings
(Ideal slow cooker size: 4-quart)

5 cups raw broccoli and cauliflower
¼ cup water
2 Tbsp. margarine
2 Tbsp. flour
½ tsp. salt
1 cup fat-free milk
1 cup fat-free shredded cheddar cheese

1. Cook broccoli and cauliflower in saucepan in water, until just crispy tender. Set aside.
2. Make white sauce by melting the margarine in another pan over Low heat. Blend in flour and salt. Add milk all at once. Cook quickly, stirring constantly until mixture thickens and bubbles. Add cheese. Stir until melted and smooth.
3. Combine vegetables and sauce in slow cooker. Mix well.
4. Cook on Low 1½ hours.

Exchange List Values:
Carbohydrate 0.5, Vegetable 1.0, Meat, lean 1.0

Basic Nutritional Values: Calories 108 (Calories from Fat 37), Total Fat 4 gm (Saturated Fat 0.8 gm, Polyunsat Fat 1.3 gm, Monounsat Fat 1.7 gm, Cholesterol 3 mg), Sodium 412 mg, Total Carbohydrate 9 gm, Dietary Fiber 2 gm, Sugars 5 gm, Protein 10 gm

Variation: Substitute green beans and carrots or other vegetables for broccoli and cauliflower.

Golden Cauliflower
Carol Peachey, Lancaster, PA

Makes 4-6 servings
(Ideal slow cooker size: 4-quart)

2 10-oz. pkgs. frozen cauliflower, thawed
2 Tbsp. light soft tub margarine, melted
1 Tbsp. flour
1 cup evaporated fat-free milk
1 oz. (¼ cup) fat-free cheddar cheese
2 Tbsp. low-fat (1%) cottage cheese
2 tsp. Parmesan cheese
4 slices bacon, crisply browned and crumbled

1. Place cauliflower in slow cooker
2. Melt margarine on stove. Add flour and evaporated milk. Heat till thickened. Add cheeses.
3. Pour sauce over cauliflower. Top with bacon.
4. Cover. Cook on High 1½ hours and then reduce to Low for an additional 2 hours. Or cook only on Low 4-5 hours.

Exchange List Values:
Carbohydrate 0.5, Meat, lean 1.0

Basic Nutritional Values: Calories 106 (Calories from Fat 37), Total Fat 4 gm (Saturated Fat 0.8 gm, Polyunsat Fat 0.6 gm, Monounsat Fat 1.9 gm, Cholesterol 5 mg), Sodium 228 mg, Total Carbohydrate 10 gm, Dietary Fiber 2 gm, Sugars 6 gm, Protein 8 gm

Quick Broccoli Fix
Willard E. Roth
Elkhart, IN

Makes 6 servings
(Ideal slow cooker size: 4-quart)

1 lb. fresh or frozen broccoli, cut up
10³/4-oz. can 98%-fat-free, reduced-sodium cream of mushroom soup
¹/4 cup fat-free mayonnaise
¹/2 cup fat-free plain yogurt
¹/2 lb. sliced fresh mushrooms
1 cup shredded fat-free cheddar cheese, divided
1 cup crushed saltine crackers with unsalted tops
sliced almonds, optional

1. Microwave broccoli for 3 minutes. Place in greased slow cooker.
2. Combine soup, mayonnaise, yogurt, mushrooms, and ¹/2 cup cheese. Pour over broccoli.
3. Cover. Cook on Low 5-6 hours.
4. Top with remaining cheese and crackers for last half hour of cooking time.
5. Top with sliced almonds, for a special touch, before serving.

Exchange List Values:
Carbohydrate 1.0, Vegetable 1.0, Meat, lean 1.0

Basic Nutritional Values: Calories 158 (Calories from Fat 28), Total Fat 3 gm (Saturated Fat 0.4 gm, Polyunsat Fat 0.8 gm, Monounsat Fat 1.0 gm, Cholesterol 3 mg), Sodium 523 mg, Total Carbohydrate 22 gm, Dietary Fiber 3 gm, Sugars 5 gm, Protein 12 gm

Eat breakfast every day. People who eat breakfast are less likely to overeat later in the day.

Broccoli and Rice Casserole
Deborah Swartz, Grottoes, VA

Makes 4-6 servings
(Ideal slow cooker size: 4-quart)

1 lb. chopped broccoli, fresh or frozen, thawed
1 medium onion, chopped
1 Tbsp. canola oil
1 cup minute rice, or 1¹/2 cups cooked rice
10³/4-oz. can 99%-fat-free, reduced-sodium cream of chicken or mushroom soup
¹/4 cup fat-free milk
1¹/3 cups fat-free cheddar cheese, shredded

1. Cook broccoli for 5 minutes in saucepan in boiling water. Drain and set aside.
2. Saute onion in oil in saucepan until tender. Add to broccoli.
3. Combine remaining ingredients. Add to broccoli mixture. Pour into greased slow cooker.
4. Cover. Cook on Low 3-4 hours.

Exchange List Values:
Starch 1.5, Vegetable 1.0, Meat, lean 1.0

Basic Nutritional Values: Calories 188 (Calories from Fat 33), Total Fat 4 gm (Saturated Fat 0.5 gm, Polyunsat Fat 1.2 gm, Monounsat Fat 1.6 gm, Cholesterol 7 mg), Sodium 404 mg, Total Carbohydrate 26 gm, Dietary Fiber 3 gm, Sugars 5 gm, Protein 13 gm

Sweet-Sour Cabbage

Irma H. Schoen
Windsor, CT

*Makes 6 servings
(Ideal slow cooker size: 4-quart)*

1 medium-sized head red,
   or green, cabbage,
   shredded
2 medium onions, chopped
4 medium tart apples,
   pared, quartered
1/2 cup raisins
1/4 cup lemon juice
1/4 cup cider, or apple juice
1 Tbsp. honey
1 Tbsp. caraway seeds
1/8 tsp. allspice
1/2 tsp. salt

1. Combine all ingredients
in slow cooker.
2. Cook on High 3-5 hours,
depending upon how crunchy
or soft you want the cabbage
and onions.

Exchange List Values:
Fruit 1.0, Vegetable 2.0

Basic Nutritional Values: Calories
112 (Calories from Fat 6), Total Fat 1
gm (Saturated Fat 0.0 gm, Polyunsat
Fat 0.3 gm, Monounsat Fat 0.1 gm,
Cholesterol 0 mg), Sodium 154
mg, Total Carbohydrate 27 gm,
Dietary Fiber 5 gm, Sugars 21 gm,
Protein 3 gm

Bavarian Cabbage

Joyce Shackelford
Green Bay, WI

*Makes 4-8 servings, depending
upon the size of the cabbage head
(Ideal slow cooker size: 4-quart)*

1 small (1 1/2 lbs.) head red
   cabbage, sliced
1 medium onion, chopped
3 medium tart apples,
   unpeeled, cored and
   quartered
1 tsp. salt
1 cup hot water
1 Tbsp. sugar
sugar substitute to equal
   1/2 Tbsp.
1/3 cup vinegar
1 1/2 Tbsp. bacon drippings

1. Place all ingredients in
slow cooker in order listed.
2. Cover. Cook on Low 8
hours, or on High 3 hours.
Stir well before serving.

Exchange List Values:
Fruit 0.5, Vegetable 1.0, Fat
0.5

Basic Nutritional Values: Calories
85 (Calories from Fat 24), Total Fat 3
gm (Saturated Fat 1.1 gm, Polyunsat
Fat 0.3 gm, Monounsat Fat 1.0 gm,
Cholesterol 2 mg), Sodium 313
mg, Total Carbohydrate 16 gm,
Dietary Fiber 3 gm, Sugars 12 gm,
Protein 1 gm

*Variation: Add 6 slices bacon,
browned until crisp and
crumbled.*

Jean M. Butzer
Batavia, NY

Cabbage Casserole

Edwina Stoltzfus, Narvon, PA

*Makes 6 servings
(Ideal slow cooker size: 4-quart)*

1 large head cabbage,
   chopped
2 cups water
3 Tbsp. margarine
1/4 cup flour
1/4 tsp. salt
1/4 tsp. pepper
1 1/3 cups fat-free milk
1 1/3 cups fat-free shredded
   cheddar

1. Cook cabbage in
saucepan in boiling water for
5 minutes. Drain. Place in
slow cooker.
2. In saucepan, melt
margarine. Stir in flour, salt,
and pepper. Add milk,
stirring constantly on Low
heat for 5 minutes. Remove
from heat. Stir in cheese.
Pour over cabbage.
3. Cover. Cook on Low 4-5
hours.

Exchange List Values:
Carbohydrate 0.5,
Vegetable 2.0, Meat, lean
1.0, Fat 0.5

Basic Nutritional Values: Calories
179 (Calories from Fat 57), Total Fat
6 gm (Saturated Fat 1.1 gm,
Polyunsat Fat 2.1 gm, Monounsat Fat
2.6 gm, Cholesterol 4 mg), Sodium
400 mg, Total Carbohydrate 19 gm,
Dietary Fiber 5 gm, Sugars 10 gm,
Protein 13 gm

*Variation: Replace cabbage
with cauliflower.*

Vegetable Curry

Sheryl Shenk
Harrisonburg, VA

Makes 8-10 servings
(Ideal slow cooker size: 4-5-quart)

16-oz. pkg. baby carrots
3 medium potatoes,
unpeeled, cubed
1 lb. fresh, or frozen, green
beans, cut in 2-inch
pieces
1 medium green pepper,
chopped
1 medium onion, chopped
1-2 cloves garlic, minced
15-oz. can garbanzo beans,
drained
28-oz. can crushed
tomatoes
3 Tbsp. minute tapioca
3 tsp. curry powder
1³⁄₄ cups boiling water
1¹⁄₂ tsp. chicken bouillon
granules

1. Combine carrots, potatoes, green beans, pepper, onion, garlic, garbanzo beans, and crushed tomatoes in large bowl.
2. Stir in tapioca and curry powder.
3. Dissolve bouillon in boiling water. Pour over vegetables. Mix well. Spoon into large cooker, or two medium-sized ones.
4. Cover. Cook on Low 8-10 hours, or High 3-4 hours. Serve with cooked rice.

Exchange List Values:
Starch 1.0, Vegetable 3.0

Basic Nutritional Values: Calories 166 (Calories from Fat 10), Total Fat 1 gm (Saturated Fat 0.1 gm, Polyunsat Fat 0.5 gm, Monounsat Fat 0.2 gm, Cholesterol 0 mg), Sodium 436 mg, Total Carbohydrate 35 gm, Dietary Fiber 8 gm, Sugars 10 gm, Protein 6 gm

Variation: Substitute canned green beans for fresh beans, but add toward the end of the cooking time.

Wild Mushrooms Italian

Connie Johnson, Loudon, NH

Makes 10 servings
(Ideal slow cooker size: 4-quart)

2 large onions, chopped
3 large red bell peppers,
chopped
3 large green bell peppers,
chopped
2 Tbsp. canola oil
12-oz. pkg. oyster
mushrooms, cleaned
and chopped
4 garlic cloves, minced
3 fresh bay leaves
10 fresh basil leaves,
chopped
1 tsp. salt
1¹⁄₂ tsp. pepper
28-oz. can Italian plum
tomatoes, crushed or
chopped

1. Saute onions and peppers in oil in skillet until soft. Stir in mushrooms and garlic. Saute just until mushrooms begin to turn brown. Pour into slow cooker.
2. Add remaining ingredients. Stir well.
3. Cover. Cook on Low 6-8 hours.

Exchange List Values:
Vegetable 3.0, Fat 0.5

Basic Nutritional Values: Calories 82 (Calories from Fat 29), Total Fat 3 gm (Saturated Fat 0.2 gm, Polyunsat Fat 1.0 gm, Monounsat Fat 1.7 gm, Cholesterol 0 mg), Sodium 356 mg, Total Carbohydrate 13 gm, Dietary Fiber 4 gm, Sugars 8 gm, Protein 3 gm

Note: Good as an appetizer or on pita bread, or serve over rice or pasta for main dish.

Stuffed Mushrooms

Melanie L. Thrower
McPherson, KS

Makes 6 servings
(Ideal slow cooker size: 3-4-quart)

12 large mushrooms
1/4 tsp. minced garlic
1 Tbsp. canola oil
dash of salt
dash of pepper
dash of cayenne pepper
1/4 cup grated reduced-fat
  Monterey Jack cheese

1. Remove stems from mushrooms and dice.
2. Heat oil in skillet. Saute diced stems with garlic until softened. Remove skillet from heat.
3. Stir in seasonings and cheese. Stuff into mushroom shells. Place in slow cooker.
4. Cover. Heat on Low 2-4 hours.

Exchange List Values:
Vegetable 1.0, Fat 0.5

Basic Nutritional Values: Calories 46 (Calories from Fat 30), Total Fat 3 gm (Saturated Fat 0.8 gm, Polyunsat Fat 0.8 gm, Monounsat Fat 1.6 gm, Cholesterol 3 mg), Sodium 39 mg, Total Carbohydrate 2 gm, Dietary Fiber 1 gm, Sugars 1 gm, Protein 3 gm

Variations:
1. Add 1 Tbsp. minced onion to Step 2.
2. Use Monterey Jack cheese with jalapenos.

Corn Pudding

Barbara A. Yoder
Goshen, IN

Makes 15 plus servings
(Ideal slow cooker size: 4-5-quart)

2 10-oz. cans whole kernel
  corn with juice
2 1 lb. cans no-added-salt
  creamed corn
2 6½-oz. boxes corn
  muffin mix, requiring
  only water
2 Tbsp. margarine
8-oz. box fat-free sour
  cream

1. Combine all ingredients in slow cooker.
2. Cover. Heat on Low 2-3 hours until thickened and set.

Exchange List Values:
Starch 2.0, Fat 0.5

Basic Nutritional Values: Calories 166 (Calories from Fat 39), Total Fat 4 gm (Saturated Fat 0.7 gm, Polyunsat Fat 0.9 gm, Monounsat Fat 1.6 gm, Cholesterol 1 mg), Sodium 456 mg, Total Carbohydrate 30 gm, Dietary Fiber 2 gm, Sugars 8 gm, Protein 4 gm

Corn on the Cob

Donna Conto
Saylorsburg, PA

Makes 6 servings
(Ideal slow cooker size: 5-6-quart)

6 small (5½-6½" long) ears
  of corn (in husk)
½ cup water

1. Remove silk from corn, as much as possible, but leave husks on.
2. Cut off ends of corn so ears can stand in the cooker.
3. Add water.
4. Cover. Cook on Low 2-3 hours.

Exchange List Values:
Starch 1.0

Basic Nutritional Values: Calories 68 (Calories from Fat 5), Total Fat 1 gm (Saturated Fat 0.1 gm, Polyunsat Fat 0.3 gm, Monounsat Fat 0.2 gm, Cholesterol 0 mg), Sodium 3 mg, Total Carbohydrate 16 gm, Dietary Fiber 2 gm, Sugars 2 gm, Protein 2 gm

Eat one more serving of vegetables today than you usually would.

Cheesy Corn

Tina Snyder
Manheim, PA
Jeannine Janzen
Elbing, KS
Nadine Martinitz
Salina, KS

Makes 10 servings
(Ideal slow cooker size: 4-quart)

3 16-oz. pkgs. frozen corn
8-oz. pkg. fat-free cream
   cheese, cubed
2 Tbsp. light soft tub
   margarine
3 Tbsp. water
3 Tbsp. fat-free milk
2 Tbsp. sugar
6 slices reduced-fat
   American cheese, cut
   into squares

1. Combine all ingredients
in slow cooker. Mix well.
2. Cover. Cook on Low 4
hours, or until heated
through and the cheese is
melted.

Exchange List Values:
Starch 2.0, Fat 0.5

Basic Nutritional Values: Calories
176 (Calories from Fat 29), Total Fat
3 gm (Saturated Fat 1.3 gm,
Polyunsat Fat 0.5 gm, Monounsat Fat
1.2 gm, Cholesterol 8 mg), Sodium
220 mg, Total Carbohydrate 33 gm,
Dietary Fiber 3 gm, Sugars 7 gm,
Protein 7 gm

Super Creamed Corn

Ruth Ann Penner
Hillsboro, KS
Alix Nancy Botsford
Seminole, OK

Makes 8-12 servings
(Ideal slow cooker size: 4-quart)

2 lbs. frozen corn
8-oz. pkg. fat-free cream
   cheese, cubed
2 Tbsp. margarine, melted
1 Tbsp. sugar
sugar substitute to equal
   ½ Tbsp.
2-3 Tbsp. water, optional

1. Combine ingredients in
slow cooker.
2. Cover. Cook on Low 4
hours.
3. Serve with meat loaf,
turkey, or hamburgers.

Exchange List Values:
Starch 1.0, Fat 0.5

Basic Nutritional Values: Calories
99 (Calories from Fat 20), Total Fat 2
gm (Saturated Fat 0.4 gm, Polyunsat
Fat 0.8 gm, Monounsat Fat 0.9 gm,
Cholesterol 2 mg), Sodium 129
mg, Total Carbohydrate 17 gm,
Dietary Fiber 2 gm, Sugars 3 gm,
Protein 5 gm

*A great addition to a holiday
that is easy and requires no
last-minute preparation. It also
frees the stove and oven for
other food preparation.*

Baked Corn

Velma Stauffer
Akron, PA

Makes 8 servings
(Ideal slow cooker size: 3-quart)

1 qt. corn, frozen or fresh
2 eggs, beaten
1 tsp. salt
1 cup fat-free milk
⅛ tsp. pepper
2 tsp. oil
1½ Tbsp. sugar
sugar substitute to equal
   2 tsp.
3 Tbsp. flour

1. Combine all ingredients
well. Pour into greased slow
cooker.
2. Cover. Cook on High
3 hours and then on Low 45
minutes.

Exchange List Values:
Starch 1.5, Fat 0.5

Basic Nutritional Values: Calories
125 (Calories from Fat 25), Total Fat
3 gm (Saturated Fat 0.7 gm,
Polyunsat Fat 0.7 gm, Monounsat Fat
1.3 gm, Cholesterol 54 mg), Sodium
324 mg, Total Carbohydrate 22 gm,
Dietary Fiber 2 gm, Sugars 6 gm,
Protein 5 gm

*Note: If you use home-grown
sweet corn, you could reduce
the amount of sugar.*

Scalloped Corn

Rebecca Plank Leichty
Harrisonburg, VA

Makes 8 servings
(Ideal slow cooker size: 4-quart)

2 eggs
10³/4-oz. can cream of
  celery soup
²/3 cup unseasoned bread
  crumbs
2 cups whole-kernel corn,
  drained, or cream-style
  corn
1 tsp. minced onion
¹/8 tsp. pepper
1 Tbsp. sugar
1 Tbsp. light, soft tub
  margarine, melted

  1. Beat eggs with fork.
Add soup and bread crumbs.
Mix well.
  2. Add remaining ingredients and mix thoroughly.
Pour into greased slow
cooker.
  3. Cover. Cook on High
3 hours or on Low 6 hours.

Exchange List Values:
Starch 1.0, Fat 1.0

Basic Nutritional Values: Calories
132 (Calories from Fat 44), Total Fat
5 gm (Saturated Fat 1.4 gm,
Polyunsat Fat 1.5 gm, Monounsat Fat
1.5 gm, Cholesterol 55 mg), Sodium
473 mg, Total Carbohydrate 19 gm,
Dietary Fiber 1 gm, Sugars 3 gm,
Protein 4 gm

Baked Corn and Noodles

Ruth Hershey
Paradise, PA

Makes 6 servings
(Ideal slow cooker size: 4-quart)

3 cups noodles, cooked al
  dente
2 cups fresh or frozen
  corn, thawed
³/4 cup grated fat-free
  cheddar cheese, or
  cubed Velveeta cheese
1 egg, beaten
2 Tbsp. light, soft tub
  margarine, melted
¹/2 tsp. salt

  1. Combine all ingredients
in slow cooker.
  2. Cover. Cook on Low 6-8
hours or on High 3-4 hours.

Exchange List Values:
Starch 2.0, Fat 0.5

Basic Nutritional Values: Calories
198 (Calories from Fat 34), Total Fat
4 gm (Saturated Fat 0.6 gm,
Polyunsat Fat 0.9 gm, Monounsat Fat
1.6 gm, Cholesterol 63 mg), Sodium
343 mg, Total Carbohydrate 32 gm,
Dietary Fiber 2 gm, Sugars 3 gm,
Protein 11 gm

Mexican Corn

Betty K. Drescher
Quakertown, PA

Makes 8 servings
(Ideal slow cooker size: 3-4-quart)

2 10-oz. pkgs. frozen corn,
  partially thawed
4-oz. jar chopped pimentos
¹/3 cup chopped green
  peppers
¹/3 cup water
1 tsp. salt
¹/4 tsp. pepper
¹/2 tsp. paprika
¹/2 tsp. chili powder

  1. Combine all ingredients
in slow cooker.
  2. Cover. Cook on High 45
minutes, then on Low 2-4
hours. Stir occasionally.

Exchange List Values:
Starch 1.0

Basic Nutritional Values: Calories
63 (Calories from Fat 3), Total Fat 0
gm (Saturated Fat 0.1 gm, Polyunsat
Fat 0.2 gm, Monounsat Fat 0.1 gm,
Cholesterol 0 mg), Sodium 298
mg, Total Carbohydrate 15 gm,
Dietary Fiber 2 gm, Sugars 2 gm,
Protein 2 gm

*Variations: For more fire, add
¹/3 cup salsa to the ingredients,
and increase the amounts of
pepper, paprika, and chili
powder to match your taste.*

Confetti Scalloped Corn

Rhoda Atzeff
Harrisburg, PA

Makes 12 servings
(Ideal slow cooker size: 4-quart)

2 eggs, beaten
1 cup fat-free sour cream
2 Tbsp. light, soft tub
   margarine, melted
1 small onion, finely
   chopped, or 2 Tbsp.
   dried chopped onion
11-oz. can Mexicorn,
   drained
14-oz. can cream-style corn
2-3 Tbsp. green jalapeno
   salsa, regular salsa, or
   chopped green chilies
8$^{1/2}$-oz. pkg. corn bread
   mix

1. Combine all ingredients.
Pour into lightly greased slow
cooker.
2. Cover. Bake on High
2-2$^{1/2}$ hours, or until corn is
fully cooked.

Exchange List Values:
Starch 2.0

Basic Nutritional Values: Calories
147 (Calories from Fat 32), Total Fat
4 gm (Saturated Fat 1.1 gm,
Polyunsat Fat 0.6 gm, Monounsat Fat
1.2 gm, Cholesterol 37 mg), Sodium
408 mg, Total Carbohydrate 29 gm,
Dietary Fiber 1 gm, Sugars 10 gm,
Protein 4 gm

Corn Bread Casserole

Arlene Groff
Lewistown, PA

Makes 16 servings
(Ideal slow cooker size: 4-quart)

1 qt. frozen whole-kernel
   corn, thawed
1 qt. creamed corn
8$^{1/2}$-oz. pkg. corn muffin
   mix
1 egg
2 Tbsp. light, soft tub
   margarine
$^{1/4}$ tsp. garlic powder
2 Tbsp. sugar
$^{1/4}$ cup fat-free milk
$^{1/2}$ tsp. salt
$^{1/4}$ tsp. pepper

1. Combine ingredients in
greased slow cooker.
2. Cover. Cook on Low
3$^{1/2}$-4 hours, stirring once
halfway through.

Exchange List Values:
Starch 2.0

Basic Nutritional Values: Calories
141 (Calories from Fat 23), Total Fat
3 gm (Saturated Fat 0.7 gm,
Polyunsat Fat 0.5 gm, Monounsat Fat
0.8 gm, Cholesterol 13 mg), Sodium
412 mg, Total Carbohydrate 31 gm,
Dietary Fiber 2 gm, Sugars 10 gm,
Protein 3 gm

Slow-Cooker Rice

Dorothy Horst
Tiskilwa, IL

Makes 20 servings
(Ideal slow cooker size: 5-6-quart)

1 Tbsp. margarine, melted
4 cups converted long
   grain rice, uncooked
10 cups water
2 tsp. salt

1. Pour margarine, rice,
water, and salt into greased
slow cooker.
2. Cover. Cook on High 2-3
hours, or until rice is tender,
but not overcooked. Stir
occasionally.

Exchange List Values:
Starch 2.0

Basic Nutritional Values: Calories
140 (Calories from Fat 7), Total Fat 1
gm (Saturated Fat 0.1 gm, Polyunsat
Fat 0.2 gm, Monounsat Fat 0.3 gm,
Cholesterol 0 mg), Sodium 241
mg, Total Carbohydrate 30 gm,
Dietary Fiber 0 gm, Sugars 0 gm,
Protein 3 gm

Fruited Wild Rice with Pecans

Dottie Schmidt
Kansas City, MO

Makes 8 servings
(Ideal slow cooker size: 4-quart)

½ cup chopped onions
1 Tbsp. canola oil
6-oz. pkg. long grain and
    wild rice
seasoning packet from
    wild rice pkg.
1½ cups hot water
⅔ cup apple juice
1 large tart apple, chopped
¼ cup raisins
¼ cup coarsely chopped
    pecans

1. Combine all ingredients except pecans in slow cooker sprayed with non-fat cooking spray.
2. Cover. Cook on High 2-2½ hours.
3. Stir in pecans. Serve.

Exchange List Values:
Starch 1.0, Fruit 1.0, Fat 0.5

Basic Nutritional Values: Calories 154 (Calories from Fat 43), Total Fat 5 gm (Saturated Fat 0.4 gm, Polyunsat Fat 1.3 gm, Monounsat Fat 2.7 gm, Cholesterol 0 mg), Sodium 237 mg, Total Carbohydrate 27 gm, Dietary Fiber 2 gm, Sugars 9 gm, Protein 3 gm

Mjeddrah

Dianna Milhizer
Brighton, MI

Makes 24 servings
(Ideal slow cooker size: 5-quart)

10 cups water
4 cups dried lentils, rinsed
2 cups uncooked brown
    rice
¼ cup olive oil
2 tsp. salt

1. Combine ingredients in large slow cooker.
2. Cover. Cook on High 8 hours, then on Low 2 hours. Add 2 more cups water, if needed, to allow rice to cook and to prevent dish from drying out.
3. This is traditionally eaten with a salad with an oil-and-vinegar dressing over the lentil-rice mixture, similar to a tostada without the tortilla.

Exchange List Values:
Starch 2.0, Fat 0.5

Basic Nutritional Values: Calories 173 (Calories from Fat 27), Total Fat 3 gm (Saturated Fat 0.4 gm, Polyunsat Fat 0.5 gm, Monounsat Fat 1.9 gm, Cholesterol 0 mg), Sodium 196 mg, Total Carbohydrate 29 gm, Dietary Fiber 7 gm, Sugars 2 gm, Protein 9 gm

Risi Bisi (Peas and Rice)

Cyndie Marrara, Port Matilda, PA

Makes 8 servings
(Ideal slow cooker size: 4-quart)

1½ cups converted long
    grain white rice,
    uncooked
¾ cup chopped onions
2 garlic cloves, minced
2 14½-oz. cans reduced-
    sodium chicken broth
⅓ cup water
¾ tsp. Italian seasoning
    (recipe on page 254)
½ tsp. dried basil leaves
½ cup frozen baby peas,
    thawed
¼ cup freshly grated
    Parmesan cheese

1. Combine rice, onions, and garlic in slow cooker.
2. In saucepan, mix together chicken broth and water. Bring to boil. Add Italian seasoning and basil leaves. Stir into rice mixture.
3. Cover. Cook on Low 2-3 hours, or until liquid is absorbed.
4. Stir in peas. Cover. Cook 30 minutes. Stir in cheese.

Exchange List Values:
Starch 2.0

Basic Nutritional Values: Calories 165 (Calories from Fat 11), Total Fat 1 gm (Saturated Fat 0.5 gm, Polyunsat Fat 0.1 gm, Monounsat Fat 0.4 gm, Cholesterol 3 mg), Sodium 409 mg, Total Carbohydrate 32 gm, Dietary Fiber 1 gm, Sugars 2 gm, Protein 6 gm

Green Rice Casserole

Ruth Hofstetter
Versailles, Missouri

Makes 6 servings
(Ideal slow cooker size: 4-quart)

1¹/3 cups fat-free evaporated milk
2 Tbsp. vegetable oil
3 eggs
one-fourth of a small onion, minced
half a small carrot, minced, optional
2 cups minced fresh parsley, or 10-oz. pkg. frozen chopped spinach, thawed and drained
1/4 tsp. salt
1/4 tsp. pepper
1 cup shredded fat-free sharp cheddar cheese
3 cups cooked long grain rice

1. Beat together milk, oil, and eggs until well combined.
2. Stir in remaining ingredients. Mix well. Pour into greased slow cooker.
3. Cover. Cook on High 1 hour. Stir. Reduce heat to Low and cook 4-6 hours.

Exchange List Values:
Starch 1.5, Milk, fat-free 0.5, Meat, medium fat 1.0, Fat 1.0

Basic Nutritional Values: Calories 264 (Calories from Fat 67), Total Fat 7 gm (Saturated Fat 1.4 gm, Polyunsat Fat 1.8 gm, Monounsat Fat 3.8 gm,

Cholesterol 109 mg), Sodium 345 mg,Total Carbohydrate 32 gm, Dietary Fiber 1 gm, Sugars 7 gm, Protein 16 gm

Wild Rice

Ruth S. Weaver
Reinholds, PA

Makes 4-5 servings
(Ideal slow cooker size: 3-4-quart)

1 cup wild rice, or wild rice mixture, uncooked
1/2 cup sliced mushrooms
1/2 cup diced onions
1/2 cup diced green, or red, peppers
1 Tbsp. oil
1/4 tsp. salt
1/4 tsp. pepper
2¹/2 cups 98%-fat-free, reduced-sodium chicken broth

1. Layer rice and vegetables in slow cooker. Pour oil, salt, and pepper over vegetables. Stir.
2. Heat chicken broth. Pour over ingredients in slow cooker.
3. Cover. Cook on High 2¹/2-3 hours, or until rice is soft and liquid is absorbed.

Exchange List Values:
Starch 2.0

Basic Nutritional Values: Calories 157 (Calories from Fat 28), Total Fat 3 gm (Saturated Fat 0.2 gm, Polyunsat Fat 1.0 gm, Monounsat Fat 1.7 gm, Cholesterol 0 mg), Sodium 370 mg,Total Carbohydrate 27 gm, Dietary Fiber 3 gm, Sugars 3 gm, Protein 6 gm

Baked Potatoes

Lucille Metzler, Wellsboro, PA
Elizabeth Yutzy, Wauseon, OH
Glenda S. Weaver, Manheim, PA
Mary Jane Musser, Manheim, PA
Esther Becker, Gordonville, PA

Makes 6 servings
(Ideal slow cooker size: 4-quart)

6 medium (5³/4 ozs.) baking potatoes
1 Tbsp. margarine

1. Prick potatoes with fork. Rub each with margarine. Place in slow cooker.
2. Cover. Cook on High 3-5 hours, or Low 6-10 hours.

Exchange List Values:
Starch 2.0

Basic Nutritional Values: Calories 147 (Calories from Fat 17), Total Fat 2 gm (Saturated Fat 0.3 gm, Polyunsat Fat 0.7 gm, Monounsat Fat 0.8 gm, Cholesterol 0 mg), Sodium 34 mg,Total Carbohydrate 29 gm, Dietary Fiber 3 gm, Sugars 3 gm, Protein 4 gm

Good snack choices include grains, fruits, and vegetables.

Pizza Potatoes

Margaret Wenger Johnson
Keezletown, VA

Makes 8 servings
(Ideal slow cooker size: 4-quart)

6 (5¾ ozs.) medium
 potatoes, sliced
1 large onion, thinly sliced
2 Tbsp. olive oil
6 ozs. (1½ cups) grated
 mozzarella fat-free
 cheese
2 ozs. sliced turkey
 pepperoni
8-oz. can pizza sauce

1. Saute potato and onion slices in oil in skillet until onions appear transparent. Drain well.
2. In slow cooker, combine potatoes, onions, cheese, and pepperoni.
3. Pour pizza sauce over top.
4. Cover. Cook on Low 6-10 hours, or until potatoes are soft.

Exchange List Values:
Starch 2.0, Meat, lean 1.0

Basic Nutritional Values: Calories 205 (Calories from Fat 43), Total Fat 5 gm (Saturated Fat 0.9 gm, Polyunsat Fat 0.8 gm, Monounsat Fat 2.9 gm, Cholesterol 12 mg), Sodium 417 mg, Total Carbohydrate 27 gm, Dietary Fiber 3 gm, Sugars 6 gm, Protein 13 gm

Potatoes O'Brien

Rebecca Meyerkorth
Wamego, KS

Makes 8 servings
(Ideal slow cooker size: 4-quart)

32-oz. pkg. shredded
 potatoes
¼ cup chopped onions
¼ cup chopped green
 peppers
¼ tsp. salt
¼ tsp. pepper
2 Tbsp. margarine
3 Tbsp. flour
½ cup fat-free milk
10¾-oz. can 98%-fat-free,
 reduced-sodium cream
 of mushroom soup
1 cup shredded fat-free
 cheddar cheese, divided

1. Place potatoes, onions, and green peppers in slow cooker. Sprinkle with salt and pepper.
2. Melt margarine in saucepan. Stir in flour; then add half of milk. Stir rapidly to remove all lumps. Stir in remaining milk. Stir in mushroom soup and ½ cup cheese. Pour over potatoes.
3. Cover. Cook on Low 4-5 hours. Sprinkle remaining cheese on top about ½ hour before serving.

Exchange List Values:
Starch 2.0, Fat 0.5

Basic Nutritional Values: Calories 193 (Calories from Fat 38), Total Fat 4 gm (Saturated Fat 1.0 gm, Polyunsat Fat 1.4 gm, Monounsat Fat 1.5 gm, Cholesterol 2 mg), Sodium 379 mg, Total Carbohydrate 30 gm, Dietary Fiber 2 gm, Sugars 3 gm, Protein 9 gm

Variation:
Add to Step 1:
 2 Tbsp. chopped
  pimento
 1 cup chopped ham

Garlic Mashed Potatoes

Katrine Rose
Woodbridge, VA

Makes 6 servings
(Ideal slow cooker size: 4-quart)

2 lbs. baking potatoes,
 unpeeled and cut into
 ½" cubes
¼ cup water
3 Tbsp. light, soft tub
 margarine
¾ tsp. salt
¾ tsp. garlic powder
¼ tsp. black pepper
1 cup 2%-milk

1. Combine all ingredients, except milk, in slow cooker. Toss to combine.
2. Cover. Cook on Low 7 hours, or on High 4 hours.
3. Add milk to potatoes during last 30 minutes of cooking time.
4. Mash potatoes with potato masher or electric mixer until fairly smooth.

Basic Nutritional Values: Calories 167 (Calories from Fat 29), Total Fat 3 gm (Saturated Fat 0.4 gm, Polyunsat Fat 0.6 gm, Monounsat Fat 1.6 gm, Cholesterol 3 mg), Sodium 361 mg, Total Carbohydrate 31 gm, Dietary Fiber 3 gm, Sugars 4 gm, Protein 4 gm

Company Mashed Potatoes

Eileen Eash
Carlsbad, NM

*Makes 12 servings
(Ideal slow cooker size: 6-quart)*

**15 (5 lbs. total) medium-sized potatoes
1 cup reduced-fat sour cream
1 small onion, diced fine
1 tsp. salt
$1/8$-$1/4$ tsp. pepper, according to your taste preference
1 cup buttermilk
1 cup fresh, chopped spinach, optional
1 cup grated Colby or cheddar cheese, optional**

1. Peel and quarter potatoes. Place in slow cooker. Barely cover with water.
2. Cover. Cook on Low 8-10 hours. Drain water.
3. Mash potatoes. Add remaining ingredients except cheese.

4. Cover. Heat on Low 4-6 hours.
5. Sprinkle with cheese 5 minutes before serving.

Basic Nutritional Values: Calories 160 (Calories from Fat 18), Total Fat 2 gm (Saturated Fat 1.1 gm, Polyunsat Fat 0.1 gm, Monounsat Fat 0.5 gm, Cholesterol 7 mg), Sodium 236 mg, Total Carbohydrate 32 gm, Dietary Fiber 3 gm, Sugars 5 gm, Protein 5 gm

---

Buttermilk gives mashed potatoes a unique flavor that most people enjoy. I often serve variations of this recipe for guests and they always ask what I put in the potatoes.

Notes:
l. I save the water drained from cooking the potatoes and use it to make gravy or a soup base.
2. Small amounts of leftovers from this recipe add a special flavor to vegetable or noodle soup for another meal.

Creamy Mashed Potatoes

Brenda S. Burkholder
Port Republic, VA

*Makes 10-12 servings
(Ideal slow cooker size: 5-quart)*

**1 tsp. salt
4 Tbsp. margarine, melted
$2^{1}/4$ cups fat-free milk
$6^{7}/8$ cups potato flakes
6 cups water
4 ozs. (approximately half of a large pkg.) fat-free cream cheese, softened
1 cup fat-free sour cream**

1. Combine first five ingredients as directed on potato box.
2. Whip cream cheese with electric mixer until creamy. Blend in sour cream.
3. Fold potatoes into cheese and sour cream. Beat well. Place in slow cooker.
4. Cover. Cook on Low 3-5 hours.

Basic Nutritional Values: Calories 173 (Calories from Fat 36), Total Fat 4 gm (Saturated Fat 0.8 gm, Polyunsat Fat 1.2 gm, Monounsat Fat 1.7 gm, Cholesterol 3 mg), Sodium 361 mg, Total Carbohydrate 29 gm, Dietary Fiber 2 gm, Sugars 4 gm, Protein 6 gm

Herbed Potatoes
Jo Haberkamp, Fairbank, IA

Makes 6 servings
(Ideal slow cooker size: 4-quart)

1½ lbs. small new potatoes
¼ cup water
¼ cup light, soft tub
  margarine, melted
3 Tbsp. chopped fresh
  parsley
1 Tbsp. lemon juice
1 Tbsp. chopped fresh
  chives
1 Tbsp. dill weed
¼-½ tsp. salt, according to
  your taste preference
⅛-¼ tsp. pepper, according
  to your taste preference

1. Wash potatoes. Peel a
strip around the center of each
potato. Place in slow cooker.
2. Add water.
3. Cover. Cook on High
2½-3 hours. Drain well.
4. In saucepan, heat
margarine, parsley, lemon
juice, chives, dill, salt, and
pepper. Pour over potatoes.
5. Serve with ham or any
meat dish that does not make
gravy.

Exchange List Values:
Starch 1.5, Fat 0.5

Basic Nutritional Values: Calories
122 (Calories from Fat 28), Total Fat
3 gm (Saturated Fat 0.0 gm,
Polyunsat Fat 0.7 gm, Monounsat Fat
1.7 gm, Cholesterol 0 mg), Sodium
163 mg, Total Carbohydrate 22 gm,
Dietary Fiber 2 gm, Sugars 2 gm,
Protein 2 gm

Onion Potatoes
Donna Lantgen
Rapid City, SD

Makes 6 servings
(Ideal slow cooker size: 4-quart)

6 medium potatoes, diced
⅓ cup olive oil
1 pkg. dry onion soup mix

1. Combine potatoes and
olive oil in plastic bag. Shake
well.
2. Add onion soup mix.
Shake well.
3. Pour into slow cooker.
4. Cover. Cook on Low 6
hours or High 3 hours.

Exchange List Values:
Starch 2.0, Fat 2.0

Basic Nutritional Values: Calories
252 (Calories from Fat 110), Total Fat
12 gm (Saturated Fat 1.6 gm,
Polyunsat Fat 1.1 gm, Monounsat Fat
8.9 gm, Cholesterol 0 mg), Sodium
465 mg, Total Carbohydrate 32 gm,
Dietary Fiber 4 gm, Sugars 5 gm,
Protein 5 gm

*Variations: Add more zest to the
potatoes by stirring in
1 small onion, chopped; 1 bell
pepper, chopped; ½ tsp. salt; and
¼ tsp. black pepper, after
pouring the potatoes into the slow
cooker. Continue with Step 4.*

Potatoes Perfect
Naomi Ressler
Harrisonburg, VA

Makes 4-6 servings
(Ideal slow cooker size: 4-quart)

¼ lb. bacon, diced and
  browned until crisp
2 medium-sized onions,
  thinly sliced
6-8 medium-sized potatoes,
  thinly sliced
4 ozs. fat-free cheddar
  cheese, thinly sliced
salt to taste
pepper to taste
2 Tbsp. light, soft tub
  margarine

1. Layer half of bacon,
onions, potatoes, and cheese
in greased slow cooker.
Season to taste.
2. Dot with margarine.
Repeat layers.
3. Cover. Cook on Low 8-
10 hours or on High 3-4
hours, or until potatoes are
soft.

Exchange List Values:
Starch 2.0, Vegetable 1.0,
Fat 1.0

Basic Nutritional Values: Calories
224 (Calories from Fat 38), Total Fat
4 gm (Saturated Fat 0.9 gm,
Polyunsat Fat 0.7 gm, Monounsat Fat
2.1 gm, Cholesterol 6 mg), Sodium
262 mg, Total Carbohydrate 35 gm,
Dietary Fiber 4 gm, Sugars 7 gm,
Protein 12 gm

Lotsa Scalloped Potatoes

Fannie Miller, Hutchinson, KS

*Makes 20-25 servings
(Ideal slow cooker size:
6-7-quart, or 2 4-5-quart cookers)*

5 lbs. potatoes, cooked and
    sliced
2 lbs. extra-lean, lower-
    sodium cooked ham,
    cubed
1/4 lb. light, soft tub
    margarine
1/2 cup flour
2 cups fat-free half-and-
    half
1/4 lb. reduced-fat mild
    cheese (your favorite),
    shredded
1/4-1/2 tsp. pepper

1. Place layers of sliced
potatoes and ham in very
large (or two smaller) slow
cooker(s).
2. Melt margarine in
saucepan on stove. Stir in
flour. Gradually add half-and-
half to make a white sauce,
stirring constantly until
smooth and thickened.
3. Stir in cheese and
pepper. Stir until cheese is
melted. Pour over potatoes
and ham.
4. Cover. Cook on Low 2-3
hours.

Exchange List Values:
Starch 1.0, Meat, lean 1.0

Basic Nutritional Values: Calories
136 (Calories from Fat 24), Total Fat
3 gm (Saturated Fat 1.0 gm,
Polyunsat Fat 0.4 gm, Monounsat Fat
0.9 gm, Cholesterol 21 mg), Sodium
379 mg, Total Carbohydrate 19 gm,
Dietary Fiber 1 gm, Sugars 4 gm,
Protein 10 gm

*Note: A great way to free up
oven space.*

Cheese Potatoes

Joyce Shackelford
Green Bay, WI

*Makes 10 servings
(Ideal slow cooker size: 5-quart)*

6 potatoes, peeled and cut
    into 1/4" strips
3 ozs. reduced-fat sharp
    cheddar cheese,
    shredded
10³/4-oz. can 98%-fat-free,
    lower-sodium cream of
    chicken soup
1 small onion, chopped
4 Tbsp. margarine, melted
1 tsp. salt
1 tsp. pepper
1 cup sour cream
2 cups seasoned stuffing
    cubes
3 Tbsp. margarine, melted

1. Toss together potatoes
and cheese. Place in slow
cooker.
2. Combine soup, onion,
4 Tbsp. margarine, salt, and
pepper. Pour over potatoes.
3. Cover. Cook on Low 8
hours.
4. Stir in sour cream.

Cover and heat for 10 more
minutes.
5. Meanwhile, toss
together stuffing cubes and
3 Tbsp. margarine. Sprinkle
over potatoes just before
serving.

Exchange List Values:
Starch 2.0, Fat 1.0

Basic Nutritional Values: Calories
190 (Calories from Fat 54), Total Fat
6 gm (Saturated Fat 1.5 gm,
Polyunsat Fat 1.2 gm, Monounsat Fat
2.5 gm, Cholesterol 10 mg), Sodium
390 mg, Total Carbohydrate 29 gm,
Dietary Fiber 2 gm, Sugars 5 gm,
Protein 7 gm

**Surround yourself
with people who care
about you and your
diabetes. They are your
very own support
network.**

Hot German Potato Salad

Judi Manos, West Islip, NY

Makes 7 servings
(Ideal slow cooker size: 4-5-quart)

5 medium-sized potatoes,
  cut ¼" thick
1 large onion, chopped
⅓ cup water
⅓ cup vinegar
2 Tbsp. flour
2 Tbsp. sugar
1 tsp. salt
½ tsp. celery seed
¼ tsp. pepper
4 slices bacon, cooked
  crisp and crumbled
chopped fresh parsley

1. Combine potatoes and onions in slow cooker.
2. Combine remaining ingredients, except bacon and parsley. Pour over potatoes.
3. Cover. Cook on Low 8-10 hours.
4. Stir in bacon and parsley.
5. Serve warm or at room temperature with grilled bratwurst or Polish sausage, dilled pickles, pickled beets, and apples.

Exchange List Values:
Starch 2.0

Basic Nutritional Values: Calories 149 (Calories from Fat 17), Total Fat 2 gm (Saturated Fat 0.6 gm, Polyunsat Fat 0.3 gm, Monounsat Fat 0.8 gm, Cholesterol 3 mg), Sodium 397 mg, Total Carbohydrate 30 gm, Dietary Fiber 3 gm, Sugars 8 gm, Protein 4 gm

Creamy Hash Browns

Judy Buller, Bluffton, OH
Elaine Patton
West Middletown, PA
Melissa Raber, Millersburg, OH

Makes 14 servings
(Ideal slow cooker size: 4-5-quart)

2 lb. pkg. frozen, cubed
  hash brown potatoes
2 cups cubed or shredded
  fat-free American cheese
12 ozs. fat-free sour cream
10¾-oz. can cream of
  celery soup
10¾-oz. can 98%-fat-free,
  lower-sodium cream of
  chicken soup
¼ lb. sliced bacon, cooked
  and crumbled
1 medium onion, chopped
2 Tbsp. margarine, melted
¼ tsp. pepper

1. Place potatoes in slow cooker. Combine remaining ingredients and pour over potatoes. Mix well.
2. Cover. Cook on Low 4-5 hours, or until potatoes are tender.

Exchange List Values:
Starch 1.0, Carbohydrate 0.5, Fat 1.0

Basic Nutritional Values: Calories 167 (Calories from Fat 44), Total Fat 5 gm (Saturated Fat 1.4 gm, Polyunsat Fat 1.5 gm, Monounsat Fat 1.6 gm, Cholesterol 9 mg), Sodium 578 mg, Total Carbohydrate 23 gm, Dietary Fiber 2 gm, Sugars 4 gm, Protein 8 gm

Candied Sweet Potatoes

Julie Weaver, Reinholds, PA

Makes 8 servings
(Ideal slow cooker size: 4-quart)

6-8 medium (6½ ozs. each)
  sweet potatoes
½ tsp. salt
2 Tbsp. margarine, melted
20-oz. can crushed
  pineapples, undrained
2 Tbsp. brown sugar
brown sugar substitute to
  equal 1 Tbsp.
1 tsp. nutmeg
1 tsp. cinnamon

1. Cook sweet potatoes until soft. Peel. Slice and place in slow cooker.
2. Combine remaining ingredients. Pour over sweet potatoes.
3. Cover. Cook on High 4 hours.

Exchange List Values:
Starch 1.5, Fruit 1.0, Fat 0.5

Basic Nutritional Values: Calories 186 (Calories from Fat 30), Total Fat 3 gm (Saturated Fat 0.7 gm, Polyunsat Fat 1.1 gm, Monounsat Fat 1.3 gm, Cholesterol 0 mg), Sodium 193 mg, Total Carbohydrate 39 gm, Dietary Fiber 3 gm, Sugars 19 gm, Protein 2 gm

Sweet Potato Casserole
Jean Butzer, Batavia, NY

Makes 10 servings
(Ideal slow cooker size: 4-5-quart)

2 29-oz. cans no-sugar-
 added sweet potatoes,
 drained and mashed
2¹⁄₂ Tbsp. light, soft tub
 margarine
1 Tbsp. sugar
1 Tbsp. brown sugar
brown sugar substitute to
 equal ¹⁄₂ tsp.
1 Tbsp. orange juice
2 eggs, beaten
¹⁄₂ cup fat-free milk
¹⁄₃ cup chopped pecans
2 Tbsp. brown sugar
brown sugar substitute to
 equal 1¹⁄₂ Tbsp.
2 Tbsp. flour
2 tsp. light, soft tub
 margarine, melted

1. Combine sweet potatoes, 2¹⁄₂ Tbsp. margarine, 1 Tbsp. sugar, 1 Tbsp. brown sugar, and sugar substitute to equal ¹⁄₂ tsp.
2. Beat in orange juice, eggs, and milk. Transfer to greased slow cooker.
3. Combine pecans, 2 Tbsp. brown sugar, sugar substitute to equal 1¹⁄₂ Tbsp., flour, and 2 tsp. margarine. Spread over sweet potatoes.
4. Cover. Cook on High 3-4 hours.

Exchange List Values:
Starch 2.0, Carbohydrate 0.5, Fat 0.5

Basic Nutritional Values: Calories 218 (Calories from Fat 51), Total Fat 6 gm (Saturated Fat 0.7 gm, Polyunsat Fat 1.4 gm, Monounsat Fat 2.9 gm, Cholesterol 43 mg), Sodium 64 mg, Total Carbohydrate 40 gm, Dietary Fiber 5 gm, Sugars 24 gm, Protein 5 gm

Glazed Sweet Potatoes
Martha Hershey
Ronks, PA

Makes 10 servings
(Ideal slow cooker size: 4-5-quart)

10 medium-sized (6¹⁄₃ ozs.
 each) sweet potatoes
¹⁄₄ cup light, soft tub
 margarine, melted
2 Tbsp. brown sugar
brown sugar substitute to
 equal 1 Tbsp.
¹⁄₂ cup orange juice
¹⁄₂ tsp. salt

1. Cook sweet potatoes until just soft. Peel and cut in half.
2. Combine remaining ingredients. Pour over potatoes.
3. Cover. Cook on High 2¹⁄₂-3 hours, or until tender but not mushy.

Exchange List Values:
Starch 2.0, Carbohydrate 0.5

Basic Nutritional Values: Calories 169 (Calories from Fat 20), Total Fat 2 gm (Saturated Fat 0.1 gm, Polyunsat Fat 0.6 gm, Monounsat Fat 1.0 gm, Cholesterol 0 mg), Sodium 171 mg, Total Carbohydrate 36 gm, Dietary Fiber 2 gm, Sugars 11 gm, Protein 2 gm

Note: The sweet potatoes can be cooked and peeled ahead of time, and frozen in a single layer. Defrost before putting in slow cooker.

These are great to serve with Thanksgiving dinner.

Orange Yams

Gladys Longacre
Susquehanna, PA

Makes 6-8 servings
(Ideal slow cooker size: 4-5-quart)

40-oz. can no-sugar-added
   yams, drained
2 apples, cored, peeled,
   thinly sliced
1 1/2 Tbsp. light, soft tub
   margarine, melted
2 tsp. orange zest
1 cup orange juice
2 Tbsp. cornstarch
1/4 cup brown sugar
brown sugar substitute to
   equal 2 Tbsp.
1 tsp. salt
dash of ground cinnamon
   and/or nutmeg

1. Place yams and apples
in slow cooker.
2. Add margarine and
orange zest.
3. Combine remaining
ingredients and pour over
yams.
4. Cover. Cook on High 1
hour and on Low 2 hours, or
until apples are tender.

Exchange List Values:
Starch 2.0, Carbohydrate
1.0

Basic Nutritional Values: Calories
199 (Calories from Fat 11), Total Fat
1 gm (Saturated Fat 0.1 gm,
Polyunsat Fat 0.4 gm, Monounsat Fat
0.5 gm, Cholesterol 0 mg), Sodium
324 mg, Total Carbohydrate 48 gm,
Dietary Fiber 4 gm, Sugars 32 gm,
Protein 3 gm

Variation: Substitute 6-8
medium-sized cooked sweet
potatoes, or approximately 4
cups cubed butternut squash,
for yams.

Sweet Potatoes and Apples

Bernita Boyts
Shawnee Mission, KS

Makes 8 servings
(Ideal slow cooker size: 4-quart)

3 large sweet potatoes,
   peeled and cubed
3 large tart and firm
   apples, peeled and
   sliced
1/2 tsp. salt
1/8-1/4 tsp. pepper
1 tsp. sage
1 tsp. ground cinnamon
4 Tbsp. light, soft tub
   margarine, melted
2 Tbsp. maple syrup
brown sugar substitute to
   equal 1 Tbsp.
toasted sliced almonds or
   chopped pecans,
   optional

1. Place half the sweet
potatoes in slow cooker.
Layer in half the apple slices.
2. Mix together dry
seasonings. Sprinkle half over
apples.
3. Mix together margarine,
maple syrup, brown sugar,
and sugar substitute. Spoon
half over seasonings.
4. Repeat layers.

5. Cover. Cook on Low 6-8
hours or until potatoes are
soft, stirring occasionally.
6. To add a bit of crunch,
sprinkle with toasted
almonds or pecans when
serving.
7. Serve with pork or
poultry.

Exchange List Values:
Starch 1.0, Fruit 1.0, Fat
0.5

Basic Nutritional Values: Calories
152 (Calories from Fat 24), Total Fat
3 gm (Saturated Fat 0.1 gm,
Polyunsat Fat 0.7 gm, Monounsat Fat
1.3 gm, Cholesterol 0 mg), Sodium
201 mg, Total Carbohydrate 32 gm,
Dietary Fiber 3 gm, Sugars 17 gm,
Protein 1 gm

**Exercise can drop
blood sugar too low, so
carry a source of sugar
with you to treat
hypoglycemia.**

Sweet Potatoes with Applesauce

Judi Manos
West Islip, NY

Makes 6-8 servings
(Ideal slow cooker size: 4-quart)

6 medium-sized sweet
  potatoes or yams
1½ cups unsweetened
  applesauce
¼ cup packed brown sugar
brown sugar substitute to
  equal 2 Tbsp.
2 Tbsp. light, soft tub
  margarine, melted
1 tsp. ground cinnamon
½ cup chopped pecans

1. Peel sweet potatoes and
cut into ½" cubes. Place in
slow cooker.
2. Combine remaining
ingredients, except nuts.
Spoon over potatoes.
3. Cover. Cook on Low 6-7
hours or until potatoes are
very tender.
4. Sprinkle with nuts.

Exchange List Values:
Starch 1.5, Fruit 1.0, Fat
1.0

Basic Nutritional Values: Calories
213 (Calories from Fat 63), Total Fat
7 gm (Saturated Fat 0.5 gm,
Polyunsat Fat 1.9 gm, Monounsat Fat
3.9 gm, Cholesterol 0 mg), Sodium
40 mg, Total Carbohydrate 37 gm,
Dietary Fiber 3 gm, Sugars 17 gm,
Protein 2 gm

Barbecued Black Beans with Sweet Potatoes

Barbara Jean Fabel
Wausau, WI

Makes 8 servings
(Ideal slow cooker size: 4-quart)

4 large (10 ozs. each) sweet
  potatoes, peeled and cut
  into 8 chunks each
15-oz. can black beans,
  rinsed and drained
1 medium onion, diced
2 ribs celery, sliced
9 ozs. Sweet Baby Ray's
  Barbecue Sauce

1. Place sweet potatoes in
slow cooker.
2. Combine remaining
ingredients. Pour over sweet
potatoes.
3. Cover. Cook on High 2-3
hours, or on Low 4 hours.

Exchange List Values:
Starch 2.5

Basic Nutritional Values: Calories
180 (Calories from Fat 10), Total Fat
1 gm (Saturated Fat 0.2 gm,
Polyunsat Fat 0.4 gm, Monounsat Fat
0.3 gm, Cholesterol 0 mg), Sodium
321 mg, Total Carbohydrate 38 gm,
Dietary Fiber 5 gm, Sugars 11 gm,
Protein 5 gm

Potato Filling

Miriam Nolt, New Holland, PA

Makes 32 servings
(Ideal slow cooker size:
2 6-7-qt. cookers)

1 cup celery, chopped fine
1 medium onion, minced
2 Tbsp. light soft tub
  margarine
2 Tbsp. canola oil
2 15-oz. pkgs. unseasoned
  bread cubes, toasted
3 eggs, beaten
4 egg whites
1 qt. fat-free milk
1 qt. mashed potatoes
2 pinches saffron
1 cup boiling water
1 tsp. pepper

1. Saute celery and onion
in margarine and canola oil in
skillet for about 15 minutes.
2. Combine sauted mixture
with bread cubes. Stir in
remaining ingredients. Add
more milk if mixture isn't
very moist.
3. Pour into slow cookers.
Cook on High 3 hours,
stirring up from bottom every
hour or so to make sure the
Filling isn't sticking.

Exchange List Values:
Starch 1.5, Fat 0.5

Basic Nutritional Values: Calories
147 (Calories from Fat 36), Total Fat
4 gm (Saturated Fat 1.5 gm,
Polyunsat Fat 1.1 gm, Monounsat Fat
1.2 gm, Cholesterol 22 mg), Sodium
280 mg, Total Carbohydrate 22 gm,
Dietary Fiber 1 gm, Sugars 4 gm,
Protein 5 gm

Mild Dressing

Jane Steiner
Orrville, OH

Makes 8 servings
(Ideal slow cooker size: 4-quart)

16-oz. loaf homemade
    white bread
2 eggs, beaten
1/2 cup celery
1/4 cup diced onions
1/4 tsp. salt
1/2 tsp. pepper
1 cup giblets, cooked and
    cut up fine
1 cup fat-free milk

1. Set bread slices out to
dry the day before using. Cut
into small cubes.
2. Combine all ingredients
except milk.
3. Moisten mixture with
enough milk to make bread
cubes soft but not soggy.
4. Pour into greased slow
cooker. Cook on Low 3 1/2
hours, stirring every hour.
When stirring, add a small
amount of milk to sides of
cooker—if needed—to keep
Dressing moist and to prevent
sticking.

Exchange List Values:
Starch 2.0, Meat, lean 1.0

Basic Nutritional Values: Calories
213 (Calories from Fat 37), Total Fat
4 gm (Saturated Fat 1.1 gm,
Polyunsat Fat 1.4 gm, Monounsat Fat
1.1 gm, Cholesterol 135 mg), Sodium
427 mg, Total Carbohydrate 31 gm,
Dietary Fiber 2 gm, Sugars 4 gm,
Protein 12 gm

Moist Poultry Dressing

Virginia Bender, Dover, DE
Josie Boilman, Maumee, OH
Sharon Brubaker, Myerstown, PA
Joette Droz, Kalona, IA
Jacqueline Stefl, E. Bethany, NY

Makes 14 servings
(Ideal slow cooker size: 6-quart)

2 4 1/2-oz. cans sliced
    mushrooms, drained
4 celery ribs, chopped
    (about 2 cups)
2 medium onions, chopped
1/4 cup minced fresh
    parsley
1/4 cup margarine
13 cups cubed day-old
    bread
1/4 tsp. salt
1 1/2 tsp. sage
1 tsp. poultry seasoning
1 tsp. dried thyme
1/2 tsp. pepper
2 eggs
14 1/2-oz. can fat-free,
    reduced-sodium chicken
    broth

1. In large skillet, saute
mushrooms, celery, onions,
and parsley in margarine
until vegetables are tender.
2. Toss together bread
cubes, salt, sage, poultry seasoning, thyme, and pepper.
Add mushroom mixture.
3. Combine eggs and broth
and add to bread mixture.
Mix well.

4. Pour into greased slow
cooker. Cook on Low 5 hours,
or until meat thermometer
reaches 160°.

Exchange List Values:
Starch 1.0, Vegetable 1.0,
Fat 1.0

Basic Nutritional Values: Calories
151 (Calories from Fat 48), Total Fat
5 gm (Saturated Fat 1.1 gm,
Polyunsat Fat 1.8 gm, Monounsat Fat
2.0 gm, Cholesterol 31 mg), Sodium
409 mg, Total Carbohydrate 20 gm,
Dietary Fiber 2 gm, Sugars 3 gm,
Protein 5 gm

*Note: This is a good way to
free up the oven when you're
making a turkey.*

Variations:
*1. Use 2 bags bread cubes for
stuffing. Make one mixed bread
(white and wheat) and the other
corn bread cubes.*
*2. Add 1/2 tsp. dried marjoram
to Step 2.*

Arlene Miller
Hutchinson, KS

Slow Cooker Stuffing

Dede Peterson
Rapid City, SD

*Makes 12 servings
(Ideal slow cooker size: 6-quart)*

12 cups toasted bread crumbs, or dressing mix
4 ozs. 50%-less-fat bulk sausage, browned and drained
2 Tbsp. canola oil
1 cup, or more, finely chopped onions
1 cup, or more, finely chopped celery
8-oz. can sliced mushrooms, with liquid
1/4 cup chopped fresh parsley
2 tsp. poultry seasoning (omit if using dressing mix)
dash of pepper
2 eggs, beaten
4 tsp. salt-free bouillon powder
4 cups water

1. Combine bread crumbs and sausage.
2. Add onions and celery to oil in skillet and saute until tender. Stir in mushrooms and parsley. Add seasonings. Pour over bread crumbs and mix well.
3. Stir in eggs and bouillon mixed with water.
4. Pour into slow cooker and bake on High 1 hour, and on Low an additional 3 hours.

Exchange List Values:
Starch 2.0, Fat 1.0

Basic Nutritional Values: Calories 209 (Calories from Fat 68), Total Fat 8 gm (Saturated Fat 1.5 gm, Polyunsat Fat 1.9 gm, Monounsat Fat 2.4 gm, Cholesterol 44 mg), Sodium 423 mg, Total Carbohydrate 28 gm, Dietary Fiber 2 gm, Sugars 4 gm, Protein 8 gm

Variations:
1. For a less spicy stuffing, reduce the poultry seasoning to 1/2 tsp.
Dolores Metzler
Mechanicsburg, PA

2. Substitute 31/2-41/2 cups cooked and diced giblets in place of sausage. Add another can mushrooms and 2 tsp. sage in Step 2.
Mrs. Don Martins
Fairbank, IA

Slow Cooker Dressing

Marie Shank
Harrisonburg, VA

*Makes 20 servings
(Ideal slow cooker size: 6-quart)*

2 (81/2 ozs.) boxes Jiffy Cornbread mix
8 slices day-old bread
3 eggs
1 onion, chopped
1/2 cup chopped celery
2 103/4-oz. cans 98%-fat-free, lower-sodium cream of chicken soup
2 tsp. salt-free chicken bouillon powder, plus 2 cups water
1/2 tsp. pepper
11/2 Tbsp. sage or poultry seasoning

1. Prepare corn bread according to package instructions.
2. Crumble corn bread and bread together.
3. In large bowl combine all ingredients and spoon into 6-qt. greased slow cooker, or 2 smaller cookers.
4. Cover. Cook on High 2-4 hours or on Low 3-8 hours.

Exchange List Values:
Starch 1.5, Fat 0.5

Basic Nutritional Values: Calories 133 (Calories from Fat 34), Total Fat 4 gm (Saturated Fat 1.5 gm, Polyunsat Fat 0.9 gm, Monounsat Fat 1.1 gm, Cholesterol 35 mg), Sodium 387 mg, Total Carbohydrate 26 gm, Dietary Fiber 1 gm, Sugars 6 gm, Protein 4 gm

Variations: Prepare your favorite corn bread recipe in an 8"-square baking pan instead of using the corn bread mix.

Serve with roast chicken or turkey drumsticks.
Helen Kenagy
Carlsbad, NM

Mashed Potato Filling

Betty K. Drescher
Quakertown, PA

Makes 8-10 servings
(Ideal slow cooker size: 6-quart)

1/2 cup diced onions
1 cup diced celery
2 Tbsp. canola oil
2 1/2 cups fat-free milk
4 large eggs, beaten
8 ozs. unseasoned bread
  cubes, toasted
4 cups mashed potatoes
3/4 tsp. salt
1/4 tsp. pepper

1. Saute onions and celery in oil in skillet for 5-10 minutes, or until vegetables are tender.
2. Combine onions and celery, milk, and eggs. Pour over bread cubes. Mix lightly to absorb liquid.
3. Stir in potatoes and seasonings. Pour into greased slow cooker.
4. Cover. Cook on Low 4 hours.

Exchange List Values:
Starch 2.0, Fat 1.0

Basic Nutritional Values: Calories 214 (Calories from Fat 54), Total Fat 6 gm (Saturated Fat 1.4 gm, Polyunsat Fat 1.6 gm, Monounsat Fat 2.7 gm, Cholesterol 88 mg), Sodium 382 mg, Total Carbohydrate 32 gm, Dietary Fiber 2 gm, Sugars 8 gm, Protein 8 gm

Variation: For more flavor, add the packet of seasoning from the bread cube package in Step 3.

Exercise with someone. It's more fun that way, and you can encourage each other when your motivation fails you.

Sweet Potato Stuffing

Tina Snyder
Manheim, PA

Makes 8 servings
(Ideal slow cooker size: 4-5-quart)

1/2 cup chopped celery
1/2 cup chopped onions
1 Tbsp. canola oil
6 cups dry bread cubes
1 large sweet potato,
  cooked, peeled, and
  cubed
1/2 cup chicken broth
1/4 cup chopped pecans
1/2 tsp. poultry seasoning
1/2 tsp. rubbed sage
1/4 tsp. salt
1/4 tsp. pepper

1. Saute celery and onion in skillet in oil until tender. Pour into greased slow cooker.
2. Add remaining ingredients. Toss gently.
3. Cover. Cook on Low 4 hours.

Exchange List Values:
Starch 1.5, Fat 1.0

Basic Nutritional Values: Calories 146(Calories from Fat 51), Total Fat 6 gm (Saturated Fat 0.5 gm, Polyunsat Fat 1.8 gm, Monounsat Fat 2.9 gm, Cholesterol 1 mg), Sodium 321 mg, Total Carbohydrate 21 gm, Dietary Fiber 2 gm, Sugars 3 gm, Protein 3 gm

Desserts

Bread Pudding

Winifred Ewy, Newton, KS
Helen King, Fairbank, IA
Elaine Patton,
West Middletown, PA

*Makes 9 servings
(Ideal slow cooker size: 4-quart)*

8 slices bread (raisin bread
  is especially good),
  cubed
3 eggs
2 egg whites
2 cups fat-free half-and-
  half
2 Tbps. sugar
sugar substitute to equal
  1 Tbsp.
¹/₂ cup raisins (use only
  ¹/₄ cup if using raisin
  bread)
¹/₂ tsp. cinnamon

Sauce:
2 Tbsp. light, soft tub
  margarine
2 Tbsp. flour

1 cup water
6 Tbsp. sugar
sugar substitute to equal
  3 Tbsp.
1 tsp. vanilla

1. Place bread cubes in
greased slow cooker.
2. Beat together eggs,
whites, and half-and-half. Stir
in sugar, sugar substitute,
raisins, and cinnamon. Pour
over bread and stir.
3. Cover and cook on High
1 hour. Reduce heat to Low
and cook 3-4 hours, or until
thermometer reaches 160°.
4. Make sauce just before
pudding is done baking.
Begin by melting margarine
in saucepan. Stir in flour until
smooth. Gradually add water,
sugar, sugar substitute, and
vanilla. Bring to boil. Cook,
stirring constantly for 2
minutes, or until thickened.
5. Serve sauce over warm
bread pudding.

Exchange List Values:
Carbohydrate 2.0, Fat 1.0

Basic Nutritional Values: Calories
200 (Calories from Fat 40), Total Fat
4 gm (Saturated Fat 1.4 gm,
Polyunsat Fat 0.6 gm, Monounsat Fat
1.7 gm, Cholesterol 75 mg), Sodium
221 mg, Total Carbohydrate 34 gm,
Dietary Fiber 1 gm, Sugars 21 gm,
Protein 6 gm

Variations:
*1. Use dried cherries instead of
raisins. Use cherry flavoring in
sauce instead of vanilla.*
Char Hagnes
Montague, MI

*2. Use ¹/₄ tsp. ground cinnamon
and ¹/₄ tsp. ground nutmeg,
instead of ¹/₂ tsp. ground
cinnamon in pudding.*

*3. Use 8 cups day-old unfrosted
cinnamon rolls instead of the
bread.*
Beatrice Orgist
Richardson, TX

*4. Use ¹/₂ tsp. vanilla and ¹/₄
tsp. ground nutmeg instead of
¹/₂ tsp. cinnamon.*
Nanci Keatley
Salem, OR

Simple Bread Pudding

Melanie L. Thrower
McPherson, KS

Makes 8 servings
(Ideal slow cooker size: 4-quart)

6-8 slices of bread, cubed
2 cups fat-free milk
2 eggs
1/4 cup sugar
1 tsp. ground cinnamon
1 tsp. vanilla

Sauce:
6-oz. can concentrated
  grape juice
1 Tbsp. cornstarch

1. Place bread in slow cooker.
2. Whisk together milk, eggs, sugar, cinnamon, and vanilla. Pour over bread.
3. Cover. Cook on High 2-2½ hours, or until mixture is set.
4. Combine cornstarch and concentrated juice in saucepan. Heat until boiling, stirring constantly, until sauce is thickened. Serve drizzled over bread pudding.
5. This is a fine dessert with a cold salad main dish.

Exchange List Values:
Carbohydrate 2.5

Basic Nutritional Values: Calories 179 (Calories from Fat 19), Total Fat 2 gm (Saturated Fat 0.7 gm, Polyunsat Fat 0.6 gm, Monounsat Fat 0.6 gm, Cholesterol 55 mg), Sodium 153 mg, Total Carbohydrate 35 gm, Dietary Fiber 1 gm, Sugars 24 gm, Protein 5 gm

Apple-Nut Bread Pudding

Ruth Ann Hoover
New Holland, PA

Makes 10 servings
(Ideal slow cooker size: 4-quart)

8 slices raisin bread, cubed
2 medium-sized tart
  apples, peeled and
  sliced
1 cup chopped pecans,
  toasted
1/2 cup sugar
sugar substitute to equal
  1/4 cup
1 tsp. ground cinnamon
1/2 tsp. ground nutmeg
1 egg, lightly beaten
3 egg whites, lightly beaten
2 cups fat-free half-and-
  half
1/4 cup apple juice
2 Tbsp. light, soft tub
  margarine, melted

1. Place bread cubes, apples, and pecans in greased slow cooker and mix together gently.
2. Combine sugar, sugar substitute, cinnamon, and nutmeg. Add remaining ingredients. Mix well. Pour over bread mixture.
3. Cover. Cook on Low 3-4 hours, or until knife inserted in center comes out clean.
4. Serve with ice cream if diet allows.

Exchange List Values:
Carbohydrate 2.0, Fat 2.0

Basic Nutritional Values: Calories 231 (Calories from Fat 87), Total Fat 10 gm (Saturated Fat 1.4 gm, Polyunsat Fat 2.3 gm, Monounsat Fat 5.1 gm, Cholesterol 25 mg), Sodium 191 mg, Total Carbohydrate 32 gm, Dietary Fiber 2 gm, Sugars 20 gm, Protein 6 gm

Mama's Rice Pudding

Donna Barnitz
Jenks, OK
Shari Jensen
Fountain, CO

Makes 8 servings
(Ideal slow cooker size: 4-quart)

1/2 cup white rice, uncooked
1/4 cup sugar
sugar substitute to equal 2
  Tbsp.
1 tsp. vanilla
1 tsp. lemon extract
1 cup plus 2 Tbsp. fat-free
  milk
1 tsp. butter
2 eggs, beaten
1 tsp. cinnamon
1/2 cup raisins
1 cup fat-free whipping
  cream, whipped
nutmeg

1. Combine all ingredients except whipped cream and nutmeg in slow cooker. Stir well.
2. Cover pot. Cook on Low 6-7 hours, until rice is tender and milk absorbed. Be sure to stir once every 2 hours during cooking.

3. Pour into bowl. Cover with plastic wrap and chill.

4. Before serving, fold in whipped cream and sprinkle with nutmeg.

Exchange List Values:
Carbohydrate 2.0

Basic Nutritional Values: Calories 148 (Calories from Fat 17), Total Fat 2 gm (Saturated Fat 0.8 gm, Polyunsat Fat 0.2 gm, Monounsat Fat 0.7 gm, Cholesterol 55 mg), Sodium 43 mg, Total Carbohydrate 28 gm, Dietary Fiber 1 gm, Sugars 15 gm, Protein 4 gm

Deluxe Tapioca Pudding
Michelle Showalter
Bridgewater, VA

Makes 16 servings
(Ideal slow cooker size: 5-quart)

2 qts. fat-free milk
3/4 cup dry small pearl tapioca
3/4 cup sugar
sugar substitute to equal 6 Tbsp.
4 eggs, beaten
2 tsp. vanilla
3 cups fat-free frozen whipped topping, thawed
chocolate candy bar, optional

1. Combine milk, tapioca, sugar, and sugar substitute in slow cooker.

2. Cook on High 3 hours.

3. Add a little of the hot milk to the eggs. Stir. Whisk eggs into milk mixture. Add vanilla.

4. Cover. Cook on High 20-30 minutes.

5. Cool. Chill in refrigerator. When fully chilled, beat with hand mixer to fluff the pudding.

6. Stir in whipped topping. Garnish with chopped candy bar.

Exchange List Values:
Carbohydrate 2.0

Basic Nutritional Values: Calories 147 (Calories from Fat 12), Total Fat 1 gm (Saturated Fat 0.6 gm, Polyunsat Fat 0.2 gm, Monounsat Fat 0.5 gm, Cholesterol 56 mg), Sodium 77 mg, Total Carbohydrate 27 gm, Dietary Fiber 0 gm, Sugars 17 gm, Protein 6 gm

Select a mix of colorful vegetables each day. Different colored vegetables provide different nutrients.

Slow-Cooker Tapioca
Nancy W. Huber
Green Park, PA

Makes 10-12 servings
(Ideal slow cooker size: 4-quart)

2 quarts fat-free milk
1 cup small pearl tapioca
1/2 cup sugar
sugar substitute to equal 1/4 cup
4 eggs, beaten
1 tsp. vanilla

1. Combine milk, tapioca, sugar, and sugar substitute in slow cooker. Cook on High 3 hours.

2. Mix together eggs, vanilla, and a little hot milk from slow cooker. Add to slow cooker. Cook on High 20 more minutes. Chill.

3. Serve with whipped cream or fruit.

Exchange List Values:
Carbohydrate 2.0

Basic Nutritional Values: Calories 160 (Calories from Fat 16), Total Fat 2 gm (Saturated Fat 0.9 gm, Polyunsat Fat 0.2 gm, Monounsat Fat 0.7 gm, Cholesterol 74 mg), Sodium 93 mg, Total Carbohydrate 28 gm, Dietary Fiber 0 gm, Sugars 17 gm, Protein 8 gm

Blushing Apple Tapioca

Julie Weaver, Reinholds, PA

Makes 8-10 servings
(Ideal slow cooker size: 4-quart)

8-10 medium tart apples
¼ cup sugar
sugar substitute to equal
   2 Tbsp.
4 Tbsp. minute tapioca
4 Tbsp. red cinnamon
   candy
½ cup water
whipped topping, optional

1. Pare and core apples.
Cut into eighths lengthwise
and place in slow cooker.
2. Mix together sugar,
sugar substitute, tapioca,
candy, and water. Pour over
apples.
3. Cook on High 3- 4
hours.
4. Serve hot or cold. Top
with whipped topping.

Exchange List Values:
Carbohydrate 2.0

Basic Nutritional Values: Calories
117 (Calories from Fat 3), Total Fat 0
gm (Saturated Fat 0.0 gm, Polyunsat
Fat 0.1 gm, Monounsat Fat 0.0 gm,
Cholesterol 0 mg), Sodium 0 mg, Total
Carbohydrate 30 gm, Dietary Fiber 2
gm, Sugars 23 gm, Protein 0 gm

Raisin Nut-Stuffed Apples

Margaret Rich
North Newton, KS

Makes 6 servings
(Ideal slow cooker size: 4-quart)

6 medium baking apples,
   cored
1½ Tbsp. light, soft tub
   margarine, melted
2 Tbsp. packed brown
   sugar
brown sugar substitute to
   equal 1 Tbsp.
¾ cup raisins
3 Tbsp. chopped walnuts
½ cup water

1. Peel a strip around each
apple about one-third of the
way below the stem end to
prevent splitting.
2. Mix together margarine,
brown sugar, and sugar
substitute. Stir in raisins and
walnuts. Stuff into apple
cavities.
3. Place apples in slow
cooker. Add water.
4. Cover and cook on Low
6-8 hours.

Exchange List Values:
Fruit 2.0, Carbohydrate
0.5, Fat 0.5

Basic Nutritional Values: Calories
187 (Calories from Fat 35), Total Fat
4 gm (Saturated Fat 0.4 gm,
Polyunsat Fat 2.1 gm, Monounsat Fat
1.0 gm, Cholesterol 0 mg), Sodium
29 mg, Total Carbohydrate 41 gm,
Dietary Fiber 5 gm, Sugars 32 gm,
Protein 2 gm

Caramel Apples

Elaine Patton
West Middletown, PA
Rhonda Lee Schmidt
Scranton, PA
Renee Shirk
Mount Joy, PA

Makes 8 servings
(Ideal slow cooker size: 4-quart)

4 very large tart apples,
   cored
½ cup apple juice
4 Tbsp. brown sugar
brown sugar substitute to
   equal 2 Tbsp.
12 hot cinnamon candies
4 Tbsp. light, soft tub
   margarine
8 caramel candies
¼ tsp. ground cinnamon
whipped cream, optinoal

1. Remove ½-inch-wide
strip of peel off the top of
each apple and place apples
in slow cooker.
2. Pour apple juice over
apples.
3. Fill the center of each
apple with 2 Tbsp. brown
sugar, sugar substitute, 3 hot
cinnamon candies, 1 Tbsp.
margarine, and 2 caramel
candies. Sprinkle with
cinnamon.
4. Cover and cook on Low
4-6 hours, or until tender.
5. Serve hot with juice
from bottom of slow cooker
and whipped cream, if you
wish.

Exchange List Values:
Carbohydrate 2.0

Basic Nutritional Values: Calories 130 (Calories from Fat 26), Total Fat 3 gm (Saturated Fat 0.6 gm, Polyunsat Fat 0.6 gm, Monounsat Fat 1.3 gm, Cholesterol 0 mg), Sodium 63 mg, Total Carbohydrate 28 gm, Dietary Fiber 3 gm, Sugars 23 gm, Protein 1 gm

Cranberry Baked Apples

Judi Manos
West Islip, NY

Makes 8 servings
(Ideal slow cooker size: 3-4-quart)

4 large cooking apples
1/3 cup packed brown sugar
1/4 cup dried cranberries
1/2 cup cranapple juice cocktail
2 Tbsp. light, soft tub margarine, melted
1/2 tsp. ground cinnamon
1/4 tsp. ground nutmeg
chopped nuts, optional

1. Core apples. Fill centers with brown sugar and cranberries. Place in slow cooker.
2. Combine cranapple juice and margarine. Pour over apples.
3. Sprinkle with cinnamon and nutmeg.
4. Cover. Cook on Low 4-6 hours.
5. To serve, spoon sauce over apples and sprinkle with nuts.
6. This is a great accompaniment to vanilla ice cream.

Exchange List Values:
Carbohydrate 2.0

Basic Nutritional Values: Calories 121 (Calories from Fat 13), Total Fat 1 gm (Saturated Fat 0.1 gm, Polyunsat Fat 0.3 gm, Monounsat Fat 0.6 gm, Cholesterol 0 mg), Sodium 27 mg, Total Carbohydrate 29 gm, Dietary Fiber 3 gm, Sugars 25 gm, Protein 0 gm

This was one of our favorite recipes while growing up. When it's cooking, the house smells delicious. I'm suddenly full of memories of days gone by and a much more relaxing time. My mother passed away in October and I re-found this recipe among her collection of favorites.

Fruit and Nut Baked Apples

Cyndie Marrara
Port Matilda, PA

Makes 4 servings
(Ideal slow cooker size: 4-quart)

4 large firm baking apples
1 Tbsp. lemon juice
1/3 cup chopped dried apricots
1/3 cup chopped walnuts, or pecans
1 1/2 Tbsp. packed brown sugar

brown sugar substitute to equal 2 tsp.
1/2 tsp. cinnamon
1 1/2 Tbsp. light, soft tub margarine
1/2 cup water, or apple juice
4 pecan halves, optional

1. Scoop out centers of apples creating a cavity 1 1/2 inches wide and stopping 1/2 inch from the bottom of each. Peel top of each apple down about 1 inch. Brush edges with lemon juice.
2. Mix together apricots, nuts, brown sugar, sugar substitute and cinnamon. Stir in margarine. Spoon mixture evenly into apples.
3. Put 1/2 cup water or juice in bottom of slow cooker. Put 2 apples in bottom, and 2 apples above, but not squarely on top of other apples. Cover and cook on Low 1 1/2-3 hours, or until tender.
4. Serve warm or at room temperature. Top each apple with a pecan half, if desired.

Exchange List Values:
Fruit 2.0, Carbohydrate 0.5, Fat 1.5

Basic Nutritional Values: Calories 212 (Calories from Fat 77), Total Fat 9 gm (Saturated Fat 0.8 gm, Polyunsat Fat 5.2 gm, Monounsat Fat 1.9 gm, Cholesterol 0 mg), Sodium 40 mg, Total Carbohydrate 36 gm, Dietary Fiber 5 gm, Sugars 28 gm, Protein 2 gm

Wagon Master Apple-Cherry Sauce

Sharon Timpe
Mequon, WI

Makes 15 servings
(Ideal slow cooker size: 4-quart)

2 21-oz. cans apple pie filling
2-3 cups frozen tart red cherries
1 Tbsp. butter or margarine
1/2 tsp. ground cinnamon
1/2 tsp. ground nutmeg
1/8 tsp. ground ginger
1/8 tsp. ground cloves

1. Combine all ingredients in slow cooker.
2. Cover. Heat on Low 3-4 hours, until hot and bubbly. Stir occasionally.
3. Serve warm over vanilla ice cream, pudding, pound cake, or shortcake biscuits. Top with whipped cream, if you wish.

Exchange List Values:
Carbohydrate 1.5

Basic Nutritional Values: Calories 97 (Calories from Fat 9), Total Fat 1 gm (Saturated Fat 0.2 gm, Polyunsat Fat 0.3 gm, Monounsat Fat 0.4 gm, Cholesterol 0 mg), Sodium 44 mg,Total Carbohydrate 23 gm, Dietary Fiber 1 gm, Sugars 18 gm, Protein 0 gm

Apple Schnitz

Betty Hostetler
Allensville, PA

Makes 10 servings
(Ideal slow cooker size: 3-4-quart)

1 qt. dried apples
3 cups water
1/4 cup sugar
sugar substitute to equal 4 Tbsp.
1 tsp. ground cinnamon
1 tsp. salt

1. Combine apples, water, sugar, sugar substitute, cinnamon, and salt in slow cooker.
2. Cover. Cook on Low 6 hours or on High 2½ hours.
3. Serve warm as a side dish with bean soup, or as filling for Half Moon Pies (see adjoining recipe).
4. To use as pie filling, remove apples from slow cooker. Mash until smooth with potato masher or put through food mill. Cool.

Exchange List Values:
Fruit 2.0

Basic Nutritional Values: Calories 105 (Calories from Fat 1), Total Fat 0 gm (Saturated Fat 0.0 gm, Polyunsat Fat 0.0 gm, Monounsat Fat 0.0 gm, Cholesterol 0 mg), Sodium 262 mg,Total Carbohydrate 28 gm, Dietary Fiber 3 gm, Sugars 21 gm, Protein 0 gm

Half Moon Pie Crust

4 cups flour
2 tsp. salt
4 Tbsp. shortening
1/4 cold water, or more

1. Combine flour and salt. Cut in shortening until mixture resembles small peas.
2. Add 1/4 cup cold water to dough, adding more by tablespoonfuls as needed to make a soft pie dough.
3. Pinch off small pieces of dough, each about the size of a large walnut. Roll into round pieces, each about 8" in diameter.
4. Jag one half of the circle a few times with a sharp fork to create holes for the steam to escape while baking. On the other half place a heaping tablespoon of Apple Schnitz filling. Fold one-half of dough up over the half holding the pie filling, shaping the pie like a half moon. Press edges of dough together. Cut off remaining dough and crimp edges.
5. Bake at 350° for 30 minutes.

On a cold winter day, Mother would prepare dried beans to make soup. After the beans were soft, she added milk to the soup pot. She heated the mixture to the boiling point, then added rivels. While the beans were cooking, she cooked dried apples until they were soft. She served these Half Moon Pies as a side dish/dessert with the soup.

Apple Crisp
Michelle Strite, Goshen, IN

*Makes 12 servings
(Ideal slow cooker size: 4-quart)*

²/₃ cup sugar
1¼ cups water
3 Tbsp. cornstarch
4 cups sliced, peeled apples
½ tsp. ground cinnamon
¼ tsp. ground allspice
¾ cup quick oatmeal
¼ cup brown sugar
brown sugar substitute to equal 2 Tbsp.
½ cup flour
¼ cup light, soft tub margarine, at room temperature

1. Combine ²/₃ cup sugar, water, cornstarch, apples, cinnamon, and allspice. Place in cooker.
2. Combine remaining ingredients until crumbly. Sprinkle over apple filling.
3. Cover. Cook on Low 2-3 hours.

Exchange List Values:
Carbohydrate 2.0

Basic Nutritional Values: Calories 134 (Calories from Fat 18), Total Fat 2 gm (Saturated Fat 0.2 gm, Polyunsat Fat 0.5 gm, Monounsat Fat 0.9 gm, Cholesterol 0 mg), Sodium 34 mg, Total Carbohydrate 29 gm, Dietary Fiber 2 gm, Sugars 15 gm, Protein 1 gm

Hot Fruit Salad
Sharon Miller, Holmesville, OH

*Makes 16 servings
(Ideal slow cooker size: 5-quart)*

25-oz. jar chunky unsweetened applesauce
21-oz. can light cherry pie filling
20-oz. can pineapple chunks, packed in juice
15½-oz. can sliced peaches, packed in juice
15½-oz. can apricot halves, packed in juice
11-oz. can mandarin oranges, packed in juice
2 Tbsp. brown sugar
brown sugar substitute to equal 1 Tbsp.
1 tsp. ground cinnamon

1. Combine fruit in slow cooker, stirring gently.
2. Combine brown sugar, sugar substitute, and cinnamon. Sprinkle over mixture.
3. Cover. Bake on Low 3-4 hours.

Exchange List Values:
Fruit 2.0

Basic Nutritional Values: Calories 105 (Calories from Fat 1), Total Fat 0 gm (Saturated Fat 0.0 gm, Polyunsat Fat 0.1 gm, Monounsat Fat 0.1 gm, Cholesterol 0 mg), Sodium 12 mg, Total Carbohydrate 27 gm, Dietary Fiber 2 gm, Sugars 24 gm, Protein 1 gm

Curried Fruit
Jane Meiser, Harrisonburg, VA

*Makes 8-10 servings
(Ideal slow cooker size: 4-5-quart)*

16-oz. can peaches, undrained
16-oz. cans apricots, undrained
16-oz. can pears, undrained
20-oz. can pineapple chunks, undrained
16-oz. can black cherries, undrained
2 Tbsp. brown sugar
brown sugar substitute to equal 1 Tbsp.
1 tsp. curry powder
3-4 Tbsp. quick-cooking tapioca, depending upon how thickened you'd like the finished dish to be
margarine, optional

1. Combine fruit. Let stand for at least 2 hours, or up to 8, to allow flavors to blend. Drain. Place in slow cooker.
2. Add remaining ingredients. Mix well. Top with margarine, if you want.
3. Cover. Cook on Low 8-10 hours.
4. Serve warm or at room temperature.

Exchange List Values:
Fruit 2.0

Basic Nutritional Values: Calories 107 (Calories from Fat 1), Total Fat 0 gm (Saturated Fat 0.0 gm, Polyunsat Fat 0.0 gm, Monounsat Fat 0.0 gm, Cholesterol 0 mg), Sodium 7 mg, Total Carbohydrate 27 gm, Dietary Fiber 2 gm, Sugars 21 gm, Protein 1 gm

Fruit Dessert Topping

Lavina Hochstedler
Grand Blanc, MI

Makes 40 (2 Tbsp.) servings
(Ideal slow cooker size: 4-quart)

3 tart apples, peeled and
   sliced
3 pears, peeled and sliced
1 Tbsp. lemon juice
2 Tbsp. brown sugar
brown sugar substitute to
   equal 1 Tbsp.
2 Tbsp. maple syrup
2 Tbsp. light, soft tub
   margarine, melted
1/2 cup chopped pecans
1/4 cup raisins
2 cinnamon sticks
1 Tbsp. cornstarch
2 Tbsp. cold water

1. Toss apples and pears in
lemon juice in slow cooker.
2. Combine brown sugar,
sugar substitute, maple syrup,
and margarine. Pour over
fruit.
3. Stir in pecans, raisins,
and cinnamon sticks.
4. Cover. Cook on Low 3-4
hours.
5. Combine cornstarch and
water until smooth. Grad-
ually stir into slow cooker.
6. Cover. Cook on High
30-40 minutes, or until thickened.
7. Discard cinnamon
sticks. Serve over pound cake
or ice cream.

Exchange List Values:
Carbohydrate 0.5

Basic Nutritional Values: Calories
33 (Calories from Fat 13), Total Fat 1
gm (Saturated Fat 0.1 gm, Polyunsat
Fat 0.4 gm, Monounsat Fat 0.8 gm,
Cholesterol 0 mg), Sodium 5 mg, Total
Carbohydrate 6 gm, Dietary Fiber 1
gm, Sugars 5 gm, Protein 0 gm

*We also like this served along
with pancakes or an egg
casserole. We always use Fruit
Topping for our breakfasts at
church camp.*

Rhubarb Sauce

Esther Porter, Minneapolis, MN

Makes 6 servings
(Ideal slow cooker size: 3-4-quart)

1 1/2 lbs. rhubarb
1/8 tsp. salt
1/2 cup water
1/2-2/3 cup sugar

1. Cut rhubarb into 1/2-inch
slices.
2. Combine all ingredients
in slow cooker. Cook on Low
4-5 hours.
3. Serve chilled.

Exchange List Values:
Carbohydrate 1.0

Basic Nutritional Values: Calories 80
(Calories from Fat 1), Total Fat 0 gm
(Saturated Fat 0.0 gm, Polyunsat Fat 0.0
gm, Monounsat Fat 0.0 gm, Cholesterol
0 mg), Sodium 54 mg, Total
Carbohydrate 20 gm, Dietary Fiber 2
gm, Sugars 17 gm, Protein 1 gm

Variation: Add 1 pint sliced
strawberries about 30 minutes
before removing from heat.

Zesty Pears

Barbara Walker
Sturgis, SD

Makes 8 servings
(Ideal slow cooker size: 3-4-quart)

6 fresh pears
1/2 cup raisins
1/4 cup brown sugar
1 tsp. grated lemon peel
1/4 cup brandy
1/2 cup sauterne wine
1/2 cup macaroon crumbs

1. Peel and core pears. Cut
into thin slices.
2. Combine raisins, sugar,
and lemon peel. Layer
alternately with pear slices in
slow cooker.
3. Pour brandy and wine
over top.
4. Cover. Cook on Low 4-6
hours.
5. Spoon into serving
dishes. Cool. Sprinkle with
macaroons. Serve plain or
topped with sour cream.

Exchange List Values:
Carbohydrate 2.0

Basic Nutritional Values: Calories
140 (Calories from Fat 13), Total Fat
1 gm (Saturated Fat 0.9 gm,
Polyunsat Fat 0.1 gm, Monounsat Fat
0.1 gm, Cholesterol 0 mg), Sodium
11 mg, Total Carbohydrate 33 gm,
Dietary Fiber 3 gm, Sugars 28 gm,
Protein 1 gm

Fruit Compote Dessert

Beatrice Orgish, Richardson, TX

Makes 8 servings
(Ideal slow cooker size: 4-quart)

2 medium tart apples,
  peeled
2 medium fresh peaches,
  peeled and cubed
2 cups unsweetened
  pineapple chunks
1¼ cups unsweetened
  pineapple juice
¼ cup honey
2 ¼-inch-thick lemon slices
3 ½-inch-long cinnamon
  stick
1 medium firm banana,
  thinly sliced
whipped cream, optional
sliced almonds, optional
maraschino cherries,
  optional

1. Cut apples into ¼-inch slices and then in half horizontally. Place in slow cooker.
2. Add peaches, pineapple chunks, pineapple juice, honey, lemon, and cinnamon. Cover and cook on Low 3-4 hours.
3. Stir in banana slices just before serving. Garnish with whipped cream, sliced almonds, and cherries, if you wish.

Exchange List Values:
Fruit 2.0

Basic Nutritional Values: Calories 117 (Calories from Fat 4), Total Fat 0 gm (Saturated Fat 0.0 gm, Polyunsat Fat 0.1 gm, Monounsat Fat 0.1 gm, Cholesterol 0 mg), Sodium 2 mg, Total Carbohydrate 31 gm, Dietary Fiber 2 gm, Sugars 27 gm, Protein 1 gm

Scandinavian Fruit Soup

Willard E. Roth, Elkhart, IN

Makes 14 servings
(Ideal slow cooker size: 4-quart)

1 cup dried apricots
1 cup dried sliced apples
1 cup dried pitted plums
1 cup canned pitted red
  cherries
½ cup quick-cooking
  tapioca
1 cup grape juice, or red
  wine
3 cups water, or more
½ cup orange juice
¼ cup lemon juice
1 Tbsp. grated orange peel
2 Tbsp. brown sugar
brown sugar substitute to
  equal 1 Tbsp.

1. Combine apricots, apples, plums, cherries, tapioca, and grape juice in slow cooker. Cover with water.
2. Cook on Low for at least 8 hours.
3. Before serving, stir in remaining ingredients.
4. Serve warm or cold, as a soup or dessert. Delicious served chilled over vanilla ice cream or frozen yogurt.

Exchange List Values:
Fruit 2.0

Basic Nutritional Values: Calories 120 (Calories from Fat 1), Total Fat 0 gm (Saturated Fat 0.0 gm, Polyunsat Fat 0.0 gm, Monounsat Fat 0.1 gm, Cholesterol 0 mg), Sodium 10 mg, Total Carbohydrate 31 gm, Dietary Fiber 2 gm, Sugars 21 gm, Protein 1 gm

Strawberry Rhubarb Sauce

Tina Snyder, Manheim, PA

Makes 8 servings
(Ideal slow cooker size: 4-quart)

6 cups chopped rhubarb
1 cup sugar
1 cinnamon stick
½ cup white grape juice
2 cups sliced strawberries

1. Place rhubarb in slow cooker. Pour sugar over rhubarb. Add cinnamon stick and grape juice. Stir well.
2. Cover and cook on Low 5-6 hours, or until rhubarb is tender.
3. Stir in strawberries. Cook 1 hour longer.
4. Remove cinnamon stick. Chill.
5. Serve over cake or ice cream.

Exchange List Values:
Carbohydrate 2.0

Basic Nutritional Values: Calories 132 (Calories from Fat 3), Total Fat 0 gm (Saturated Fat 0.0 gm, Polyunsat Fat 0.1 gm, Monounsat Fat 0.0 gm, Cholesterol 0 mg), Sodium 5 mg, Total Carbohydrate 33 gm, Dietary Fiber 3 gm, Sugars 29 gm, Protein 1 gm

Spiced Applesauce
Judi Manos, West Islip, NY

Makes 12 servings
(Ideal slow cooker size: 4-quart)

12 cups cored, pared, thinly sliced, medium cooking apples
¼ cup sugar
sugar substitute to equal 2 Tbsp.
½ tsp. cinnamon
1 cup water
1 Tbsp. lemon juice
freshly grated nutmeg, optional

1. Place apples in slow cooker.
2. Combine sugar, sugar substitute, and cinnamon. Mix with apples. Stir in water and lemon juice, and nutmeg, if desired.
3. Cover. Cook on Low 5-7 hours, or High 2½-3½ hours.
4. Stir for a chunky sauce. Serve hot or cold.

Exchange List Values:
Carbohydrate 1.0

Basic Nutritional Values: Calories 75 (Calories from Fat 3), Total Fat 0 gm (Saturated Fat 0.0 gm, Polyunsat Fat 0.1 gm, Monounsat Fat 0.0 gm, Cholesterol 0 mg), Sodium 0 mg, Total Carbohydrate 20 gm, Dietary Fiber 2 gm, Sugars 18 gm, Protein 0 gm

> **Physical activity is essential to weight control.**

Quick Yummy Peaches
Willard E. Roth
Elkhart, IN

Makes 8 servings
(Ideal slow cooker size: 4-quart)

⅓ cup buttermilk baking mix
⅔ cup dry quick oats
¼ cup brown sugar
brown sugar substitute to equal 2 Tbsp.
1 tsp. cinnamon
4 cups sliced peaches (canned or fresh)
½ cup peach juice, or water

1. Mix together baking mix, oats, brown sugar, sugar substitute, and cinnamon in greased slow cooker.
2. Stir in peaches and peach juice.
3. Cook on Low for at least 5 hours. (If you like a drier cobbler, remove lid for last 15-30 minutes of cooking.)
4. Serve with frozen yogurt or ice cream.

Exchange List Values:
Carbohydrate 2.0

Basic Nutritional Values: Calories 131 (Calories from Fat 11), Total Fat 1 gm (Saturated Fat 0.1 gm, Polyunsat Fat 0.5 gm, Monounsat Fat 0.4 gm, Cholesterol 0 mg), Sodium 76 mg, Total Carbohydrate 29 gm, Dietary Fiber 3 gm, Sugars 20 gm, Protein 2 gm

Scalloped Pineapples
Shirley Hinh
Wayland, IA

Makes 8 servings
(Ideal slow cooker size: 4-quart)

½ cup sugar
sugar substitute to equal ¼ cup
3 eggs
¼ cup light, soft tub margarine, melted
¾ cup milk
20-oz. can crushed pineapple, drained
8 slices bread (crusts removed), cubed

1. Mix together all ingredients in slow cooker.
2. Cook on High 2 hours. Reduce heat to Low and cook 1 more hour.
3. Delicious served as a side dish to ham or poultry, or as a dessert served warm or cold. Eat hot or chilled with vanilla ice cream or frozen yogurt.

Exchange List Values:
Carbohydrate 2.0, Fat 0.5

Basic Nutritional Values: Calories 181 (Calories from Fat 44), Total Fat 5 gm (Saturated Fat 1.1 gm, Polyunsat Fat 1.1 gm, Monounsat Fat 2.1 gm, Cholesterol 81 mg), Sodium 176 mg, Total Carbohydrate 30 gm, Dietary Fiber 1 gm, Sugars 21 gm, Protein 5 gm

Black and Blue Cobbler

Renee Shirk, Mount Joy, PA

Makes 12 servings
(Ideal slow cooker size: 5-quart)

1 cup flour
6 Tbsp. sugar
sugar substitute to equal
  3 Tbsp.
1 tsp. baking powder
1/4 tsp. salt
1/4 tsp. ground cinnamon
1/4 tsp. ground nutmeg
2 eggs, beaten
2 Tbsp. milk
2 Tbsp. vegetable oil
2 cups fresh, or frozen,
  blueberries
2 cups fresh, or frozen,
  blackberries
3/4 cup water
1 tsp. grated orange peel
6 Tbsp. sugar
sugar substitute to equal
  3 Tbsp.
whipped topping, or ice
  cream, optional

1. Combine flour, 6 Tbsp. sugar, baking powder, salt, cinnamon, and nutmeg.

2. Combine eggs, milk, and oil. Stir into dry ingredients until moistened.

3. Spread the batter evenly over bottom of greased 5-quart slow cooker.

4. In saucepan, combine berries, water, orange peel, 6 Tbsp. sugar, and sugar substitute to equal 3 Tbsp. Bring to boil. Remove from heat and pour over batter. Cover.

5. Cook on High 2-2 1/2 hours, or until toothpick inserted into batter comes out clean. Turn off cooker.

6. Uncover and let stand 30 minutes before serving. Spoon from cooker and serve with whipped topping or ice cream, if desired.

Exchange List Values:
Carbohydrate 2.0, Fat 0.5

Basic Nutritional Values: Calories 170 (Calories from Fat 31), Total Fat 3 gm (Saturated Fat 0.5 gm, Polyunsat Fat 0.9 gm, Monounsat Fat 1.7 gm, Cholesterol 36 mg), Sodium 92 mg, Total Carbohydrate 34 gm, Dietary Fiber 2 gm, Sugars 23 gm, Protein 3 gm

Cranberry Pudding

Margaret Wheeler
North Bend, OR

Makes 12 servings
(Ideal slow cooker size: 4-5-quart)

Pudding:
1 1/3 cups flour
1/2 tsp. salt
2 tsp. baking soda
1/3 cup boiling water
6 Tbsp. dark molasses
2 cups whole cranberries
1/2 cup chopped walnuts
1/2 cup water

Butter Sauce:
1 cup confectioners sugar
1/2 cup fat-free half-and-half

4 Tbsp. light, soft tub margarine
1 tsp. vanilla

1. Mix together flour and salt.

2. Dissolve soda in boiling water. Add to flour and salt.

3. Stir in molasses. Blend well.

4. Fold in cranberries and nuts.

5. Pour into well greased and floured bread or cake pan that will sit in your cooker. Cover with greased tin foil.

6. Pour 1/2 cup water into cooker. Place foil-covered pan in cooker. Cover with cooker lid and steam on High 3 to 4 hours, or until pudding tests done with a wooden pick.

7. Remove pan and uncover. Let stand 5 minutes, then unmold.

8. To make butter sauce, mix together all ingredients in saucepan. Cook, stirring over medium heat until sugar dissolves.

9. Serve warm butter sauce over warm cranberry pudding.

Exchange List Values:
Carbohydrate 2.0, Fat 0.5

Basic Nutritional Values: Calories 177 (Calories from Fat 46), Total Fat 5 gm (Saturated Fat 0.5 gm, Polyunsat Fat 2.7 gm, Monounsat Fat 1.3 gm, Cholesterol 1 mg), Sodium 355 mg, Total Carbohydrate 31 gm, Dietary Fiber 1 gm, Sugars 18 gm, Protein 3 gm

Slow Cooker Pumpkin Pie Pudding

Joette Droz
Kalona, IA

Makes 8 servings
(Ideal slow cooker size: 4-quart)

15-oz. can solid pack
   pumpkin
12-oz. can fat-free
   evaporated milk
1/2 cup sugar
sugar substitute to equal
   2 Tbsp.
1/2 cup buttermilk baking
   mix
2 eggs, beaten
2 Tbsp. light, soft tub
   margarine, melted
1 Tbsp. pumpkin pie spice
2 tsp. vanilla

1. Mix together all ingredients. Pour into greased slow cooker.
2. Cover and cook on Low 6-7 hours, or until thermometer reads 160°.
3. Serve in bowls topped with fat-free whipping topping, if you wish.

Exchange List Values:
Carbohydrate 2.0, Fat 0.5

Basic Nutritional Values: Calories 171 (Calories from Fat 36), Total Fat 4 gm (Saturated Fat 0.7 gm, Polyunsat Fat 0.9 gm, Monounsat Fat 1.6 gm, Cholesterol 53 mg), Sodium 203 mg, Total Carbohydrate 28 gm, Dietary Fiber 2 gm, Sugars 19 gm, Protein 6 gm

Low-Fat Apple Cake

Sue Hamilton
Minooka, IL

Makes 10 servings
(Ideal slow cooker size: 4-quart)

1 cup flour
3/4 cup sugar
sugar substitute to equal
   2 Tbsp.
2 tsp. baking powder
1 tsp. ground cinnamon
1/4 tsp. salt
4 medium-sized cooking
   apples, chopped
2 eggs, beaten
2 tsp. vanilla

1. Combine flour, sugar, sugar substitute, baking powder, cinnamon, and salt.
2. Add apples, stirring lightly to coat.
3. Combine eggs and vanilla. Add to apple mixture. Stir until just moistened. Spoon into lightly greased slow cooker.
4. Cover. Bake on High 2 1/2-3 hours.
5. Serve warm. Top with frozen whipped topping, thawed, or ice cream and a sprinkle of cinnamon, if you wish.

Exchange List Values:
Carbohydrate 2.0

Basic Nutritional Values: Calories 152 (Calories from Fat 11), Total Fat 1 gm (Saturated Fat 0.4 gm, Polyunsat Fat 0.2 gm, Monounsat Fat

0.4 gm, Cholesterol 43 mg), Sodium 144 mg, Total Carbohydrate 33 gm, Dietary Fiber 2 gm, Sugars 22 gm, Protein 3 gm

Variation: Stir 1/2 cup broken English or black walnuts, or 1/2 cup raisins, into Step 2.

The slow cooker is great for baking desserts. Your guests will be pleasantly surprised to see a cake coming from your slow cooker.

Creamy Orange Cheesecake

Jeanette Oberholtzer
Manheim, PA

Makes 10 servings
(Ideal slow cooker size: 5-6-quart)

Crust:
3/4 cup graham cracker
   crumbs
2 Tbsp. sugar
3 Tbsp. light, soft tub
   margarine, melted

Filling:
2 8-oz. pkgs. fat-free cream
   cheese, at room temperature
2/3 cup sugar
2 eggs
1 egg yolk
1/4 cup frozen orange juice
   concentrate
1 tsp. orange zest
1 Tbsp. flour
1/2 tsp. vanilla

1. Combine crust ingredients. Pat into 7" or 9" springform pan, whichever size fits into your slow cooker.

2. Cream together cream cheese and sugar. Add eggs and yolk. Beat for 3 minutes.

3. Beat in juice, zest, flour, and vanilla. Beat 2 minutes.

4. Pour batter into crust. Place pan on rack in slow cooker.

5. Cover. Cook on High 2½-3 hours. Turn off and let stand for 1-2 hours, or until cool enough to remove from cooker.

6. Cool completely before removing sides of pan. Chill before serving.

7. Serve with thawed frozen whipped topping and fresh or mandarin orange slices, if you wish.

Exchange List Values:
Carbohydrate 1.5, Meat, lean 1.0

Basic Nutritional Values: Calories 159 (Calories from Fat 23), Total Fat 3 gm (Saturated Fat 0.7 gm, Polyunsat Fat 0.6 gm, Monounsat Fat 1.1 gm, Cholesterol 69 mg), Sodium 300 mg, Total Carbohydrate 25 gm, Dietary Fiber 0 gm, Sugars 19 gm, Protein 9 gm

Lemon Pudding Cake

Jean Butzer, Batavia, NY

Makes 6 servings
(Ideal slow cooker size: 3-4-quart)

3 eggs, separated
1 tsp. grated lemon peel
¼ cup lemon juice
1 Tbsp. light, soft tub margarine, melted
1½ cups fat-free half-and-half
½ cup sugar
sugar substitute to equal 2 Tbsp.
¼ cup flour
⅛ tsp. salt

1. Beat eggs whites until stiff peaks form. Set aside.

2. Beat eggs yolks. Blend in lemon peel, lemon juice, margarine, and half-and-half.

3. In separate bowl, combine sugar, sugar substitute, flour, and salt. Add to egg-lemon mixture, beating until smooth.

4. Fold into beaten egg whites.

5. Spoon into slow cooker.

6. Cover and cook on High 2-3 hours.

7. Serve from cooker.

Exchange List Values:
Carbohydrate 2.0, Fat 0.5

Basic Nutritional Values: Calories 169 (Calories from Fat 37), Total Fat 4 gm (Saturated Fat 1.5 gm, Polyunsat Fat 0.5 gm, Monounsat Fat 1.4 gm, Cholesterol 111 mg), Sodium 185 mg, Total Carbohydrate 27 gm, Dietary Fiber 0 gm, Sugars 20 gm, Protein 5 gm

Dump Cake

Janice Muller
Derwood, MD

Makes 15 servings
(Ideal slow cooker size: 4-5-quart)

20-oz. can crushed pineapple
21-oz. can light blueberry, or cherry, pie filling
18½-oz. pkg. yellow cake mix
cinnamon
⅓ cup light, soft tub margarine
⅓ cup chopped walnuts

1. Grease bottom and sides of slow cooker.

2. Spread layers of pineapple, blueberry pie filling, and dry cake mix. Be careful not to mix the layers.

3. Sprinkle with cinnamon.

4. Top with thin layers of margarine chunks and nuts.

5. Cover. Cook on High 2-3 hours.

6. Serve with vanilla ice cream, if you wish.

Exchange List Values:
Carbohydrate 2.5, Fat 1.0

Basic Nutritional Values: Calories 219 (Calories from Fat 57), Total Fat 6 gm (Saturated Fat 1.5 gm, Polyunsat Fat 2.4 gm, Monounsat Fat 2.2 gm, Cholesterol 0 mg), Sodium 250 mg, Total Carbohydrate 41 gm, Dietary Fiber 1 gm, Sugars 28 gm, Protein 2 gm

Variation: Use a pkg. of spice cake mix and apple pie filling.

Carrot Cake

Colleen Heatwole, Burton, MI

Makes 10 servings
(Ideal slow cooker size: 4-5-quart)

1/3 **cup canola oil**
2 **eggs**
1 **Tbsp. hot water**
1/2 **cup grated raw carrots**
3/4 **cup flour**
3/4 **cup sugar**
1/2 **tsp. baking powder**
1/8 **tsp. salt**
1/4 **tsp. ground allspice**
1/2 **tsp. ground cinnamon**
1/8 **tsp. ground cloves**
1/2 **cup chopped nuts**
1/2 **cup raisins or chopped dates**
2 **Tbsp. flour**

1. In large bowl, beat oil, eggs, and water for 1 minute.
2. Add carrots. Mix well.
3. Stir together 3/4 cup flour, sugar, baking powder, salt, allspice, cinnamon, and cloves. Add to creamed mixture.
4. Toss nuts and raisins in bowl with 2 Tbsp. flour. Add to creamed mixture. Mix well.
5. Pour into greased and floured 3 lb. shortening can or slow cooker baking insert. Place can or baking insert in slow cooker.
6. Cover insert with its lid, or cover can with 8 paper towels, folded down over edge of slow cooker to absorb moisture. Cover paper towels with cooker lid. Cook on High 3-4 hours.
7. Remove can or insert from cooker and allow to cool on rack for 10 minutes. Run knife around edge of cake. Invert onto serving plate.

Exchange List Values:
Carbohydrate 2.0, Fat 3.0

Basic Nutritional Values: Calories 274 (Calories from Fat 147), Total Fat 16 gm (Saturated Fat 1.5 gm, Polyunsat Fat 6.4 gm, Monounsat Fat 7.6 gm, Cholesterol 43 mg), Sodium 66 mg, Total Carbohydrate 30 gm, Dietary Fiber 1 gm, Sugars 20 gm, Protein 4 gm

The key to weight loss is simple: burn more calories than you eat.

Chocolate Peanut Butter Cake

Ruth Ann Gingrich
New Holland, PA

Makes 11 servings
(Ideal slow cooker size: 4-quart)

2 **cups (half a package) milk chocolate cake mix**
1/2 **cup water**
1/4 **cup peanut butter**
1 **egg**
2 **egg whites**
6 **Tbsp. chopped walnuts**

1. Combine all ingredients. Beat 2 minutes in electric mixer.
2. Pour into greased and floured 3 lb. shortening can. Place can in slow cooker.
3. Cover top of can with 8 paper towels.
4. Cover cooker. Bake on High 2-3 hours.
5. Allow to cool for 10 minutes. Run knife around edge and invert cake onto serving plate. Cool completely before slicing and serving.

Exchange List Values:
Carbohydrate 1.5, Fat 1.5

Basic Nutritional Values: Calories 165 (Calories from Fat 75), Total Fat 8 gm (Saturated Fat 1.5 gm, Polyunsat Fat 3.6 gm, Monounsat Fat 2.8 gm, Cholesterol 19 mg), Sodium 255 mg, Total Carbohydrate 20 gm, Dietary Fiber 1 gm, Sugars 11 gm, Protein 4 gm

Harvey Wallbanger Cake

Roseann Wilson
Albuquerque, NM

Makes 18 servings
(Ideal slow cooker size: 4-5-quart)

Cake:
16-oz. pkg. pound cake mix
1/3 cup vanilla instant pudding (reserve rest of pudding from 3-oz. pkg. for glaze)
2 Tbsp. canola oil
3 eggs
2 Tbsp. Galliano liqueur
2/3 cup orange juice

Glaze:
remaining pudding mix
2/3 cup orange juice
1 Tbsp. Galliano liqueur

1. Mix together all ingredients for cake. Beat for 3 minutes. Pour batter into greased and floured bread or cake pan that will fit into your slow cooker. Cover pan.

2. Bake in covered slow cooker on High 2½-3½ hours.

3. Invert cake onto serving platter.

4. Mix together glaze ingredients. Spoon over cake.

Basic Nutritional Values: Calories 165 (Calories from Fat 49), Total Fat 5 gm (Saturated Fat 1.5 gm, Polyunsat Fat 0.8 gm, Monounsat Fat 2.1 gm, Cholesterol 36 mg), Sodium 168 mg, Total Carbohydrate 28 gm, Dietary Fiber 0 gm, Sugars 19 gm, Protein 2 gm

Graham Cracker Cookies

Cassandra Ly, Carlisle, PA

Makes 96 (1 cookie) servings
(Ideal slow cooker size: 4-quart)

12-oz. pkg. (2 cups) semi-sweet chocolate chips
2 1-oz. squares unsweetened baking chocolate, shaved
2 14-oz. cans fat-free sweetened condensed milk
3¾ cups crushed graham cracker crumbs, divided
1 cup finely chopped walnuts

1. Place chocolate in slow cooker.

2. Cover. Cook on High 1 hour, stirring every 15 minutes. Continue to cook on Low heat, stirring every 15 minutes, or until chocolate is melted (about 30 minutes).

3. Stir milk into melted chocolate.

4. Add 3 cups graham cracker crumbs, 1 cup at a time, stirring after each addition.

5. Stir in nuts. Mixture should be thick but not stiff.

6. Stir in remaining graham cracker crumbs to reach consistency of cookie dough.

7. Drop by heaping teaspoonfuls onto lightly greased cookie sheets. Keep remaining mixture warm by covering and turning the slow cooker to warm.

8. Bake at 325° for 7-9 minutes, or until tops of cookies begin to crack. Remove from oven. Cool 1-2 minutes before transferring to waxed paper.

Basic Nutritional Values: Calories 65 (Calories from Fat 23), Total Fat 3 gm (Saturated Fat 0.9 gm, Polyunsat Fat 0.8 gm, Monounsat Fat 0.9 gm, Cholesterol 0 mg), Sodium 29 mg, Total Carbohydrate 10 gm, Dietary Fiber 0 gm, Sugars 8 gm, Protein 1 gm

Note: These cookies freeze well.

This delectable fudge-like cookie is a family favorite. The original recipe (from my maternal grandmother) was so involved and yielded so few cookies that my mom and I would get together to make a couple of batches only at Christmas-time. Adapting the recipe for using a slow cooker, rather than a double boiler, allows me to prepare a double batch without help.

Apple Peanut Crumble

Phyllis Attig, Reynolds, IL
Joan Becker, Dodge City, KS
Pam Hochstedler, Kalona, IA

*Makes 8 servings
(Ideal slow cooker size: 4-quart)*

4 medium cooking apples, peeled and sliced
1/3 cup packed brown sugar
brown sugar substitute to equal 3 Tbsp.
1/2 cup flour
1/2 cup quick-cooking dry oats
1/2 tsp. cinnamon
1/4-1/2 tsp. nutmeg
1/4 cup light, soft tub margarine, softened
2 Tbsp. peanut butter
ice cream, or whipped cream, optional

1. Place apple slices in slow cooker.
2. Combine brown sugar, sugar substitute, flour, oats, cinnamon, and nutmeg.
3. Cut in margarine and peanut butter. Sprinkle over apples.
4. Cover cooker and cook on Low 5-6 hours.
5. Serve warm or cold, plain or with ice cream or whipped cream.

Exchange List Values:
Carbohydrate 2.0, Fat 0.5

Basic Nutritional Values: Calories 164 (Calories from Fat 45), Total Fat 5 gm (Saturated Fat 0.7 gm, Polyunsat Fat 1.3 gm, Monounsat Fat 2.4 gm, Cholesterol 0 mg), Sodium 71 mg, Total Carbohydrate 29 gm, Dietary Fiber 2 gm, Sugars 18 gm, Protein 3 gm

Cherry Delight
Anna Musser
Manheim, PA
Marianne J. Troyer
Millersburg, OH

*Makes 10-12 servings
(Ideal slow cooker size: 4-quart)*

20-oz. can cherry pie fillng, light
1/2 pkg. yellow cake mix
1/4 cup light, soft tub margarine, melted
1/3 cup walnuts, optional

1. Place pie filling in greased slow cooker.
2. Combine dry cake mix and margarine (mixture will be crumbly). Sprinkle over filling. Sprinkle with walnuts.
3. Cover and cook on Low 4 hours, or on High 2 hours.
4. Allow to cool, then serve in bowls with dips of ice cream, if you wish.

Exchange List Values:
Carbohydrate 2.0

Basic Nutritional Values: Calories 137 (Calories from Fat 33), Total Fat 4 gm (Saturated Fat 0.9 gm, Polyunsat Fat 0.9 gm, Monounsat Fat 1.6 gm, Cholesterol 0 mg), Sodium 174 mg, Total Carbohydrate 26 gm, Dietary Fiber 1 gm, Sugars 19 gm, Protein 1 gm

Hot Fudge Cake
Maricarol Magil, Freehold, NJ

*Makes 10 servings
(Ideal slow cooker size: 4-quart)*

1/2 cup packed brown sugar
brown sugar substitute to equal 1/4 cup
1 cup flour
3 Tbsp. unsweetened cocoa powder
2 tsp. baking powder
1/2 tsp. salt
1/2 cup fat-free half-and-half
2 Tbsp. melted butter
1/2 tsp. vanilla
6 Tbsp. brown sugar
brown sugar substitute to equal 3 Tbsp.
1/4 cup unsweetened cocoa powder
1 3/4 cups boiling water

1. Mix together 1/2 cup brown sugar, brown sugar substitute to equal 1/4 cup, flour, 3 Tbsp. cocoa, baking powder, and salt.
2. Stir in half-and-half, butter, and vanilla. Spread over the bottom of slow cooker.
3. Mix together 6 Tbsp. brown sugar, brown sugar substitute to equal 3 Tbsp., and 1/4 cup cocoa. Sprinkle over mixture in slow cooker.
4. Pour in boiling water. Do not stir.
5. Cover and cook on High 2-3 hours, or until a toothpick inserted comes out clean.

6. Serve warm with vanilla ice cream, if diets allow.

Exchange List Values:
Carbohydrate 2.0

Basic Nutritional Values: Calories 143 (Calories from Fat 11), Total Fat 1 gm (Saturated Fat 0.4 gm, Polyunsat Fat 0.2 gm, Monounsat Fat 0.4 gm, Cholesterol 1 mg), Sodium 226 mg, Total Carbohydrate 32 gm, Dietary Fiber 2 gm, Sugars 21 gm, Protein 2 gm

Chocolate Pudding Cake

Lee Ann Hazlett
Freeport, IL
Della Yoder
Kalona, IA

Makes 24 servings
(Ideal slow cooker size: 4-5-quart)

18^{1}/$_2$-oz. pkg. chocolate cake mix
3.9-oz. pkg. instant chocolate pudding mix
2 cups (16 ozs.) fat-free sour cream
4 eggs
1 cup water
^{1}/$_2$ cup canola oil
2 Tbsp. semisweet chocolate chips

1. Combine cake mix, pudding mix, sour cream, eggs, water, and oil in electric mixer bowl. Beat on medium speed for 2 minutes. Stir in chocolate chips.
2. Pour into greased slow cooker. Cover and cook on Low 6-7 hours, or on High 3-4 hours, or until toothpick inserted near center comes out with moist crumbs.
3. Serve with whipped cream or ice cream, if you wish.

Exchange List Values:
Carbohydrate 1.5, Fat 1.5

Basic Nutritional Values: Calories 186 (Calories from Fat 83), Total Fat 9 gm (Saturated Fat 1.5 gm, Polyunsat Fat 2.6 gm, Monounsat Fat 4.6 gm, Cholesterol 37 mg), Sodium 280 mg, Total Carbohydrate 24 gm, Dietary Fiber 1 gm, Sugars 13 gm, Protein 3 gm

Peanut Butter and Hot Fudge Pudding Cake

Sara Wilson
Blairstown, MO

Makes 6 servings
(Ideal slow cooker size: 4-quart)

^{1}/$_2$ cup flour
^{1}/$_4$ cup sugar
sugar substitute to equal 2 Tbsp.
^{3}/$_4$ tsp. baking powder
^{1}/$_3$ cup fat-free milk
1 Tbsp. canola oil
^{1}/$_2$ tsp. vanilla
^{1}/$_4$ cup peanut butter
^{1}/$_4$ cup sugar
3 Tbsp. unsweetened cocoa powder
1 cup boiling water

1. Combine flour, ^{1}/$_4$ cup sugar, sugar substitute, and baking powder. Add milk, oil, and vanilla. Mix until smooth. Stir in peanut butter. Pour into slow cooker.
2. Mix together ^{1}/$_4$ cup sugar and cocoa powder. Gradually stir in boiling water. Pour mixture over batter in slow cooker. Do not stir.
3. Cover and cook on High 2-3 hours, or until toothpick inserted comes out clean.
4. Serve warm with ice cream, if you wish.

Exchange List Values:
Carbohydrate 2.0, Fat 1.0

Basic Nutritional Values: Calories 197 (Calories from Fat 73), Total Fat 8 gm (Saturated Fat 1.1 gm, Polyunsat Fat 2.1 gm, Monounsat Fat 4.2 gm, Cholesterol 0 mg), Sodium 92 mg, Total Carbohydrate 29 gm, Dietary Fiber 2 gm, Sugars 18 gm, Protein 5 gm

Seven Layer Bars
Mary W. Stauffer
Ephrata, PA

Makes 18 servings
(Ideal slow cooker size: 4-5-quart)

2 Tbsp. light, soft tub
  margarine, melted
1/2 cup graham cracker
  crumbs
1/4 cup chocolate chips
2 Tbsp. butterscotch chips
1/4 cup flaked coconut
1/2 cup chopped pecans
1/2 cup fat-free sweetened
  condensed milk

1. Layer ingredients in a
bread or cake pan that fits in
your slow cooker, in the order
listed. Do not stir.
2. Cover and bake on High
2-3 hours, or until firm.
Remove pan and uncover.
Let stand 5 minutes.
3. Unmold carefully on
plate and cool.

Exchange List Values:
Carbohydrate 0.5, Fat 1.0

Basic Nutritional Values: Calories
87 (Calories from Fat 42), Total Fat 5
gm (Saturated Fat 1.4 gm, Polyunsat
Fat 0.9 gm, Monounsat Fat 2.3 gm,
Cholesterol 0 mg), Sodium 37
mg,Total Carbohydrate 11 gm,
Dietary Fiber 1 gm, Sugars 9 gm,
Protein 1 gm

Chocolate Rice Pudding
Michele Ruvola
Selden, NY

Makes 12 servings
(Ideal slow cooker size: 3-4-quart)

4 cups cooked white rice
1/2 cup sugar
sugar substitute to equal
  2 Tbsp.
1/4 cup baking cocoa
  powder
2 Tbsp. light, soft tub
  margarine, melted
1 tsp. vanilla
2 12-oz. cans fat-free
  evaporated milk
whipped cream, optional
sliced toasted almonds,
  optional
maraschino cherries,
  optional

1. Combine first 7
ingredients in greased slow
cooker.
2. Cover. Cook on Low
2½-3½ hours, or until liquid
is absorbed.
3. Serve warm or chilled.
Top individual servings with
a dollop of whipped cream,
sliced toasted almonds, and a
maraschino cherry, if you
wish

Exchange List Values:
Carbohydrate 2.5

Basic Nutritional Values: Calories
180 (Calories from Fat 15), Total Fat
2 gm (Saturated Fat 0.3 gm,
Polyunsat Fat 0.3 gm, Monounsat Fat
0.8 gm, Cholesterol 0 mg), Sodium
104 mg,Total Carbohydrate 35 gm,
Dietary Fiber 1 gm, Sugars 18 gm,
Protein 7 gm

Water is the best
thing to drink when
you're exercising for less
than an hour.

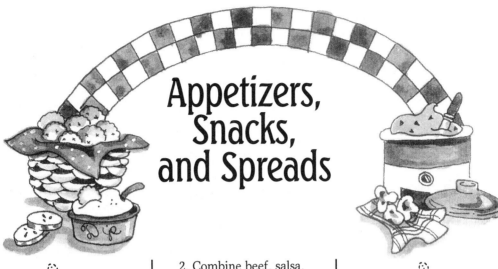

Appetizers, Snacks, and Spreads

Quick and Easy Nacho Dip

Kristina Shull, Timberville, VA

Makes 20 servings
(Ideal slow cooker size: 3-quart)

½ lb. 85%-lean ground
  beef
salt, optional
pepper, optional
onion powder, optional
2 garlic cloves, minced,
  optional
2 16-oz. jars salsa (as hot
  or mild as you like)
15-oz. can fat-free refried
  beans
1½ cups fat-free sour
  cream
1½ cups shredded
  reduced-fat sharp
  cheddar cheese, divided

1. Brown ground beef in
skillet. Drain. Add salt,
pepper, onion powder, and
minced garlic.

2. Combine beef, salsa,
beans, sour cream, and 1 cup
cheese in slow cooker.
3. Cover. Heat on Low 2
hours. Just before serving
sprinkle with ½ cup cheese.
4. Serve with tortilla chips.

Exchange List Values:
Carbohydrate 0.5, Meat,
lean 1.0

Basic Nutritional Values: Calories
80 (Calories from Fat 27), Total Fat 3
gm (Saturated Fat 1.5 gm, Polyunsat
Fat 0.2 gm, Monounsat Fat 1.0 gm,
Cholesterol 14 mg), Sodium 298
mg,Total Carbohydrate 8 gm, Dietary
Fiber 2 gm, Sugars 3 gm, Protein 6
gm

Red Pepper Cheese Dip

Ann Bender, Ft. Defiance, VA

Makes 12-15 servings
(Ideal slow cooker size: 3-4-quart)

2 Tbsp. olive oil
4 large red peppers, cut
  into 1″ squares
4 ozs. feta cheese

1. Pour oil into slow
cooker. Stir in peppers.
2. Cover. Cook on Low 2
hours.
3. Serve with feta cheese
on crackers.

Exchange List Values:
Vegetable 1.0, Fat 0.5

Basic Nutritional Values: Calories
49 (Calories from Fat 32), Total Fat 4
gm (Saturated Fat 1.4 gm, Polyunsat
Fat 0.3 gm, Monounsat Fat 1.7 gm,
Cholesterol 7 mg), Sodium 86 mg,Total
Carbohydrate 3 gm, Dietary Fiber 1
gm, Sugars 2 gm, Protein 2 gm

Hamburger Cheese Dip

Julia Lapp
New Holland, PA

Makes 20 servings
(Ideal slow cooker size: 1-quart)

3/4 lb. ground beef,
 browned and crumbled
 into small pieces
1/8 tsp. salt
1/2 cup chopped green
 peppers
3/4 cup chopped onion
8-oz. can no-sugar-added
 tomato sauce
4-oz. can green chilies,
 chopped
1 Tbsp. Worcestershire
 sauce
1 Tbsp. brown sugar
8 ozs. Velveeta Light
 cheese, cubed
1 Tbsp. paprika
red pepper

1. Combine beef, salt,
green peppers, onion, tomato
sauce, green chilies,
Worcestershire sauce, and
brown sugar in slow cooker.
 2. Cover. Cook on Low 2-3
hours. During the last hour
stir in cheese, paprika, and
red pepper.
 3. Serve with tortilla chips.

Basic Nutritional Values: Calories
64 (Calories from Fat 27), Total Fat 3
gm (Saturated Fat 1.5 gm, Polyunsat
Fat 0.1 gm, Monounsat Fat 1.1 gm,
Cholesterol 14 mg), Sodium 231
mg, Total Carbohydrate 4 gm, Dietary
Fiber 1 gm, Sugars 3 gm, Protein 6 gm

---

*Variation: Prepare recipe using
only 1/3-1/2 lb. ground beef.*

Mexican Chip Dip Olé

Joy Sutter, Iowa City, IA

Makes 32 servings
(Ideal slow cooker size: 3-quart)

1 1/2 lbs. ground turkey
1 large onion, chopped
15-oz. can tomato sauce
4-oz. can green chilies,
 chopped
3-oz. can jalapeno peppers,
 chopped
1 lb. Velveeta Light cheese,
 cubed

1. Brown turkey and
onion. Drain.
 2. Add tomato sauce,
chilies, jalapeno peppers, and
cheese. Pour into slow cooker.
 3. Cover. Cook on Low 4
hours, or High 2 hours.
 4. Serve warm with tortilla
chips.

Basic Nutritional Values: Calories
75 (Calories from Fat 32), Total Fat 4
gm (Saturated Fat 1.5 gm, Polyunsat
Fat 0.6 gm, Monounsat Fat 1.2 gm,
Cholesterol 21 mg), Sodium 339
mg, Total Carbohydrate 3 gm, Dietary
Fiber 0 gm, Sugars 3 gm, Protein 8 gm

Pizza Fondue

Lisa Warren
Parkesburg, PA

Makes 18 servings
(Ideal slow cooker size: 3-quart)

1/2 lb. 85%-lean ground
 beef
2 15-oz. cans pizza sauce
 with cheese
4 ozs. grated fat-free
 cheddar cheese
4 ozs. grated reduced-fat
 mozzarella cheese
1 tsp. dried oregano
1/2 tsp. fennel seed,
 optional
1 Tbsp. cornstarch

1. Brown beef, crumble
fine, and drain.
 2. Combine all ingredients
in slow cooker.
 3. Cover. Heat on Low 2-3
hours.
 4. Serve with tortilla chips.

Basic Nutritional Values: Calories
76 (Calories from Fat 34), Total Fat 4
gm (Saturated Fat 1.4 gm, Polyunsat
Fat 0.9 gm, Monounsat Fat 0.9 gm,
Cholesterol 13 mg), Sodium 392
mg, Total Carbohydrate 4 gm, Dietary
Fiber 0 gm, Sugars 3 gm, Protein 6
gm

Good 'n Hot Dip

Joyce B. Suiter
Garysburg, NC

Makes 40 servings
(Ideal slow cooker size: 3-quart)

³/4 **lb. ground beef**
³/4 **lb. bulk pork sausage**
10³/4-oz. can 98%-fat-free,
lower-sodium cream of
chicken soup
10³/4-oz. can cream of
celery soup
24-oz. jar salsa (use hot for
some zing)
10 ozs. Velveeta Light
cheese, cubed

1. Brown beef and
sausage, crumbling into small
pieces. Drain.
2. Combine meat, soups,
salsa, and cheese in slow
cooker.
3. Cover. Cook on High 1
hour. Stir. Cook on Low until
ready to serve.
4. Serve with chips.

Exchange List Values:
Meat, lean 1.0

Basic Nutritional Values: Calories
60 (Calories from Fat 31), Total Fat 3
gm (Saturated Fat 1.5 gm, Polyunsat
Fat 0.5 gm, Monounsat Fat 1.3 gm,
Cholesterol 12 mg), Sodium 291
mg, Total Carbohydrate 3 gm, Dietary
Fiber 0 gm, Sugars 1 gm, Protein 4
gm

Hot Cheese and Bacon Dip

Lee Ann Hazlett
Freeport, IL

Makes 25 servings
(Ideal slow cooker size: 1-quart)

9 slices bacon, diced
2 8-oz. pkgs. fat-free cream
cheese, cubed and
softened
8 ozs. shredded reduced-fat
mild cheddar cheese
1 cup fat-free half-and-half
2 tsp. Worcestershire sauce
1 tsp. dried minced onion
¹/2 tsp. dry mustard
¹/2 tsp. salt
2-3 drops Tabasco

1. Brown and drain bacon.
Set aside.
2. Mix remaining ingredi-
ents in slow cooker.
3. Cover. Cook on Low 1
hour, stirring occasionally
until cheese melts.
4. Stir in bacon.
5. Serve with fruit slices or
French bread slices. (Dip fruit
in lemon juice to prevent
browning.)

Exchange List Values:
Meat, lean 1.0

Basic Nutritional Values: Calories
54 (Calories from Fat 28), Total Fat 3
gm (Saturated Fat 1.5 gm, Polyunsat
Fat 0.2 gm, Monounsat Fat 1.1 gm,
Cholesterol 11 mg), Sodium 273
mg, Total Carbohydrate 2 gm, Dietary
Fiber 0 gm, Sugars 1 gm, Protein 6
gm

Cheesy Hot Bean Dip

John D. Allen
Rye, CO

Makes 20 servings
(Ideal slow cooker size: 3-quart)

16-oz. can refried beans
1 cup salsa
2 cups (8 ozs.) shredded
reduced-fat Monterey
Jack and reduced-fat
cheddar cheeses, mixed
1 cup fat-free sour cream
3-oz. pkg. fat-free cream
cheese, cubed
1 Tbsp. chili powder
¹/4 tsp. ground cumin

1. Combine all ingredients
in slow cooker.
2. Cover. Cook on High 2
hours. Stir 2-3 times during
cooking.
3. Serve warm from the
cooker with chips.

Exchange List Values:
Carbohydrate 0.5, Fat 0.5

Basic Nutritional Values: Calories
65 (Calories from Fat 22), Total Fat 2
gm (Saturated Fat 1.5 gm, Polyunsat
Fat 0.1 gm, Monounsat Fat 0.7 gm,
Cholesterol 11 mg), Sodium 275
mg, Total Carbohydrate 6 gm, Dietary
Fiber 1 gm, Sugars 2 gm, Protein 6
gm

This bean dip is a favorite.
Once you start on it, it's hard
to leave it alone. We have been
known to dip into it even when
it's cold.

Refried Bean Dip

Maryann Markano
Wilmington, DE

Makes 12 servings
(Ideal slow cooker size: 3-quart)

20-oz. can fat-free refried
  beans
1 cup shredded fat-free
  cheddar cheese
1/2 cup chopped green
  onions
2-4 Tbsp. bottled taco
  sauce (depending upon
  how spicy a dip you
  like)

1. Combine beans, cheese,
onions, and taco sauce in
slow cooker.
2. Cover. Cook on Low
2-2½ hours, or cook on High
30 minutes and then on Low
30 minutes.
3. Serve with tortilla chips.

Exchange List Values:
Starch 0.5, Meat, very lean
1.0

Basic Nutritional Values: Calories
56 (Calories from Fat 0), Total Fat 0
gm (Saturated Fat 0.0 gm, Polyunsat
Fat 0.0 gm, Monounsat Fat 0.0 gm,
Cholesterol 1 mg), Sodium 270
mg,Total Carbohydrate 8 gm, Dietary
Fiber 2 gm, Sugars 1 gm, Protein 5
gm

Short-Cut Fondue Dip

Jean Butzer
Batavia, NY

Makes 20 servings
(Ideal slow cooker size: 1-quart)

2 10¾-oz. cans condensed
  cheese soup
3½ ozs. grated reduced-fat
  sharp cheddar cheese
1 Tbsp. Worcestershire
  sauce
1 tsp. lemon juice
2 Tbsp. dried chopped
  chives
celery sticks
cauliflower florets
corn chips

1. Combine soup, cheese,
Worcestershire sauce, lemon
juice, and chives in slow
cooker.
2. Cover. Heat on Low
2-2½ hours. Stir until smooth
and well blended.
3. Serve warm dip with
celery sticks, cauliflower, and
corn chips.

Exchange List Values: Fat
1.0

Basic Nutritional Values: Calories
44 (Calories from Fat 27), Total Fat 3
gm (Saturated Fat 1.5 gm, Polyunsat
Fat 0.6 gm, Monounsat Fat 0.9 gm,
Cholesterol 8 mg), Sodium 322
mg,Total Carbohydrate 3 gm, Dietary
Fiber 0 gm, Sugars 1 gm, Protein 2
gm

Reuben Spread

Clarice Williams
Fairbank, IA
Julie McKenzie
Punxsutawney, PA

Makes 52 servings
(Ideal slow cooker size: 3-quart)

1/2 lb. corned beef,
  shredded or chopped,
  all visible fat removed
16-oz. can sauerkraut, well
  drained
1 cup shredded Swiss
  cheese
1 cup shredded cheddar
  cheese
1 cup mayonnaise
Thousand Island dressing,
  optional

1. Combine all ingredients
except Thousand Island
dressing in slow cooker. Mix
well.
2. Cover. Cook on High 1-2
hours until heated through,
stirring occasionally.
3. Turn to Low and keep
warm in cooker while serving. Put spread on bread
slices. Top individual servings
with Thousand Island dressing, if desired.

Exchange List Values:
Fat 1.0

Basic Nutritional Values: Calories
58 (Calories from Fat 49), Total Fat 5
gm (Saturated Fat 1.5 gm, Polyunsat
Fat 1.9 gm, Monounsat Fat 1.6 gm,
Cholesterol 10 mg), Sodium 113
mg,Total Carbohydrate 1 gm, Dietary
Fiber 0 gm, Sugars 0 gm, Protein 2
gm

Note: Low-fat cheese and mayonnaise are not recommended for this spread.

Variation: Use dried beef instead of corned beef.

TNT Dip
Sheila Plock
Boalsburg, PA

Makes 32 (1/4 cup) servings (Ideal slow cooker size: 4-quart)

1 1/4 lbs. ground beef, browned
10 3/4-oz. can 98%-fat-free, reduced-sodium cream of mushroom soup
1/4 cup light, soft tub margarine, melted
3/4 lb. Velveeta Light, cubed
1 cup salsa
2 Tbsp. chili powder

1. Combine all ingredients in slow cooker.
2. Cover. Cook on High 1-1 1/4 hours, or until cheese is melted, stirring occasionally.
3. Serve with tortilla chips, corn chips, or party rye bread.

Exchange List Values:
Meat, medium fat 1.0

Basic Nutritional Values: Calories 62 (Calories from Fat 32), Total Fat 4 gm (Saturated Fat 1.5 gm, Polyunsat Fat 0.3 gm, Monounsat Fat 1.4 gm, Cholesterol 14 mg), Sodium 215 mg, Total Carbohydrate 2 gm, Dietary Fiber 0 gm, Sugars 1 gm, Protein 5 gm

---

My son has hosted a Super Bowl party for his college friends at our house the past two years. He served this dip the first year, and the second year it was requested. His friends claim it's the best dip they've ever eaten. With a bunch of college kids it disappears quickly.

Hearty Beef Dip Fondue
Ann Bender
Ft. Defiance, VA
Charlotte Shaffer
East Earl, PA

Makes 10 (1/4 cup) servings (Ideal slow cooker size: 3-quart)

1 cup fat-free milk
3/4 cup fat-free half-and-half
2 8-oz. pkgs. fat-free cream cheese, cubed
2 tsp. dry mustard
1/4 cup chopped green onions
2 1/2 ozs. sliced dried beef, shredded or torn into small pieces

1. Heat milk and half-and-half in slow cooker on High.
2. Add cheese. Stir until melted.
3. Add mustard, green onions, and dried beef. Stir well.
4. Cover. Cook on Low for up to 6 hours.

5. Serve by dipping toasted bread pieces on long forks into mixture.

Exchange List Values:
Carbohydrate 0.5, Meat, very lean 1.0

Basic Nutritional Values: Calories 72 (Calories from Fat 6), Total Fat 1 gm (Saturated Fat 0.1 gm, Polyunsat Fat 0.0 gm, Monounsat Fat 0.1 gm, Cholesterol 10 mg), Sodium 508 mg, Total Carbohydrate 6 gm, Dietary Fiber 0 gm, Sugars 4 gm, Protein 10 gm

---

Variations: Add 1/2 cup chopped pecans, 2 Tbsp. chopped olives, or 1 tsp. minced onion in Step 3.

I make this on cold winter evenings, and we sit around the table playing games.

Don't wear new exercise shoes for prolonged exercise. Break them in gradually.

Hot Crab Dip
Cassandra Ly
Carlisle, PA
Miriam Nolt
New Holland, PA

Makes 15-20 servings
(Ideal slow cooker size: 3-4-quart)

1/2 cup milk
1/3 cup salsa
3 8-oz. pkgs. fat-free cream
cheese, cubed
2 8-oz. pkgs. imitation
crabmeat, flaked
1 cup thinly sliced green
onions
4-oz. can chopped green
chilies

1. Combine milk and salsa.
Transfer to greased slow
cooker.
2. Stir in cream cheese,
crabmeat, onions, and chilies.
3. Cover. Cook on Low 3-4
hours, stirring every 30
minutes.
4. Serve with crackers or
bread.

Exchange List Values:
Carbohydrate 0.5, Meat,
very lean 1.0

Basic Nutritional Values: Calories
60 (Calories from Fat 4), Total Fat 0
gm (Saturated Fat 0.1 gm, Polyunsat
Fat 0.2 gm, Monounsat Fat 0.1 gm,
Cholesterol 9 mg), Sodium 410
mg, Total Carbohydrate 5 gm, Dietary
Fiber 0 gm, Sugars 4 gm, Protein 8
gm

Liver Paté
Barbara Walker
Sturgis, SD

Makes 12 (2 Tbsp.) servings
(Ideal slow cooker size: 3-quart)

1 lb. chicken livers
1/2 cup dry wine
1 tsp. instant chicken
bouillon
1 tsp. minced parsley
1 Tbsp. instant minced
onion
1/4 tsp. ground ginger
1/2 tsp. seasoning salt
1 Tbsp. light soy sauce
1/4 tsp. dry mustard
1/4 cup light, soft tub
margarine
1 Tbsp. brandy

1. In slow cooker, combine
all ingredients except
margarine and brandy.
2. Cover. Cook on Low 4-5
hours. Let stand in liquid
until cool.
3. Drain. Place in blender
or food grinder. Add mar-
garine and brandy. Process
until smooth.
4. Serve with crackers or
toast.

Exchange List Values:
Meat, lean 1.0

Basic Nutritional Values: Calories
61 (Calories from Fat 28), Total Fat 3
gm (Saturated Fat 0.6 gm, Polyunsat
Fat 0.6 gm, Monounsat Fat 1.2 gm,
Cholesterol 137 mg), Sodium 235
mg, Total Carbohydrate 1 gm, Dietary
Fiber 0 gm, Sugars 0 gm, Protein 6
gm

Cheesy New Orleans Shrimp Dip
Kelly Evenson, Pittsboro, NC

Makes 20 servings
(Ideal slow cooker size: 1-quart)

1 slice bacon
3 medium onions, chopped
1 garlic clove, minced
4 jumbo shrimp, peeled
and deveined
1 medium tomato, peeled
and chopped
7 ozs. (1 3/4 cups) reduced-
fat Monterey Jack
cheese, shredded
4 drops Tabasco sauce
1/8 tsp. cayenne pepper
dash of black pepper

1. Cook bacon until crisp.
Drain on paper towel.
Crumble.
2. Saute onion and garlic
in skillet sprayed with non-fat
cooking spray. Drain on
paper towel.
3. Coarsely chop shrimp.
4. Combine all ingredients
in slow cooker.
5. Cover. Cook on Low 1
hour, or until cheese is
melted. Thin with milk if too
thick. Serve with chips.

Exchange List Values:
Meat, lean 1.0

Basic Nutritional Values: Calories
43 (Calories from Fat 18), Total Fat 2
gm (Saturated Fat 1.5 gm, Polyunsat
Fat 0.1 gm, Monounsat Fat 0.6 gm,
Cholesterol 13 mg), Sodium 90
mg, Total Carbohydrate 2 gm, Dietary
Fiber 0 gm, Sugars 2 gm, Protein 4
gm

Roasted Pepper and Artichoke Spread

Sherril Bieberly, Salina, KS

Makes 24 servings
(Ideal slow cooker size: 1-quart)

1 cup grated Parmesan cheese
1/2 cup reduced-fat mayonnaise
8-oz. pkg. fat-free cream cheese, softened
1 garlic clove, minced
14-oz. can artichoke hearts, drained and chopped finely
1/3 cup finely chopped roasted red bell peppers (from 71/4-oz. jar)

1. Combine Parmesan cheese, mayonnaise, cream cheese, and garlic in food processor. Process until smooth. Place mixture in slow cooker.
2. Add artichoke hearts and red bell peppers. Stir well.
3. Cover. Cook on Low 1 hour. Stir again.
4. Use as spread for crackers, cut-up fresh vegetables, or snack-bread slices.

Exchange List Values: Fat 1.0

Basic Nutritional Values: Calories 49 (Calories from Fat 29), Total Fat 3 gm (Saturated Fat 1.3 gm, Polyunsat Fat 0.7 gm, Monounsat Fat 0.9 gm, Cholesterol 8 mg), Sodium 209 mg, Total Carbohydrate 2 gm, Dietary Fiber 0 gm, Sugars 1 gm, Protein 4 gm

Broccoli Cheese Dip

Carla Koslowsky
Hillsboro, KS

Makes 24 servings
(Ideal slow cooker size: 3-quart)

1 cup chopped celery
1/2 cup chopped onion
10-oz. pkg. frozen chopped broccoli, cooked
1 cup cooked rice
103/4-oz. can 98%-fat-free, lower-sodium cream of mushroom soup
15 slices fat-free American cheese, melted and mixed with 2/3 cup fat-free half-and-half

1. Combine all ingredients in slow cooker.
2. Cover. Heat on Low 2 hours.
3. Serve with snack breads or crackers.

Exchange List Values: Carbohydrate 0.5

Basic Nutritional Values: Calories 44 (Calories from Fat 4), Total Fat 0 gm (Saturated Fat 0.2 gm, Polyunsat Fat 0.1 gm, Monounsat Fat 0.1 gm, Cholesterol 3 mg), Sodium 234 mg, Total Carbohydrate 6 gm, Dietary Fiber 1 gm, Sugars 2 gm, Protein 4 gm

Chili Nuts

Barbara Aston
Ashdown, AR

Makes 80 (1 Tbsp.) servings
(Ideal slow cooker size: 3-quart)

1/4 cup melted butter
2 12-oz. cans cocktail peanuts
15/8-oz. pkg. chili seasoning mix

1. Pour butter over nuts in slow cooker. Sprinkle in dry chili mix. Toss together.
2. Cover. Heat on Low 2-21/2 hours. Turn to High. Remove lid and cook 10-15 minutes.
3. Serve warm or cool.

Exchange List Values: Fat 1.0

Basic Nutritional Values: Calories 56 (Calories from Fat 43), Total Fat 5 gm (Saturated Fat 1.0 gm, Polyunsat Fat 1.4 gm, Monounsat Fat 2.3 gm, Cholesterol 2 mg), Sodium 104 mg, Total Carbohydrate 2 gm, Dietary Fiber 1 gm, Sugars 0 gm, Protein 2 gm

Baked Brie with Cranberry Chutney

Amymarlene Jensen
Fountain, CO

Makes 25 servings
(Ideal slow cooker size: 1-quart)

1 cup fresh, or dried,
  cranberries
1/2 cup brown sugar
1/3 cup cider vinegar
2 Tbsp. water, or orange
  juice
2 tsp. minced crystallized
  ginger
1/4 tsp. cinnamon
1/8 tsp. ground cloves
oil
8-oz. round of Brie cheese
1 Tbsp. sliced almonds,
  toasted

1. Mix together cran-
berries, brown sugar, vinegar,
water or juice, ginger,
cinnamon, and cloves in slow
cooker.
2. Cover. Cook on Low 4
hours. Stir once near the end
to see if it is thickening. If
not, remove top, turn heat to
High and cook 30 minutes
without lid.
3. Put cranberry chutney
in covered container and chill
for up to 2 weeks. When
ready to serve, bring to room
temperature.
4. Brush ovenproof plate
with vegetable oil, place
unpeeled Brie on plate, and
bake uncovered at 350° for 9
minutes, until cheese is soft

and partially melted. Remove
from oven.
5. Top with half the
chutney and garnish with
almonds. Serve with crackers.

Exchange List Values: Fat
1.0

Basic Nutritional Values: Calories
38 (Calories from Fat 23), Total Fat 3
gm (Saturated Fat 1.5 gm, Polyunsat
Fat 0.1 gm, Monounsat Fat 0.8 gm,
Cholesterol 8 mg), Sodium 67 mg, Total
Carbohydrate 3 gm, Dietary Fiber 0
gm, Sugars 3 gm, Protein 1 gm

Curried Almonds

Barbara Aston, Ashdown, AR

Makes 64 (1 Tbsp.) servings
(Ideal slow cooker size: 3-quart)

2 Tbsp. melted butter
1 Tbsp. curry powder
1/2 tsp. seasoned salt
1 lb. blanched almonds

1. Combine butter with
curry powder and seasoned
salt.
2. Pour over almonds in
slow cooker. Mix to coat well.
3. Cover. Cook on Low 2-3
hours. Turn to High. Uncover
cooker and cook 1-1 1/2 hours.
4. Serve hot or cold.

Exchange List Values: Fat
1.0

Basic Nutritional Values: Calories
45 (Calories from Fat 36), Total Fat 4
gm (Saturated Fat 0.5 gm, Polyunsat

Fat 0.9 gm, Monounsat Fat 2.4 gm,
Cholesterol 1 mg), Sodium 18 mg, Total
Carbohydrate 1 gm, Dietary Fiber 1
gm, Sugars 0 gm, Protein 2 gm

Hot Artichoke Dip

Mary E. Wheatley, Mashpee, MA

Makes 30 (1/4 cup) servings
(Ideal slow cooker size: 4-quart)

2 14 3/4-oz. jars marinated
  artichoke hearts,
  drained
1 cup fat-free mayonnaise
1 cup fat-free sour cream
1 cup water chestnuts,
  chopped
2 cups freshly grated
  Parmesan cheese
1/4 cup finely chopped
  scallions

1. Cut artichoke hearts
into small pieces. Add
mayonnaise, sour cream,
water chestnuts, cheese, and
scallions. Pour into slow
cooker.
2. Cover. Cook on High 1-2
hours or on Low 3-4 hours.
3. Serve with crackers or
crusty French bread.

Exchange List Values:
Carbohydrate 0.5, Fat 0.5

Basic Nutritional Values: Calories
57 (Calories from Fat 26), Total Fat 3
gm (Saturated Fat 1.2 gm, Polyunsat
Fat 0.7 gm, Monounsat Fat 0.9 gm,
Cholesterol 6 mg), Sodium 170
mg, Total Carbohydrate 5 gm, Dietary
Fiber 0 gm, Sugars 2 gm, Protein 3 gm

Artichokes

Susan Yoder Graber, Eureka, IL

Makes 4 servings
(Ideal slow cooker size: 3-quart)

4 artichokes
1 tsp. salt
2 Tbsp. lemon juice

1. Wash and trim artichokes by cutting off the stems flush with the bottoms of the artichokes and by cutting 3/4-1 inch off the tops. Stand upright in slow cooker.
2. Mix together salt and lemon juice and pour over artichokes. Pour in water to cover 3/4 of artichokes.
3. Cover. Cook on Low 8-10 hours, or High 2-4 hours.
4. Serve with melted butter. Pull off individual leaves and dip bottom of each into butter. Using your teeth, strip the individual leaf of the meaty portion at the bottom of each leaf.

Exchange List Values:
Vegetable 3.0

Basic Nutritional Values: Calories 60 (Calories from Fat 2), Total Fat 0 gm (Saturated Fat 0.0 gm, Polyunsat Fat 0.1 gm, Monounsat Fat 0.0 gm, Cholesterol 0 mg), Sodium 397 mg, Total Carbohydrate 13 gm, Dietary Fiber 6 gm, Sugars 1 gm, Protein 4 gm

Note: 3 vegetable exchanges = 1 carbohydrate exchange

All-American Snack

Doris M. Coyle-Zipp
South Ozone Park, NY
Melissa Raber
Millersburg, OH
Ada Miller
Sugarcreek, OH
Nanci Keatley
Salem, OR

Makes 48 (1/4 cup) servings
(Ideal slow cooker size: 4-quart)

3 cups thin pretzel sticks
4 cups Wheat Chex
4 cups Cheerios
12-oz. can salted peanuts
1/4 cup melted butter, or margarine
1 tsp. garlic powder
1 tsp. celery salt
1/2 tsp. seasoned salt
2 Tbsp. grated Parmesan cheese

1. Combine pretzels, cereal, and peanuts in large bowl.
2. Melt butter. Stir in garlic powder, celery salt, seasoned salt, and Parmesan cheese. Pour over pretzels and cereal. Toss until well mixed.
3. Pour into large slow cooker. Cover. Cook on Low 2½ hours, stirring every 30 minutes. Remove lid and cook another 30 minutes on Low.
4. Serve warm or at room temperature. Store in tightly covered container.

Exchange List Values:
Starch 0.5, Fat 1.0

Basic Nutritional Values: Calories 77 (Calories from Fat 44), Total Fat 5 gm (Saturated Fat 1.2 gm, Polyunsat Fat 1.2 gm, Monounsat Fat 2.1 gm, Cholesterol 3 mg), Sodium 174 mg, Total Carbohydrate 7 gm, Dietary Fiber 1 gm, Sugars 1 gm, Protein 3 gm

Variations:
1. Use 3 cups Wheat Chex (instead of 4 cups) and 3 cups Cheerios (instead of 4 cups). Add 3 cups Corn Chex.
Marcia S. Myer
Manheim, PA

2. Alter the amounts of pretzels, cereal, and peanuts to reflect your preferences.

Use moisturizing soaps instead of deodorant soaps to avoid drying out your skin.

233

Snack Mix

Yvonne Boettger
Harrisonburg, VA

Makes 28 servings
(Ideal slow cooker size: 5-quart)

8 cups Chex cereal, of any
  combination
6 cups from the following:
  pretzels, snack crackers,
  goldfish, Cheerios, nuts,
  bagel chips, toasted corn
6 Tbsp. light, soft tub
  margarine, melted
2 Tbsp. Worcestershire
  sauce
1 tsp. seasoning salt
1/2 tsp. garlic powder
1/2 tsp. onion salt
1/2 tsp. onion powder

1. Combine first two
ingredients in slow cooker.
  2. Combine margarine and
seasonings. Pour over dry
mixture. Toss until well
mixed.
  3. Cover. Cook on Low
2 hours, stirring every 30
minutes.

Exchange List Values:
Starch 1.0, Fat 1.0

Basic Nutritional Values: Calories
110 (Calories from Fat 48), Total Fat
5 gm (Saturated Fat 1.3 gm,
Polyunsat Fat 1.1 gm, Monounsat Fat
2.9 gm, Cholesterol 1 mg), Sodium
278 mg, Total Carbohydrate 14 gm,
Dietary Fiber 2 gm, Sugars 2 gm,
Protein 2 gm

Rhonda's Apple Butter

Rhonda Burgoon
Collingswood, NJ

Makes 24 (2 Tbsp.) servings
(Ideal slow cooker size: 3-quart)

4 lbs. apples
2 tsp. cinnamon
1/2 tsp. ground cloves

1. Core, peel, and slice
apples. Place in slow cooker.
  2. Cover. Cook on High 2-3
hours. Reduce to Low and
cook 8 hours. Apples should
be a rich brown and be
cooked down by half.
  3. Stir in spices. Cook on
High 2-3 hours with lid off.
Stir until smooth.
  4. Pour into freezer containers and freeze, or into
sterilized jars and seal.

Exchange List Values:
Fruit 0.5

Basic Nutritional Values: Calories
37 (Calories from Fat 2), Total Fat 0
gm (Saturated Fat 0.0 gm, Polyunsat
Fat 0.1 gm, Monounsat Fat 0.0 gm,
Cholesterol 0 mg), Sodium 0 mg, Total
Carbohydrate 10 gm, Dietary Fiber 1
gm, Sugars 8 gm, Protein 0 gm

Shirley's Apple Butter

Shirley Sears
Tiskilwa, IL

Makes 96 (2 Tbsp.) servings
(6 pints total)
(Ideal slow cooker size: 6-quart)

4 qts. peeled tart apples,
  finely chopped
1 1/2 cups sugar
sugar substitute to equal
  3/4 cup
2 3/4 tsp. cinnamon
1/4 tsp. ground cloves
1/8 tsp. salt

1. Pour apples into slow
cooker.
  2. Combine remaining
ingredients. Drizzle over
apples.
  3. Cover. Cook on High 3
hours, stirring well with a
large spoon every hour.
Reduce heat to Low and cook
10-12 hours, until butter
becomes thick and dark in
color. Stir occasionally with a
strong wire whisk for smooth
butter.
  4. Freeze or pour into sterilized jars and seal.

Exchange List Values:
Carbohydrate 0.5

Basic Nutritional Values: Calories
24 (Calories from Fat 1), Total Fat 0
gm (Saturated Fat 0.0 gm, Polyunsat
Fat 0.0 gm, Monounsat Fat 0.0 gm,
Cholesterol 0 mg), Sodium 3 mg, Total
Carbohydrate 6 gm, Dietary Fiber 0
gm, Sugars 6 gm, Protein 0 gm

Ann's Apple Butter
Ann Bender
Ft. Defiance, VA

*Makes 32 (2 Tbsp.) servings
(Ideal slow cooker size: 3-quart)*

7 cups unsweetened
   applesauce
1 cup sugar
sugar substitute to equal
   1/2 cup
2 tsp. cinnamon
1 tsp. ground nutmeg
1/4 tsp. allspice

1. Combine all ingredients
in slow cooker.
2. Put a layer of paper
towels under lid to prevent
condensation from dripping
into apple butter. Cook on
High 8-10 hours. Remove lid
during last hour. Stir occasionally.

Exchange List Values:
Carbohydrate 1.0

Basic Nutritional Values: Calories
48 (Calories from Fat 1), Total Fat 0
gm (Saturated Fat 0.0 gm, Polyunsat
Fat 0.0 gm, Monounsat Fat 0.0 gm,
Cholesterol 0 mg), Sodium 1 mg, Total
Carbohydrate 13 gm, Dietary Fiber 1
gm, Sugars 11 gm, Protein 0 gm

*Variation: Use canned
peaches, pears, or apricots in
place of applesauce.*

Pear Butter
Betty Moore
Plano, IL

*Makes 40 (2 Tbsp.) servings
(Ideal slow cooker size: 4-quart)*

10 large pears (about 4
   lbs.)
1 cup orange juice
1 cup sugar
sugar substitute to equal
   1/2 cup
1 tsp. ground cinnamon
1 tsp. ground cloves
1/2 tsp. ground allspice

1. Peel and quarter pears.
Place in slow cooker.
2. Cover. Cook on Low 10-
12 hours. Drain and then
discard liquid.
3. Mash or puree pears.
Add remaining ingredients.
Mix well and return to slow
cooker.
4. Cover. Cook on High 1
hour.
5. Place in hot sterile jars
and seal. Process in hot water
bath for 10 minutes. Allow to
cool undisturbed for 24
hours.

Exchange List Values:
Carbohydrate 1.0

Basic Nutritional Values: Calories
56 (Calories from Fat 2), Total Fat 0
gm (Saturated Fat 0.0 gm, Polyunsat
Fat 0.0 gm, Monounsat Fat 0.0 gm,
Cholesterol 0 mg), Sodium 0 mg, Total
Carbohydrate 14 gm, Dietary Fiber 1
gm, Sugars 13 gm, Protein 0 gm

Peach or Apricot Butter
Charlotte Shaffer
East Earl, PA

*Makes 48 (2 Tbsp.) servings
(Ideal slow cooker size: 4-quart)*

4 1-lb. 13-oz. cans peaches,
   or apricots
1 1/2 cups sugar
sugar substitute to equal
   3/4 cup
2 tsp. cinnamon
1 tsp. ground cloves

1. Drain fruit. Remove
pits. Puree in blender. Pour
into slow cooker.
2. Stir in remaining ingredients.
3. Cover. Cook on High
8-10 hours. Remove cover
during last half of cooking.
Stir occasionally.

Exchange List Values:
Carbohydrate 0.5

Basic Nutritional Values: Calories
39 (Calories from Fat 0), Total Fat 0
gm (Saturated Fat 0.0 gm, Polyunsat
Fat 0.0 gm, Monounsat Fat 0.0 gm,
Cholesterol 0 mg), Sodium 2 mg, Total
Carbohydrate 10 gm, Dietary Fiber 1
gm, Sugars 10 gm, Protein 0 gm

*Note: Spread on bread, or use
as a topping for ice cream or
toasted pound cake.*

Beverages

Hot Mulled Cider

Phyllis Attig, Reynolds, IL
Jean Butzer, Batavia, NY
Doris G. Herr, Manheim, PA
Mary E. Martin, Goshen, IN
Leona Miller, Millersburg, OH
Marjora Miller, Archbold, OH
Janet L. Roggie, Lowville, NY
Shirley Sears, Tiskilwa, IL
Charlotte Shaffer, East Earl, PA
Berenice M. Wagner,
Dodge City, KS
Connie B. Weaver,
Bethlehem, PA
Maryann Westerberg,
Rosamond, CA
Carole Whaling, New Tripoli, PA

Makes 16 (1/2 cup) servings
(Ideal slow cooker size: 4-quart)

1/4 cup brown sugar
2 quarts apple cider
1 tsp. whole allspice
1 1/2 tsp. whole cloves
2 cinnamon sticks
2 oranges sliced, with peels
  on

1. Combine brown sugar and cider in slow cooker.
2. Put spices in tea strainer or tie in cheesecloth. Add to slow cooker. Stir in orange slices.
3. Cover and simmer on Low 2-8 hours.

Exchange List Values:
Fruit 1.0

Basic Nutritional Values: Calories 76 (Calories from Fat 1), Total Fat 0 gm (Saturated Fat 0.0 gm, Polyunsat Fat 0.0 gm, Monounsat Fat 0.0 gm, Cholesterol 0 mg), Sodium 5 mg, Total Carbohydrate 19 gm, Dietary Fiber 0 gm, Sugars 18 gm, Protein 0 gm

Variation: Add a dash of ground nutmeg and salt.
Marsha Sabus
Fallbrook, CA

Cider Snap

Cathy Boshart, Lebanon, PA

Makes 16 servings
(Ideal slow cooker size: 4-quart)

2 qts. apple cider or apple
  juice
4 Tbsp. red cinnamon
  candies
at least 16 apple slices
at least 16 cinnamon sticks

1. Combine cider and cinnamon candies in slow cooker.
2. Cover. Cook on High for 2 hours until candies dissolve and cider is hot.
3. Ladle into mugs and serve with apple slice floaters and cinnamon stick stirrers.

Exchange List Values:
Fruit 1.5

Basic Nutritional Values: Calories 81 (Calories from Fat 1), Total Fat 0 gm (Saturated Fat 0.0 gm, Polyunsat Fat 0.0 gm, Monounsat Fat 0.0 gm, Cholesterol 0 mg), Sodium 4 mg,Total Carbohydrate 20 gm, Dietary Fiber 0 gm, Sugars 18 gm, Protein 0 gm

This is a cold-winter-night luxury. Make it in the morning and keep it on Low throughout the day so its good fragrance fills the house.

Apple-Honey Tea
Jeanne Allen, Rye, CO

*Makes 12 (1/2 cup) servings
(Ideal slow cooker size: 3-4-quart)*

**12-oz. can frozen apple juice/cider concentrate
2 Tbsp. instant tea powder
1 Tbsp. honey
1/2 tsp. ground cinnamon**

1. Reconstitute the apple juice/cider concentrate according to package directions. Pour into slow cooker.
2. Add tea powder, honey, and cinnamon. Stir to blend.
3. Heat on Low 1-2 hours. Stir well before serving since cinnamon tends to settle on bottom.

Exchange List Values:
Fruit 1.0

Basic Nutritional Values: Calories 66 (Calories from Fat 1), Total Fat 0 gm (Saturated Fat 0.0 gm, Polyunsat Fat 0.0 gm, Monounsat Fat 0.0 gm, Cholesterol 0 mg), Sodium 8 mg,Total Carbohydrate 16 gm, Dietary Fiber 0 gm, Sugars 16 gm, Protein 0 gm

Maple Mulled Cider
Leesa Lesenski
Wheately, MA

*Makes 10 servings
(Ideal slow cooker size: 4-quart)*

**1/2 gallon cider
3-4 cinnamon sticks
2 tsp. whole cloves
2 tsp. whole allspice
1-2 Tbsp. orange juice concentrate, optional
1 Tbsp. maple syrup, optional**

1. Combine ingredients in slow cooker.
2. Cover. Heat on Low for 2 hours. Serve warm.

Exchange List Values:
Fruit 1.5

Basic Nutritional Values: Calories 98 (Calories from Fat 1), Total Fat 0 gm (Saturated Fat 0.0 gm, Polyunsat Fat 0.1 gm, Monounsat Fat 0.0 gm, Cholesterol 0 mg), Sodium 7 mg,Total Carbohydrate 25 gm, Dietary Fiber 0 gm, Sugars 23 gm, Protein 0 gm

Serve at Halloween, Christmas caroling, or sledding parties.

Deep Red Apple Cider
Judi Manos
West Islip, NY

*Makes 16 (1/2 cup) servings
(Ideal slow cooker size: 4-quart)*

**5 cups apple cider
3 cups dry red wine
1/4 cup brown sugar
1/2 tsp. whole cloves
1/4 tsp. whole allspice
1 stick cinnamon**

1. Combine all ingredients in slow cooker.
2. Cover. Cook on Low 3-4 hours.
3. Remove cloves, allspice, and cinnamon before serving.

Exchange List Values:
Fruit 1.0

Basic Nutritional Values: Calories 58 (Calories from Fat 1), Total Fat 0 gm (Saturated Fat 0.0 gm, Polyunsat Fat 0.0 gm, Monounsat Fat 0.0 gm, Cholesterol 0 mg), Sodium 7 mg,Total Carbohydrate 14 gm, Dietary Fiber 0 gm, Sugars 14 gm, Protein 0 gm

Variation: You can use 8 cups apple cider and no red wine.

> **Try growing your own food—the closer to the ground it is, the better your food is going to be.**

Hot Mulled Apple Tea
Barbara Tenney
Delta, PA

*Makes 16 1-cup servings
(Ideal slow cooker size: 5-quart)*

¹/₂ gallon apple cider
¹/₂ gallon strong tea
1 sliced lemon
1 sliced orange
3 3-inch cinnamon sticks
1 Tbsp. whole cloves
1 Tbsp. allspice

1. Combine all in slow cooker.
2. Heat on Low 2 hours.

Exchange List Values:
Fruit 1.0

Basic Nutritional Values: Calories 59 (Calories from Fat 1), Total Fat 0 gm (Saturated Fat 0.0 gm, Polyunsat Fat 0.0 gm, Monounsat Fat 0.0 gm, Cholesterol 0 mg), Sodium 7 mg, Total Carbohydrate 15 gm, Dietary Fiber 0 gm, Sugars 13 gm, Protein 0 gm

Spiced Apple Cider
Janice Muller
Derwood, MD

*Makes 40 servings
(Ideal slow cooker size: 5-6-quart)*

2 sticks cinnamon
1 cup orange juice
1 tsp. cinnamon
1 tsp. ground cloves
¹/₄ cup lemon juice
2 tsp. whole cloves
1 gallon apple cider
2 tsp. ground nutmeg
¹/₂ cup pineapple juice
1 tsp. ginger
1 tsp. lemon peel
¹/₄ cup sugar
sugar substitute to equal
    ¹/₄ cup

1. Mix all ingredients in 5-6-quart slow cooker.
2. Simmer on Low 4-6 hours.

Exchange List Values:
Fruit 1.0

Basic Nutritional Values: Calories 58 (Calories from Fat 1), Total Fat 0 gm (Saturated Fat 0.0 gm, Polyunsat Fat 0.0 gm, Monounsat Fat 0.0 gm, Cholesterol 0 mg), Sodium 4 mg, Total Carbohydrate 14 gm, Dietary Fiber 0 gm, Sugars 13 gm, Protein 0 gm

Hot Wassail Drink
Dale Peterson, Rapid City, SC

*Makes 54 (¹/₂ cup) servings
(Ideal slow cooker size: 6-quart)*

12-oz. can frozen orange juice
12-oz. can frozen lemonade
2 qts. apple juice
1 cup sugar
sugar substitute to equal
    ¹/₂ cup
3 Tbsp. whole cloves
2 tbsp. ground ginger
4 tsp. ground cinnamon
10 cups hot water
6 cups strong tea

1. Mix juices, sugar, sugar substitute, and spices in slow cooker.
2. Add hot water and tea.
3. Heat on High until Hot (1-2 hours), then on Low while serving.

Exchange List Values:
Fruit 1.0

Basic Nutritional Values: Calories 61 (Calories from Fat 1), Total Fat 0 gm (Saturated Fat 0.0 gm, Polyunsat Fat 0.0 gm, Monounsat Fat 0.0 gm, Cholesterol 0 mg), Sodium 3 mg, Total Carbohydrate 16 gm, Dietary Fiber 0 gm, Sugars 15 gm, Protein 0 gm

Note: To garnish wassail with an orange, insert 10-12 ¹/₂"-long whole cloves halfway into orange. Place studded orange in flat baking pan with ¹/₄ cup water. Bake at 325°-350° for 30 minutes. Just before serving, float orange on top of wassail.

Orange Cider Punch

Naomi Ressler
Harrisonburg, VA

*Makes 16 (½ cup) servings
(Ideal slow cooker size: 4-quart)*

½ cup sugar
sugar substitute to equal
    ¼ cup
2 cinnamon sticks
1 tsp. whole nutmeg
2 cups apple cider or apple
    juice
6 cups orange juice
fresh orange

1. Combine ingredients in slow cooker.
2. Cover. Cook on Low 4-10 hours or High 2-3 hours.
3. Float thin slices of an orange in cooker before serving.

Exchange List Values:
Fruit 1.5

Basic Nutritional Values: Calories 81 (Calories from Fat 2), Total Fat 0 gm (Saturated Fat 0.0 gm, Polyunsat Fat 0.1 gm, Monounsat Fat 0.0 gm, Cholesterol 0 mg), Sodium 2 mg, Total Carbohydrate 20 gm, Dietary Fiber 0 gm, Sugars 19 gm, Protein 1 gm

Hot Cranberry Cider

Kristi See
Weskan, KS

*Makes 20 (½ cup) servings
(Ideal slow cooker size: 4-quart)*

2 qts. apple cider or apple
    juice
1 pt. cranberry juice
    cocktail
¼ cup sugar
2 cinnamon sticks
1 tsp. whole allspice
1 orange, studded with
    whole cloves
sweetener to equal 2 Tbsp.

1. Put all ingredients in slow cooker.
2. Cover. Cook on High 1 hour, then on Low 4-8 hours. Serve warm.
3. Serve with finger foods.

Exchange List Values:
Fruit 1.0

Basic Nutritional Values: Calories 71 (Calories from Fat 1), Total Fat 0 gm (Saturated Fat 0.0 gm, Polyunsat Fat 0.0 gm, Monounsat Fat 0.0 gm, Cholesterol 0 mg), Sodium 4 mg, Total Carbohydrate 18 gm, Dietary Fiber 0 gm, Sugars 17 gm, Protein 0 gm

Note: I come from a family of eight children, and every Christmas we all get together. We eat dinner, and then set around playing games and drinking Hot Cranberry Cider.

Fruity Wassail

Kelly Evenson, Pittsboro, NC

*Makes 20 servings
(Ideal slow cooker size: 6-quart)*

6 cups apple cider
1 cinnamon stick
¼ tsp. ground nutmeg
¼ cup honey
3 Tbsp. lemon juice
1 tsp. grated lemon rind
46-oz. can pineapple juice

1. Combine ingredients in slow cooker.
2. Cover. Cook on Low 1-2 hours.
3. Serve warm from slow cooker.

Exchange List Values:
Fruit 1.5

Basic Nutritional Values: Calories 85 (Calories from Fat 1), Total Fat 0 gm (Saturated Fat 0.0 gm, Polyunsat Fat 0.0 gm, Monounsat Fat 0.0 gm, Cholesterol 0 mg), Sodium 4 mg, Total Carbohydrate 21 gm, Dietary Fiber 0 gm, Sugars 20 gm, Protein 0 gm

Variation: Use 3 cups cranberry juice and reduce the amount of pineapple juice by 3 cups, to add more color and to change the flavor of the wassail.

Johnny Appleseed Tea

Sheila Plock, Boalsburg, PA

Makes 9 cups
(Ideal slow cooker size: 4-quart)

2 qts. water, divided
6 tea bags of your favorite
  flavor
6 ozs. frozen apple juice,
  thawed
3 Tbsp. packed brown
  sugar
brown sugar substitute to
  equal 2 Tbsp.

1. Bring 1 quart water to boil. Add tea bags. Remove from heat. Cover and let steep 5 minutes. Pour into slow cooker.
2. Add remaining ingredients and mix well.
3. Cover. Heat on Low until hot. Continue on Low while serving from slow cooker.

Exchange List Values:
Fruit 1.0

Basic Nutritional Values: Calories 60 (Calories from Fat 1), Total Fat 0 gm (Saturated Fat 0.0 gm, Polyunsat Fat 0.0 gm, Monounsat Fat 0.0 gm, Cholesterol 0 mg), Sodium 12 mg, Total Carbohydrate 15 gm, Dietary Fiber 0 gm, Sugars 14 gm, Protein 0 gm

I serve this wonderful hot beverage with cookies at our Open House Tea and Cookies afternoon, which I host at Christmas-time for friends and neighbors.

Hot Fruit Tea

Kelly Evenson
Pittsboro, NC

Makes 20 servings
(Ideal slow cooker size: 5-quart)

5-6 tea bags, fruit flavor of
  your choice
2 cups boiling water
³/₄ cup sugar
sugar substitute to equal
  ¹/₂ cup
2 cinnamon sticks
2¹/₂ qts. water
1¹/₄ tsp. vanilla
1¹/₄ tsp. almond extract
juice of 3 lemons
juice of 3 oranges

1. Steep tea bags in boiling water for 5 minutes.
2. Bring tea water, sugar, sugar substitute, cinnamon sticks, and 2¹/₂ qts. water to boil in saucepan. Remove from heat and add remaining ingredients.
3. Pour tea into slow cooker and keep warm there while serving.

Exchange List Values:
Carbohydrate 0.5

Basic Nutritional Values: Calories 38 (Calories from Fat 0), Total Fat 0 gm (Saturated Fat 0.0 gm, Polyunsat Fat 0.0 gm, Monounsat Fat 0.0 gm, Cholesterol 0 mg), Sodium 4 mg, Total Carbohydrate 10 gm, Dietary Fiber 0 gm, Sugars 9 gm, Protein 0 gm

Variation: Float thinly cut fresh lemon and/or orange slices in tea.

Spicy Autumn Punch

Marlene Bogard
Newton, KS

Makes 16 servings
(Ideal slow cooker size: 4-quart)

2 oranges
8 whole cloves
6 cups apple juice
1 cinnamon stick
¹/₄ tsp. ground nutmeg
3 Tbsp. lemon juice
¹/₄ cup honey
2¹/₄ cups pineapple juice

1. Press cloves into oranges. Bake at 325°-350° for 30 minutes.
2. Meanwhile, combine apple juice and cinnamon stick in slow cooker.
3. Cover. Cook on High 1 hour.
4. Add remaining ingredients except oranges.
5. Cover. Cook on Low 2-3 hours. Add oranges at end, either whole or in quarters.

Exchange List Values:
Fruit 1.5

Basic Nutritional Values: Calories 80 (Calories from Fat 1), Total Fat 0 gm (Saturated Fat 0.0 gm, Polyunsat Fat 0.0 gm, Monounsat Fat 0.0 gm, Cholesterol 0 mg), Sodium 4 mg, Total Carbohydrate 20 gm, Dietary Fiber 0 gm, Sugars 19 gm, Protein 0 gm

Hot Cranberry Tea

Sherrill Bieberly
Salina, KS

Makes 21 (²/₃-cup) servings
(Ideal slow cooker size: 4-5-quart)

¹/₂ cup sugar
sugar substitute to equal
    ¹/₄ cup
2 qts. water
3 cinnamon sticks
1 qt. cranberry juice
6-oz. can frozen orange
    juice
1¹/₄ cups water
3 Tbsp. lemon juice
fresh lemon and/or orange
    slices

1. In saucepan, mix
together sugar, sugar
substitute, 2 quarts water,
and cinnamon sticks. Bring to
boil.
2. Pour into slow cooker
along with remaining ingredients. Cover and cook on High
1 hour. Turn to Low. Serve
warm.

Exchange List Values:
Carbohydrate 1.0

Basic Nutritional Values: Calories
58 (Calories from Fat 1), Total Fat 0
gm (Saturated Fat 0.0 gm, Polyunsat
Fat 0.0 gm, Monounsat Fat 0.0 gm,
Cholesterol 0 mg), Sodium 1 mg, Total
Carbohydrate 15 gm, Dietary Fiber 0
gm, Sugars 15 gm, Protein 0 gm

Hot Cranberry Punch

Janie Steele
Moore, OK

Makes 24 (²/₃ cup) servings
(Ideal slow cooker size: 5-quart)

1 cup water
¹/₂ cup brown sugar
brown sugar substitute to
    equal ¹/₄ cup
³/₈ tsp. salt
³/₈ tsp. nutmeg
³/₈ tsp. cinnamon
³/₄ tsp. allspice
1¹/₈ tsp. cloves
46-oz. can unsweetened
    pineapple juice
64-oz. bottle cranberry
    juice cocktail
rum flavoring, optional
red food coloring, optional
24 cinnamon sticks

1. Combine water, sugar,
and sugar substitute in slow
cooker. Bring to boil.
2. Place salt and spices in
bag or tea ball. Add spice ball
to cooker.
3. Cover. Cook on High 1
hour.
4. Add juices, and rum
flavoring and food coloring, if
desired.
5. Cover. Cook on High 2-3
hours until hot.
6. Serve in cups, each with
a cinnamon-stick stirrer.

Exchange List Values:
Fruit 1.5

Basic Nutritional Values: Calories
92 (Calories from Fat 2), Total Fat 0
gm (Saturated Fat 0.0 gm, Polyunsat
Fat 0.1 gm, Monounsat Fat 0.0 gm,
Cholesterol 0 mg), Sodium 42
mg, Total Carbohydrate 23 gm,
Dietary Fiber 0 gm, Sugars 22 gm,
Protein 0 gm

Mulled Wine

Julie McKenzie
Punxsutawney, PA

Makes 8 1-cup servings
(Ideal slow cooker size: 3-4-quart)

¹/₂ cup sugar
1¹/₂ cups boiling water
half a lemon, sliced thin
3 cinnamon sticks
3 whole cloves
1 bottle red dinner wine
    (burgundy or claret)

1. Dissolve sugar in boiling
water in saucepan.
2. Add remaining ingredi-
ents.
3. Pour into slow cooker.
Heat on Low for at least 1
hour, until wine is hot. Do
not boil.
4. Serve from cooker into
mugs.

Exchange List Values:
Carbohydrate 1.0

Basic Nutritional Values: Calories
91 (Calories from Fat 1), Total Fat 0
gm (Saturated Fat 0.0 gm, Polyunsat
Fat 0.1 gm, Monounsat Fat 0.0 gm,
Cholesterol 0 mg), Sodium 6 mg, Total
Carbohydrate 14 gm, Dietary Fiber 0
gm, Sugars 13 gm, Protein 0 gm

Christmas Wassail

Dottie Schmidt, Kansas City, MO

Makes 10 servings
(Ideal slow cooker size: 4-quart)

2 cups cranberry juice
  cocktail
3¼ cups hot water
3 Tbsp. sugar
sugar substitute to equal
  1½ Tbsp.
6-oz. can lemonade
  concentrate
1 stick cinnamon
5 whole cloves
2 oranges, cut in 10 thin
  slices

1. Combine all ingredients
except oranges in slow
cooker. Stir until sugar and
sugar substitute are dissolved.
2. Cover. Cook on High
1 hour. Strain out spices.
3. Serve hot with an orange
slice floating in each cup.

Exchange List Values:
Carbohydrate 1.5

Basic Nutritional Values: Calories
90 (Calories from Fat 3), Total Fat 0
gm (Saturated Fat 0.1 gm, Polyunsat
Fat 0.1 gm, Monounsat Fat 0.0 gm,
Cholesterol 0 mg), Sodium 5 mg, Total
Carbohydrate 24 gm, Dietary Fiber 0
gm, Sugars 22 gm, Protein 0 gm

Almond Tea

Frances Schrag
Newton, KS

Makes 12 1-cup servings
(Ideal slow cooker size: 4-quart)

10 cups boiling water
1 Tbsp. instant tea
⅔ cup lemon juice
½ cup sugar
½ cup Splenda
1 tsp. vanilla
1 tsp. almond extract

1. Mix together all ingredients in slow cooker.
2. Turn to High and heat
thoroughly (about 1 hour).
Turn to Low while serving.

Exchange List Values:
Carbohydrate 0.5

Basic Nutritional Values: Calories
40 (Calories from Fat 0), Total Fat 0
gm (Saturated Fat 0.0 gm, Polyunsat
Fat 0.0 gm, Monounsat Fat 0.0 gm,
Cholesterol 0 mg), Sodium 3 mg, Total
Carbohydrate 10 gm, Dietary Fiber 0
gm, Sugars 9 gm, Protein 0 gm

Hot (Buttered) Lemonade

Janie Steele
Moore, OK

Makes 6 servings
(Ideal slow cooker size: 4-quart)

4½ cups water
6 Tbsp. sugar
sugar substitute to equal
  3 Tbsp.
1½ tsp. grated lemon peel
¾ cup lemon juice
2 Tbsp. light, soft tub
  margarine
6 cinnamon sticks

1. Combine water, sugar,
sugar substitute, lemon peel,
lemon juice, and margarine in
slow cooker.
2. Cover. Cook on High for
2½ hours, or until well
heated through.
3. Serve very hot with a
cinnamon stick in each mug.

Exchange List Values:
Carbohydrate 1.0

Basic Nutritional Values: Calories
69 (Calories from Fat 13), Total Fat 1
gm (Saturated Fat 0.1 gm, Polyunsat
Fat 0.3 gm, Monounsat Fat 0.8 gm,
Cholesterol 0 mg), Sodium 36
mg, Total Carbohydrate 15 gm,
Dietary Fiber 0 gm, Sugars 14 gm,
Protein 0 gm

**Seek support from
family, friends, and
coworkers.**

Hot Chocolate with Stir-Ins

Stacy Schmucker Stoltzfus
Enola, PA

Makes 12 96-oz. servings
(Ideal slow cooker size: 4-5-quart)

9½ cups water
1½ cups hot chocolate mix
Stir-ins:
    smooth peanut butter
    chocolate-mint candies, chopped
    candy canes, broken
    assorted flavored syrups: hazelnut, almond, raspberry, Irish creme
    instant coffee granules
    cinnamon
    nutmeg
whipped topping
candy sprinkles

1. Pour water into slow cooker. Heat on High 1-2 hours. (Or heat water in tea kettle and pour into slow cooker.) Turn cooker to Low to keep hot for hours.
2. Stir in hot chocolate mix until blended.
3. Arrange stir-ins in small bowls.
4. Instruct guests to place approximately 1 Tbsp. of desired stir-in in mug before ladling in hot chocolate. Stir well.
5. Top with whipped topping and candy sprinkles.

Exchange List Values:
Carbohydrate 1.0

Basic Nutritional Values: Calories 63 (Calories from Fat 14), Total Fat 2 gm (Saturated Fat 0.3 gm, Polyunsat Fat 0.4 gm, Monounsat Fat 0.7 gm, Cholesterol 0 mg), Sodium 32 mg, Total Carbohydrate 12 gm, Dietary Fiber 0 gm, Sugars 3 gm, Protein 1 gm

Note: 1 serving of each stir-in was used in the nutritional analysis.

Crockery Cocoa

Betty Hostetler
Allensville, PA

Makes 12 servings, depending on size of mugs
(Ideal slow cooker size: 4-5-quart)

½ cup sugar
½ cup unsweetened cocoa powder
2 cups boiling water
3½ cups nonfat dry milk powder
6 cups water
1 tsp. vanilla
1 tsp. ground cinnamon

1. Combine sugar and cocoa powder in slow cooker. Add 2 cups boiling water. Stir well to dissolve.
2. Add dry milk powder, 6 cups water, and vanilla. Stir well to dissolve.
3. Cover. Cook on Low 4 hours or High 1-1½ hours.

4. Before serving, beat with rotary beater to make frothy. Ladle into mugs. Top with marshmallows and sprinkle with cinnamon, if you wish.

Exchange List Values:
Milk, fat-free 1.0,
Carbohydrate 0.5

Basic Nutritional Values: Calories 111 (Calories from Fat 6), Total Fat 1 gm (Saturated Fat 0.3 gm, Polyunsat Fat 0.0 gm, Monounsat Fat 0.2 gm, Cholesterol 4 mg), Sodium 110 mg, Total Carbohydrate 21 gm, Dietary Fiber 1 gm, Sugars 19 gm, Protein 8 gm

Variations:
1. Add ⅛ tsp. ground nutmeg, along with ground cinnamon in Step 4.
2. Mocha-style—Stir ¾ tsp. coffee crystals into each serving in Step 4.
3. Coffee-Cocoa—Pour half-cups of freshly brewed, High quality coffee; top with half-cups of Crockery Cocoa.

Breakfast

Welsh Rarebit

Sharon Timpe
Mequon, WI

Makes 16 servings
(Ideal slow cooker size: 3-4-quart)

12-oz. can beer
1 Tbsp. dry mustard
1 tsp. Worcestershire sauce
1/8 tsp. black, or white, pepper
8 ozs. reduced-fat American cheese, cubed
8 ozs. reduced-fat sharp cheddar cheese, cubed
English muffins, or toast, optional
bacon, cooked until crisp, optional
tomato slices, optional
fresh steamed asparagus spears, optional

1. In slow cooker, combine beer, mustard, Worcestershire sauce, and pepper.
2. Cover and cook on High 1-2 hours, until mixture boils.
3. Add cheese, a little at a time, stirring constantly until all the cheese melts.
4. Heat on High 20-30 minutes with cover off, stirring frequently.
5. Serve hot over toasted English muffins or over toasted bread cut into triangles. Garnish with strips of crisp bacon and tomato slices or asparagus spears.

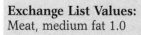

Exchange List Values:
Meat, medium fat 1.0

Basic Nutritional Values: Calories 69 (Calories from Fat 46), Total Fat 5 gm (Saturated Fat 3.0 gm, Polyunsat Fat 0.1 gm, Monounsat Fat 1.5 gm, Cholesterol 17 mg), Sodium 317 mg, Total Carbohydrate 2 gm, Dietary Fiber 0 gm, Sugars 2 gm, Protein 6 gm

Note: If Rarebit is left in slow cooker after it has cooked (Step 4), it will begin to curdle.

This is a good dish for brunch with fresh fruit, juice, and coffee. Also makes a great lunch or late-night light supper. Serve with a tossed green salad, especially fresh spinach and orange slices with a vinaigrette dressing.

Cheese Souffle Casserole

Iva Schmidt, Fergus Falls, MN

Makes 6 servings
(Ideal slow cooker size: 3-4-quart)

8 slices bread (crusts removed), cubed or torn into squares
2 cups (8 ozs.) grated fat-free cheddar cheese
1 cup cooked, chopped extra-lean, lower-sodium ham
4 eggs
1 cup fat-free half-and-half
1 cup fat-free evaporated milk
1 Tbsp. parsley
paprika

1. Lightly grease slow cooker. Alternate layers of bread and cheese and ham.
2. Beat together eggs, half-and-half, milk, and parsley. Pour over bread in slow cooker.
3. Sprinkle with paprika.
4. Cover and cook on Low 3-4 hours. (The longer cooking time yields a firmer, dryer dish.)
5. About 30 minutes before finish, increase temperature to High and remove lid.

Exchange List Values:
Starch 1.0, Milk, fat-free 0.5, Meat, lean 2.0

Basic Nutritional Values: Calories 233 (Calories from Fat 46), Total Fat 5 gm (Saturated Fat 1.9 gm, Polyunsat Fat 0.9 gm, Monounsat Fat 1.6 gm, Cholesterol 159 mg), Sodium 650 mg, Total Carbohydrate 22 gm, Dietary Fiber 0 gm, Sugars 9 gm, Protein 23 gm

Breakfast Casserole

Shirley Hinh
Wayland, IA

Makes 10 servings
(Ideal slow cooker size: 4-quart)

4 eggs, beaten
4 egg whites, lightly beaten
1/3 lb. little smokies (cocktail wieners)
1 1/2 cups fat-free milk
1 cup shredded fat-free cheddar cheese
8 slices bread, torn into pieces
1/2 tsp. dry mustard
1 cup shredded reduced-fat mozzarella cheese

1. Mix together all ingredients except cheese. Pour into greased slow cooker.
2. Sprinkle mozzarella cheese over top.
3. Cover and cook 2 hours on High, and then 1 hour on Low.

Exchange List Values:
Starch 1.0, Meat, medium fat 1.0, Fat 1.0

Basic Nutritional Values: Calories 194 (Calories from Fat 76), Total Fat 8 gm (Saturated Fat 3.4 gm, Polyunsat Fat 1.2 gm, Monounsat Fat 3.1 gm, Cholesterol 103 mg), Sodium 485 mg, Total Carbohydrate 13 gm, Dietary Fiber 0 gm, Sugars 4 gm, Protein 15 gm

Egg and Cheese Bake

Evie Hershey
Atglen, PA

Makes 6 servings
(Ideal slow cooker size: 4-quart)

3 cups toasted bread cubes
1 1/2 cups shredded reduced-fat sharp cheddar cheese
fried, crumbled bacon, or ham chunks, optional
4 eggs, beaten
4 egg whites
3 cups fat-free milk
1/4 tsp. pepper

1. Combine bread cubes, cheese, and meat in greased slow cooker.
2. Mix together eggs, milk, and pepper. Pour over bread.
3. Cook on Low 4-6 hours.

Exchange List Values:
Starch 1.0, Milk, fat-free 0.5, Meat, medium fat 1.0

Basic Nutritional Values: Calories 193 (Calories from Fat 65), Total Fat 7 gm (Saturated Fat 3.3 gm, Polyunsat Fat 1.0 gm, Monounsat Fat 2.3 gm, Cholesterol 155 mg), Sodium 377 mg, Total Carbohydrate 18 gm, Dietary Fiber 1 gm, Sugars 8 gm, Protein 16 gm

Egg and Broccoli Casserole

Joette Droz
Kalona, IA

Makes 8 servings
(Ideal slow cooker size: 4-quart)

24-oz. carton small-curd low-fat (1% milkfat) cottage cheese
10-oz. pkg. frozen chopped broccoli, thawed and drained
1½ cups (6 ozs.) shredded cheddar cheese
6 eggs, beaten
⅓ cup flour
2 Tbsp. canola oil
3 Tbsp. finely chopped onion
shredded cheese, optional

1. Combine first 7 ingredients. Pour into greased slow cooker.
2. Cover and cook on High 1 hour. Stir. Reduce heat to Low. Cover and cook 2½-3 hours, or until temperature reaches 160° and eggs are set.
3. Sprinkle with cheese, if you wish, and serve.

Exchange List Values:
Carbohydrate 0.5, Meat, lean 3.0

Basic Nutritional Values: Calories 211 (Calories from Fat 74), Total Fat 8 gm (Saturated Fat 2.3 gm, Polyunsat Fat 1.6 gm, Monounsat Fat 3.7 gm, Cholesterol 165 mg), Sodium 550 mg, Total Carbohydrate 10 gm, Dietary Fiber 1 gm, Sugars 5 gm, Protein 23 gm

Breakfast Skillet

Sue Hamilton
Minooka, IL

Makes 6 servings
(Ideal slow cooker size: 4-quart)

3 cups non-fat milk
5½-oz. box au gratin potatoes
1 tsp. hot sauce
5 eggs, lightly beaten
1 Tbsp. prepared mustard
4-oz. can sliced mushrooms
4 slices bacon, fried and crumbled
1 cup fat-free cheddar cheese, shredded

1. Combine milk, au gratin-sauce packet, hot sauce, eggs, and mustard.
2. Stir in dried potatoes, mushrooms, and bacon.
3. Cover. Cook on High 2½-3 hours or on Low 5-6 hours.
4. Sprinkle cheese over top. Cover until cheese melts.

Exchange List Values:
Starch 1.5, Milk, fat-free 0.5, Meat, lean 2.0

Basic Nutritional Values: Calories 251 (Calories from Fat 67), Total Fat 7 gm (Saturated Fat 3.1 gm, Polyunsat Fat 0.9 gm, Monounsat Fat 2.9 gm, Cholesterol 185 mg), Sodium 941 mg, Total Carbohydrate 29 gm, Dietary Fiber 2 gm, Sugars 9 gm, Protein 20 gm

Western Omelet Casserole

Mary Louise Martin
Boyd, WI

Makes 10 servings
(Ideal slow cooker size: 4-5-quart)

32-oz. bag frozen hash brown potatoes
8 ozs. extra lean, lower sodium cooked ham, cubed
1 medium onion, diced
1½ cups shredded fat-free cheddar cheese
12 eggs
1 cup fat-free milk
½ tsp. salt
1 tsp. pepper

1. Layer one-third each of frozen potatoes, ham, onions, and cheese in bottom of slow cooker. Repeat 2 times.
2. Beat together eggs, milk, salt, and pepper. Pour over mixture in slow cooker.
3. Cover. Cook on Low 8-9 hours.
4. Serve with orange juice and fresh fruit.

Exchange List Values:
Starch 1.5, Meat, lean 2.0

Basic Nutritional Values: Calories 237 (Calories from Fat 63), Total Fat 7 gm (Saturated Fat 2.7 gm, Polyunsat Fat 1.2 gm, Monounsat Fat 2.5 gm, Cholesterol 268 mg), Sodium 563 mg, Total Carbohydrate 24 gm, Dietary Fiber 2 gm, Sugars 5 gm, Protein 20 gm

Mexican-Style Grits

Mary Sommerfeld
Lancaster, PA

Makes 10-12 servings
(Ideal slow cooker size: 4-quart)

1¹/₂ cups instant grits
4 ozs. fat-free cheddar
   cheese, cubed
¹/₂ tsp. garlic powder
2 4-oz. cans diced chilies
2 Tbsp. light, soft tub
   margarine

1. Prepare grits according to package directions.
2. Stir in cheese, garlic powder, and chilies, until cheese is melted.
3. Stir in margarine. Pour into greased slow cooker.
4. Cover. Cook on High 2-3 hours or on Low 4-6 hours.

Exchange List Values:
Starch 1.0

Basic Nutritional Values: Calories 91 (Calories from Fat 9), Total Fat 1 gm (Saturated Fat 0.1 gm, Polyunsat Fat 0.3 gm, Monounsat Fat 0.5 gm, Cholesterol 1 mg), Sodium 167 mg, Total Carbohydrate 16 gm, Dietary Fiber 2 gm, Sugars 0 gm, Protein 5 gm

Creamy Old-Fashioned Oatmeal

Mary Wheatley
Mashpee, MA

Makes 5 servings
(Ideal slow cooker size: 3-quart)

1¹/₃ cups dry old-fashioned
   rolled oats
2¹/₂ cups, plus 1 Tbsp.,
   water
dash of salt

1. Mix together cereal, water, and salt in slow cooker.
2. Cook on Low 6 hours.

Exchange List Values:
Starch 1.0

Basic Nutritional Values: Calories 83 (Calories from Fat 12), Total Fat 1 gm (Saturated Fat 0.3 gm, Polyunsat Fat 0.5 gm, Monounsat Fat 0.4 gm, Cholesterol 0 mg), Sodium 1 mg, Total Carbohydrate 14 gm, Dietary Fiber 2 gm, Sugars 0 gm, Protein 3 gm

Variation: Before cooking, stir in a few chopped dates or raisins for each serving, if you wish.
Cathy Boshart
Lebanon, PA

> **Get plenty of sleep—it revitalizes your body and your mind.**

Apple Oatmeal

Frances B. Musser
Newmanstown, PA

Makes 4-5 servings
(Ideal slow cooker size: 3-quart)

2 cups fat-free milk
1 Tbsp. honey
1 Tbsp. light, soft tub
   margarine
¹/₄ tsp. salt
¹/₂ tsp. cinnamon
1 cup dry old-fashioned
   oats
1 cup chopped apples
¹/₂ cup chopped walnuts
1 Tbsp. brown sugar
brown sugar substitute to
   equal ¹/₂ Tbsp.

1. Mix together all ingredients in greased slow cooker.
2. Cover. Cook on Low 5-6 hours.
3. Serve with milk or ice cream.

Exchange List Values:
Carbohydrate 2.0, Fat 1.5

Basic Nutritional Values: Calories 220 (Calories from Fat 89), Total Fat 10 gm (Saturated Fat 1.1 gm, Polyunsat Fat 6.3 gm, Monounsat Fat 1.9 gm, Cholesterol 2 mg), Sodium 180 mg, Total Carbohydrate 28 gm, Dietary Fiber 3 gm, Sugars 15 gm, Protein 8 gm

Variation: Add ¹/₂ cup light or dark raisins to mixture.
Jeanette Oberholtzer
Manheim, PA

Peanut Butter Granola

Dawn Ranck, Harrisonburg, VA

Makes 26 servings
(Ideal slow cooker size: 5-quart)

6 cups dry oatmeal
1/2 cup wheat germ
1/4 cup toasted coconut
1/4 cup sunflower seeds
1/2 cup raisins
8 Tbsp. light, soft tub
   margarine
3/4 cup peanut butter
1/2 cup brown sugar
brown sugar substitute to
   equal 4 Tbsp.

1. Combine oatmeal, wheat germ, coconut, sunflower seeds, and raisins in large slow cooker.
2. Melt together margarine, peanut butter, brown sugar, and sugar substitute. Pour over oatmeal in cooker. Mix well.
3. Cover. Cook on Low 1 1/2 hours, stirring every 15 minutes.
4. Allow to cool in cooker, stirring every 30 minutes or so, or spread onto cookie sheet. When thoroughly cooled, break into chunks and store in airtight container.

Exchange List Values:
Starch 0.5, Carbohydrate 1.0, Fat 1.5

Basic Nutritional Values: Calories 179 (Calories from Fat 73), Total Fat 8 gm (Saturated Fat 1.5 gm, Polyunsat Fat 2.8 gm, Monounsat Fat 3.3 gm, Cholesterol 0 mg), Sodium 70 mg, Total Carbohydrate 22 gm, Dietary Fiber 3 gm, Sugars 7 gm, Protein 6 gm

Breakfast Apple Cobbler

Anona M. Teel
Banga, PA

Makes 6-8 servings
(Ideal slow cooker size: 4-5-quart)

8 medium apples, cored, peeled, sliced
2 Tbsp. sugar
sugar substitute to equal 1 Tbsp.
dash of cinnamon
juice of 1 lemon
2 Tbsp. light, soft tub margarine, melted
2 cups granola

1. Combine ingredients in slow cooker.
2. Cover. Cook on Low 7-9 hours (while you sleep!), or on High 2-3 hours (after you're up in the morning).

Exchange List Values:
Starch 1.5, Fruit 1.5, Fat 1.0

Basic Nutritional Values: Calories 221 (Calories from Fat 57), Total Fat 6 gm (Saturated Fat 2.1 gm, Polyunsat Fat 1.9 gm, Monounsat Fat 1.7 gm, Cholesterol 0 mg), Sodium 102 mg, Total Carbohydrate 42 gm, Dietary Fiber 4 gm, Sugars 29 gm, Protein 2 gm

Dulce Leche (Sweet Milk)

Dorothy Horst, Tiskilwa, IL

Makes 38 (1 Tbsp.) servings
(Ideal slow cooker size: 3-4-quart)

2 14-oz. cans fat-free sweetened condensed milk

1. Place unopened cans of milk in slow cooker. Fill cooker with warm water so that it comes above the cans by 1 1/2-2 inches.
2. Cover cooker. Cook on High 2 hours.
3. Cool unopened cans.
4. When opened, the contents should be thick and spreadable. Use as a filling between 2 cookies or crackers.

Exchange List Values:
Carbohydrate 1.0

Basic Nutritional Values: Calories 58 (Calories from Fat 0), Total Fat 0 gm (Saturated Fat 0.0 gm, Polyunsat Fat 0.1 gm, Monounsat Fat 0.5 gm, Cholesterol 0 mg), Sodium 21 mg, Total Carbohydrate 13 gm, Dietary Fiber 0 gm, Sugars 13 gm, Protein 2 gm

When on a tour in Argentina, we were served this at breakfast-time as a spread on toast or thick slices of bread. We were also presented with a container of prepared Dulce Leche as a parting gift to take home. This dish also sometimes appears on Mexican menus.

Breads

Boston Brown Bread

Jean Butzer
Batavia, NY

Makes 21 servings (3 loaves)
(Ideal slow cooker size: 6-quart)

3 16-oz. vegetable cans,
    cleaned and emptied
1/2 cup rye flour
1/2 cup yellow cornmeal
1/2 cup whole wheat flour
3 Tbsp. sugar
1 tsp. baking soda
3/4 tsp. salt
1/2 cup chopped walnuts
1/2 cup raisins
1 cup low-fat buttermilk*
1/3 cup molasses

1. Spray insides of
vegetable cans, and one side
of 3 6"-square pieces of foil,
with nonstick cooking spray.
Set aside.
2. Combine rye flour,
cornmeal, whole wheat flour,
sugar, baking soda, and salt
in a large bowl.
3. Stir in walnuts and
raisins.
4. Whisk together
buttermilk and molasses. Add
to dry ingredients. Stir until
well mixed. Spoon into
prepared cans.
5. Place one piece of foil,
greased side down, on top of
each can. Secure foil with
rubberbands or cotton string.
Place upright in slow cooker.
6. Pour boiling water into
slow cooker to come halfway
up sides of cans. (Make sure
foil tops do not touch boiling
water).
7. Cover cooker. Cook on
Low 4 hours, or until skewer
inserted in center of bread
comes out clean.
8. To remove bread, lay
cans on their sides. Roll and
tap gently on all sides until
bread releases. Cool
completely on wire racks.
9. Serve with butter or
cream cheese and bowls of
soup.

Exchange List Values:
Carbohydrate 1.0, Fat 0.5

Basic Nutritional Values: Calories
85 (Calories from Fat 20), Total Fat 2
gm (Saturated Fat 0.2 gm, Polyunsat
Fat 1.4 gm, Monounsat Fat 0.3 gm,
Cholesterol 0 mg), Sodium 158
mg, Total Carbohydrate 16 gm,
Dietary Fiber 2 gm, Sugars 8 gm,
Protein 2 gm

** To substitute for buttermilk,
pour 1 Tbsp. lemon juice into
1-cup measure. Add enough
milk to fill the cup. Let stand 5
minutes before mixing with
molasses.*

**Make one meal today
free of meat and cheese.
Your heart will thank
you.**

Healthy Whole Wheat Bread

Esther Becker,
Gordonville, PA

Makes 16 servings
(Ideal slow cooker size: 5-6-quart)

**2 cups warm reconstituted
fat-free powdered milk
($^2/_3$ cup powder to
1$^1/_3$ cups water)
2 Tbsp. canola oil
$^1/_4$ cup honey, or brown
sugar
$^3/_4$ tsp. salt
1 pkg. active dry yeast
2$^1/_2$ cups whole wheat
flour
1$^1/_4$ cups white flour**

1. Mix together milk, oil, honey or brown sugar, salt, yeast, and half the flour in electric mixer bowl. Beat with mixer for 2 minutes. Add remaining flour. Mix well.

2. Place dough in well-greased bread or cake pan that will fit into your cooker. Cover with greased tin foil. Let stand for 5 minutes. Place in slow cooker.

3. Cover cooker and bake on High 2$^1/_2$-3 hours. Remove pan and uncover. Let stand for 5 minutes. Serve warm.

Exchange List Values:

Basic Nutritional Values: Calories 142 (Calories from Fat 20), Total Fat 2 gm (Saturated Fat 0.1 gm, Polyunsat Fat 0.7 gm, Monounsat Fat 1.1 gm, Cholesterol 1 mg), Sodium 126 mg, Total Carbohydrate 27 gm, Dietary Fiber 3 gm, Sugars 6 gm, Protein 5 gm

Corn Bread From Scratch

Dorothy M. Van Deest
Memphis, TN

Makes 9 servings
(Ideal slow cooker size: 6-quart)

**1$^1/_4$ cups flour
$^3/_4$ cup yellow cornmeal
$^1/_4$ cup sugar
4$^1/_2$ tsp. baking powder
$^1/_2$ tsp. salt
1 egg, slightly beaten
1 cup fat-free milk
$^1/_4$ cup melted canola oil**

1. In mixing bowl sift together flour, cornmeal, sugar, baking powder, and salt. Make a well in the center.

2. Pour egg, milk, and oil into well. Mix into the dry mixture until just moistened.

3. Pour mixture into a greased 2-quart mold that will fit into your cooker. Cover with a plate. Place on a trivet or rack in the bottom of slow cooker.

4. Cover. Cook on High 2-3 hours.

Exchange List Values:
Starch 2.0, Fat 1.0

Basic Nutritional Values: Calories 200 (Calories from Fat 64), Total Fat 7 gm (Saturated Fat 0.7 gm, Polyunsat Fat 2.1 gm, Monounsat Fat 4.0 gm, Cholesterol 24 mg), Sodium 330 mg, Total Carbohydrate 29 gm, Dietary Fiber 1 gm, Sugars 7 gm, Protein 4 gm

Lemon Bread

Ruth Ann Gingrich
New Holland, PA

Makes 12 servings
(Ideal slow cooker size: 4-quart)

**$^1/_4$ cup canola oil
6 Tbsp. sugar
sugar substitute to equal
3 Tbsp.
2 eggs, beaten
1$^2/_3$ cups flour
1$^2/_3$ tsp. baking powder
$^1/_2$ tsp. salt
$^1/_2$ cup fat-free milk
4 ozs. chopped walnuts
grated peel from 1 lemon**

**Glaze:
$^1/_4$ cup powdered sugar
juice of 1 lemon**

1. Cream together oil, sugar, and sugar substitute. Add eggs. Mix well.

2. Sift together flour, baking powder, and salt. Add flour mixture and milk alternately to shortening mixture.

3. Stir in nuts and lemon peel.

4. Spoon batter into well-greased 2-pound coffee can and cover with well-greased tin foil. Place in cooker set on High for

2-2¹/₄ hours, or until done. Remove bread from coffee can.

5. Mix together powdered sugar and lemon juice. Pour over loaf.

6. Serve plain or with cream cheese.

Exchange List Values:
Starch 1.5, Fat 1.0

Basic Nutritional Values: Calories 176 (Calories from Fat 66), Total Fat 7 gm (Saturated Fat 0.9 gm, Polyunsat Fat 2.7 gm, Monounsat Fat 3.3 gm, Cholesterol 37 mg), Sodium 168 mg, Total Carbohydrate 24 gm, Dietary Fiber 1 gm, Sugars 10 gm, Protein 4 gm

Broccoli Corn Bread

Winifred Ewy
Newton, KS

Makes 10 servings
(Ideal slow cooker size: 3-4-quart)

3 Tbsp. light, soft serve margarine, melted
10-oz. pkg. chopped broccoli, cooked and drained
1 medium onion, chopped
8¹/₂-oz. box corn bread mix
1 egg, well beaten
3 egg whites
8 ozs. 1% fat cottage cheese
¹/₈ tsp. salt

1. Combine all ingredients. Mix well.

2. Pour into greased slow cooker. Cook on Low 6 hours, or until toothpick inserted in center comes out clean.

3. Serve like spoon bread, or invert the pot, remove bread, and cut into wedges.

Exchange List Values:
Starch 1.0, Vegetable 1.0, Fat 0.5

Basic Nutritional Values: Calories 119 (Calories from Fat 34), Total Fat 4 gm (Saturated Fat 1.4 gm, Polyunsat Fat 0.6 gm, Monounsat Fat 1.4 gm, Cholesterol 22 mg), Sodium 370 mg, Total Carbohydrate 20 gm, Dietary Fiber 2 gm, Sugars 7 gm, Protein 7 gm

Date and Nut Loaf

Jean Butzer, Batavia, NY

Makes 20 servings
(Ideal slow cooker size: 6-quart)

1¹/₂ cups boiling water
1¹/₂ cups chopped dates
³/₄ cup sugar
sugar substitute to equal ¹/₄ cup
1 egg
2 tsp. baking soda
¹/₂ tsp. salt
1 tsp. vanilla
1 Tbsp. melted, light, soft tub margarine
2¹/₂ cups flour
1 cup walnuts, chopped
2 cups hot water

1. Pour 1¹/₂ cups boiling water over dates. Let stand 5-10 minutes.

2. Stir in sugar, sugar substitute, egg, baking soda, salt, vanilla, and margarine.

3. In separate bowl, combine flour and nuts. Stir into date mixture.

4. Pour into 2 greased 11¹/₂-oz. coffee cans or one 8-cup baking insert. If using coffee cans, cover with foil and tie. If using baking insert, cover with its lid. Place cans or insert on rack in slow cooker. (If you don't have a rack, use rubber jar rings instead.)

5. Pour hot water around cans, up to half their height.

6. Cover slow cooker tightly. Cook on High 3¹/₂-4 hours.

7. Remove cans or insert from cooker. Let bread stand in coffee cans or baking insert for 10 minutes. Turn out onto cooling rack. Slice. Spread with butter, cream cheese, or peanut butter, if you wish.

Exchange List Values:
Carbohydrate 2.0, Fat 0.5

Basic Nutritional Values: Calories 168 (Calories from Fat 41), Total Fat 5 gm (Saturated Fat 0.5 gm, Polyunsat Fat 3.0 gm, Monounsat Fat 0.8 gm, Cholesterol 11 mg), Sodium 193 mg, Total Carbohydrate 30 gm, Dietary Fiber 2 gm, Sugars 17 gm, Protein 3 gm

Banana Loaf

Sue Hamilton, Minooka, IL

Makes 10 servings
(Ideal slow cooker size: 4-5-quart)

3 very ripe, medium
  bananas
1/4 cup margarine, softened
2 eggs
1 tsp. vanilla
1/2 cup sugar
sugar substitute to equal
  1/4 cup
1 cup flour
1 tsp. baking soda

1. Combine all ingredients
in an electric mixing bowl.
Beat 2 minutes or until well
blended. Pour into well
greased 2-lb. coffee can.
2. Place can in slow cooker.
Cover can with 6 layers of
paper towels between cooker
lid and bread.
3. Cover cooker. Bake on
High 2-2 1/2 hours, or until
toothpick inserted in center
comes out clean. Cool 15
minutes before removing
from can.

Exchange List Values:
Carbohydrate 2.0, Fat 1.0

Basic Nutritional Values: Calories
177 (Calories from Fat 53), Total Fat 6
gm (Saturated Fat 1.3 gm, Polyunsat Fat
1.7 gm, Monounsat Fat 2.5 gm,
Cholesterol 43 mg), Sodium 192
mg, Total Carbohydrate 29 gm, Dietary
Fiber 1 gm, Sugars 16 gm, Protein 3 gm

Cheery Cherry Bread

Shirley Sears
Tiskilwa, IL

Makes 10 servings
(Ideal slow cooker size: 4-5-quart)

6-oz. jar maraschino
  cherries
1 1/2 cups flour
1 1/2 tsp. baking powder
1/4 tsp. salt
2 eggs
6 Tbsp. sugar
sugar substitute to equal
  3 Tbsp.
3/4 cup coarsely chopped
  pecans

1. Drain cherries,
reserving 1/3 cup syrup. Cut
cherries in pieces. Set aside.
2. Combine flour, baking
powder, and salt.
3. Beat eggs, sugar, and
sugar substitute together until
thickened.
4. Alternately add flour
mixture and cherry syrup to
egg mixture, mixing until well
blended after each addition.
5. Fold in cherries and
pecans. Spread in well
greased and floured baking
insert or 2-lb. coffee can. If
using baking insert, cover
with its lid; if using a coffee
can, cover with 6 layers of
paper towels. Set in slow
cooker.
6. Cover cooker. Cook on
High 2-3 hours.
7. Remove from slow
cooker. Let stand 10 minutes

before removing from pan.
  8. Cool before slicing.

Exchange List Values:
Carbohydrate 2.0, Fat 1.5

Basic Nutritional Values: Calories
213 (Calories from Fat 70), Total Fat
8 gm (Saturated Fat 1.0 gm,
Polyunsat Fat 2.1 gm, Monounsat Fat
4.3 gm, Cholesterol 43 mg), Sodium
126 mg, Total Carbohydrate 31 gm,
Dietary Fiber 2 gm, Sugars 15 gm,
Protein 4 gm

Gingerbread with Lemon Sauce

Jean Butzer, Batavia, NY
Marie Shank, Harrisonburg, VA

Makes 16 servings
(Ideal slow cooker size: 4-5-quart)

1/4 cup margarine, softened
1/4 cup sugar
sugar substitute to equal
  2 Tbsp.
1 egg, lightly beaten
1 cup sorghum molasses
2 1/2 cups flour
1 1/2 tsp. baking soda
1 tsp. cinnamon
2 tsp. ground ginger
1/2 tsp. ground cloves
1/2 tsp. salt
1 cup hot coffee, or hot
  water
1/2 cup powdered sugar
2 tsp. cornstarch
pinch of salt
juice of 2 lemons
1/2 cup water
1 Tbsp. butter
powdered sugar for garnish

1. Cream together ¼ cup margarine, sugar, and sugar substitute.

2. Add egg. Mix well.

3. Add molasses. Mix well.

4. Sift together flour, baking soda, cinnamon, ginger, cloves, and salt. Stir into creamed mixture.

5. Add coffee or 1 cup water. Beat well.

6. There are two ways to bake the gingerbread:

a. If you have a baking insert, or a 2-lb. coffee can, grease and flour the inside of it. Pour in batter. Place in slow cooker. Pour water around insert or coffee can. Cover insert with its lid, or cover coffee can with 6-8 paper towels.

b. Cut waxed paper or parchment paper to fit bottom of slow cooker. Place in bottom of cooker. Spray paper and sides of cooker's interior with nonstick cooking spray. Pour batter into preheated slow cooker.

7. Cover cooker with its lid slightly ajar to allow excess moisture to escape. Cook on High 1¾-2 hours, or on Low 3-4 hours, or until edges are golden and knife inserted in center comes out clean.

8. If you used a baking insert or coffee can, remove from cooker. Cool on cake rack. Let stand 5 minutes before running knife around outer edge of cake and inverting onto serving plate.

If you baked the gingerbread directly in the cooker, cut the cake into wedges after allowing it to cool for 30 minutes, and

carefully lift the wedges out of the cooker onto serving plates.

9. In saucepan, mix together ½ cup powdered sugar, cornstarch, and salt. Add lemon juice and ½ cup water, stirring with each addition. Cook over medium heat until thick and bubbly, about 1 minute. Remove from heat. Stir in butter.

10. If gingerbread has been cooling on a rack, cut it into wedges. To serve, top with sauce and sprinkle with powdered sugar.

Exchange List Values:
Carbohydrate 2.5, Fat 0.5

Basic Nutritional Values: Calories 198 (Calories from Fat 37), Total Fat 4 gm (Saturated Fat 1.1 gm, Polyunsat Fat 1.1 gm, Monounsat Fat 1.6 gm, Cholesterol 15 mg), Sodium 239 mg, Total Carbohydrate 38 gm, Dietary Fiber 1 gm, Sugars 23 gm, Protein 2 gm

Old-Fashioned Gingerbread

Mary Ann Westerberg
Rosamond, CA

Makes 16 servings
(Ideal slow cooker size: 4-quart)

4 Tbsp. margarine, softened
4 Tbsp. sugar
sugar substitute to equal
    2 Tbsp.
1 egg
1 cup light molasses
2½ cups flour

1½ tsp. baking soda
1 tsp. ground cinnamon
2 tsp. ground ginger
½ tsp. ground cloves
½ tsp. salt
1 cup hot water
warm applesauce, optional
whipped cream, optional
nutmeg, optional

1. Cream together margarine, sugar, and sugar substitute. Add egg and molasses. Mix well.

2. Stir in flour, baking soda, cinnamon, ginger, cloves, and salt. Mix well.

3. Add hot water. Beat well.

4. Pour batter into greased and floured 2-lb. coffee can.

5. Place can in cooker. Cover top of can with 6-8 paper towels. Cover cooker and bake on High 2½-3 hours.

6. Serve with applesauce. Top with whipped cream and sprinkle with nutmeg.

Exchange List Values:
Carbohydrate 2.0, Fat 0.5

Basic Nutritional Values: Calories 168 (Calories from Fat 30), Total Fat 3 gm (Saturated Fat 0.7 gm, Polyunsat Fat 1.0 gm, Monounsat Fat 1.4 gm, Cholesterol 13 mg), Sodium 235 mg, Total Carbohydrate 32 gm, Dietary Fiber 1 gm, Sugars 16 gm, Protein 2 gm

Low-Sodium Mixes and Sauce

Italian Seasoning Mix

Madelyn L. Wheeler, Zionsville, IN

Makes 13 (1 Tbsp.) servings

6 tsp. marjoram, dried
6 tsp. thyme leaves, dried
6 tsp. rosemary, dried
6 tsp. savory, ground
3 tsp. dry sage, ground
6 tsp. oregano leaves, dried
6 tsp. basil leaves, dried

Combine all ingredients.

Exchange List Values:
Vegetable 2.0, Meat, lean 4.0

Basic Nutritional Values: Calories 8 (Calories from Fat 2), Total Fat 0 gm (Saturated Fat 0.1 gm, Polyunsat Fat 0.1 gm, Monounsat Fat 0.0 gm, Cholesterol 0 mg), Sodium 1 mg, Total Carbohydate 2 gm, Dietary Fiber 1 gm, Sugars 0 gm, Protein 0 gm

This recipe should be made with dried leaves if available, rather than ground, except for the savory and sage.

Taco Seasoning Mix, Low-Sodium

Madelyn L. Wheeler, Zionsville, IN

Makes 3 servings; serving size is 1/3 of recipe (about 7 tsp.)

6 tsp. chili powder
5 tsp. paprika
4 1/2 tsp. cumin seed
3 tsp. onion powder
1 tsp. garlic powder
2/3 Tbsp. dry cornstarch

1. Combine all ingredients in bowl.
2. One-third of mix (about 7 tsp.) is equivalent to 1 pkg. (1.25 oz.) purchased taco seasoning mix.

Exchange List Values:
Carbohydrate 0.5

Basic Nutritional Values: Calories 56 (calories from Fat 19), Total Fat 2 gm (Saturated Fat 0.0 gm, Polyunsat Fat 0.9 gm, Monounsat Fat 0.7 gm, Cholesterol 0 mg), Sodium 61 mg, Total Carbohydrate 10 gm, Dietary Fiber 3 gm, Sugars 3 gm, Protein 2 gm

Onion Soup Mix, Salt-Free

Madelyn L. Wheeler, Zionsville, IN

Makes 1 serving (equivalent to 1 pkg. purchased dry onion soup mix)

2 2/3 Tbsp. dried onion, minced, flaked, or chopped
4 tsp. beef instant bouillon powder, sodium-free
1 tsp. onion powder
1/4 tsp. celery seed

Combine all ingredients.

Exchange List Values:
Carbohydrate 1.5

Basic Nutritional Values: Calories 106 (calories from Fat 2), Total Fat 0 gm (Saturated Fat 0.0 gm, Polyunsat Fat 0.1 gm, Monounsat Fat 0.1 gm, Cholesterol 0 mg), Sodium 5 mg, Total Carbohydrate 23 gm, Dietary Fiber 2 gm, Sugars 11 gm, Protein 2 gm

Phyllis' Homemade Barbecue Sauce

Phyllis Barrier
Little Rock, AR

Makes 16 (2 Tbsp.) servings

2 8-oz. cans tomato sauce, no-added-salt
1/4 cup cider vinegar
brown sugar substitute to equal 2 Tbsp.
1/2 cup fresh onions, minced
1 tsp. garlic powder
1/2 tsp. dry mustard powder
6 tsp. chili powder
1/8 tsp. Tabasco sauce
1/2 tsp. black pepper
6 tsp. Worcestershire sauce
1 tsp. paprika
1 tsp. liquid smoke
1/4 tsp. salt

Mix all ingredients together and cook in microwave until minced onion is tender and sauce has thickened.

Exchange List Values:
Carbohydrate 0.5

Basic Nutritional Values: Calories 24 (calories from Fat 2), Total Fat 0 gm (Saturated Fat 0.0 gm, Polyunsat Fat 0.1 gm, Monounsat Fat 0.0 gm, Cholesterol 0 mg), Sodium 81 mg, Total Carbohydrate 5 gm, Dietary Fiber 1 gm, Sugars 5 gm, Protein 0 gm

A Week of Menus

If you're trying to stick to a daily meal plan with a specific number of calories, here is help. Each day in this Week of Menus is designed with 3 meals and 2 snacks, for a total of about 1500 calories.

One or two recipes each day comes from this *Fix-It and Forget-It Diabetic Cookbook,* making it easy to eat healthfully, despite busy lives and chaotic schedules.

You'll quickly see the Exchange Value for each part of the meal, as well as the nutritional breakdown of each food. In addition, the total number of nutrients for each day's menu is given, and then compared to healthy, nutritional goals. You'll soon see how easy it is to eat well.

Saturday

Food Item	Amount to Serve	Exchanges	Cal	Carb(g)	Prot(g)	Fat(g)	Sod(mg)
BREAKFAST							
Milk, fat-free (nonfat, skim)	1 cup	1 Milk, fat-free	83	12	8	0	108
Kashi, puffed cereal	1 cup	1 Starch	70	13	3	1	2
Apricots, dried	8 halves	1 Fruit	67	18	1	0	3
Almonds, dry roasted	6 almonds	1 Fat	48	2	2	4	0
Wheat bread, toasted	1 slice		65	12	2	1	132
			333	**56**	**17**	**6**	**245**
MORNING SNACK							
Banana, fresh	1 extra small	1 Fruit	75	19	1	0	1
			75	**19**	**1**	**0**	**1**
LUNCH							
Slow-Cooker Minestrone (p 134) —lower-sodium	1 serving	1 Starch 2 Vegetable 1 Meat, lean	183	21	17	4	413
Crackers, whole wheat, reduced fat	5 Triscuits	1 Starch	80	15	2	2	110
Apple, with peel	1 small (2½" d)	1 Fruit	55	15	0	0	1
			318	**51**	**19**	**6**	**524**
AFTERNOON SNACK							
Popcorn, popped, no salt/fat added	3 cups	1 Starch	92	19	3	1	1
Nuts, mixed	6 nuts	1 Fat	37	1	1	3	26
			129	**20**	**4**	**4**	**27**
DINNER							
Pot Roast (p 12)	1 serving	1 Starch 1 Vegetable 3 Meat, lean	219	14	26	6	361
Roll, multi-grain	1 roll, medium	1½ Starch	125	23	3	2	244
Margarine, light soft tub	1 Tbsp.	1 Fat	40	0	0	4	90
Salad greens mix	2 cups	1 Vegetable	15	3	1	0	15
Salad dressing, Italian, fat-free	1 Tbsp.	Free food	7	2	0	0	155
Fresh fruit mix	¾ cup	1 Fruit	61	15	1	0	4
			468	**57**	**31**	**13**	**869**

EVENING SNACK

Milk, fat-free (nonfat, skim)	1 cup	1 Milk, fat-free	83	12	8	0	108
Oatmeal, cooked	½ cup	1 Starch	73	13	3	1	1
			156	**25**	**11**	**1**	**109**

Saturday—Totals for the Day

Nutrient	Quantity		DRI Comparison (- = Under)	% of Day's Calories	Goals
Calories	1479				1450 to 1550
Fat	31	grams		18 %	0 to 30 %
Saturated fat	8	grams		4 %	0 to 10 %
Polyunsat fat	7	grams		4 %	
Monounsat fat	14	grams		8 %	More than 10 %
Cholesterol	126	milligrams			Less than 300 mg
Sodium	1775	milligrams			0 to 2400 mg
Carbohydrate	228	grams		60 %	150 to 230 grams
Dietary fiber	30	grams			More than 17 gm
Sugars	94	grams			Less than 150 gm
Protein	82	grams	32	22 %	12 to 20 %
Calcium	726	milligrams	-474		More than 1200 mg
Carb (Breakfast)	56	grams			
Carb (AM Snack)	19	grams			
Carb (Lunch)	51	grams			
Carb (PM Snack)	20	grams			
Carb (Dinner)	57	grams			
Carb (EV Snack)	25	grams			
Glycemic index	42				
Starch	83	grams			
Phosphorus	1339	milligrams	639		More than 700 mg
Potassium	3197	milligrams			

Sunday

Food Item	Amount to Serve	Exchanges	Cal	Carb(g)	Prot(g)	Fat(g)	Sod(mg)
BREAKFAST							
Breakfast Skillet (p 246) lower fat, sat fat	1 serving	1½ Starch ½ Milk, fat-free 2 Meat, lean	251	29	20	7	941
Fresh fruit mix	¾ cup	1 Fruit	61	15	1	0	4
			312	44	21	8	945
LUNCH							
Pita bread, whole wheat	1 pita	2 Starch	140	30	5	1	130
Ham, boneless, extra-lean, lower-sodium, roasted	1 oz.	1 Meat, vy lean	30	1	5	1	230
Cheese, Monterey Jack, reduced fat	1 oz.	1 Meat, med fat	81	0	9	5	222
Tomato, cucumber, onion mix, raw	1 cup	1 Vegetable	30	7	1	0	9
Orange, fresh	1 orange	1 Fruit	62	15	1	0	0
			342	53	22	7	592
AFTERNOON SNACK							
Yogurt, nonfat, vanilla,	1 container (6 oz.)	1 Milk, fat-free	90	16	6	0	95
			90	16	6	0	95
DINNER							
Savory Slow-Cooker Chicken (p 72) —lower-sodium	1 serving	2 Vegetable 3 Meat, lean	230	11	30	7	427
Potato, mashed	½ cup	1 Starch	85	19	2	0	12
Roll, multi-grain	1 roll, medium	1½ Starch	125	23	3	2	244
Margarine, light soft tub	1 Tbsp.	1 Fat	40	0	0	4	90
Watermelon, fresh	1¼ cups	1 Fruit	61	14	1	1	4
			541	67	36	15	777
EVENING SNACK							
Milk, fat-free (nonfat, skim)	1 cup	1 Milk, fat-free	83	12	8	0	108
Wheaties	¾ cup	1 Starch	80	18	2	1	163
			163	30	11	1	271

Sunday—Totals for the Day

Nutrient	Quantity		DRI Comparison (- = Under)	% of Day's Calories	Goals
Calories	1449				1450 to 1550
Fat	31	grams		19 %	0 to 30 %
Saturated fat	11	grams		7 %	0 to 10 %
Polyunsat fat	6	grams		3 %	
Monounsat fat	11	grams		7 %	More than 10 %
Cholesterol	310	milligrams			Less than 300 mg
Sodium	2680	milligrams			0 to 2400 mg
Carbohydrate	210	grams		56 %	150 to 230 grams
Dietary fiber	20	grams			More than 17 gm
Sugars	93	grams			Less than 150 gm
Protein	95	grams	45	25 %	12 to 20 %
Calcium	1088	milligrams	-112		More than 1200 mg
Carb (Breakfast)	44	grams			
Carb (AM Snack)	0	grams			
Carb (Lunch)	53	grams			
Carb (PM Snack)	16	grams			
Carb (Dinner)	67	grams			
Carb (EV Snack)	30	grams			
Glycemic index	41				
Starch	97	grams			
Phosphorus	1602	milligrams	902		More than 700 mg
Potassium	2806	milligrams			

Monday

Food Item	Amount to Serve	Exchanges	Cal	Carb(g)	Prot(g)	Fat(g)	Sod(mg)
BREAKFAST							
Bagel, plain	½ large (4" dia)	2 Starch	155	30	6	1	302
Cream cheese, reduced-fat (neufchatel)	1½ Tbsp.	1 Fat	54	1	2	5	92
Milk, fat-free (nonfat, skim)	1 cup	1 Milk, fat-free	83	12	8	0	108
Orange juice, fresh	½ cup	1 Fruit	56	13	1	0	1
			348	**56**	**17**	**6**	**502**
LUNCH							
Southwestern Bean Soup with Cornmeal Dumpling (page 130)	1 serving	2 Starch 2 Vegetable	197	39	9	1	367
Nuts, mixed	6 nuts	1 Fat	37	1	1	3	26
Fresh fruit mix	¾ cup	1 Fruit	61	15	1	0	4
Cheese, cheddar, reduced fat	2 ozs.	2 Meat, med fat	115	1	14	12	480
			410	**56**	**25**	**17**	**877**
AFTERNOON SNACK							
Crackers, whole wheat, reduced fat (Triscuits)	5 triscuits	1 Starch	80	15	2	2	110
Sunflower seeds, dry roasted	1 Tbsp.	1 Fat	47	2	2	4	0
			127	**17**	**3**	**6**	**110**
DINNER							
Snapper, cooked	4 ozs.	4 Meat, vy lean	145	0	30	2	65
Beans, green, fresh, cooked	1 cup	2 Vegetable	44	10	2	0	4
Potato, baked with skin	6 ozs.	2 Starch	158	36	4	0	17
Margarine, light soft tub,	1 Tbsp.	1 Fat	40	0	0	4	90
Pear, fresh	½ pear	1 Fruit	62	16	0	0	0
			449	**62**	**37**	**7**	**176**
EVENING SNACK							
Yogurt, nonfat, vanilla,	1 container (6 oz.)	1 Milk, fat-free	90	16	6	0	95
Walnuts, English	4 halves	1 Fat	52	1	1	5	0
			142	**17**	**7**	**6**	**95**

Monday—Totals for the Day

Nutrient	Quantity		DRI Comparison (- = Under)	% of Day's Calories	Goals
Calories	1476				1450 to 1550
Fat	42	grams		24 %	0 to 30 %
Saturated fat	14	grams		8 %	0 to 10 %
Polyunsat fat	12	grams		7 %	
Monounsat fat	12	grams		7 %	More than 10 %
Cholesterol	117	milligrams			Less than 300 mg
Sodium	1760	milligrams			0 to 2400 mg
Carbohydrate	208	grams		53 %	150 to 230 grams
Dietary fiber	26	grams			More than 18 gm
Sugars	76	grams			Less than 150 gm
Protein	90	grams	40	23 %	12 to 20 %
Calcium	1117	milligrams	-83		More than 1200 mg
Carb (Breakfast)	56	grams			
Carb (AM Snack)	0	grams			
Carb (Lunch)	56	grams			
Carb (PM Snack)	17	grams			
Carb (Dinner)	62	grams			
Carb (EV Snack)	17	grams			
Glycemic index	46				
Starch	104	grams			
Phosphorus	1672	milligrams	972		More than 700 mg
Potassium	3855	milligrams			

Tuesday

Food Item	Amount to Serve	Exchanges	Cal	Carb(g)	Prot(g)	Fat(g)	Sod(mg)
BREAKFAST							
Wheat bread, toasted	2 slices	2 Starch	130	24	5	2	265
Margarine, light soft tub	1 Tbsp.	1 Fat	40	0	0	4	90
Jelly/preserves, low or reduced sugar	2 tsps.	Free food	16	4	0	0	0
Fresh fruit mix	¾ cup	1 Fruit	61	15	1	0	4
Milk, fat-free (nonfat, skim)	1 cup	1 Milk, fat-free	83	12	8	0	108
			330	**55**	**14**	**7**	**467**
MORNING SNACK							
Cranberries, dried	3 Tbsp.	1 Fruit	66	16	0	1	0
Walnuts, English	4 halves	1 Fat	52	1	1	5	0
			119	**17**	**1**	**6**	**0**
LUNCH							
Cottage cheese, low-fat, 1% milkfat	½ cup	2 Meat, vy lean	81	3	14	1	459
Crackers, whole wheat, reduced fat (Triscuits)	10 Triscuits	2 Starch	160	30	4	4	220
Grapes, fresh seedless, small	17 grapes	1 Fruit	60	15	1	0	2
Tomato, raw	3 slices, medium		13	3	0	0	5
			314	**51**	**19**	**6**	**686**
AFTERNOON SNACK							
Milk, fat-free (nonfat, skim)	1 cup	1 Milk, fat-free	83	12	8	0	108
Popcorn, popped, no salt/fat added	3 cups	1 Starch	92	19	3	1	1
			175	**31**	**11**	**1**	**109**
DINNER							
Turkey and Sweet Potato Casserole (page 96)	1 serving	2 Starch 1 Vegetable 4 Meat, vy lean	318	35	37	3	473
Salad greens mix	2 cups	1 Vegetable	15	3	1	0	15
Salad dressing, Italian, fat-free	1 Tbsp.	Free food	7	2	0	0	155
Cantaloupe melon, fresh	1 cup	1 Fruit	56	13	1	0	14
			397	**53**	**40**	**3**	**657**

EVENING SNACK

Crackers, graham	3 crackers	1 Starch	89	16	1	2	127
Peanut butter, smooth/crunchy	1 Tbsp.	1 Meat, high fat	96	3	4	8	80
			185	**19**	**5**	**10**	**207**

Tuesday—Totals for the Day

Nutrient	Quantity		DRI Comparison (- = Under)	% of Day's Calories	Goals
Calories	1520				1450 to 1550
Fat	34	grams		19 %	0 to 30 %
Saturated fat	7	grams		4 %	0 to 10 %
Polyunsat fat	12	grams		7 %	
Monounsat fat	12	grams		7 %	More than 10 %
Cholesterol	107	milligrams			Less than 300 mg
Sodium	2126	milligrams			0 to 2400 mg
Carbohydrate	226	grams		58 %	150 to 230 grams
Dietary fiber	24	grams			More than 18 gm
Sugars	102	grams			Less than 150 gm
Protein	90	grams	40	23 %	12 to 20 %
Calcium	755	milligrams	-445		More than 1200 mg
Carb (Breakfast)	55	grams			
Carb (AM Snack)	17	grams			
Carb (Lunch)	51	grams			
Carb (PM Snack)	31	grams			
Carb (Dinner)	53	grams			
Carb (EV Snack)	19	grams			
Glycemic index	37				
Starch	81	grams			
Phosphorus	1309	milligrams	609		More than 700 mg
Potassium	2755	milligrams			

Wednesday

Food Item	Amount to Serve	Exchanges	Cal	Carb(g)	Prot(g)	Fat(g)	Sod(mg)
BREAKFAST							
Oatmeal, cooked	1 cup	2 Starch	145	25	6	2	2
Raisins, dark, seedless	2 Tbsp.	1 Fruit	54	14	1	0	2
Almonds, dry roasted	6 almonds	1 Fat	48	2	2	4	0
Milk, fat-free (nonfat, skim)	1 cup	1 Milk, fat-free	83	12	8	0	108
			330	**53**	**17**	**7**	**112**
MORNING SNACK							
Snack Mix (p 234)	1 serving	1 Starch	110	14	2	5	278
		1 Fat					
			110	**14**	**2**	**5**	**278**
LUNCH							
Bread, whole wheat	2 slices	2 Starch	138	26	5	2	295
Tuna salad, fresh	½ cup	½ Carbohydrate	192	10	16	9	412
		2 Meat, lean					
		1 Fat					
Lettuce, leaf	2 leaves	2	0	0	0	1	
Tomato, raw	3 slice, medium		13	3	0	0	5
Apple, with peel	1 small (2½" d)	1 Fruit	55	15	0	0	1
			399	**53**	**23**	**12**	**714**
DINNER							
Beef, chuck, lean only (extras from Saturday)	4 ozs.	4 Meat, lean	245	0	37	9	75
Hot German Potato Salad (page 200)	1 serving	2 Starch	149	30	4	2	397
Cabbage, red, cooked, shredded	1 cup	2 Vegetable	44	10	2	0	12
Applesauce, unsweetened	½ cup	1 Fruit	52	14	0	0	2
			490	**54**	**44**	**11**	**486**
EVENING SNACK							
Gingersnap cookies, regular	3 cookies	1 Carbohydrate	87	16	1	2	137
Milk, fat-free (nonfat, skim)	1 cup	1 Milk, fat-free	83	12	8	0	108
			170	**28**	**9**	**2**	**245**

Wednesday—Totals for the Day

Nutrient	Quantity		DRI Comparison (- = Under)	% of Day's Calories	Goals
Calories	1499				1450 to 1550
Fat	38	grams		22 %	0 to 30 %
Saturated fat	9	grams		5 %	0 to 10 %
Polyunsat fat	9	grams		5 %	
Monounsat fat	16	grams		10 %	More than 10 %
Cholesterol	141	milligrams			Less than 300 mg
Sodium	1836	milligrams			0 to 2400 mg
Carbohydrate	203	grams		53 %	150 to 230 grams
Dietary fiber	23	grams			More than 18 gm
Sugars	83	grams			Less than 150 gm
Protein	96	grams	46	25 %	12 to 20 %
Calcium	719	milligrams	-481		More than 1200 mg
Carb (Breakfast)	53	grams			
Carb (AM Snack)	14	grams			
Carb (Lunch)	53	grams			
Carb (PM Snack)	0	grams			
Carb (Dinner)	54	grams			
Carb (EV Snack)	28	grams			
Glycemic index	46				
Starch	83	grams			
Phosphorus	1463	milligrams	763		More than 700 mg
Potassium	3093	milligrams			

Thursday

Food Item	Amount to Serve	Exchanges	Cal	Carb(g)	Prot(g)	Fat(g)	Sod(mg)
BREAKFAST							
Egg, scrambled with	1 egg	1 Meat, med fat	75	1	6	5	63
pepper, green bell, raw	⅛ cup, sliced	⅛ Vegetable	2	1	0	0	0
onions, fresh	⅛ cup	⅛ Vegetable	7	2	0	0	1
Salsa	¼ cup	Free food	15	3	1	0	168
English muffin, whole wheat	1 muffin	2 Starch	126	25	5	1	220
Margarine, light soft tub	1 Tbsp.	1 Fat	40	0	0	4	90
Orange juice, fresh	½ cup	1 Fruit	56	13	1	0	1
			322	**44**	**14**	**11**	**543**
MORNING SNACK							
Milk, fat-free (nonfat, skim)	1 cup	1 Milk, fat-free	83	12	8	0	108
			83	**12**	**8**	**0**	**108**
LUNCH							
Pirate Stew (p 144) lower-sodium	1 serving	2 Starch 1 Vegetable 2 Meat, lean ½ Fat	310	38	22	8	611
Papaya, fresh	1 cup	1 Fruit	55	14	1	0	4
			365	**52**	**23**	**8**	**615**
AFTERNOON SNACK							
Snack Mix (page 234) (extras from a previous day)	1 serving 1 Fat	1 Starch	110	14	2	5	278
			110	**14**	**2**	**5**	**278**
DINNER							
Salmon, fresh, broiled or baked	3 ozs.	3 Meat, lean	183	0	23	9	56
Vegetables, mixed (with corn), frozen cooked	1 cup	1 Starch	80	18	4	0	80
Roll, multi-grain	1 roll, medium	1½ Starch	125	23	3	2	244
Margarine, light soft tub	1 Tbsp.	1 Fat	40	0	0	4	90
Salad greens mix	2 cups	1 Vegetable	15	3	1	0	15

Salad dressing, Italian, fat-free	2 Tbsp.	Free food	15	3	0	0	310
Banana, fresh	1 extra small	1 Fruit	75	19	1	0	1
			533	**66**	**32**	**17**	**796**

EVENING SNACK

Yogurt, nonfat, vanilla,	1 container (6 oz.)	1 Milk, fat-free	90	16	6	0	95
			90	**16**	**6**	**0**	**95**

Thursday—Totals for the Day

Nutrient	Quantity		DRI Comparison (- = Under)	% of Day's Calories	Goals
Calories	1503				1450 to 1550
Fat	42	grams		25 %	0 to 30 %
Saturated fat	10	grams		6 %	0 to 10 %
Polyunsat fat	8	grams		5 %	
Monounsat fat	19	grams		11 %	More than 10 %
Cholesterol	341	milligrams			Less than 300 mg
Sodium	2435	milligrams			0 to 2400 mg
Carbohydrate	204	grams		53 %	150 to 230 grams
Dietary fiber	24	grams			More than 18 gm
Sugars	86	grams			Less than 150 gm
Protein	85	grams	35	22 %	12 to 20 %
Calcium	858	milligrams	-342		More than 1200 mg
Carb (Breakfast)	44	grams			
Carb (AM Snack)	12	grams			
Carb (Lunch)	52	grams			
Carb (PM Snack)	14	grams			
Carb (Dinner)	66	grams			
Carb (EV Snack)	16	grams			
Glycemic index	48				
Starch	92	grams			
Phosphorus	1548	milligrams	848		More than 700 mg
Potassium	3874	milligrams	.		

Friday

Food Item	Amount to Serve	Exchanges	Cal	Carb(g)	Prot(g)	Fat(g)	Sod(mg)
BREAKFAST							
Mexican-Style Grits (p 247) lower-fat	2 servings	2 Starch	182	32	9	2	334
Fresh fruit mix	¾ cup	1 Fruit	61	15	1	0	4
Milk, fat-free (nonfat, skim)	1 cup	1 Milk, fat-free	83	12	8	0	108
			326	**59**	**18**	**3**	**445**
LUNCH							
Soy patty, chicken flavor,	1 patty	1 Starch	150	12	13	6	470
1 Meat, med fat							
Pita bread, whole wheat	½ pita	1 Starch	70	15	3	1	65
Tomato, cucumber, onion mix raw	1 cup	1 Vegetable	30	7	1	0	9
Lettuce, leaf	2 leaves	2	0	0	0	1	
Salad dressing, ranch, light	1 Tbsp.	1 Fat	40	2	0	4	140
Plum, fresh	2 plums	1 Fruit	73	17	1	1	0
			365	**53**	**19**	**11**	**685**
AFTERNOON SNACK							
Yogurt, nonfat, vanilla,	1 container (6 oz.)	1 Milk, fat-free	90	16	6	0	95
			90	**16**	**6**	**0**	**95**
DINNER							
Mjeddrah (page 170)	1 serving	2 Starch ½ Fat	173	29	9	3	196
Meatless burger, soy-based	2½ cup	1 Carbohydrate 2 Meat, vy lean	140	14	22	1	440
Raisins, dark, seedless	2 Tbsp.	1 Fruit	54	14	1	0	2
Cashews, unsalted	1 Tbsp.	1 Fat	52	3	1	4	1
Carrots, fresh cooked	1 cup	2 Vegetable	70	16	2	0	102
			488	**76**	**34**	**9**	**742**

EVENING SNACK

Tortilla chips, baked (lowfat)	¾ oz	1 Starch	83	18	2	1	150
Hummus	⅓ cup	1 Starch 1 Fat	137	12	7	8	313
			219	**30**	**9**	**9**	**463**

Friday—Totals for the Day

Nutrient	Quantity		DRI Comparison (- = Under)	% of Day's Calories	Goals
Calories	1489				1450 to 1550
Fat	31	grams		18 %	0 to 30 %
Saturated fat	5	grams		3 %	0 to 10 %
Polyunsat fat	10	grams		6 %	
Monounsat fat	11	grams		7 %	More than 10 %
Cholesterol	12	milligrams			Less than 300 mg
Sodium	2430	milligrams			0 to 2400 mg
Carbohydrate	233	grams		60 %	150 to 230 grams
Dietary fiber	38	grams			More than 18 gm
Sugars	78	grams			Less than 150 gm
Protein	86	grams	36	22 %	12 to 20 %
Calcium	841	milligrams	-359		More than 1200 mg
Carb (Breakfast)	59	grams			
Carb (AM Snack)	0	grams			
Carb (Lunch)	53	grams			
Carb (PM Snack)	16	grams			
Carb (Dinner)	76	grams			
Carb (EV Snack)	30	grams			
Glycemic index	35				
Starch	117	grams			
Phosphorus	1823	milligrams	1123		More than 700 mg
Potassium	2422	milligrams			

Averages—for the Week

Nutrient	Quantity		DRI Comparison (- = Under)	% of Day's Calories	Goals
Calories	1488				1450 to 1550
Fat	36	grams		21 %	0 to 30 %
Saturated fat	9	grams		5 %	0 to 10 %
Polyunsat fat	9	grams		5 %	
Monounsat fat	14	grams		8 %	More than 10 %
Cholesterol	165	milligrams			Less than 300 mg
Sodium	2149	milligrams			0 to 2400 mg
Carbohydrate	216	grams		56 %	150 to 230 grams
Dietary fiber	26	grams			More than 18 gm
Sugars	88	grams			Less than 150 gm
Protein	89	grams	39	23 %	12 to 20 %
Calcium	872	milligrams	-328		More than 1200 mg
Carb (Breakfast)	52	grams			
Carb (AM Snack)	9	grams			
Carb (Lunch)	53	grams			
Carb (PM Snack)	16	grams			
Carb (Dinner)	62	grams			
Carb (EV Snack)	24	grams			
Glycemic index	42				
Starch	94	grams			
Phosphorus	1537	milligrams	837		More than 700 mg
Potassium	3143	milligrams			

10 Most Asked Questions about Diabetes

1. Can people with diabetes eat sugar?

Yes, they can. Sugar is just another carbohydrate to the body. All carbohydrates, whether they come from dessert, breads, or carrots, raise blood sugar. An equal serving of brownie and of baked potato raise your blood sugar the same amount. If you know that a rise in blood sugar is coming, it is wise to focus on the size of the serving.

The question of "how much sugar is too much?" has to be answered by each one of us. No one who wants to be healthy eats a lot of sugar.

2. Do people with diabetes have to eat a special diet?

No, they should eat the same foods that are healthy for everyone—whole grains, vegetables, fruit, and small portions of lean meat. Like everyone else, people with diabetes should eat breakfast, lunch, and dinner and not put off eating until dinnertime. By then, you are ravenous and will eat too much. This sends the blood sugar levels soaring in people with diabetes, and doesn't allow them to feel hungry for breakfast the next morning.

Some people (with or without diabetes) do best when they eat five or six tiny meals or snacks a day.

3. What is diabetes?

Let's begin with insulin. It is a hormone that is produced in the pancreas, which is an organ located near your stomach. When you eat food, it is digested and broken down into glucose, a sugar. In this form it can travel around to feed all the cells in your body by way of the bloodstream. But the glucose cannot get into your cells unless insulin is there to open the door. Without insulin, the glucose stays in the bloodstream. And each time you eat, more glucose goes into your bloodstream. High levels of blood glucose or blood sugar is the sign that you have diabetes.

In type 1 diabetes, the body cannot produce insulin at all. Something has caused the body to destroy the cells in the pancreas that make insulin. People with type 1 diabetes must have insulin injections or use an insulin pump to stay alive.

In type 2 diabetes, the body is either not making enough insulin or not using it well. People can help their bodies use the insulin more effectively by losing weight and being active every day. Some people have to take diabetes pills or insulin to get their blood sugar levels back to normal.

4. What causes diabetes?

To start with, you need to have the gene for diabetes. Then there has to be something that triggers the gene. For many people who develop type 2 diabetes, the trigger is being overweight and sedentary. For others, it might be a stress on the body such as pregnancy or a serious accident requiring surgery.

For a child with type 1 diabetes, a virus may have confused the immune system into identifying the beta cells in the pancreas as part of the virus, and so the immune system destroyed the beta cells and stopped the production of insulin.

5. How many people have diabetes in the United States?

About 18 million people have diabetes in the U.S., but 8 million of those don't know it. There are 1 million new cases of diabetes diagnosed every year. The most distressing of these are the growing number of teens and older children who are developing type 2 diabetes—which usually occurs much later in life.

6. Why don't people know that they have diabetes?

The people who develop type 1 diabetes know because it comes on quickly and the symptoms are serious. But it affects only about 10 percent of the people with diabetes.

Type 2 accounts for the other 90 percent. Because it doesn't hurt and the symptoms come on gradually, people have usually had type 2 diabetes for 7 to 10 years when they get diagnosed.

7. Is there a cure for diabetes?

Not yet. Some people with type 2 diabetes may seem to have cured it by losing weight and getting regular daily exercise, because their blood sugar returns to normal levels and stays there. This may continue for years, but eventually the pancreas just wears out, and they will need medication to manage their blood sugar levels.

A small number of people with type 1 diabetes who have had a successful pancreas or islet cell transplant no longer have diabetes because their bodies are producing insulin again. However, they have to take powerful immunosuppressant drugs for the rest of their lives to prevent their bodies from rejecting the transplant.

8. Is there a type of diabetes that only happens when a woman is pregnant?

Yes, it is called gestational diabetes. After the baby is born, the woman no longer has diabetes, but she needs to take care to be active and to maintain a healthy weight or she might develop type 2 diabetes later on in life. During the last two months of her pregnancy, she will need to follow a meal plan to keep her blood sugar in normal ranges, or her baby may grow too big, causing problems for her and the baby during the birth process.

9. Does diabetes hurt?

High blood sugar can make you feel tired and irritable, but it comes on so gradually that you may not realize what is happening. It can blur your vision. That's on the outside. On the inside, constantly high blood sugar levels are silently damaging your blood vessels and nerves and can cause problems everywhere from your eyes to your feet, and especially to your heart. If diabetes starts hurting, damage has already been done.

10. Is there any way to avoid the damage that diabetes can do to the body?

Yes. We now know how to manage blood sugar levels, and persons with diabetes can learn what to do to keep healthy. Working with dietitians to develop a meal plan of foods that they like helps them get the nutrients their bodies need and not eat too much carbohydrate at any one meal or snack. Checking their blood sugar, in the morning or two hours after a meal for example, with a small glucose meter gives them and their health care providers information about how high their blood sugar is going and when, and about the effect of any diabetes medication they are taking. A daily 30- to 45-minute walk is another simple but powerful way to lower blood sugar and to be healthier all over.

Learning to bring blood sugar levels back to normal every day is the key to preventing diabetes from doing any damage. We have extensive research to show that this is true. People can even prevent diabetes from developing at all by taking the same steps of eating healthy meals and getting daily exercise. These are also the tools that can reverse some of the damage that might have already been done.

Index

Index

Index

Index

Index

Recommended Reading List
(ADA is the American Diabetes Association.)

Diabetes Burnout: What to Do When You Can't Take it Anymore, William H. Polonsky, Ph.D.; CDE, 2001, 350 pages. Also available on audio cassette.

Diabetes Meal Planning Made Easy, 2nd ed., Hope Warshaw, MMSc, RD, CDE, BC-ADM; ADA, 2000, 235 pages.

Dr. Gavin's Health Guide for African Americans, Small Steps Press, 2004, 285 pages.

A Field Guide to Type 1 Diabetes, ADA, 2003, 210 pages.

A Field Guide to Type 2 Diabetes, ADA, 2004, 295 pages.

Help! My Underwear is Shrinking! Jo Ann Hattner, MPH, RD; Ann Coulston, MS, RD; and E. Michael Goodkind, BA; ADA, 2003, 140 pages.

Mastering Your Diabetes (before diabetes masters you), Janette Kirkham, RN, CDE, EMT; ADA, 2003, 132 pages.

The Official Pocket Guide to Diabetic Exchanges, 2nd ed., ADA, 2003, 64 pages.

Playing the Numbers: How to Make Sense of Your Blood Sugar Levels, ADA, 2003, 64 pages.

What to Do When You Have Type 2 Diabetes, ADA, 2002, 64 pages.

About the Author

Phyllis Pellman Good is a *New York Times* bestselling author whose books have sold more than 7 million copies.

Good also authored the *New York Times* bestselling ***Fix-It and Forget-It Lightly: Healthy, Low-Fat Recipes for Your Slow Cooker.*** She co-authored the national #1 bestselling cookbook (with Dawn J. Ranck) ***Fix-It and Forget-It Cookbook: Feasting with your Slow Cooker***, which appeared on *The New York Times* Best Sellers list, as well as the best seller lists of *USA Today, Publishers Weekly,* and Book Sense. In addition, Good authored ***Fix-It and Forget-It Recipes for Entertaining: Slow Cooker Favorites for All the Year Round,*** also in the series (with Ranck).

Good's other cookbooks include ***The Best of Amish Cooking, The Best of Mennonite Fellowship Meals, The Central Market Cookbook,*** and ***Favorite Recipes with Herbs.***

Phyllis Pellman Good is Senior Editor at Good Books. She received her B.A. and M.A. in English from New York University. She and her husband, Merle, live in Lancaster, Pennsylvania. They are the parents of two young-adult daughters.

For a complete listing of books by Phyllis Pellman Good, as well as excerpts and reviews, visit www.goodbks.com.